To my Mississippi Friends

CONTENTS

ILLUSTRATIONS

following page 147

ACKNOWLEDGMENTS

ANYONE who has written a book knows that the task involved is by no means a solo one. Numerous people, many unwittingly, are drawn into the effort, one that is at times hellish and at other times a labor of love. Mine was mostly the latter. Still, I put many people through hell, and to these people and others I owe my gratitude.

The person most responsible for getting me started in this business is Ray Arsenault. He is in every respect a mentor, selfless friend, and fellow Devil Rays fan. My debt to him can never be repaid. The same heartfelt thanks go to Jacqueline Jones. Like Ray, her friendship, exemplary scholarship, and encouragement helped light the end of the tunnel.

Several people gave their time to read all or part of the manuscript. Their comments were invaluable, and I take the rap for any flaws and purple prose. Much gratitude goes to Morton Keller, Harvard Sitkoff, Neil McMillen, James Cobb, Richard King, Nancy Hewitt, Jeffrey Adler, Don Simonton, Steve Whitfield, Rae Nell Presson, Melisandre Hilliker, Vernon Burton, Melissa Seixas, and Jane Morgan. Mimi Miller, Ellen Babb, and Sharon Meckel read nearly every word of final drafts, and David Oshinsky did read every word. Chris Warren brainstormed the book title, but I then gave him one back.

A debt of gratitude is owed as well to a repertoire of friends, teachers, classmates, and colleagues who offered suggestions, encouragement, or a willing ear. They include: Jill Bennett, Jim Connolly, Peter Hansen, Sarah Redfield, Ann Plane, Grant Rice, Denise Frontel, Neil Kamel, Mitchell Snay, Lee Whitfield, David Hackett Fischer, Jay Malone, Houston Robison, Steve Classen, Christine Heyrman, Tom Carter, Gary Mormino, Dave McCally,

Acknowledgments

Andy Doyle, Sudye Cauthen, Art Budros, Carolyn Johnston, Peter Rinaldi, Tara Zachary, Claire Schen, Warren Ellem, Stephanie Saul, and all the members of the Dead Historian Society. Thank you, Ray Mohl, Colin Davis, Karen Utz, Sam Webb, Debbie Givens, Elaine Cardin, Pamela Valentine, Julie Valentine, students at the University of Alabama at Birmingham, the superb editorial staff of the *Vulcan Historical Review,* and especially Sonya Rudenstine for keeping me sane in Birmingham.

Numerous librarians and archivists have been indispensable. Many thanks to staff members at Brandeis University, the Atlanta University Center, Millsaps College, Eckerd College, University of Mississippi, University of Southern Mississippi, Georgia State University, University of South Florida, Harvard University, the Library of Congress, Saint Mary's Parish Archives, the Natchez–Adams County Board of Education, and Jan Hillegas of the Freedom Information Service. Jim Cobb said it best when he wrote that research at the Mississippi Department of Archives and History is "like a visit with old friends." I owe an incalculable debt to Anne Lipscomb Webster, Nancy Bounds, Betty Robinson, Vera Richardson, Sara Clark, Victor Bailey, Joyce Dixon, Mickey Hennen, Hank Holmes, Jan May, Elaine Owens, Joyce Black-Smith, Jenny Biggers, and J. V. Lewis. Standouts at the Eudora Welty Public Library in Jackson were Charlie Brenner and Michelle Hudson. Anyone researching in Natchez is grateful for the generosity of Mimi and Ron Miller of the Historic Natchez Foundation. Without the kind cooperation of the many people of Natchez who granted interviews, this book could not have been written.

Grants from the Brandeis University Irving and Rose Crown Foundation, Eckerd College, and the Graduate School at the University of Alabama at Birmingham helped defray research costs. Thanks also to Maureen Hewitt and the Louisiana State University Press for their confidence in this project. While flagging factual errors, misspellings, malapropisms, and purple prose, Jean C. Lee made copyediting a valuable and pleasant experience.

In my travels, many people provided shelter, food, and warm company. My grandmother Eleanor Palmer, my mother Becky Davis (Devil Rays fan supreme), my sister and brother-in-law Wendy and David

Keller, Jill Vandenboogaart and friends Christine Heyrman and Tom Carter, Brian and Beth Hancock, Jim and Ruth Basinger, Jean Stegall, Anna Furr, and Mimi and Ron Miller always opened their doors to me.

Throughout this project, the people of Mississippi have been hosts, friends, and surrogate family. This book is for them. They include especially: Lorraine Redd Allen, Charlie Brenner, Mary Jane Hall, Jean Stegall, Michelle Hudson, Anne Lipscomb Webster, Jan Hillegas, Joseph Dumas, Anna Furr, Rae Nell and Bill Presson, Victor Bailey, Jonathan Hamilton, Craig Bodenhorn, David and Annie Debauche, Jamie and Sharon Bush, Evelyn Redd, Adelaide Fletcher, Mark and Kathy Greenberg, Jane Morgan (and Spring), and George and Ann Schimmel.

RACE AGAINST TIME

"I've hunted and fished this land since I was a child," he says. "This land is composed of two different cultures: a white culture and a black culture. And I've lived close to them all of my life. But I'm told now that we've mistreated them and that we must change. And these changes are coming faster than I expected. And I'm required to make decisions on the basis of a new way of thinking, and it's difficult. It's difficult for me, and it's difficult for all southerners."[1]

These are revealing words. Although the interview takes place in the Delta, a plantation region of alluvial soil located north of Natchez, the subject community of this book, the hunter expresses the basic concerns shared by most Mississippi whites. The traditional racial order of white over black and the predictability of the white southerner's way of life will be no longer. Until this day, the past had been a guide to a predictable future, something understood and embraced. Challenged one hundred years before by the Civil War and Reconstruction, timeworn sensibilities that were taken for granted now collide with the civil rights movement. The certainty of change casts a gray cloud over the hunter's future, that of his fellow white Mississippians, and all the white South. His black neighbors, most of whom live and labor much as blacks had since emancipation, welcome that change. The enduring struggle to survive, known to every generation back to the first ancestors retrieved from Africa and enshackled in slavery, has escalated into an unstoppable organized movement for equal humanity. Initiated by blacks themselves, change represents hope for a better life.

It is noteworthy that the hunter's dialogue does not include the word "race." There is no taboo against using the word. He simply knows the two racial groups as separate and different cultures: "a white culture and a black culture." Natchez and Mississippi whites, and blacks for that matter, cared as much about a person's cultural distinctions as his or her race. Simply put, southerners identified culture with each racial group. Doing so steered the fate of race relations in southern society.

This study rests on the premise that there was a socially significant cultural dimension in the southern white construction of race and in conceptions of inferiority and superiority. Historians have failed to give importance to that construction or have overlooked it altogether. Scholarship in the last few decades has expanded the knowledge of race in America in new and significant ways. But in the worthy zeal to transcend

(ULTUℝE AND ℨEPAℝATION

IN the opening clip of the "Mississippi" episode of the highly acclaimed documentary *Eyes on the Prize*, two hunters have perched themselves along a riverbank for the day's pursuit. The waters below are muddy and sleepy, like those of many rivers in Mississippi. A bobwhite calls its name from beneath the thinning canopy of trees in the backdrop. Cast against clear skies, the scene suggests a warm autumn day early in the hunting season. Even so, the two southerners wear caps and jackets, perhaps hoping to create the illusion of ideal hunting conditions—gray, damp, and chilled. Every Mississippi man and boy knows that pleasant weather makes for poor hunting.

For the moment, though, fortunes and misfortunes of weather seem secondary to another and larger illusion—that of holding on to the white southern way of life. The South as a whole is embroiled in the civil rights struggle, and Mississippi occupies center stage for these two white men. A diligent news reporter has tracked them down (evidently looking for rural Mississippi's equivalent to the man in the street) and distracted them with a question about the ongoing race conflict. The hunter in the foreground turns toward a film camera to talk. His face is contemplative, and he speaks with eloquence and equanimity.

the biases of earlier generations and elevate the black experience historically—that is, to recognize black agency—historians of race relations
have been less diligent in addressing important questions about the white
meaning of race.

The social meaning of race has never been static and transhistorical. It
has its own history, one in which the meaning of race has changed to
conform to different social imperatives in different eras and different
places. By the mid–twentieth century, the meaning of race in white Mississippi no longer revolved solely around biological traits; cultural traits
had moved to the center. To southerners, culture was the embodiment of
a group's observable customs, physical artifacts and behavior, and identifiable social expressions, such as speech, dress, music, and cuisine. Not
confining culture to these surface expressions, southerners also associated culture with the collective cluster of values, norms, beliefs, ethical
rules, and priorities that yielded a group's distinctive integration.[2] Still
around and still plentiful were whites who believed that biological imperatives predetermined one's cultural development (because blacks were
biologically inferior, they were naturally culturally inferior). But this
train of thought was increasingly abandoned for the belief that African
antecedents, as well as the conditions of slavery, had arrested the development of black culture. The common variable between those whites
who believed in biological predeterminates and those who no longer did
was the notion of cultural difference, defined ultimately as cultural inferiority.[3]

The idea that environmental or social conditions undermined
healthy cultural development reflected a once similar way of thinking of
experts. Social scientists and some black intellectuals of the early and mid–
twentieth century, as well as liberal scholars of later years, believed that
slavery, and later segregation, retarded the progress of black culture,
making it in fact pathological. Even Natchez native Richard Wright,
who, while rejecting the concept of biological inferiority, "brooded" over
what he described as "the cultural barrenness of black life" in America.
Racial discrimination, in other words, had prevented blacks from being
able "to catch the full spirit of Western civilization." Although in the minority, some social scientists, such as E. Franklin Frazier and W. E. B.
DuBois, challenged convention by arguing that discriminatory social

3

conditions impeded, not cultural development, but access to a quality of life equal to the abilities of black culture. The black and white cultures were more alike than not, and whatever dissimilarities existed did not represent inferiority.[4]

Perhaps to some—social scientist and southern white—associating inferiority with culture rather than the physicality of race seemed less damning. The cultural argument, after all, might imply the possibility of escape for the individual who could rise above debilitating group trappings; the biological carried a life sentence without possibility of release. The seemingly benign nature of the cultural argument, however, made it that much more insidious. There was in fact no escape. First, white southerners were unwilling to acknowledge their own blackness, that their culture over the centuries had borrowed liberally from black culture. Second, regardless of personal striving and success, one was always associated with the culture of one's ancestors. As long as black culture existed, anyone identified as black faced a stigma of inferiority that was no less virulent than the stigma of biological inferiority.

Beneath the rot of prejudice—ethnocentrism, racism, and even class elitism—from which such stigmas fester, has always been cultural difference, real and perceived. In Western tradition, observes Pierre van den Burghe, planting the idea of inherent racial differences in the social consciousness has traditionally required the recognition of not only physical differences between groups but also cultural ones. Since ancient history, culture has served as a reference by which all human groups identify others. The very idea of cultural diversity predates the development of social classes and the social engineering of race. Frequently, difference seen in one group by another has been translated into deficiency. To associate cultural difference with cultural inferiority has not been an uncommon response of a group with ideas about its own superiority. Nor has that response been solely the doing of oppressing groups. Many Native Americans, to cite one example, were struck by the oddness of English settlers; their work habits, sexual division of labor, and their practice of overdressing and underbathing were all seen as strange and thus evidence of a culturally inferior people.[5]

Citizenship in this country was, and perhaps still is, defined as much by cultural values as by ethnic and linguistic origins.[6] The federal government's handling of the "Indian problem," for instance, historically shifted between a policy of extermination and acculturation, the process of stripping Native Americans of their supposedly less-advanced cultures and teaching them the ways of the supposedly advanced white culture. Acculturation as a policy failed, and Native Americans were the last group to gain the rights of citizenship. More successful has been the acculturation of so-labeled ethnic immigrants, who were forced to melt into the dominant culture before enjoying complete acceptance in American society. Being white, English, and Protestant indicated that one possessed the prequalifying traits for being a "true" American. All other peoples were required to waive their ethnic and cultural identity, to discard values viewed as inferior and political allegiances labeled subversive. Even blacks born and reared Christian on American soil were obliged to show they were more white than black, in terms of habits and manners, before attaining some semblance of citizenship.[7]

In Mississippi, the fruits of full citizenship were determined by one's correspondence to the dominant Anglo-Christian culture, to what some scholars call whiteness. Although the popular mind typically paints an image of Mississippi's population with only two colors, black and white, life there reflects a much richer ethnic heritage. "It was a true melting pot," said writer Shelby Foote of his native Greenville, Mississippi. "Here they are bragging about moonlight and magnolias and pure blood lines. It's all foolishness. It's the exact opposite." Historic populations of Choctaws, Jews, Chinese, Lebanese, Germans, Slavonians, French, Acadian French, and more recently, Asian Indian and Vietnamese have over the years complemented Mississippi's British and African descendants.[8]

Within this multiethnic environment, Mississippi Anglo whites traditionally located themselves and others in social categories by cultural traits, as well as by race and lineage. Jews, for instance, were accepted as white, meaning they were welcomed into the dominant culture. Jews were physically white, of course. But what was equally important was that even as they retained many Old World traditions, they revealed ideals, values, and beliefs (excluding some religious beliefs, but including racial beliefs) that were seen as virtually consistent with Anglo culture, values that were rooted in family, education, and work, not to mention honor and loyalty. With few exceptions, Jews reaped the loftier advantages of membership in Mississippi's white social body. This was especially true in Natchez. To quote K. Anthony Appiah, "With whiteness, as with American Express, membership has its privileges."[9]

The same privileges were not extended to blacks. Not only did they constitute a physical contrast to whiteness; their cultural distinctions— their blackness—remained more pronounced in the white normative gaze than did those of nineteenth-century immigrants and their descendants. With great resolve, whites sought to isolate black culture, first with the slave quarters and slave codes and then with residential and school segregation and Jim Crow laws. Even as many blacks before and after the Civil War made overtures toward whiteness, the dominant culture sent such aspirants, sometimes obligingly and sometimes violently, back to their proverbial place.

Blacks themselves played an active part in this cultural separation. Before and after the war, they willfully retreated into their own world, where they could find emotional and intellectual sustenance apart from the inhospitableness of white-controlled society. Enslaved blacks freshly separated from their African roots brought together elements of various European, Native American, and African cultures to devise a unique and vital African American culture with its own forms of English, storytelling, cuisine, music, and Christian worship. During Reconstruction, with the ostensible rights of citizenship, blacks tried to assimilate themselves into the economic system and the political process. At the same time, they held fast to their culture, organizing new and reinforcing old institutions that were uniquely black. The most notable of these institutions were churches, and social, civic, and educational organizations. Ironically, what whites would argue in defense of Jim Crow in later years, blacks determined immediately after the Civil War: separation was necessary for cultural survival.[10]

By no means, of course, was cultural isolation complete. If, as mentioned, African American culture borrowed from European cultures, it also complemented American white culture. African words passed freely into American English; African rhythms inspired indigenous American music forms; African farming techniques helped sustain the South's agrarian economy; African food and cooking fed the white population; and the list of African influences goes on. Not only was white culture more black than whites cared to acknowledge; America was dependent on black culture to define a national culture that was distinct from, and therefore considered superior to, the mother cultures of Europe.[11]

Even beyond the expressive forms of culture, blacks and whites had much in common. As historian Jacqueline Jones writes, "The white middle class has had no monopoly on the virtues of hard work, love of family, and commitment to schooling for their children."[12] Aspirations of a stable and fulfilling life—a secure job, decent education, and an enduring family environment—and sacrificing to attain that life was as much a part of black culture as white culture. Blacks had indeed caught the "spirit of Western civilization." They confronted, though, a discriminatory system that militated against the full expression of black culture. Where desire existed for full expression of values, ideals, and priorities, opportunity often did not. Blacks were subjected to a white criteria of standards but were not granted the equal opportunities to meet them.

Fusing culture with race carried significant implications for black-white relations in post–1930 Natchez. While many whites fixated on real and imagined biological distinctions between the races, behavioral traits combined with outward physical qualities confirmed the idea of cultural differences. Whites then converted those differences into hierarchical measures of inferiority and superiority. Black speech seemed comparatively crude, black dress usually untidy. Even the black walk seemed not quite a walk; to whites, it was a shuffle, a strut, or a contemptuous swagger. Though many whites enjoyed it, black music resonated with a "jungle rhythm" that carried the white imagination to the darkest recesses of Africa, which purportedly had never produced a civilized culture; nor were whites willing to compare black music to the great symphonies of civilization's masters such as Brahms, Beethoven, and Tchaikovsky. Sophistication was, of course, in the mind (or the imagination) of the white beholder, and in that mind it seemed reasonable that underlying black surface traits was an unsophisticated framework of black values, ideals, and initiatives.

The very idea of a fully equipped black culture stained the white reality. As was true with any culture, a tautology of myth and truth colored the white perception of what was real and what was not. Myths occupied a central and natural place in the lives of the people of Natchez, as was true elsewhere. The white order of reality embodied the idea of distinctive cultures and the meaning of race, which together influenced racial attitudes.

Race itself is a myth. It is an invention, a mere social construction that reduces people to simplified categories. But in the white reality, the concept of race was fact. As Robert Ezra Park noted, "Race relations . . . are not so much the relations that exist between individuals of different races as between individuals conscious of these differences." Whites attributed solid values to a few exceptional black individuals but not to black culture as a whole. One of the unfortunate realities is that whites associated the black cultural norm with the failings within the black community, not with the successes.[13]

The idea of racial inferiority and superiority was not only in the mind or in the human motivation; it arose, historian Thomas Holt argues, "from viral growths within the living whole." In other words, everyday experiences "naturalized" racism. Reaffirming concepts about race, the false concepts that underlay racism evolved from the white individual's daily encounters with symbols, racial discourse, images, and what Holt calls the "racial Other." In Natchez, written and public history, political rhetoric, white social privilege, segregation, and the sometimes wretched social conditions of blacks naturalized white racial attitudes and behavior and cemented the importance of white cultural hegemony. Within this social milieu, the white notion of race-distinctive cultures, nourished in everyday experiences, shaped and affirmed the racial order of Natchez society. In essence, discrimination reinforced segregation.[14] Like the banker who lends new money to a debtor to repay a debt, but ultimately perpetuates that debt, white treatment of blacks fortified discriminatory racial beliefs.[15]

Any one thing or condition that heightened the consciousness of racial differences also strengthened the desire for social distance. In the end, racial segregation secured for whites and denied to blacks more than political, social, and economic privileges. Jim Crow ensured cultural dominance, a hierarchy of not only race but of values, ideals, and moral priorities. Behind the segregationist's vitriol that physical commingling would despoil the purity of the great race was the belief that cultural commingling would imperil society at large. Separating the races was imperative to safeguarding whites against the influences of black

CRITICAL

"perversions" and white culture against the sullying impress of the "defective" black culture. The subordination of blacks and their culture assured the hegemony of white culture and all that flowed from it: economic, political, and social achievements. In turn, these fruits of cultural dominance were devices that, once secured, also perpetuated that dominance.

Whites believed that the fundamental preservation of civilization itself depended on separating the races. Mississippi senator Theodore Bilbo enunciated a commonly held white assumption when in 1944 he said, "The white race has founded, developed, and maintained every civilization known to the human race." As the myth went, black culture simply could not sustain the arts of civilized society, which had flowered from white culture. The validation of that myth carried the stamp of history. "For in the annals," the *Natchez Democrat* noted four years later, "we can find no basis for assuming that all races of people have the same qualities, the same ingenuity, the same ambitions, the same capacities for development." Mississippi writer Stark Young, who had ancestral and literary ties to Natchez, took the civilization argument one step further. According to him, the white "South had a civilization once, the only clearly defined and frankly admitted system that we ever had in this country of ours."[16]

Before desegregation—"the change," as Mississippians call it—white southerners were at peace in a stable place of the familiar and the predictable. Social harmony, conjured the white mind, would prevail as long as blacks maintained their physical and cultural distance and continued to shuffle about in their separate world. White dominance of political and economic institutions, and black exclusion from these institutions, was part of the larger systematic process of keeping black culture at one remove from white culture and, thus, civilization safe. By contrast, black equality promised social disruption and uncertainty. Once free to fully express itself, black culture would contaminate society with a lesser standard of values—lowering moral and ethical norms, diminishing individual initiative and responsibility, disrupting social institutions, and ultimately retarding, if not reversing, the advance of civilization. The southern way of life, the familiar and predictable, would disappear into the chaos.

*   *   *

9

In examining the cultural basis of race relations, this book covers six decades of history, through the present. Although whites remained firmly attached to racial traditions during much of that time, Natchez was swept up in broader currents of historical change. Beginning in the 1930s, modern manufacturing transformed Natchez, as did tourism, and later civil rights, school integration, and federal social programs. All represented forces of modernity often at war with local race relations. Each of those forces also serves as a subtheme of this book while providing a window into white myths and reality, the cultural dynamic of race relations, and the nature of white racial attitudes in Natchez.

As a subject of study, Natchez has attained a special status among academicians. Nine scholarly books have been devoted to Natchez—this one makes ten (coincidentally, three other Davises have written books about Natchez). Only two of the nine books deal specifically with life in the twentieth century, and those two concentrate on the 1930s. The most famous of them is that of social anthropologists Allison Davis and Burleigh and Mary Gardner, *Deep South: A Social Anthropological Study of Caste and Class*. Davis and the Gardners were interested primarily in examining the social dynamics of a biracial society. They found in 1930s Natchez a social ordering that they described as a caste system. They were among the first social scientists to apply the caste concept (a theoretical model originally used to describe the historical system of India) to a southern community.[17]

It seemed to fit Natchez. In this semiremote city of 13,500 residents, race served as an insurmountable barrier separating blacks and whites into an upper-caste group (white) and a lower-caste group (black). A black man could be educated, wealthy, and an upstanding member in the community, and he was still only a second-class citizen. By rule, economic or educational advancement elevated blacks within their caste group but not out of it. Birth and race, not accomplishment, determined one's unalterable caste membership. Occasionally, light-skinned blacks deceived the system by "passing" as white; otherwise, blacks could never transcend the caste divide. For their part, whites used the legal system, economic coercion, property ownership, and physical violence to preserve white supremacy and to attain certain racial/caste-exclusive social, political, and sexual privileges.

Before *Deep South,* few studies described so thoroughly and comprehensively the workings of caste society in a southern community. The authors tackled their questions expertly, and their conclusions have become an established and accessible part of the historical record. Although pioneering scholarship, *Deep South* is a work about a concentrated period when cotton and timber were still the main staples of the economy and, with the exception of federal public policy dealing with the national depression, Natchez was free of external forces that in later years pressed for social change.

The book in hand builds on the classic work of Davis and the Gardners. It does not pretend to be a full-scale follow-up of an anthropological study of black and white life in a segregated community. Up to five people conducted the research for *Deep South,* while only one did so for this book, and did so with no illusions of creating a work that equals the extraordinary product in *Deep South.* The new work, for instance, does not examine as closely the social dynamics within the black community or intra- and inter-racial class relationships. It is chiefly concerned with the evolution of race relations—the point where blacks and whites interacted in ways that affected their own lives and the structure and direction of larger society—over more than six decades of change. Even with this work's completion, one could write a book about the civil rights movement in Natchez and still offer something original.

This book has been written, however, with the hope that historians will be prompted to approach the scholarship of race from a new direction. Traditionally, studies on twentieth-century race relations have been devoted almost exclusively either to the black or the white side of the equation. Those that look at the white side typically examine the practice of white supremacy and the economic and political benefits of racism while failing to fully answer the question of why whites segregated. This study follows the belief that before we can know exactly what blacks were (and are) battling against, we have to know the organic nature of the phenomenon we call racism, which, this study contends, is deeper than the political economy and the racial dynamic of sex. One objective of this book then is to illuminate the continuities and discontinuities in white behavior and attitudes—without ignoring the black experience or black agency—while tracing the caste system evolving in the context of broader historical developments. Natchezians accepted and invited many of those developments, even as whites stubbornly resisted change in the racial hierarchy.

In the end, change in the social order did come. As the hunter sitting on the riverbank prophesied, experiencing it was indeed difficult for Mississippians, white and black.

GOING TO NATCHEZ

When people ask me what it was like to live and research in Mississippi, I tell them that it was a fascinating and enriching experience. Then I'm eager to add that I loved living there and found Mississippians to be among the friendliest people I have ever met. That comment always draws looks of disbelief. How could anyone like Mississippi, they seem to be asking themselves. It's an ungodly place with uncharitable rednecks running around lynching innocent blacks and anyone else who is offended by the word "nigger."

Many Yankee friends actually worried when I first moved to the "land of the benighted" in December 1991. One called Mississippi "the heart of darkness" and wondered whether I would make it out safely. Even my father, a dyed-in-the-wool southerner born and reared in Alabama, cautioned me before my first trip to Natchez. Knowing that I would be asking locals sensitive questions about race, he said, "Son, make sure you use a southern accent and let them know you're a southerner." He coached me to say "How you" to everyone I met when stopping for gas and to pronounce Natchez with a soft "z," as in "matches." The wrong pronunciation would surely mark me as an outsider.

Nor was I, a person who prides himself in being open-minded, going to Natchez without apprehensions. Reflecting back on my childhood in Alabama in the early 1960s, when George Corley Wallace ruled the state with the zeal of a southern xenophobic, I remembered how we in the "Heart of Dixie" looked down upon our next-door neighbor to the west as a wasteland of ignorance and hate. Mississippi was our scapegoat, while we were oblivious to our own state's racial evils.

Just how mythic that image of Mississippi was became evident thirty years later when I drove across the state line. A lush landscape mixed with newly paved and broad highways, sleek industrial parks, and garish national franchises both greeted and shocked me. I had expected backwardness, not symbols of modernity. My anxiety about stopping to buy food or gas was quickly dissolved by friendly greetings that preempted every one of my "How you's." Still, I remained guarded and unconvinced as I proceeded to Natchez.

With a population of roughly twenty thousand, Natchez seems more like a town than a city, though it is one of significant size by Mississippi standards. The oldest city in the state, it sits nobly on tall bluffs overlooking the Mississippi River and the Louisiana Delta across the water. The history of every living and every lost city and settlement along its banks is defined in some way by that imperious river. Richard Wright, literary son of Natchez, used the river to describe one of the "coded meanings" of his early childhood: "There was the vague sense of the infinite as I looked down upon the yellow, dreaming river waters of the Mississippi River from the verdant bluffs of Natchez." In an earlier epoch, Indians stood atop the bluffs first, then the French, British, Spanish, and finally Americans. Among the latter group were master, mistress, and slaves; then later landlord, merchant, sharecropper; and in the most recent epoch the old-family elite and factory worker.[1]

The only incorporated municipality in Adams County, Natchez today, as it has always been, is an urban island in a rural sea that unfolds to all points of the compass. To the east stands a national forest of loblolly pine, long the profitable stock of corporate druids and the habitat of the hired timber folk. Flat, unobstructed fields of soy and cotton land, toiled by generations of the same families, black and white, open to the west horizon and the setting sun. Dividing the contrasting landscapes is the serpentine river and its virtually uninhabitable floodplain, curbed intermittently on the east bank by bluffs like those elevating Natchez. In the midst of this pastoral expanse, one comes upon the sometimes real, sometimes pretended, urbanity of Natchez, for all roads lead to the bluff city. Natchez native Don Simonton, who writes about the people, his people, who dwell in the outlying areas, notes that "the population to whom events in Natchez mattered a great deal was larger than that of a small river town."[2]

By modern transportation standards, Natchez is isolated, probably more so than in the days when the Mississippi River was the continent's chief superhighway. Interstate highway planners ignored Natchez in the 1960s, Amtrak rolls past it more than fifty miles away to the east, and only charter and private planes navigate into its general aviation airport. There is the Natchez Trace. Carved by Native Americans, it originated as a rugged trade and travel route that connected early Natchez to lower Tennessee.[3] It is now a pristine two-lane national parkway, a sanctuary to deer and the occasional wayward hunting dog lost during the chase through the thickly forested wilderness that advances to within feet of the asphalt. The Trace's fifty-mile-an-hour speed limit tends to steer hurried travelers to other routes; the best are U.S. highways 84 and 61, which intersect at Natchez. Old Highway 61 is the famous artery that once delivered blacks from the Jim Crow South to the so-called Promised Land of the urban North. An uncertain number traveled up from Natchez, tired of the white man's imposed sense of social order.

Within Natchez's physical setting, its architecture, and its people, one finds the romantic's sense of Old South grandeur. The WPA guide to Mississippi noted in 1938, "So deeply has the patina of the past been impressed on Natchez that it is the modern rather than the aged that stand out as anomalies." Until recent years, highway billboards promoted Natchez as the place "Where the Old South Still Lives." Contrasting with Natchez's modern side—the every-small-city-U.S.A. side with strip malls, plastic fast-food franchises, discount chains, and nondescript suburban homes—are a magnificent pageant of antebellum mansions and countless stories of chivalrous ancestors. The people of the surrounding counties and parishes, says Simonton, "spoke of Natchez and its grand houses and its nabobs as a Yorkshireman might speak of London—that great, large place full of kings and courtiers."[4]

This is the Natchez that nostalgic yet business-minded whites prefer; it is the staple of life in the old river city. White Natchez fanaticizes history like other southern communities do high-school football. White Natchez not only worships the days of the more pleasant past; it has commodified history, converted it into the city's chief business concern. In 1968 a northern visitor said of Natchez: "Here I drank in the atmosphere, culture and stability of true southerners."[5]

When I first encountered the Old South nostalgia, I understood what Robert Penn Warren meant when in the 1950s he called Natchez a "fantasia." There is indeed a fantasy world in which life wants to float with the gentle rhythms of a motionless and mythic time. The dominant historical memory, which is still shaped by an old-family elite and other white citizens, begins with noble European settlers of the early 1700s, maneuvers delicately around the sensitive subject of slavery, and then stops at some vague time in the mid–nineteenth century when Natchez was the "queen city" of the Old South. With few exceptions, white Natchez today is like a nonagenarian who forgets what happened yesterday but remembers the distant, clearer days. The city itself is an enclave of legendary gentility, still a land of balls, promenades, and cotillions, with hoopskirts and azaleas gracing a backdrop of white-columned affluence, unlikely and unwilling to look away from Dixieland. The more recent history, the days of Jim Crow and civil rights, disappears behind wistful reflections of earlier times. Like the great bluff above the flow of the river, Natchez has tried to stand above the currents of history. This all fascinated me as a researcher, and I liked to think that I could see through the moonlight-on-magnolias veneer.

My arrival in Natchez soon awakened another white southern stereotype that I had not associated with Natchez. My first morning in town, I ate breakfast at a fast-food restaurant. I took a table across from four white men smoking cigarettes and drinking coffee. They looked like workers from the local tire plant or paper mill. Behind the cloak of antebellum gentility, Natchez hid a modest but economically important manufacturing base. Its secret was given away by the inescapable rotten-egg odor that spoiled the air and the visible working class that combed the Wal-Mart and the fast-food joints. The four men were the type, a Mississippi friend would say, who grew up on white bread and potted meat. Their blend of Mississippi and Louisiana dialect was thick with working-class conjugations. They were Mississippi "rednecks," I surmised—intractable, ignorant, hatemongers with John Deere ball caps perched high on their heads.

After a while three of them left. The remaining "redneck" chatted with the black woman cleaning tables. After she moved on, he twisted around in his seat and said, "How you," with a disarming drawl and a smile etched at the corner of his eyes. I would time and again discover the same dissolving warmth in other Mississippians, black and white.

We "visited," as Mississippians like to call it, for several minutes. He had me pegged as an outsider even before we spoke. He asked my place of origin and destination, and my purpose in Natchez. I suspected that I had not been the only one engaged in secret scrutiny. Or was this genuine friendliness? Or some combination of both? I had lived in many places where friendliness often breeds suspicion, and I had nearly forgotten about the amicable nature of southerners. If the man's friendliness concealed an underlying suspicion of me, I could not deny the existence of my preconceptions about him. While I was willing to judge him only from a silent distance, he reached out with a greeting and created the opportunity to make a new friend.

Gestures such as his began to tear at the fabric of negative stereotypes I had woven around white Mississippians. The rest of the country has looked down upon their state as an American aberration, a barefooted, slack-jawed, clay-eating, race-hating embarrassment. It was not surprising to learn that white Mississippians often exhibit a defensive side to their personality. They still see their state as the "whipping boy" of a duplicitous nation unable to solve its own race problem.

In some ways their observation is justified (though behavior of the past certainly is not). Racial discrimination travels with blacks wherever they go in this country. White Mississippians are impatient with the Yankee self-righteousness that damns southern race relations with evangelical fervor. The outsider (a federal investigator or a research scholar) might regard the defensive personality as, or confuse it with, obstructionist or reactionary behavior. But from the standpoint of the white southerner, the defensive personality is shielding those closest to it from gratuitous vilification: distortions, exaggeration, innuendoes, bald-faced lies, or anything else that might unfairly sully a personal reputation, a family name, or the regional image.

In Mississippi, the defensive personality most often arises when dealing with the state's record on race. The prescribed defense in such cases is to forget the past. My brand of historical inquiry represented the resurrection of best-forgotten times, and in my endeavors in Natchez, the defensive personality usually exhibited either polite evasiveness or apologetic amnesia. I encountered the former early in my research when I tried to collect data on the percentage of black voters in Natchez and Adams County before the Voting Rights Act of 1965. When I asked for that data from registration records at the city clerk's office, an assistant explained that the city never identified the race of its voters. I did not push the issue, even after I later learned that the city charter once required that voters be recorded by race.[6]

Thinking I might have better luck with county records, I found myself in the basement of the courthouse. It was the bowels of the county seat, windowless, dim, and dank. Four workers and one visitor, whom I happened to know, greeted me in a cramped room. I made my inquiry with a heavyset man who appeared to be the registrar. "The justice department has made several requests for the same information," he said, "and we can't give it to them because it doesn't exist." He explained that Adams County never distinguished its voters by race. "I can tell you that blacks were always welcome to register in Adams County."

To confirm his claim, he turned to a black assistant who had been working quietly at her desk. He asked her when she had first registered. The woman was old enough to have qualified to vote more than a decade before the civil rights movement. Never looking up from her work, she answered quietly, "1965." The registrar must have been unaware that 1965 was the year of the first federal Voting Rights Act and was, in fact, a significant year to disfranchised blacks. Apparently believing he had proven his point, he looked at me and smiled with a hint of satisfaction.

Four years later I discovered the county poll books safely stored in the basement of the Historic Natchez Foundation, an independent nonprofit organization located two blocks from the courthouse. In the books dated before the 1960s, the race of each registered voter was meticulously recorded with a W for white and a C for colored.

The southern white memory of the past can be conveniently faulty, for recent historical interpretation has made the past a controversial one. It is little wonder then that Mississippians are sensitive about how they are portrayed in the annals. History itself—accurate history—can be seen as an assault on the local community if it fails to conform to local codes of trust and loyalty.

Scholarly studies such as mine tend to violate the local white trust. Preceding me, there have been many violators who dredged up a past that some locals would prefer left buried beneath the sludge of amnesia. The pioneers were Davis and the Gardners with their 1941 book *Deep South*. Davis and Burleigh Gardner were Harvard graduate students of the famous community-study scholar W. Lloyd Warner. In the early 1930s, Warner began looking for a southern community where he could apply the participant-observer methods of social anthropology to study black-white relationships. To white southerners, he wisely pitched his proposed project as an examination of the economic, political, and social life of a community.

When he went to Mississippi in 1933 searching for that community, his diplomacy was finely tuned. State officials in Jackson suggested he explore southwestern Mississippi, the oldest part of the state. Unsuspecting whites there indulged the Yankee scholar. The *Woodville Republican*, the local newspaper in Wilkinson County just south of Natchez, said of Warner: "He is a most elegant gentleman and a cordial welcome will be accorded him at any time." In Natchez, Warner made a point to meet the police chief, sheriff, and key political leaders.

He even dined with the Natchez mayor at the Robert E. Lee Hotel in Jackson. Speaking the language of the Natchez white leadership, Warner said he had chosen their city as the subject community "because of the fine relations between the two races, which seems to me to be essential for any work that would be done in studying a total southern community."[7]

Warner then turned the field research over to Davis and Gardner. They in turn recruited their wives, Elizabeth and Mary, into the project to form two husband-and-wife teams, one black and the other white. Warner sharpened his tactfulness. He presented Burleigh Gardner, who was white, as the research-team leader. Southern custom would have disallowed that role to the black Allison Davis, even though he was more experienced and better educated. In a letter introducing the researchers to the mayor, Warner assured city leaders that the "colored man from Virginia" was "a thoroughly reliable, trustworthy individual."[8]

The biracial team of researchers did not try to conceal their roles as social scientists. Nor did they reveal the true purpose of their study: to explore race and class relationships. The Gardners limited their research to the white community, while the Davises kept their work, residence, and social life properly confined to the black community. The project resulted in the writing of *Deep South,* which is a brutally honest and unflattering interpretation of the social dynamics of oppression. The authors consequently gave Natchez the fictitious name of "Old City" and chose not to identify the people they interviewed.

Their study virtually disappeared from the public consciousness in Natchez. While doing my own research, I found no trace of *Deep South* in local documents, in the newspapers, or in the memories of Natchez whites. A few blacks knew of the Davis study, but they were generally older people who remembered the researchers coming to Natchez.

The white ignorance of *Deep South* is hardly surprising in a place that has only recently acknowledged its most famous native, Richard Wright, even though Mississippi is typically proud of its distinguished literary heritage. Like any self-conscious community, Natchez seeks greatness in the celebrity of individuals it claims as a son or daughter. Until 1991 when the Mississippi Department of Archives and History planted a historic marker recognizing Wright, Natchez whites had all but shut out the writer's accomplishments. Clearly, recognition would risk affirming his piercing prose indicting white America.

I was reminded of white Natchez's selective memory and its sensitivity to controversial history when I inquired about *Deep South* at a locally owned bookstore. The clerk was not familiar with the book and asked about its topic. When I told her Natchez race relations in the 1930s, her face dropped into a faint expression of concern. She explained that customers probably would not care for the book. Then the defensive personality surfaced. She asked if someone else had written a more recent history, as if such a study would exonerate Mississippi in the eyes of the world. Apparently, I made the wrong impression, because her look of concern returned when I smiled and said that I was presently doing one.

It later occurred to me that my study was not about a dead past. It was about a viable community, contemporary and alive with real people. To the citizens of Natchez, to the woman in the bookstore, my book would not be the literary reconstruction of a remote time that could be closed easily between two covers and slipped onto a bookshelf, forgotten among other stories. Nor could it be dismissed as an imaginary interlude that ended with the lives of distant ancestors. The chronological scope of my study was too recent. For many people of Natchez, where the historical vision is fixed on the antebellum South, it defies convention to associate history with the time of a parent or, especially, oneself. History of this type fails to conform to the vernacular. It becomes intrusive, in some cases suspect, and even blasphemous. History in Natchez has traditionally been something that evokes pride, not something that unearths community conflict.

Yet for Natchez blacks, public history's antiseptic purpose represents its great failing. The few blacks I met who knew of Davis's book also appreciated its worth; others recognized a value in its type of study. The prevailing public history mostly ignores Natchez blacks, casting all aside like a collective Richard Wright. The recent decades, the tumultuous years of civil rights and black political empowerment, are the most meaningful to Natchez blacks. Those years represent a time of courage and triumph, and blacks believe that much has yet to be said, like the cold, hard truth.

In a sense, Natchez has continued to live with the burdens of its history. For the research scholar looking for fresh material, this is a plus. Natchez is a history laboratory, where live historical figures walk the streets like apparitions before historical places, and the passerby of the present can interact with the barely faded past.

On each trip to Natchez, this blend of past and present tested my objectivity as a researcher. The scholar and the reader typically approach Mississippi with opinions informed by the biases of the media, popular film, folklore, and by a nation's struggle with racial guilt, all of which have narrowed the American image of Mississippi to surface realities. Until recent years, Mississippi's record on race relations ranked at the bottom of a national record that in itself is appalling. While never feeling the compulsion to be sympathetic toward those who denied others their freedom, I did learn that Mississippi is more than hate and prejudice, power and oppression.[9] These are generalizations, just as "nigger" and "redneck" are stereotypes. They are not the sinew and bone of the complex, multidimensional Mississippi I sought to understand after going to Natchez. Nor are they wholly the Mississippi one should expect to encounter in this book, which was written, and might be best read, with an awareness of one's personal preconceptions and biases.

CHAPTER ONE

HISTORY LESSONS

Perpetuating Myths and Values

The Toyota station wagon turned off the road and edged onto the dirt driveway. "Stop here," the elderly landlady instructed, the car barely off the blacktop. She sat in the passenger seat proper-like, with hands folded across the purse in her lap. White athletic shoes offered a practical complement to her navy-blue dress and dress coat. "Look at this stuff," she said with as much wonder as disgust, gazing out the car window. Around the old tenant farmer's house, the yard was littered with a washing machine, lawnmowers, car parts, and other abandoned materials, remnants of bartering, bargaining, and attempts at moneymaking. All now were rusted markings of the tenant's domain. "And those columns," she added. Four white columns salvaged from a former structure of grandeur had been cut down to size and crudely fitted to the front porch, creating an odd contrast to the ramshackle house sagging on blocks and bricks.

The occupant was the last of the landlady's tenant farmers. In 1992 he was in his eighties and retired from the fields. In the spirit of noblesse oblige, the landlady was allowing him to live on her property until his death. The two were contemporaries but not social equals. Their families went back several generations. Her ancestors had owned his. She was one of the wealthiest women in Mississippi; he one of Mississippi's poorest. She was white; he was black.

She climbed out of the car, fixed her slight frame behind the open door, and let out a vigorous "Whooooop! . . . Whooooop!" No one emerged from within or around the house. She called again, "Whooooop! . . . Whooooop!" It became clear that someone would have to approach the house. She waited by the car while her escort maneuvered through the yard and on to the front porch.

Rumbling broke out from inside at the first knock. A moment passed before a throaty voice called back, "Who is it?" The door opened a crack and a head pushed through. "My God!" said the man with more than a hint of irritation. "That woman's gonna outlive us all." At eleven in the morning, his eyes were bloodshot and tired. White stubble sparkled his dark face. "Let me get my hat."

The three then gathered near the car. The landlady looked even smaller before the tenant, himself bent and of modest height. But she was clearly in charge as they respected a dated racial etiquette still observed by many blacks and whites their age. "This gentleman would like to talk to you," she said to her tenant, who removed his hat. "I suggest you make an appointment with him." The retired farmer apologized repeatedly for his unshaven face. "How about three o'clock?" she prodded. "Yes, ma'am," he said, adding he would be more presentable that afternoon.

At three, he sat waiting in a lawn chair in his driveway. He was a living symbol, a history lesson of an earlier age. Clean shaven with a self-assurance not seen earlier that day, he held a half-smoked cigar aloft in one hand and gripped a paper-sacked bottle in the other. "My white folks," he said referring to the landlady and her family, "have always taken good care of me."

SYMBOLS of the past had always been plentiful in Natchez, cropping up seemingly everywhere with their sometimes hidden, sometimes obvious, meanings. "One thing that we never sang," said Virginia Beltzhoover Morrison, speaking of her school days in Natchez during the 1940s, "was the 'Battle Hymn of the Republic.' That was a northern song. We stood up when we sang 'Dixie.'" Many of the songs that once filled the classrooms of southern white school children— "Bonnie Blue Flag" and "Swanee River," for instance—were the very ones that members of the United Daughters of the Confederacy sang at their own functions. "Dixie," which carried the most intense historical meaning of all the songs, served as the anthem of southern white culture. In

Morrison's day, the classroom was considered the proper place for ceremonious expressions of white heritage.[1] The children of the two races
took their lessons under different roofs, and there were no black students
at her school to feel the sting of alabaster rituals. This arrangement alone
provided an important lesson for larger life, which the songs and related
rituals reinforced: the races had their appointed places—separated and
stratified, white on top of black.[2]

When Bill Hanna attended Natchez schools a generation later in the
1960s, the lessons and rituals and the segregation were the same. Southern white heritage took center stage of the great theater of learning, and
every fall, eyes shifted to the football stadium of the Natchez High
Rebels. In the larger spectacle of the football game were the lessons of
history. Spectators witnessed on the field the regeneration of their culture
through boys who choreographed the virtuous qualities of manhood—
strife, force, and justifiable violence. The sport itself enlisted the players
into strategies and emotions that resembled those of war, and it had been
"the" war that was the defining historical event in forming the southern
white identity. When the high-school marching band played "Dixie,"
Hanna remembered, the school mascot Colonel Reb stood at attention in
his gray and gold Confederate uniform before a backdrop of fluttering
Rebel flags. The scene that unfolded was one of an entire stadium of
white southerners rising in tribute to not only the school and players but
to the memory of the Old South.[3]

Natchez was not necessarily a timeless place in the twentieth century.
The city of fewer than twenty thousand welcomed some change, such as
industry, tourism, and commercial progress. But it could be timeless in
some respects, and self-consciously so, especially when and where social
relations were concerned, or when the white population revered its past,
particularly the era before the Civil War. It was a blissful era in Natchez,
by some accounts, one of prominence, wealth, and important men, of
cotton plantations, slaves, and clearly delineated social positions. The
local infatuation with the Old South was captured in a popular anecdote.
As the story went, when a northern visitor asked a Natchez girl about
her dog's breed, she replied that it was nothing special—"Just a little old
ante-bellum dog."[4]

Since the Civil War, white southerners as a whole had exhibited a profound attachment to the antebellum era. Wilbur J. Cash observed that

the conscious mind of the southern white was "continuous with the past," perhaps informed more by history than by change and modernity. Within the regional milieu of heightened historical consciousness, twentieth-century Natchez was an exceptionally nostalgic city. When W. Lloyd Warner chose Natchez for the community study, he said, "We felt that the tradition of the 'Old South' had carried on much better and with far greater security than any other place we could find in the deep south." Warner was telling locals what they already knew. "There's a continuity here," said Grace MacNeil, whose great-great-grandfather settled in the area in the eighteenth century. "Young people here grow up with a sense of history, and that's a big word."[5]

Everyday life in Natchez delivered history lessons offering an intellectual as well as an emotional continuity with the traditions, ideals, and values of the past. Hundreds of white families lived surrounded by the artifacts, stories, and memories of their ancestors who, with the labor of slaves, had built the houses and public buildings, bricked the streets, and chartered the government of Natchez. History to these people was personal and integral, and with a gallery of rituals, ceremonies, icons, and written texts, they kept history alive and pressed upon the public consciousness. Containing the cultural and psychological building blocks that nourished individual and group identity, history was central to the white reality, giving it a self-protective sense of permanence and predictability. Whites looked at history like they looked into a mirror, to see who they were—and how they looked. Whatever displeased them, they could change. Just as they could straighten an unruly curl or cover an ugly blemish, they rewrote the story or left parts out.[6]

Natchez whites were perhaps no more imaginative than other southerners in their interpretation of the past. But the potency of historical myths was exceptional and ultimately proportional to the imposition of history. As late as the 1990s the historical setting in Natchez was so prepossessing that it was apt to envelop the human consciousness in a tangled reality. "Southerners who live in this region," Mississippi writer Margaret Walker Alexander said while speaking in Natchez in 1991, "rarely think of its dual nature—fact and fiction, reality and fantasy— and . . . seldom, if ever, recognize or consider the effects of the region on our lives and our personalities." As Walker knew, the power of the region on the culture was deeply rooted in the collective sense of the past.

Even without the taint of myth, the history of Natchez was rich with accounts of social conflict, conspiracies, and affluence. Twentieth-century Natchezians indeed had much to preserve in the way of material artifacts and deep family roots. They also had much of the stuff of mythmaking, which informed their daily lives.[7]

As virtually any local could tell the visitor, Natchez was one of the first cities settled on the Mississippi River. It "absorbed the best and the worst of" the region's pioneer days, according to one source. The district's bottom lands, open to the flooding waters of the Mississippi and its tributaries, Second and Saint Catherine's Creeks, were rich and dark; by the nineteenth century those lands were producing cotton and millionaires and demanding enslaved labor. Rolling hills of yellow loam, less suitable for cotton, otherwise dominated the landscape immediately around Natchez. In the twentieth century, erosion caused by intensive agriculture and timbering gouged the hills open, turning them into smaller inland versions of the natural river bluffs that stood like a fortress against the Mississippi. Two centuries earlier, the French had recognized a strategic benefit in the bluffs and built a fort, Fort Rosalie, atop them in 1716. By slaughter and disease, the settler-soldiers eventually eradicated the native inhabitants, *les Natchez,* who had refused French attempts to convert them to Catholicism. Alternating Spanish and British occupations followed the French before Mississippi became a United States territory in 1798. Natchez served as the first territorial capital before the center of government moved in 1802 to the hamlet of Washington, east of Natchez in Adams County. Style and grace and wealth remained with the river city.[8]

By the early nineteenth century, Natchez had fostered a constant stream of entrepreneurs who made great fortunes speculating in the mercantile trades, cotton, credit, and slaves. Parvenus rather than descended Old World nobility, the Natchez wealthy were known as nabobs. In manners and pretensions they exhibited an Americanized version of European sophistication. They were the nominal aristocracy of the district. Some came to Natchez with the advantage of experience and established reputations, such as French sea captain Pierre Surget who obtained a land grant of 2,500 acres in the 1780s when Natchez was a part of Spanish West Florida. Using the labor of enslaved Africans, he built a plantation and named it Cherry Grove. Before his death in 1796, he had acquired more than 7,000 acres and given his three sons a head start in life. Two, Frank and James, married and invested smartly. Between them, they controlled nearly 100,000 acres and more than a thousand slaves on several plantations scattered throughout parts of Mississippi, Arkansas, and Louisiana. Much of the more productive land of Natchez's resident elite was located in the fertile alluvial region across the river in Louisiana, which meant that profits made elsewhere came back to Natchez in the form of personal fortunes. Because the nabobs preferred to keep their wealth close, they tended to intermarry, creating small clans among forty or so families that formed the stock of a local aristocracy.[9]

They were never a ruling elite, but their affluence was inseparable from the city's image. By directing their slaves to build grand mansions, the nabobs contributed to their own and Natchez's physical conspicuousness. As a busy river city, Natchez did have a more socially varied side, which was manifested in less-affluent itinerant peddlers, slave traders, backwoodsmen, boatmen, Indians, free blacks, and others. Beneath the great houses, physically and socially, was Natchez-under-the-Hill, the river wharf, notorious for drunken brawls, gambling, and prostitution. But as long as social boundaries were respected, the river rabble did not concern "the society of the great plantation houses." By the second quarter of the nineteenth century, wealthy Natchezians had fashioned their city into a "sweet spot," as one observer described it, that stood out from the other "wretched-looking" villages and towns along the Mississippi.[10]

As Natchez burgeoned into a commercial center, the nabobs developed lucrative business alliances with the North. Many educated their children at the better universities in the Northeast and maintained a second or third residence there. Jacob, the brother of Frank and James Surget, lived full time in New York. When the threat of war loomed, peace and union obviously served the best interests of his brothers and their social equals, who questioned secession and remained loyal to the Whigs until the eve of conflict.[11]

For them and all other southerners, the Civil War turned life in the South upside down and left an aftermath of uncertainty. Only a semblance of the old social order survived. The economic wreckage combined with the destruction of slavery ruined many accumulated fortunes and in some cases forced the sale or division of great landholdings. Natchez would experience an economic resurgence in the late nineteenth century, but the old river city never recovered its prewar cultural and commercial prominence—or its "regal opulence," as one Natchezian put it. Yet in some ways it was luckier than most southern cities. Local northern sympathies during the war, as well as the Confederate decision against establishing defenses in Natchez, saved the prepossessing homes of the nabobs from Union torches, allowing an unsurpassed collection of antebellum mansions to be passed on to future generations.[12]

Perhaps equally important to some whites was the bequest of a prominent family name. Good bloodlines in Natchez came in surnames, such as Minor, Duncan, Ogden, Ellis, Surget, or Dunbar. Whether wealthy or poor, one required only the right family membership in the twentieth century to retain rank among the aristocracy. Owning a mansion was not enough; nor was it a prerequisite. Manners, bearing, taste, refinement, and self-control were all important prequalifications of a reputation for gentility. Once established, the reputation was carried forward in a family name. Mississippi newspaperman Hodding Carter found family continuity in Natchez so striking eight decades after the Civil War that he noted: The present-day Natchez aristocracy has been "persistent in survival here, where fewer surnames than homes have vanished." The contention of W. J. Cash, the South's own dispenser of hard truth, that white southerners actually came from a bloodline of coon hunters rather than fox hunters was more accurate than many white Natchezians would have cared to discuss.[13] Disregarding historical truth, these same whites were professing by the late nineteenth century that they descended from "chivalrous settlers who planted the banner of civilization and progress on the hills of Natchez." The continued presence of elite families was the power behind the myth of cultural exceptionalism and community greatness.[14]

After the Civil War, history assumed a new cultural importance.[15] Still raw from defeat, white southerners were trying to hold on to their social and family status while also dealing with the uncertainties and chaos of social and economic change. The Union had destroyed the South's economic structure and labor system, and Radical Republicans had disfranchised Confederate patriots and forced black equality upon them. The weight of shame from defeat in a region of honor had nearly crushed the southern white spirit. Yet southern white righteousness had endured, and restoring the regional hegemony of white culture had never been questioned. With the fall of the Confederacy, Robert Penn Warren wrote, "the Solid South was born—not only the witless automatism of fidelity to the Democratic Party but the mystique of prideful 'difference,' identity, and defensiveness." Wresting economic and political control from the carpetbagger invaders and scalawag turncoats eventually secured the dominance of southern white ideals and values. Precisely because whites could never again take for granted their supremacy, they embarked on an extraordinary venture of historical creativity that reinvented the values and behavioral norms of southern white culture.[16]

By setting their story in not a wholly historical past but in a mythic one, whites found renewed possibility in a narrative that allowed them to take control of their regional consciousness.[17] The war had dislodged the relevant myths that had provided them with the idealized conception of themselves as the denizens of a new Eden. But after the war new and amended myths soon materialized to cushion the iconoclastic impact of defeat. Without the availability of believable myths to give blueprint to their mission and their self-righteousness, whites could not have restored confidence and esteem lost with Lee's surrender at Appomatox. Nor could they have recovered their sense of innocence when the national cultural convention was to award that essential virtue to the victorious. Myth assured the regeneration of a modified, but self-sustaining, regional character and protected the vision of idealism from the destructive forces of truth. History became the vehicle carrying the new mythic patterns that made the past intelligible; it moved traumatized white southerners through the uncertainties of the present and forward into a coherent future. With the reordering of their past and present reality, whites rose above the threat of a collective cynicism and once again took stock in their destiny and celebrated their past as a unified people.[18]

To this end, history in Natchez constituted the near apotheosis of white culture, baldly professing white achievements and exceptionalism. White Natchez readily accepted the transcultural belief that cultural continuity required a group's exaltation and dominance. It was upon this ideological foundation that "Major" Stephen F. Power, a veteran of the Mexican and Civil Wars and longtime resident of Natchez, penned his view of the past. In 1897 he noted: "The aristocracy of Natchez was proud, exclusive, highly cultivated, and possessed of an amount of wealth and absolute leisure that enabled them to reach the highest pinnacle of civilization." Titled *The Memento,* Power's tract belonged to the genre of civic histories in memoir that were popular in the postbellum South and intended to excite pride in community and heritage. In his role as gentleman scholar, Power established a filiopietistic style that served as a model for local historians who followed in the next century.[19]

Functioning as moral arbiters of culture, those historians of later years tailored a celebratory history for a biracial society. Their history was white by design; it was about, produced for, and controlled by whites. In its lessons was the intellectual basis for the racially stratified social order, lessons that celebrated white culture and professed its elevation over black culture. "History shows conclusively," a 1948 *Natchez Democrat* editorial noted, "that certain individuals and certain races are superior to others." Of the old elements retained in the new and amended myths, the belief in white cultural superiority was the most relevant to the new order. History ordained whites as the architects of civilized life, while at the same time it mostly ignored the contributions of others. From the public rituals and symbols then, and from their high-school history lessons, Morrison and Hanna learned that the heritage of their black counterparts was one of ignorance and dependence. The subtextual message of the accepted version of past reality was uncomplicated and unchanging: white and black cultures were different and separate; that was the way it had always been, and that was the way it would remain.[20]

Protecting white culture's hegemony was a public undertaking that required unmitigated vigilance. Using history as a prop for white culture's continued dominance began in earnest in the 1880s with the rise of the Lost Cause creed. That creed propagated a mythic history that interpreted the white South's struggle and subsequent defeat in the Civil War as one of a cause upholding the country's founding principles against northern tyranny. The mortar securing the universal acceptance of those principles was states' rights, which had been threatened by the North's "jealousy," as one Natchez Lost Cause speaker put it in 1912, "of the refinement, wealth and progress of the South." When unscrupulous northerners "violated the most solemn guarantees" of the Constitution and tried to impose a new and corrupt vision on the country, the southern states were "driven, actually driven, to the last resort" to secede and to defend their right to do so. In the end, the North's greater resources allowed the Yankees to triumph militarily but not ideologically, for the South's noble cause would live on in white hearts and minds through the "dark days" of Reconstruction.[21]

In essence, the history lessons of the Lost Cause helped make life in the postbellum South somewhat familiar and predictable again for whites. Lost Cause history reconciled military defeat with notions of regional eminence and rescued the white South from a miasma of shame and uncertainty and returned it to a recognizable, though mythic, course rising toward the highest planes of civilization. Cultural greatness was an unquestioned fact to white southerners, and the Lost Cause affirmed the righteousness of that fact. In biracial society, the uplifting messages of the Lost Cause translated into white supremacy.

Whites considered few among their own as more supreme than those who had given their lives for the cause. A cemetery for the war dead and for veterans was the first physical expression of the Lost Cause in Natchez. Locals would eventually boast having five Confederate generals among their cemetery's subterranean occupants. Natchez also joined the rest of the white South in recognizing an annual Confederate Memorial Day. The April celebration brought together adults and school children in a daylong program of activities. Memorial services traditionally opened with High Mass at Saint Mary's Cathedral, Natchez's white Catholic church. Then followed a procession of Confederate veterans parading in dress uniform through the streets of Natchez to a gathering of citizens at the city cemetery. The climax came with the oratory of local Civil War heroes, who praised not only the dead but frequently "the culture and refinement of the [white] citizens of Natchez."[22]

At the 1890 Memorial Day celebration, white Natchezians dedicated a Confederate monument. Atop the granite obelisk and facing the north, an impassive Confederate soldier stood as a permanent symbol of the Lost Cause creed and of the sacredness of southern white civilization. Historian Gaines M. Foster notes that the Confederate monuments that multiplied across the South in the late nineteenth and early twentieth centuries were meant not to elicit mourning so much as to evoke histori-

cal memory—to remind white passersby of who they were and from whence they came.[23]

The primary movers in the campaign to erect a monument in Natchez were white women. Mostly middle class with some elite among them, they proved to be worthy champions of the gospel of historical preservation and cultural continuance. They served as officers in the Natchez Confederate Memorial Association (CMA), the organization sponsoring the monument campaign. By organizing raffles, picnics, and concerts, they collected the donations needed to fund the monument, an undertaking at which the men of the CMA had miserably failed.[24]

With the Lost Cause, women secured their role in Natchez society as the guiding spirit and principal guardians of heritage and public history. Melody Kubassek, who has studied the "feminization" of the Lost Cause in Natchez, explains that the public rituals "enabled women noncombatants to lay claim to the most important event in Southern history," the Civil War. One might add that their experiences even as noncombatants made them bona fide veterans of the war and its aftermath. Perhaps the Scarlett O'Haras who secretly welcomed war and death as a substitute for divorce actually existed. But for most women, sending a husband or son off to battle was a patriotic duty that bore the painful reality of the conflict; their men, in fact, were three times less likely than Union soldiers to return home. During and after the war, white women were left with having to deal with the dreadful Yankees who trampled their farms and their constitutional rights and who with the promise of freedom turned their slaves, in white eyes, into a roaming mass of unpredictability.[25]

Simply being female, white, and southern pushed women into the ideological fold of the Lost Cause. Their responsibility as custodians of the Confederate ideal actually began during the fight for southern independence. The exigencies of war forced a marriage between the public and private venues that compelled society's primary spiritual guardians to defend the moral order of home and community against the threat of social dislocations. Guarding the portals of the past was not only consistent with traditional gender expectations; female activities in the community's ceremonies and rituals constituted a natural extension of the woman's accustomed role as the culture's conservator of western traditions and

morals. The very ideals and values, including that of white cultural superiority, that mothers instilled in their children at home were packaged in the messages of public history. Well through contemporary times, white Natchez women continued to oversee the public production and dissemination of the culture's collective memory.[26]

In 1899, a number of the women of the CMA organized a Natchez chapter of the United Daughters of the Confederacy (UDC). Ideologically, it was a natural transition to make. The Natchez UDC thanked God for "Confederate History" and "for its pure record of virtue, valor and sacrifice." Steeping itself in the glory of the Lost Cause, the membership vowed to pay "homage to the memory of our gallant Confederate soldiers," with a purpose "to perpetuate the fame of their noble deeds unto the third and fourth generation." Embodied in the UDC's pledge of allegiance to the Mississippi state flag was a ritualistic reminder of the cultural commitment to God, region, and history:[27] "I salute the Flag of Mississippi and the sovereign state for which it stands with pride in her history and achievements and with confidence in her future under the guidance of Almighty God."[28]

At the regional level, the UDC organized in 1894 and immediately took the lead in the South's monument movement. The organization was able to muster an enthusiasm in activities and membership—which peaked at 100,000 in the early twentieth century—that its brother counterpart, Sons of Confederate Veterans, could never match. The membership was typically composed of women of self-proclaimed goodwill and high standards who had the time, energy, and resources to make their organizations into pivotal forces in the community.[29]

One of the primary concerns of the UDC was the "correct, fair, and unbiased" teaching of history in southern schools. A cofounder of the UDC gave top priority to "the selection of histories for the children of the South and the rejection of histories seeking sale which misrepresent the facts." The possibility that southern posterity might encounter in textbooks or the classroom the intolerable suggestion that the South had been wrong and the North right frightened the keepers of the Confederate legacy. Every year for several years, the Natchez chapter sponsored a contest for the best history essay at the grade-school level. The women of the UDC, whose motto was "Loyalty to the Truth of Confed-

erate History," chose the subject of the essay (usually a hero of the Confederacy or a circumstance associated with the Lost Cause). They then judged the essays for historical accuracy and objectivity, both of which revealed a peculiar white southern bias.[30]

Many UDC members also belonged to the Natchez Daughters of the American Revolution, which began sponsoring a similar essay contest in 1958. In addition, it presented an annual "Good Citizen" award to high-school students who best exemplified "qualities of good citizenship, dependability, service, and patriotism." The DAR, which like the UDC regarded itself as an arbiter of historical accuracy, made a policy of screening school textbooks for prointegration and politically "subversive" language.[31]

Both the DAR and UDC believed that a primary objective of the classroom and history textbook was to mold the minds of young Mississippians. Natchezian Amanda Geisenberger laid out the cultural function of history lessons when she quoted a "noted" historian (one of uncertain identity): "[T]he most important event in Mississippi education is the teaching of history in our high schools. Citizenship is a direct product. Our history courses are also the basis of culture. . . . Underlying all other outward manifestations of culture must be a deep sense of that community pictured by history. And history has more to do with the creation of character than any other subject taught. It alone presents ideals and men who gave their lives to them for them. The mere fact that such men and women lived and wrought is inspiration to all."[32]

Children formed their first and arguably most lasting impressions about their heritage and the larger southern experience from their history lessons in public schools. Following the Mississippi state-accredited course curriculum guidelines, Natchez school districts required students to take a full year of Mississippi history. Over the course of several decades, it was offered variously in the sixth, seventh, or ninth grade and was always taught around the subject of the Civil War. Classrooms served as the authoritative venues that legitimized a group's heritage and permanence, while the imprimaturs of the history textbook bestowed greater currency to the myth and lore that permeated the southern history narrative. Assessing the history of America's history textbooks, Frances Fitzgerald found that they were traditionally "written not to explore but to instruct—to tell children what their elders want them to know about their country. . . . Like time capsules, the texts contain the truths selected for posterity." Several generations of history textbooks in Mississippi schools did more than impart historical information.[33]

The earlier generations of texts set forth the agenda of character building and cultural transmission that was consistent with the conventions of the Lost Cause. Their narratives are selective and exclusionary, rather than comprehensive and inclusive, and they reveal a pedagogical continuity in their southernization of history. Often sharpened with exaggeration, fabrication, and omissions, their message about the righteousness of white supremacy and black subordination is unmistakable. Although the textbooks were used in both black and white schools, the few black historical participants that appear in the narratives are not allotted the personalized nomenclature Mississippian, which meant white. All the texts incorporate narratives with a we/them dichotomy when discussing different groups—with "we" and "our" referring to whites, and "they" and "them" serving as exclusionary pronouns for blacks (and Native Americans). Blacks assume an implicit nonperson status and are portrayed as two-dimensional in being: evil when not subservient to whites and happy when they were. At the same time that the books emphasize harmony between the races and between the southern states, they treat the historical relationship between the North and South as an interminable conflict. The homeland is cast as a national victim of constant Yankee meddling while it continued to exhibit the utmost honorable behavior in all its affairs, internal and national.[34]

In their pursuit to keep textbooks ideologically pure, the UDC and DAR gained a powerful ally in the state of Mississippi. In 1940, lawmakers enacted legislation to provide free textbooks for Mississippi's children. Sworn into office that year, Governor Paul B. Johnson had run on a populist platform to improve the state's ailing public education system, ranked at the bottom in the nation. The legislation he signed created a ratings committee that convened annually to review textbooks and recommend selections for the textbook board's approval. During the 1950s, the state superintendent of education, who was also vice-chairman of the board, reminded the ratings committee each year that "the boys and girls of Mississippi are the ones to be benefited or harmed by your decisions." He instructed committee members to "[l]ook closely for any expressed or implied statement suggestive of subversive principles, Communistic propaganda or any ideas that connote alien ideologies antagonistic to the basic principles of our political faith or way of life."[35]

Despite these clearly articulated instructions, the ratings committee apparently failed on occasion to live up to the high standards of some of the state's more circumspect citizens. In 1959, the state DAR joined forces with the American Legion and the Citizens' Council to charge that forty-four of the textbooks used in Mississippi schools failed to teach adequately states' rights and racial integrity and instead tacitly endorsed the philosophies of socialism, communism, and "one-world-isms." The DAR claimed that one of the books had wrongly concluded "that Negro people have done much to develop themselves." An American Legion resolution concurring with the DAR findings publicly condemned the textbooks for allegedly advocating racial integration and amalgamation, as well as the dissolution of state sovereignty. As chairman of the textbook board and with the support of the self-appointed censors, Mississippi's segregationist Governor Ross Barnett seized responsibility for selecting history books for the public schools. We must "clean up our textbooks," Barnett declared in spring 1960. "Our children must be properly informed of the southern and true American way of life."[36]

The Barnett-UDC-DAR version of history became the state's official version of history. Its sanitized narrative was the creation of writers who, while not necessarily prone to fiction, were sympathetic to the ideals of the white southern way of life, such as segregation and limited black franchise. Like the symbols and rituals that raised the image of the Old South to a romantic plane, history written within the purview of white southern correctness extolled reverent images of a defeated though virtuous people. Akin to the regional tradition of storytelling, the texts wove a tapestry of folktales that validated the world of southern whites and reconciled their staunch commitment to democratic principles in a racially divided society. The result was a history self-consciously written to elevate and explain the past rather than to interpret it critically and objectively.[37]

One book that met the approval of the censors was written by the head of the history department at Natchez High School, Pearl Guyton. For more than a quarter of a century, beginning in 1935, her book *Our Mississippi* served as the standard of historical wisdom in Natchez classrooms. A smallish and impassioned woman who came from an academic, though racially conservative, family of northeast Mississippi, Guyton diverted from the southern woman's expected course of marriage and domesticity and instead devoted her adult life to teaching. Hundreds of children passed through her classroom over the years, and thousands studied her text. Popular among her students, Guyton earned a lasting reputation for being a model teacher. "She had a heart of gold," remembered Katherine Blankenstein. "We all were fond of Miss Guyton." Whether written or spoken, her word carried the considerable weight of a teacher and published author.[38]

As a scholar she demonstrated a steadfast loyalty to the cultural ideals of her race. Economic decisions had kept her book off the textbook board's approval list until 1952. Ideologically, however, the book was sound; it resonates with the Stars-and-Bars patriotism of the UDC. Its loyalties are quickly affirmed in the introduction, which was written by her brother, David E. Guyton, a professor of history at Blue Mountain College in Mississippi. Settled by "men and women of the purest Anglo-Saxon stock," the professor wrote, Mississippi has risen "steadily, proudly and majestically onward and upward" from a "peerless heritage." An even "nobler day" lies ahead, for the "White Race and Negroes" dwell together in "mutual good will." From cover to cover, Pearl Guyton carefully crafted southern and state loyalty and pride of this magnitude. So unfailingly faithful was she in her labor that in the index under the subject "Civil War," she directed readers to the regionally correct phrase, "War Between the States."[39]

Likewise, her interpretation of Reconstruction was in keeping with the white regional memory. Predisposed to crime, laziness, and irresponsibility, the author and teacher argued, the former slaves would not work unless forced to and consequently lacked the capacity to support themselves in freedom. This was the very basis of the Black Code of 1865 that, to paraphrase her book, impressed restrictions that all but restored slavery—for the "good" of the desultory and the ignorant. The Reconstruction government that eventually abolished the Black Code had taken "the power from the hands of able men and put it in the hands of people who were incompetent and uneducated." What followed were insufferable years of social disruption brought on by the abject failure of black political leadership, a time when the inept and corrupt occupied the legislative halls. In Guyton's reckoning, "it is a wonder that anything constructive was accomplished" at the constitutional convention of 1868. "The first move by representatives was to vote themselves huge salaries and to make ridiculously large appropriations of money for the care of freed Negroes." Guyton concluded: "No one at the convention seems to have worried as to where all this money was coming from." (It was an argument that presaged criticisms of the federal social-welfare programs of the 1960s.)[40]

The Natchez High School teacher was especially mindful of the ancestors who redeemed the South. Guyton had grown up only miles from the home of Nathan Bedford Forrest, founder of the first Ku Klux Klan, and her book's rendition of southern Restoration is the stuff of Thomas Dixon, one of the creative minds behind *The Birth of a Nation*. Honorable white southerners, she wrote, banded together and organized the Ku Klux Klan to save their beloved South from ruin. The white-robed defenders of civilization were committed to protecting "weak, innocent, and defenseless people, especially the widows and orphans of the Confederate soldiers." The Klan's was a "worthy aim," Guyton contended, which was united with another equally commendable purpose: "that of restoring the political power in the South to the educated and responsible white men who formerly held it." To accomplish that end, the Klan "visited," as Guyton worded it, "not only the Negroes but also the carpetbaggers and scalawags." Upon the establishment of Democratic government, overburdening taxes were reduced, the agricultural economy was revived, and "the hard feelings that existed between the blacks and whites during reconstruction times gave way to understanding and cooperation." Guyton's Dixonesque Restoration was a fanciful epilogue of understanding and cooperation that in reality translated into black disfranchisement and obeisance.[41]

Like their colleague Pearl Guyton, Natchez teachers recognized the broader cultural importance of history. Schools charged teachers with cultivating moral values and political ideals, and in the classroom they served as the authoritative enunciators of selected truths. The pedagogical approach Natchez teachers followed complied with the idea that schools were character builders, serving the community and posterity, with history as one of the building blocks. In the mid-1960s, for instance, junior-high schoolteachers proclaimed in a report to the Southern Association of Schools and Colleges that they "realize that the teaching of social studies is more than the 'reconstruction of the past,' it is a display of patriotism and loyalty." The report's authors listed twelve objectives in their roles as teachers, including: "To develop respect and understanding of our heritage"; "Create a more effective feeling of patriotism"; and "To enable students to recognize and analyze propaganda." The report reflected in part a fear of the communist menace. But in counteracting communist propaganda, Natchez teachers were peddling ideals themselves with an idealized history that influenced attitudes and world views of Natchez youth.[42]

History served a valuable social utility in just this way. As the editor of the *Natchez Democrat* put it: "The minds of the little fellows who trudge off to the classrooms every day are completely in the hands of the forces administering it." When in 1940 the editor decried German schools for propagating Nazism, for instance, he proposed a countermeasure that was not unlike the German offensive method itself. He called for U.S. schools to "inculcate more strongly in the mind of the impressionable student the value of democracy." To emphasize his point, the editor added that "[w]ithout the influence of American schools, it would be much more difficult to combat the teachings of alien ideologies." Ironically, the Nazification of German history and the intellectual dissemination of Aryan racial attributes were of the same propaganda form as were the myth-imbued Mississippi history textbooks and their less-than-subtle message of white homogeneity and racial superiority. Corroborating the power of the written message was the authoritarian atmosphere of the classroom, where passive learning was the norm.[43]

Guyton retired from the classroom in 1953, still committed to the same ideals, and another decade passed before her book went out of print. In its place, the state adopted John K. Bettersworth's *Mississippi: Yesterday and Today.* A 1937 Duke University Ph.D. and history professor at Mississippi State University for more than thirty years, Bettersworth refrained from using the same sort of misty, romantic prose that characterized his predecessors' work. But to a large degree, Bettersworth's book is the sum of the interpretations and ideals of Guyton and others. Had he chosen to draw on the important historical evidence presented in the pathbreaking works of Mississippi historians such as Vernon L. Wharton, author of the seminal *Negro in Mississippi, 1865–1890,* and David Donald, who won a Pulitzer Prize for his *Charles Sumner and the*

Coming of the Civil War, he would have demonstrated a genuine departure from the traditionalists. Yet the Jackson native constructed an exclusionary narrative that pushes blacks to an inert fringe of the white experience. Reconstruction in Bettersworth follows the traditionalist theme. In another telling example, Ross Barnett, who as governor flouted constitutional authority by trying to stop James Meredith's enrollment at the University of Mississippi in 1962, emerges as a nationally recognized defender of constitutional government.[44]

The Bettersworth version of history was the only option given to public schools during the late 1960s and 1970s, even though the Mississippi State Textbook Purchasing Board could approve up to five history texts. By that time, Bettersworth had attracted the censure of revisionists, who distrusted his white patriarchal narrative and who labeled the senior scholar "a 'safe' Mississippi historian." They contended that the state's only approved Mississippi history text presented a picture of the past that was incomplete and clearly outdated, especially in the aftermath of the civil rights movement, a subject that Bettersworth glossed over in his 1975 edition. The critics' complaints were directed at the state textbook board, which had refused to approve a new book, *Mississippi: Conflict and Change.*[45]

First published in 1974, *Conflict and Change* introduced a racial balance not found in Bettersworth. Most of the authors of the revisionist book had been educated or had taught in Mississippi, but it represented a generational advance in history scholarship that was born in the political liberalization of academics in the 1960s. They recognized blacks as vital participants in the state's history and incorporated new themes that sat poorly with traditional white southern sensibilities: labor unrest, lynching, poverty, convict-leasing, political corruption, and racial conflict.

The book drew high praise in academic circles. Historian Paul Gaston applauded its bold perspective yet accurately predicted it could expect "a future of controversy." The title itself suggested as much. Despite capturing the 1975 Lillian Smith Award for Best Southern Nonfiction, *Conflict and Change* required legal intervention to win state approval. After years of delay, the authors, with the legal help of the NAACP, won a U.S. district court decision in 1980 ordering the state to add *Conflict and Change* to its list of approved texts. Following the decision, only 20 of Mississippi's 153 school districts indicated that they would use the book. The Natchez–Adams County school district was not among them.[46]

No less than its predecessors, *Conflict and Change* did more than narrate history. For good or bad, it propagated a structured set of beliefs and values in an attempt to fix the historical record. With the book's publication, history became an ideological battleground between new and old ways of thinking. Other texts seeking a moderate interpretation of Mississippi's past were introduced as alternatives to the two in conflict.[47] By simply bringing a sense of wholeness to Mississippi's written history, *Conflict and Change* could be regarded as a threat to the social ordering of society in Natchez and elsewhere in Mississippi. The traditional interpretation of history legitimized the existing social, political, and cultural status quo of whites. Giving blacks an important role in history was de facto recognition of them as valid citizens in contemporary society. Equally unsettling to many whites, *Conflict and Change* dismantled much of the historical myth and lore that for generations had formed the ideological foundation of the southern white experience and identity. Probably in no other Mississippi community had the southernization of history been more essential to social and cultural identity than in the state's oldest city, Natchez.[48]

The selection of truths that determined classroom pedagogy and that shaped the textbook narrative began at the point of origin of evidence gathering. In the zeal to preserve the official version of history and to pass it on to those who would read and perhaps teach it, the efforts of the researcher-writer sometimes went beyond censorship to include outright corruption of evidence. Teachers could not always know whether they were encountering historical fact or fiction in textbooks and other sources. How many cared is debatable. Objectivity mattered less than subjectivity, truth less than message.

A case in point is the ex-slave narratives of the Federal Writers Project (FWP). Compiled in the 1930s mostly by writers employed by the FWP, the narratives were the product of thousands of interviews conducted across the South with blacks born in slavery. In later years, scholars wanting to restore historical agency to blacks have depended heavily on the narratives. At the same time, cautious observers have pointed out that elderly blacks were recollecting racially sensitive events seven decades or more old, doing so usually before white interviewers, and doing so during the uncertainties of the Great Depression, when the old predictability of slave life might have held a nostalgic attraction. Scholars, therefore, should question the narratives' reliability.[49]

The methods employed in Mississippi to record data should indeed give scholars reason for pause. An all-white team of federal writers conducted more than five hundred interviews. Of those, only twenty-six narratives were sent to the Library of Congress while the project was in operation. Four decades later, two researchers, Ken Lawrence and Jan Hillegas, a former Mississippi Summer Project activist, unearthed the missing narratives buried in boxes at the Mississippi state archives in Jackson. From originals found at the archives, Lawrence and Hillegas learned that a dozen narratives sent to Washington contained numerous distortions. Descriptive adjectives such as "good," for master, and "happy," for slave, were added to give the impression that slavery was a benign and beneficent institution and that the contemporary racial order was a model of virtuousness. Three of the Library of Congress narratives came from Natchez, and all of them contained points of departure from the originals.[50]

The supervisor of the FWP office in Natchez was Edith Wyatt Moore, a Georgia native who moved to the river city in 1919. During most of her years in Natchez, Moore remained active in community affairs. She was "Official lecturer" and historian of the Natchez Garden Club and founder of the Old Natchez District Historical Society. She also played an instrumental role in the discovery and the transfer of the private diary of William Johnson, antebellum Natchez's most renowned free-black resident, to the public domain. In later years, Natchez schools identified her as the chief authority teachers should consult about Natchez history. As district supervisor for the FWP, one of her responsibilities required collecting local historical data for the WPA *Guide to Mississippi*. Much of that material later became the genesis of a sensational tale she wrote about Natchez-under-the-Hill.[51]

Under Moore's supervision, the FWP interviewers, which included Moore, manipulated the ex-slave testimonies conducted in Adams County. As did other FWP staff members working on the ex-slave narratives, those workers in Natchez had a list of prepared questions, and as whites they had their own ideas about the answers expected from their black respondents. The narratives prepared by the Natchez staff affirm the white conception of blacks as childlike and tolerable when deferential, misguided and intolerable when not. Every respondent, for instance, was asked for an opinion about younger blacks, who whites generally considered more predisposed to social deviance.

Adams County ex-slave Charlie Davenport apparently was a favorite of the interviewers. He had been a slave of Gabriel Shields on Aventine Plantation, which belonged in the Surget family. He undoubtedly offered Moore an acceptable response when he told her, "Most of the young niggers is headed straight fur hell." Moore recorded him saying, "All dey think about is drinkin hard liquor, goin to dance halls en gettin a ole rattletrap automobile. . . . Hit beats all how dey brags en wastes things. Dey ain't one whit happier den de folks wuz in my day. . . . 'Course schools has done a heap towards givin colored folks book learnin. But hit looks to me like all dey is studying 'bout is how to git out ob honest labor."[52]

This passage was included in both the original manuscript and the copy sent to Washington. What the Library of Congress copy did not include, what apparently had been deliberately removed from the original manuscript, was the following addendum to Davenport's testimony of young blacks: "Dey is all in debt en chained down to somethin same ez us slaves wuz. . . . Dat ain't no such thing as freedom. Us is all tied down to something." Moore conducted the interview and transcribed it to longhand, and the account that later went to Washington was rewritten by Pauline Loveless and edited by Clara E. Stokes. It is unclear who was responsible for the distortions, but the practice was both common and advocated in Mississippi.[53]

Less controvertible evidence indicates that one passage in the Davenport narrative was completely fabricated. During the interview, Davenport told Moore about a planned slave uprising in Adams County.[54] According to the Library of Congress narrative, the motivations of the slave rebels puzzled Davenport. He allegedly said: "But what us want to kill Marster an' take de lan' when dey was de bes' frien's us had?" This sentence was not part of Moore's handwritten original and was added to the Library of Congress version for obvious reasons. The narrative of another ex-slave, James Lucas, contains a similar gratuity. Moore noted in her unedited copy that Lucas said: "Folks dat aint ebber bin free don't rightly know de feel ob bein free or de meanin ob hit." Between the edited and unedited accounts a sentence was attached apparently for the benefit of correcting any misguided notions (outside the South) about the relationship between slave and master. It has Lucas saying: "Slaves like us, what was owned by quality-folks, was sati'fied an' didn' sing none of dem freedom songs."[55]

In the data Moore collected for other FWP writing projects, her perspective of history was always in the tradition established by her Lost Cause predecessors. Like many of her white neighbors, she had a dreamy image of the Old South, especially of Natchez. In a short paper describing the "spectacular beauty" of her adopted home, she mentioned: "When the Creator made the Natchez country he truly clothed it in lordly raiment." Her longer essay "History of Natchez" is trimmed with similar fanciful impressions: "Hospitality in Natchez seemed to have no limit," she wrote. "Guests sometimes came for a day but remained a year. Chivalry took deep root and duels became frequent occurrences. . . . When war finally broke out . . . Natchez and vicinity furnished hundreds of soldiers to the Lost Cause." Her rendition of white southern gallantry and patrician dignity smacked of Guyton-style narrative. Moore wrote: "During their [masters'] absence may it be said to the everlasting credit of the colored race that crimes were infrequent and plantations were still cultivated. . . . Reconstruction was far more deadly than war. . . . Man power was decimated, slaves were freed and the whole social system tottering." Moore expanded the lore in the written historical record with another WPA essay, which requires nothing more mentioned than its title: "Heroes and Heroines."[56]

The icon building that is so evident in Moore's writing typified the literary style of her contemporaries of letters. Old South novels enjoyed a widespread audience in the late nineteenth century, when southern whites needed a psychological palliative to help survive military defeat, economic decline, and social change—not to mention continued Yankee assaults on southern character. Postbellum "Cavalier" literature rescued the image of the Old South patrician class from the social, economic, and humanitarian decadence northern histories and literature ascribed to it. Thus from the sentimental perspective of the southern literary tradition, there would have been no noble society in America if the Southland had not been graced with the presence of the patrician ken and kind. Educated in the classics and endowed with chivalric virtues, the gentleman southerner of the romance novel assumed the characteristics of the English squire. He was a sophisticated student and citizen of the world, at once a wise businessman and a vigorous sportsman, a man of honor in all arenas. He was benevolent toward his loyal subordinates, intolerant of social deviance. The women in his life were his abiding complement. They were ladies of chivalry and respectability, trained as the gatekeepers of proper manners and moral rectitude. They were gentle and pious yet pleasantly firm in conviction. They were smart, though dutifully self-effacing. With their men they were portrayed as the standard-bearers of southern and American culture.[57]

By the 1920s, southern writers of the so-called Literary Renaissance gave rise to new forms that broke with the genteel image of the Old South. Yet even while the likes of Faulkner, a pivotal figure in the emerging genre, kept Mississippi society and conventions in the spotlight of literary criticism, Natchez continued to inspire the traditionalists. The most famous example is Stark Young and his *So Red the Rose,* a classic Civil War fiction set in the grandeur of old Natchez. An enormously successful book that sold 400,000 copies the first month of its publication in 1934, *So Red the Rose* manifests the material elegance and cultural preeminence that prevailed in the Old South literature, and in the historical memories of white Natchezians. Although Young was whetted by such memories, he insisted that his book was about the South in general and only about Mississippi and Natchez incidentally.[58]

Nevertheless, white Natchez vainly regarded his work as a deserving tribute to a model community that a worldwide readership could and should acknowledge. In *So Red the Rose* locals could find an affirmation of life like that rendered in their own version of history. The Natchez mansions mentioned in the book were the very ones they saw every day. Place and family names were the same. The actions and behavior of Young's "darkeys" were how Natchez whites imagined that of "their" blacks. Young himself was a native Mississippian, born in Como in the northeast region of the state, and the son of a Confederate veteran. On his mother's side he was related to the McGehees, a large and socially prominent family of the state and of the Natchez district. The McGehees provided Young with a cast of characters for many of his novels, including his most popular. As he acknowledged, *So Red the Rose* is based on the lives of his own "blood" ancestors.[59]

The book is an imaginative treatment of the white elite who lived in and around Natchez and suffered the impact of the war and its aftermath. Fellow southern novelist Ellen Glasgow gave *So Red the Rose* high marks as the "most completely realized novel of the Deep South in the Civil War." What impressed her equally so was the book's success at conveying a "special sense of time and place," as well as "some larger habit of mind, some abstract fidelity." Young's story is actually less about war than about the values and customs that forged white southern civilization and sustained its continuity—the "whole Southern cultural idea," as Young put it. He said of his book: "I am making it a comment on civilization and living questions. . . . I want it to be a large, rich and beautiful canvas."[60]

Although implicitly, which was the author's method, Young conveyed that lesson to his readers through the words of Hugh McGehee, the wealthy family scion (and Young's real-life granduncle). The patriarch of Montrose tells his son Edward: "Our ideas and instincts work upon our memory of these people who have lived before us, and so they take on some clarity and outline. It's not to our credit to think we began today, and it's not to our glory to think we end today." The continuum of which McGehee speaks begins with an earlier generation, and if not for that generation's own accomplishments and foresight, the past would hold for Hugh and Edward no answers to the "living questions" of civilization. History would lose its cultural meaning. It is not the mansions, the family names, or even the agreeable servants that bring the fictional Natchez closest to real life and to the authentic Natchez. It is the cultural significance of history, the fidelity to continuity, and the ancestor worship.[61]

Like the real Natchez, the civilization of Young's fiction is one constantly drawn into "battle between tradition and anti-tradition." The conflict represents one constant in the continuum and, according to Donald Davidson, a persistent theme in the novel.[62] Like Davidson, Young was an unwary Agrarian Radical and a contributor to *I'll Take My Stand,* the reactionary 1930 manifesto that questioned the rationale of Yankeefied change in the South.[63] Young's broader convictions about his southland emerge in *So Red the Rose*'s narrative but fall short of the point of intrusive personal politics or emotion. In the incendiary figure of William Tecumseh Sherman, for instance, Young skillfully plants the force of northern conquest and aggression. The Union general is the composite of the military enemy and the cultural antagonist who clashes with the old southern traditions embodied in the person of Duncan Bedford, one of Young's southern heroes. At the story's climax, Young symbolizes the intended destruction of the nobler society with black Federal troops sacking and burning the McGehees' Montrose. Hugh McGehee contends that the new, imposed order will bring "the debasement of the social sense."[64]

Ultimately, the common bonds of family, friendship, attitudes, and traditions sustain Young's main characters and save their civilization—that of the white South and of Natchez. Its continuity in defiance of a bleak future is symbolized in the novel's last pages with a double wedding that further cements the incestuous ties of the elite families (a similar theme is found in D. W. Griffith's *The Birth of a Nation*). Young then closes his novel with Agnes McGehee caught in a grievous reflection of her son's death at Shiloh. It is 1866 and three years after Edward left her; yet she visualizes the shapes of the wounded and dead on the battlefield green; their "groans and cries" come back to her. She then looks down and into the ecstatic face of her young nephew. She is for the moment suspended between the past, represented in her son's memory, and the future, seen in her nephew. The scene is a metaphoric prelude to the Lost Cause creed.[65]

It is perhaps unfair to dismiss *So Red the Rose* as an Old South Gothic. Young researched local family records, journals, newspapers, and letters; he strove for historical authenticity and hoped to avoid the suggestion that he had composed a "mere romance" novel. He chose Natchez in part for that reason. With its antebellum mansions, old family heritage, and history, Natchez offered a place with the real physical setting and life of the Old South. "I wanted that life thus created to be true to its original," he said, "but at the same time essentially free of time and place." Seeming to oblige him at the very time that Young was researching his book between 1932 and 1934, white Natchez was building a tourist industry, using its antebellum homes, that did much to preserve the artifacts, particularly the antebellum homes, of that past life. Young not only believed that with Natchez he had satisfied his objective; he claimed that many historians, including Henry Steele Commager and Allan Nevins, praised *So Red the Rose* for its adherence to historical authenticity.[66]

One might question such a validation. The works of Commager and Nevins themselves reflected the patrician's bias toward the "dominant" culture, which may have been partially responsible for the professional respect that they commanded and that Young valued. His fellow Agrarian and friend Donald Davidson was of a different mind from the historians. As he saw it, the novel that presumably pleased the annalists is at bottom "literature, not documentation." Like most southern fictions, *So Red the Rose* draws on fact and blends in fantasy. As does the historian, the novelist rearranges the chaos of real-life events into an intelligible order. For both scholar and artist, the process is a creative and imaginative one, and the result is an admixture of truth and illusion. To borrow the words of Margaret Walker Alexander, who was speaking about the mythic power of Natchez, "The world of fiction is one of myth, not history. . . . Sometimes the fantasy of fiction seems as real as history, and sometimes the reality seems absolutely fantastic."[67]

How many Natchezians ultimately read Young's book and were affected by it is not important. What matters is that *So Red the Rose* projected an invented image that flowed from the remembered past as well as from the contemporary environment in which the author created his work. That environment bore the continuity of life, an "abstract fidelity" to the past, for which Young so desperately struggled. The book ultimately fails because the centrality of history in the fictional Natchez provides the strongest link to the real Natchez—the recent, not the old, Natchez. As Stark Young scholar John Pilkington notes, "One could say that the real dates of the work should be not 1860–65 but 1932–34." *So Red the Rose* is less the product of the era it portrays than the reflection of the attitudes, beliefs, and myths—indeed the sense of reality—of its creator and his fellow white Mississippians.[68]

Whether writing about or from Natchez, patrons of southernized history did not see themselves as overzealous censors or distorters of truth. Through the emotional prism of the writer, teacher, historian, and memorial group—cultural guardians all—they were setting straight a historical record that could otherwise impugn their sense of past reality, and thus their identity as a people. Like any cultural group, white southerners wanted to celebrate their heritage, and it was natural that they relied on selectivity and myth when reconstructing history. But in projecting powerful images of white achievements, inventiveness, and survival—of white superiority—southernized history conferred legitimacy to preexisting racial attitudes. It widened the conceptual gap between black and white cultures and strengthened the pretext for white superiority and racial separation. White Natchezians were like other southerners when it came to inventing history and taking identity from history. The difference lay in the fanatical intensity with which white Natchez continued to celebrate its heritage well beyond the twilight of the Lost Cause in the 1910s.[69]

More than seventy years later, Virginia Morrison and Bill Hanna could attest to history's perpetual power in Natchez. By that time blacks attended their alma mater with whites, and many of the old symbols and rituals were gone. Still, other tangibles of faith were plentiful. At the time, the Natchez area claimed five official historic districts, more than five hundred pre–Civil War buildings, twelve National Historic Landmarks, and eighty-two homes on the National Register of Historic Places, reputedly more per square mile than any other southern city. A second Confederate monument stood before the county courthouse, dedicated in 1950 by the UDC. Near the original monument in Memorial Park, a vintage cannon was aimed defiantly to the north, perhaps not ironically like the granite soldier. With the development of a major local tourist industry in the 1930s that extolled Old South greatness, the symbols and ceremonies of the white reality of the past had acquired an economic value that made them ever more sacred and powerful.

Women were responsible for turning history into a tourist attraction, just as they had been responsible for enhancing history's social importance after the Civil War. They romanticized the past and made it sacred, and in turn their history consecrated southern white culture. It was indeed their history, for they had seized the initiative from men and taken the lessons and meaning of the past into their protective purview. In a land of chivalry, they transformed public history into a white matriarchy. Ultimately, they were plotting an important course for future generations of women of the their race and class in public life in Natchez.

CHAPTER TWO

PILGRIMAGE TO THE PAST

Public History, Women, and the Racial Order

With cameras in hand, clusters of sightseers tramped the sidewalks in search of scenes of the Old South. Natchez was a tourist town, a veritable time capsule conveying visitors back to an idealized past of opulence and courtly grace. Every spring during Pilgrimage week, locals dressed in period clothing and put their city's unrivaled preserve of antebellum homes on public display. Theirs was the second-oldest house tour in the country. Most of the Natchez homes were privately owned by descendants of the Old South elite, most were mansions, and all had names.

At Monmouth, a little girl dressed in white pantaloons and a flower-print dress looked picturesque in the vernal sunlight. Next to her was a grandmotherly woman wearing a hoopskirt. Their costumes lacked a certain precision. The woman wore plastic-framed glasses with a trendy flare at the temples. The girl's "pantaloons" were not pantaloons at all but white slacks, and the basket she held in her left hand contained not spring flowers but ticket stubs. The inaccuracies did not seem to trouble the tourists who gathered around them like starstruck fans, many of them perching cameras before their faces.

Across town at another mansion, a tall cast-iron fence encircling it kept the tourists at bay, at least on this particular day. The 1830s estate occupied half a city block. Blooming azalea bushes skirted the house; old live oaks shaded the rest of the grounds, their branches twisting outward and downward. As did the house, their antiquity awakened the mind to history. Inside, three generations shared the home's spaciousness; their family had lived there since 1849. The house was their anchor, an integral part of the family history, an assurance of their perpetuity.

Three women joined in the conversation outside. They sat on the back terrace overlooking a shaded courtyard mottled with yellow sunlight. Yes, they agreed, "elite" is an accurate label to describe the social class of some of the local garden club women, many of whom own a historic house. That's right, there are no black members in either of the garden clubs. People become comfortable with a particular pattern of life, and they just don't like change.

As the conversation neared its end, the busy sounds of the black cook preparing the evening meal carried from the kitchen through a screen door and across the terrace. Beyond the old house's cast-iron fence, the tourists still tramped. Natchez was a romance novel brought to life, a wish, perhaps, that the present had not happened.

NATCHEZ Pickaninnies," reads the caption of the circa-1930s black and white photograph found in a local history monograph. In it four black children, with arms wrapped around their knees, are huddled together on the side of a downed tree. Their clothes are worn and tattered and bear the look of hand-me-downs. All four are barefooted and obviously poor. The faces of three share the same dispassionate expressions. The fourth, the biggest boy, wears a floppy hat smartly cocked back on his crown, and he reveals a faint grin. Presumably, they were not accustomed to being in the focal point of a camera lens. It is also safe to assume that they were unaware that the camera would make them part of the local historical record, one that today is recognizably incomplete and misinformed.[1]

The photograph comes from a small book titled *Natchez of Long Ago and the Pilgrimage,* by Katherine Grafton Miller. In itself, the photograph is not degrading. But within the context of Miller's 1938 book, it assumes a specific social meaning and purpose. The Natchez pickaninnies are alone among the book's fifty-three other photographs ennobling whites and antebellum traditions: hoopskirted belles, aristocratic men, magnolia-shaded mansions, and black mammies and footmen tending to all. Miller's account of historic Natchez and "the golden days of the Old South" offered to white readers an inflated conception of their heritage and culture. The compliant servants and the barefooted pickaninnies render the book's only images of black life. Their unflattering contrast to the white material elegance carries a subtextual message that undoubtedly reinforced the assumption of difference between two cultures.[2]

Miller likely was not interested in subtextual messages. She wrote her book as a tribute to the Natchez Pilgrimage, a weeklong spring event in which private antebellum homes were opened to the public for an admission price. Miller was a founder and the exalted empress of the Pilgrimage, which began in the early 1930s and ultimately evolved into a community mnemonic more powerful than the Lost Cause creed, history textbooks, or any other local ritual or ceremony. It was the consummate history lesson—animated, inspiring, and righteous. During Pilgrimage week, Natchez became a fantasy world in which the past seemed to coexist with the present. One could hardly know Natchez without knowing the Pilgrimage. The latter was the undergirding of a burgeoning local tourist industry, an industry that quickly grew to rival farming and manufacturing and eventually to surpass both.

Along with Miller, fellow members of the all-female Natchez Garden Club created the Pilgrimage and oversaw its operations. They elevated their spring event to a commanding status in the community by selling nostalgia to locals and tourists; it was an elixir in great demand. In a sense, the garden club women privatized public history. Yet their efforts went beyond profitmaking. In the tradition of their nineteenth-century foremothers, they served as the trustees of the local historical memory, and with their Pilgrimage, they raised the historical consciousness of Natchezians. Indeed, public history in Natchez is noteworthy for the expanded moral force it gave women. They were the trusted keepers of white culture and the vessels of its regeneration. They "sanctified history," said a longtime Natchez resident. "They've made it holy; they've made a religion out of it."[3]

Theirs was a civil religion given to value consensus rather than spiritual truth-seeking. It tolerated and nurtured only pleasant images of and messages about white heritage. Pilgrimage festivities dwelled on themes of innocence, simplicity, family, and virtue, and they brought to life a vision of the Old South that was deeply embedded in the regional imagination. David Donald, a native Mississippian, describes that vision as one of "magnolia-shaded plantations, where young gallants rode to foxes, cheered on by damsels in hoops and crinolines, and where happy pickaninnies divided their time between eating watermelons and serving mint juleps to the Old Massa." If that South, as Donald contends, "never existed outside of fiction," then by way of historical depiction, fiction flourished in Natchez. History's chief fabricators, the garden club women resurrected with their Pilgrimage a dream world of the past that shaped beliefs and perceptions in modern-day Natchez.[4]

In the qualities of spirit, Natchez and the Pilgrimage were one. The city, in fact, appropriated as its own the motto garden club members adopted in the 1930s for their annual Pilgrimage. "Natchez, 'Where the Old South Still Lives'" summed up concisely the image both wanted to convey to the world and did so with extraordinary success. As one observer of the Pilgrimage remarked in 1935, there is a "sense of timeless quality about this romantic little town." More than four decades later, the Pilgrimage moved a *Boston Herald* writer to describe Natchez as a page out of *Gone with the Wind*. "[D]uring Pilgrimage," the author noted, "it is possible to believe that there is still a land of cotton, where old times are truly not forgotten."[5]

The Pilgrimage indeed assured that the past would be not forgotten and thus sustained history's role as a social determinant. Like the photograph of pickaninnies that provided a visual reference from which whites could contrast their imagined cultural elevation, the Pilgrimage animated an age of unquestioned white virtuousness. It was an age when the racial order allowed white southerners to march civilization to a pinnacle of greatness never reached before or after. This was the Pilgrimage myth. It was also the cultural reality that defined whites' social standing, as well as that of blacks, in southern life. The Pilgrimage myth was not created to justify racial traditions or to placate white guilt over the treatment of blacks. The former did not carry the latter, but the Pilgrimage did create a context that heightened the sense of whiteness and of a racial other. The spring event was a product of preexisting myths, a producer of new ones, and a disseminator of both.

* * *

The myths begin with the popular story of the events that stimulated the idea for the Pilgrimage. That version maintains that the events happened by chance, unfolding out of a minor but portentous crisis that descended on the 1931 second annual convention of the Mississippi State Confederation of Garden Clubs. It was held in Natchez that year from March 19 to 21. As host, the Natchez Garden Club was responsible for organizing the event, which included excursions of immaculately maintained public and private flower gardens. Natchez had long been renowned for its japonicas, camellias, and azaleas. In the early nineteenth century, travelers through the old region found Natchez to be a "garden paradise" nestled in the middle of rugged and unforgiving country. But in 1931 an untimely frost destroyed many of Natchez's treasured blossoms. Having received its federation charter only two years earlier, the Natchez Garden Club was "most anxious to put its best foot forward," a garden club publication recounted. Unfortunately, "its best foot was frost-bitten." As the story goes, the club president, Katherine Miller, responded to the crisis with steadfast leadership and the inspired idea to substitute tours of Natchez's antebellum mansions for the garden excursions. Reluctantly, the other members went along and hastily prepared their homes as a collective retreat from the cold.[6]

Conventioneers did arrive in Natchez under winterlike skies. But contrary to popular memory, garden club members met nearly two weeks before the convention and discussed plans to offer a tour of the homes. Nine days later and a week before the convention, the president of the state garden club federation told the planning committee in Natchez that the city's old homes should not be "hidden away" during the upcoming event. Some eighty federation members from around the state attended the convention, and each received a preprinted program guide listing twenty homes on tour.[7]

Whatever the truth of the early events, the conventioneers were taken with the historic houses, their antique furnishings, and the family stories. Afterward, the visitors congratulated the Natchez Garden Club for a successful convention. Local and family history had proven to be a popular attraction, and the favorable outcome of the convention boded future possibilities. Someone (just who is a matter of discussion in garden club circles) suggested opening the old homes the next spring for paid tours to the general public.

It is clear that Natchez Garden Club president Katherine Miller liked the idea and pursued it doggedly. A handsome, not-yet-middle-aged woman with dark eyes and hair, Miller was a self-proclaimed dreamer known for a streak of independence, which was served well by a polite aggressiveness. She was the unconventional conventional southern lady with the faculties of both the progressive and the reactionary. A conservative in politics and principles, she possessed a truly perceptive vision. She had the gift to foresee and champion the need for change, but only for the purpose of maintaining social stability and continuity.[8]

Miller and some of her fellow garden club members solicited the support of businesses and civic and city leaders. They wanted "to invite the world to come see [the homes] for an admission fee." The river city had for years served as a minor convention locale for business and fraternal groups from around the country, and yet it had never taken the extra step toward developing a major tourist trade. Supporters of Miller's vision were plentiful. But with the country crippled by the Great Depression, the idea of an annual Pilgrimage drew many skeptics as well. Even some among the garden club membership of seventy or so could not imagine visitors willing to pay to see the old homes, many of which were in disrepair. The "ladies in Natchez really didn't know what they had," remembered one Natchez resident. "They just accepted grandma's vase and thought nothing of it."[9]

In actuality, Miller and others believed grandma's vase had possibilities. The garden club ultimately found enough community leaders and homeowners who recognized in Miller's proposal the potential for boosting the ailing local economy with outside dollars. Twenty-six homes were signed on for a six-day tour in March 1932. Miller included her own eighteenth-century home, Hope Farm, which she and her husband bought some years before. As a final measure to enhance the Old South nostalgia, Miller convinced the homeowners and hostesses greeting guests to wear hoopskirts.[10]

The year of cleaning and repairing houses, fitting costumes, and attending meetings paid off. On the first day of the "Garden Pilgrimage Week," as the event was styled, the *Natchez Democrat* published a special pull-out "pink edition" describing scheduled events and the histories of the homes on tour. The first official Pilgrimage was a greater success than even Miller had expected. Visitors came from thirty-seven states, creating a demand that persuaded their hosts to extend the Pilgrimage an extra day. Natchez was "agog with excitement," Miller recalled in later years, conceding her own nervousness on the eve of the unprecedented event. According to a Natchez Garden Club assessment report, tourists spent fifty thousand dollars during the Pilgrimage. They crowded Natchez hotels, restaurants, filling stations, and retail shops. Within the rarely used dank and dark rooms and parlors of their mansions, the women of the garden club had discovered a commercial value in old family furniture, artifacts, and photo albums, as well as family lore. Noted the report, "The dreamy old town felt the thrill of renewed life" in the midst of the country's economic crisis.[11]

The 1932 Pilgrimage was indeed the beginning of a success story for the garden club and for Natchez. The spring event was expanded to four weeks and advertised nationally. It was repeatedly featured in major magazines, including *National Geographic*. In 1939, Metro Goldwyn Mayer produced a ten-minute movie short about the Pilgrimage that was eventually shown in seventeen thousand theaters across the continent. Miller and Edith Wyatt Moore traveled around the country promoting Natchez and the Pilgrimage as a "royal splendor." Before her audiences, Miller preferred words such as "guests," "visitors," and "friends" to the less genial expression of "tourists" to describe those who came to the Pilgrimage. Among those guests over the years were foreign dignitaries, members of royal families, and American luminaries, including Eleanor Roosevelt, Douglas MacArthur, and Lady Bird Johnson. Civic groups from other cities consulted with the Natchez Garden Club in the hopes of creating their own success stories, and by the 1940s the Mississippi Federation of Garden Clubs was sponsoring a statewide pilgrimage featuring gardens and historic homes.[12]

Across the country, historical pageantry entered a new era of popularity after the nation's centennial and peaked at the turn of the century. Most pageants tended to be onetime spectacles rather than annual events. But even among annual events, the Natchez Pilgrimage was distinctive for opening up private spaces of family homes and for the central role it played in the local economy. While other annual pageants, especially those outside the South, typically illuminated the "separate worlds" of the present and bygone days—suggesting the respective community's progress—Natchez embraced a seamless continuity with the past. Pilgrimage participants were celebrating the lives of their own blood ancestors, and the idea of bygone days amounted to a lament for what had been lost rather than a celebration for what had been gained.[13]

The civic benefits of its model event could "hardly be estimated," proclaimed the Natchez Garden Club. Profits from the Pilgrimage afforded the restoration of Natchez's antebellum architecture and the continued tenancy of the old families, many of whom had been edging toward financial ruin. The entire city got a facelift. "Cultural and citizenship standards were raised," said the 1933 garden club report; "community teamwork increased; disfiguring advertising signs were permanently removed from the roadways, and the whole town cleaned up as if on dress parade." "Old Natchez lives, breathes, and is happy again," observed one national publication five years later. The editor of the *Natchez Democrat* bubbled with equal enthusiasm. The women of the Natchez Garden Club, he wrote, by virtue of their "intelligence, enthusiasms, culture and appreciative viewpoint," had done Natchez a great community service.[14]

With the Pilgrimage, the club's civic duties expanded significantly. Organized in 1928, the garden club adopted as its principal objective the establishment of a city "beautification program" to "promote the planting of shrubbery and trees" and flower gardens. Recreating history and celebrating heritage had not been a part of the club's original vision.[15] In later years, women with no interest in flowers but one in history joined the garden club. Roane Fleming Byrnes, an influential local plantation owner and charter member of the Natchez Garden Club, remembered that the Pilgrimage shifted club goals to include stimulating "civic interest in the town's rich inheritance from the past, and [making] Natchez a mecca for students of America's life and development and thus bring[ing] improvement and increased prosperity to the whole community."[16]

The Pilgrimage had been sold to the city on the promise of increased tourist revenue. But the monetary infusion that benefited the community and the individual homeowners also sustained the more fundamental and dynamic social purpose "to perpetuate the history, traditions and architecture of the Southern [antebellum] period in Natchez." Part of fulfilling that purpose was manifested in the practice of distributing complimentary Pilgrimage tickets to local teachers and students and exposing them to the artifacts and animated exhibitions of the past—albeit a selected past. A Meridian, Mississippi, man congratulated the Pilgrimage women for realizing their social objective of "doing very splendid work in educating the people to the fact that your section holds a heritage second to none in all America."[17]

In the vision of many, the Pilgrimage mission had an intergenerational and cultural purpose. In a speech commemorating the tenth anniversary of the Pilgrimage, Miller outlined public history's mission in Natchez. "You will always keep [Natchez] a national shrine," she told a group of garden club women, "recreating each spring the life, the customs, the wealth and culture of a section of our nation which once bordered upon a separate kingdom so great was the power of its affluent splendor. Some day we shall pass on. Others will take our place. But the flame of your torch shall never be extinguished."[18]

The torchbearers remained committed to their purpose, but not without conflict. As often happens with success, that of the Pilgrimage led to dissension and eventually to a schism within the leadership and ranks of the garden club. Styled by the unfailingly frank Ernie Pyle and other national media people as the "war of the hoopskirts," the conflict centered around a disagreement over how Pilgrimage profits should be distributed. In the first four years, the Pilgrimage earned the garden club $33,014 after expenses. More than $14,000 went to the homeowners, leaving the garden club nearly $19,000. Part of the membership favored using net proceeds to purchase and restore historic sites. Their warring opponents wanted to increase the percentage of the proceeds going to the homeowners, who had to keep the old houses presentable to tourists. The houses "were the merchandise on the shelves," said Miller, a homeowner supporter. After a string of failed compromises, Miller led a dissenting faction to secede in June 1936 and to form the Pilgrimage Garden Club. The renegades took seventeen of the twenty-six tour homes and organized a separate Pilgrimage.[19]

The tumult polarized friends, families, and business relationships for nearly ten years. Even writer Stark Young, who had donated *So Red the Rose* memorabilia to a local history museum at the garden club's Connelly's Tavern, ranted about "that famous row." The city that he had once revered in his writing receded in his opinion into a "rotten old place!" and some of the garden club women, whom he had elevated to the pinnacle of civilization, plummeted to "the bottom of all ignorance." The secession of Miller's faction prompted the Natchez Garden Club to seek an injunction against the Pilgrimage Garden Club. Both clubs then filed suit against the other for damages. Meanwhile, separate, overlapping pilgrimages competed for tourists. World War II suspended the pilgrimages for three years, and then the coming of world peace disposed the garden clubs to mediate their own. In October 1946, they agreed to merge the respective pilgrimages into one overseen by a joint board of directors. The clubs would split expenses and proceeds and then distribute monies as each saw fit.[20]

Reconciliation was important to the general interest of the community as well as to the continued success of Natchez's newest industry. Within a decade of its inception, the Pilgrimage had grown into a major tourist event of the Southeast. Miller and the Pilgrimage organizers were credited with developing a tourist trade at a time when travel agents described Mississippi as underdeveloped and wanting for interesting places. Each year, the hostesses of the Natchez homes were "receiving" an increasing number of visitors, and in 1977 a fall Pilgrimage was added. By the 1980s, a half million tourists were flocking to Natchez annually to see living history, and each year homeowners earned several thousand dollars for opening their private lives to visitors. "You didn't have a half a dozen houses fit to come see," said former mayor Troy B. Watkins of the early years. With the Pilgrimage, the garden club women made "a success out of nothing. And it was nothing."[21]

Natchez always had its history and tradition though. Miller and the others turned both into a livelihood, and Natchez seemed to have regained the prominence it formerly commanded in the antebellum South. In later years, the 1930s in Natchez were remembered not only for their economic hard times, but for a "Renaissance" in commercial and cultural life initiated by the founding of the Pilgrimage. The garden clubs were, by Watkins's account, "probably more responsible for bringing Natchez out of the doldrums back in the 30s. That was a bunch of determined women at the time."[22]

The evidence of a local revival was in the restored physical elegance of the mansions. Most of the homes on tour were of early to mid-nineteenth-century vintage. One of Natchez's great contributions to that period was its grand domestic architecture. The inclusion of Federal and Greek Revival forms gave Natchez an architectural grandeur that compared to its celebrated citizenry. The local nabobs engaged local master builders, many originally from the East, who duplicated a national trend of integrating classical forms, common in public architecture, into domestic design. Many of the skilled workers in wood and plaster, as well as the landscape gardeners, were both locals and European immigrants. Slaves lent their own carpentry and bricklaying skills and, of course, their muscle. Clay and timber were the principal building materials and were available locally. Decorative work came from abroad: iron from Spain and Belgium and stained glass from the latter. The nabobs furnished their mansions with French and English pieces and Italian paintings. Elevated locations enhanced the stately appearance of the houses, removed residents and guests from mosquito-infested bottomlands, and provided the master with a perch from which he could watch over his labor. The mansion was his most prominent expression of success and social rank. He built it on the idea of familial permanence and social continuity, bequeathed it as a home place and symbol of status to be possessed by his children and grandchildren. Like a surname it was part of his legacy.[23]

One of the mansions that contributed to Natchez's larger legacy and that represented local architecture "at its best" evolved in part from the efforts of a woman, Jane Surget White. Eldest daughter of Pierre Surget, she gave her hand to John Hampton White, a shrewd and consequently wealthy land speculator previously from North Carolina; it was a strategic union for both White and the Surgets. Sometime around 1816 they commissioned the construction of a new mansion, which she named Arlington. Her husband died in 1819 during a yellow-fever epidemic. Yet evidence indicates that she had been the original force behind Arlington's planning and construction. The Whites hired an architect-contractor, who was probably from Philadelphia, and they apparently allowed him to study existing local design before beginning his own Natchez project. What he created reflected a "Southern Colonial" form that would become commonplace in Natchez.[24]

The result was a sturdy, two-story brick structure of Georgian precision. Inside were seventeen-and-a-half-foot ceilings, eight rooms, including a music room and library, and a rear gallery. Handcarved rosewood furniture complemented cornices of like design above the windows and interior doors. Up- and downstairs front entrances, with fanlighted transoms and glass side panels, led in from a large portico, fronted by four Tuscan columns supporting a frieze-trimmed pediment. The white-pillared facade, which later came to epitomize the southern mansion in the popular imagination, had not reached most other parts of the South at the time of Arlington's construction. White did not live long enough to realize her own role in helping to establish a trend in southern architecture. Legend has it that she hosted a ball to celebrate the opening of her new home, was overcome by the festivities, and died in her sleep that night. Whatever the circumstances of her death, she foreshadowed an architectural matriarchy that characterized twentieth-century Natchez. Her family descendants would help build the Pilgrimage and would display their own homes.[25]

In those later years, the great houses such as Arlington were tangible reminders of the South's unique past. On speaking tours promoting the Pilgrimage, Miller said Natchez's "houses show history-making events and epochs." In the minds of white southerners, such homes conjured up the style of life of a "vanished culture" that prevailed when graciousness and an easy pace defined the norm, when the South commanded a certain sense of order, permanence, and leadership.[26]

Even after the Civil War assailed the South's sense of itself, the surviving mansions stood as the ultimate vestiges of security and restoration. Perhaps the best known example of this symbolism is the place of Tara in *Gone with the Wind*. In the climax of Margaret Mitchell's romance, after Sherman's fiery procession sweeps through Atlanta, Scarlett retreats to the family plantation in the North Georgia countryside. Her life and livelihood have been ravaged by the war. But there the family home, Tara, still stands, cast in immortality. Its very survival of the war is portentous. It is the nourishment of Scarlett's being, easing her despair and granting her hope and a future. Without such great houses as Tara in their stories, southern writers of the early tradition could not have conveyed the desired sense of place and ordered civilization, not to mention romance, to their readers.[27]

Before Mitchell's *Gone with the Wind,* Mississippi's Stark Young recognized the singular importance of the stately residence as a device to establish the setting of an Old South novel of popular appeal. He chose

Natchez as the setting of *So Red the Rose* in part because he saw its ante-bellum mansions as "the richest things of their kind in America." They were rich in visual splendor, family and regional heritage, and symbol-ism. Young, in fact, began research on his book the year of the first offi-cial Pilgrimage, and for the 1935 Pilgrimage, Scribner issued a special five-hundred-copy Natchez Trace, autographed edition of *So Red the Rose*; it sold out instantly. In actuality, columned mansions of Natchez's collection and plantation houses of Tara's cinematic magnificence did not dominate the architectural landscape of the Old South; they represented the exception—and Natchez's exceptionalism.[28]

Mitchell herself understood this historic fact. She fought vigorously with Hollywood filmmakers to keep columns off Tara. Writing a close friend, she said she wanted to keep it consistent with "the healthy, hearty, country and somewhat crude civilization" of North Georgia, the book's setting for Tara. She had found the domestic scenery in the film adaptation of *So Red the Rose* overly spectacular and artificial. One re-viewer referred to the 1935 movie as "history-in-hoopskirts." That Holly-wood and the moviegoing public confused the Natchez houses on the screen with an architectural standard of the Old South truly grieved her. She did not "know whether to laugh or to throw up" at the thought that the producers of *Gone with the Wind* might try to duplicate the showy grandeur of Natchez.[29]

But Mitchell was waging a losing battle against a powerful cultural myth. Fellow southerners of her and Young's day and race saw white-columned mansions as a lost norm and attached a meaning to them that went beyond mere shelter, taste, and even wealth; they were manifest proof of the ascendancy of southern white civilization over all other civ-ilized societies. One society that offered an acceptable comparison to the grand Old South was that of the Athenian Greeks, whose architectural style provided a source of inspiration for the latter-day civilization.[30]

The women of the Pilgrimage believed that the great homes continued to bestow the same meaning of prestige and social position as they did for the original occupants. To the garden clubs, Natchez's architectural contribution to the nineteenth century also belonged to the twentieth. This was the legacy of Jane Surget White and the others, or at least that was how the Pilgrimage women perceived it, and they undertook the re-sponsibility of perpetuating it. They looked upon that responsibility as a cultural mission defined by history. As the organizers of the Pilgrimage, they were also prophets of white cultural integrity. History played an integral role in their collective stewardship.

The mansions of Natchez provided the visual props to the mythic story of their idealized culture. When Mississippi newspaperman and writer Hodding Carter visited the Spring Pilgrimage in the early 1940s, he observed that each mansion "has its unending story of hope and change and lost greatness and despair." Another observer attributed Natchez's far-reaching attraction to not only its "hallowed atmosphere" of "august abodes" but also to the Pilgrimage's success at preserving "the spirit of the Old South." He called Natchez's tourists "culture-seekers" and described the old river city as a last remnant of "the cream of American culture."[31]

The more pleasant scenes of that Old South civilization were brought to life every spring in the Confederate Pageant, a stage production that became part of the Pilgrimage in the early years. The pageant was first performed at Natchez's resplendent but confining Memorial Hall. The garden club later moved the affair to the city auditorium, where nearly a thousand people could be accommodated. Visitors were treated to "beauteous" southern belles in hoopskirts, pantaloons, and ball gowns, and stalwart young beaux in frock coats, military dress, and fox-hunting jodhpurs. All graced a series of animated tableaux that composed the pageant. Locals from every generation performed in skits and dances celebrating antebellum culture. With the musical score dominated by songs of Stephen Foster (a southern favorite who was actually a Yankee), the whole effect gave profound life to moonlight-on-magnolia romanticism.[32]

The pageant was a myth-building reenactment of an "enchanted way of life," to which whites held an intransigent faith, even though it never truly existed. The tableaux avoided the tender subjects of southern defeat and intolerance and instead followed a patriotic thematic line—from the "Unfurling of Old Glory" to the wedding of Jefferson Davis and Natchez's Varina Howell to past time soirees and a Confederate farewell ball. The pageant pointedly associated Natchez with "great" men of history, however indirect the connections with those men, including Jefferson Davis, John James Audubon, and the infamous but honorable Aaron Burr. "[A]ll these are Natchez," proclaimed the 1992 pageant program guide, as were "Romance, grandeur, chivalry, wealth," and "Adventure, action, boldness, strength."[33]

The cultural heroes and the self-congratulatory images were parts of the social relationship that twentieth-century white southerners forged with the past. That relationship gave meaning to life, while it substituted for the larger and elusive American relationship with economic prosperity, educational prominence, military success, and national respect. One might interpret the ceremonious exaltation of the mythic past as the collective yearning to inhabit it, to turn back the calendar far enough to escape the feeling of loss, which was heightened by conditions breeding runaway social change: the Great Depression, World War II, and later the cold war and the civil rights movement. "We, as a new generation in a changing South," noted the program for the 1940 pageant, "take pride in preserving that which seems best in our glorious heritage."[34]

Along with the grandeur, one outstanding feature of the pageant was the presence of children. Participation in the pageant was a family tradition, with two or three generations taking the stage together year after year. No less than Little League or the Girl Scouts, the pageant was part of the upbringing of children of garden club members. For example, one six-year-old girl whose family regularly devoted itself to Pilgrimage activities was described in 1984 as being "like any other little girl," except that she had a large bedroom with twelve-foot ceilings, a closet with hoopskirts and pantalets hanging among her blue jeans, and a dresser covered with countless Pilgrimage party invitations. Children were groomed at an early age for a succession of parts in the pageant, often starting as a young maypole dancer and working up to a member of the royal court.[35]

Every pageant had two royal courts—each representing a garden club. Presiding over the courts were a king and queen. It was not unusual to find in some families a mother who had passed along her queen's tiara and scepter to her daughter, or a boy who had followed in his older brother's footsteps as king. Candidates for royal couple were required to be students and were judged on citizenship, academic achievements, and, of course, family and background. Once the couples were chosen and announced, an anticipated moment in some circles, the local newspaper played up the qualifications of the selectees. As was tradition, the respective royal couples were honored at a private "Royal Ball" of pageant participants. They were then introduced to the public at the Confederate Pageant, where family and friends sat conspicuously in the "Royal Box" along with the garden club presidents. The women wore hoopskirts and the men equivalent formal attire. In the closing tableau, the royal families and guests stood in glorification of the not-forgotten South to honor the king and queen, cueing the rest of the audience to rise as the music of "Dixie" filled the auditorium.[36]

From the pageant and Pilgrimage came a palatable history of order, innocence, and leisure. As one garden club member put it, the Pilgrimage organizers were "trying to make something pleasant and happy. They are not trying to show anything that was unattractive. Most of the things they have researched." In researching local history, one was looking at one's ancestors, and in being selective rather than comprehensive, the result was a Shintoistic interpretation of the past. In the Pilgrimage version of antebellum Natchez, society was a natural bias born out of family loyalty and regional and racial pride. That version was codified into law in 1940 when the garden clubs persuaded city aldermen to institute an ordinance mandating the licensing of all tour guides. Applicants were required to pass an exam, developed by the two clubs, in local history, horticulture, architecture, and "cultural facts." Violators of the ordinance could be fined up to fifty dollars and jailed up to ten days.[37]

Historical truth that subverted vaunted images of bravery, honor, and solidarity had no place in Pilgrimage lore. By means of omission and hyperbole, the historical message of the spring ritual insulated the dominant culture from scurrilous realities and extolled ideal group values and virtues. Tourists did learn about the rowdy river life at Natchez-under-the-Hill, but the local trustees of history humorously sloughed it off as a bawdy other world worthy only for its contrast to the culture on top of the hill. Not completely taken in by the pomp and ceremony of the Pilgrimage, Hodding Carter understood that the stories of the Natchez elite were festooned in myth, like moss on the oak trees that shaded them. "It is pleasant and easier," he wrote, "to fit old Natchez to a pattern of brave gentility shrouded in candlelight, and of quiet breeding that is the presently dismissed handmaiden of wealth, and of community integrity as unassailable as the classic proportions of a Corinthian pillar."

Carter knew that tourists encountered a portraiture of Natchez life in the Old South that was incomplete.[38]

One of the Pilgrimage's more egregious omissions was an explanation of how Natchez's extraordinary collection of mansions escaped Yankee pyromania during the "War between the States." What the Pilgrimage did not tell tourists is that Natchez had the distinction of surrendering on two separate occasions to Union forces. Following the forty-four-day struggle required to seize Vicksburg, Natchez submitted to Union occupation without a fight. Natchezians welcomed their enemy, according to historian Ronald Davis, with "waving handkerchiefs and unfurled American flags." They then turned their mansions into "perfect hotel[s]" for high-ranking officers. More than a century after embers cooled in Vicksburg, residents there would remember Natchez's wartime hospitality as a traitorous deed.[39]

What the Pilgrimage did promote was the idea of a surviving aristocracy. However one wishes to define aristocracy, in Natchez the word was associated with wealth, intelligence, family, and continuity. One early sentimental historian said of old Natchez that men of only the best breeding populated the region, talented men "of education and high social standing." These were the words of "Major" Steve Power, whose work Miller consulted when forming her own vision of Natchez past. The myth of local exceptionalism was so enduring that Natchez society impressed even H. L. Mencken, whose haughty standards not even the Anglo Saxons themselves could meet. He called the old Natchez elite "one of the best the Western Hemisphere has seen" and thus propagated the myth himself. Long after the deaths of its originators, the myth betrayed itself in a 1992 Pilgrimage program guide that described old Natchez as "an early magnet for men with a lust for life. . . . A bustling river town full of passion, power, and paradise."[40]

The elite of Natchez were not without wealth, of course. Even before the founding of the Pilgrimage, locals habitually boasted that antebellum Natchez was unsurpassed in terms of personal fortune. That claim contained, to quote one recent historian, "elements of mythmaking that would take on new dimensions with the introduction of the 'Natchez Pilgrimage.'" Antebellum Natchez had been indeed a cosmopolitan city, and concentrated within the district was an impressive number of family fortunes. This was the era that the Pilgrimage resurrected, when Natchez could lay claim to a portion of estates valued over $100,000 that was greater than that held by America's wealthy in Newport, Rhode Island, and in the Eighteenth Ward of New York City. Yet the so-called local nabobery was a group constantly in flux, with shallow, mostly early nineteenth-century roots. If there were those who inherited wealth—and thus social status—and those who brought their wealth when they came to Natchez, there were also the *nouveau riche,* those who rose to social prominence by way of successful business ventures. Such traits might ordinarily be considered commendable, but the Pilgrimage preferred the inherited qualities of bloodline over those acquired by way of common ambition.[41]

In sensing something extraordinary about their history and community, Pilgrimage folks showed an almost messianic fervor in their resolve to share Natchez with the rest of the world. "It is 'noblesse oblige,' " noted a local history, "on the part of the members of the Garden Club, who work and give that their good purposes may be served." Beyond the Pilgrimage's economic benefits was the self-gratification that Natchez's reborn greatness would not go unrecognized in other corners of the globe. If Yankees could not respect the modern South, their enthusiasm for the Pilgrimage revealed an enduring appreciation for what the South had once been. Natchez is a "modern miracle," noted a writer in *Better Homes and Gardens.* Those who have made it so "deserve a nation's thanks," for one "will come away with a feeling of awe, and a prayer for the perpetuation of such haunting sweetness." A 1935 *New York Times* article complimented Natchez as a "romantic little town . . . tinged with a nostalgia for days and manners that are gone; with regret that this culture went down in ruin."[42]

Even the image of Katherine Miller in the founding of the Pilgrimage was tinged with mythic nostalgia. Considered the personification of Natchez itself, Miller in organizing the first Pilgrimage was acclaimed as a brave woman who singlehandedly overcame mountainous obstacles of public pessimism and complacency to restore Natchez to its former glory. One Natchez historian, Harnett T. Kane, described Miller as having "the pent-up energy of a buzz-bomb . . . a combination of Miss Nelly of N'Orleans and Tallulah Bankhead, with a slight dash of P. T. Barnum." With Natchez caught in the economic grip of the depression and teeter-

ing at the brink of financial ruin, Miller made the momentous decision to
sell, by another observer's account, "the last thing that we have left to
sell of our Past: the Past itself." With Miller at the helm, the opening day
of the first official Pilgrimage in 1932 was depicted as an epochal event,
a cataclysm in the course of Natchez's future that occurred with the redemption of its history. The garden club women invested time, sweat,
money, and new gray hairs in preparing for the opening day, with no assurance of success. Failure would mean shame. "Suddenly it happened,"
wrote Kane, reconstructing the first day into a great climax. "From all
directions, by car, bus, and train, people were pouring in."[43]

The romantic genesis also included stories of families and their ancestral mansions being delivered from the insuperable depths of ruin. Many
of the families indeed had suffered depression-wrought hardships, and
their houses consequently fell into disrepair. Pilgrimage profits afforded
the restoration of Natchez's antebellum architecture and the continued
tenancy of the old families. Yet in Pilgrimage lore, a commiserating eyebrow was raised to those whites who had fallen from luxury to live in reduced circumstances. The Grecian columns and white porticoes had become a mere facade behind which families survived without the usual
platoon of servants and with, instead, plenty of bare cupboard space and
tax bills. The image that was projected smacked of a modern-day Lost
Cause comparable to the suffering of ancestors who forfeited their slaves
and fortunes during the Civil War. It was another chapter of pathos in
the South's beleaguered history, one that ignored the perpetual economic
instability of blacks and many whites. In his sentimental rendition of the
elite's misfortunes, Kane wrote that the downtrodden elite "had only the
house, a place they could not afford to heat in the winter, in which they
must live through the summer without ice." They were "too poor to
paint, too proud to whitewash," he wrote in hackneyed description of
the South's evanescent fortunes. "Granddaughters of mansion builders
walked a mile or so into town from the big house to save a nickel."[44]

The myth of genteel poverty and the founding of the Pilgrimage was
so profound that in 1950 it became the material of a modern romance
novel. In *The Natchez Woman,* Alice Graham (a descendent of an old
Natchez family) forges fiction with real-life themes, such as love, divorce,
death, tragedy, ruin, and the Pilgrimage founding. All add up to a soppy
melodrama. Graham depicts the Pilgrimage founding as a fateful turn of

events that spared many elite from economic privation and public embarrassment. The book's protagonist is Jane Elliston, the archetypical garden club woman. Jane finds her ancestral home slipping from her financial grasp, and transforming, Graham writes, "like a coagulation of leaves in the swamp, disintegrating, giving out an unhealthy atmosphere." Jane grows increasingly disillusioned with the burdens of an elite life. "I had to fight the house," she says, "just as I had to fight the land. Rule it, not let it rule me." She and her husband cannot seem to turn a profit from their five plantations, so they subject themselves to accepting tourism as a necessary means of living. Her husband, Alec, moans about their shifting existence. "I feel harried," he says. "We have to skimp and save and almost starve ourselves here at home to put on a show, then we work ourselves to rags over the plantations." Jane complains, too, but she sees a "certain brilliance" in the Pilgrimage that offers a way out of her family's economic plight. "I don't want to live in a measly way," she says. "I want to live in a grand way, and to do that we have to have money."[45]

The theme Graham explores here is one of survival, which in Pilgrimage lore was an attribute attached to beleaguered mansion owners. During the Great Depression, poverty among the elite took on an elevated class distinction of sorts. Dire straits were associated with virtuosity for the old families who withstood the test of character by weathering the destabilizing atmosphere of the national economic crisis. Not all made it; many lost their homes. But those who did lose, as the tale went, were victims of incontrovertible conditions. They had, after all, come from good stock, where estimable values and upstanding character had been part of their upbringing. Their impoverishment was, as Pilgrimage folk saw it, the consequence of circumstance, or in the worst case, individual failure—but not culture.[46]

The Natchez elite failed to rationalize poverty among nonelite poor, black and white, in the same fashion. The cause of one group's poverty was different from the other's, as whites saw it, and was related to the cultures of the respective races and an individual's relationship with his or her culture. The southernized version of history communicated and legitimized the ideas of a culture of poverty (essentially black) and a culture of prosperity (essentially white), while the Pilgrimage did its part by celebrating whiteness and keeping history in the mind's eye. When whites glimpsed at history through the animation of the Pilgrimage, they saw a society and omnipotent culture that heralded traditional values of work, family, and education, those values believed to be central to the progress of civilization. "You have some values that are not based on money alone," said Grace MacNeil, scion of the Surget family. Whites saw themselves as the progenitors of fundamental American values and the lone human embodiment of those values.[47]

Probably the most crucial source in the South for taught values was the family, a central theme in the Pilgrimage. As one observer of Mississippi culture put it, "Families carry on the rich and vital culture which nourishes the spirit of their kin, molding, reshaping, and renewing them . . . in generation after generation." Family was an individual's strongest link with the past, and out of the repository of history came one's heritage and ultimately one's identity. Family represented continuity over change, tradition over innovation, and security over disruption; and the integrity of family assured the continuing stability of culture and society. Mississippi had a relatively small population (2.5 million in 1980), and all but one city (Jackson) had populations of fewer than 50,000. Family and kinship ties that laced this small-town state formed the cohesive fabric of Mississippi society. The Pilgrimage indeed paid elegant tribute, as one Confederate Pageant narrator put it, to "continuity of family and homeland across the generations."[48]

By no coincidence, family and social relationships have traditionally been favorite themes of some of Mississippi's fiction writers. Among those writers is novelist Ellen Douglas (pen name for Josephine Haxton), a native of Natchez and a descendent of its antebellum homes. Many of her stories are set in the imaginary town of Homochitto, a place that holds fast to social traditions. When writing about the fictitious community, she is often describing the manners and culture of her birthplace. She does just that in her first book, A Family's Affair, published in 1962 to positive reviews after winning the Houghton Mifflin–Esquire Fellowship Award. "At its best," one reviewer noted, A Family's Affair "projects the sights, sounds, and rhythms of true Mississippi life." Fleshing out the central themes in Douglas's fiction reveals much about the actual in Natchez.[49]

In A Family's Affair, the varied lives of Douglas's characters come together in a saga about family life. She carries her story from the early twentieth century through three generations of the Andersons and Mc-Governs, a clan of cousin intermarriages and of Scotch ancestry. At its core, the book is both a testament to and a study of the value and meaning of family: an individual's need of a support structure, despite that person's own inner strengths; the complex patterns of kinship relationships and choosing an acceptable mate; and the utility of and emphasis on family loyalty.[50]

The women of Douglas's novel are the heart and soul of family life. They do not simply belong to their respective family; their own strengths are its foundation of stability. The book's story revolves primarily around the life of Kate Anderson, beginning with her acceptance of widowhood and forfeiture of remarriage to plan instead the futures of her three daughters. After her husband's death, Kate tried to keep the family plantation going. But "flood had compounded debt," forcing Kate to move her daughters and son to her mother's house in town. Although their financial stability is in question, their social status is not. They are among the impoverished elite. In Homochitto, as in Natchez, "poverty was more than respectable . . . and by its inverse standards the Andersons were the last word in aristocracy." A firmly determined woman, Kate Anderson knows that if she raises her three daughters within the dictates of their social class, they can still marry well.[51]

Family perpetuity and continuity serves as an important subtheme in Douglas's narrative. The Anderson and McGovern women cast their vision toward the future, which counterbalances that of the more present-minded men. In choosing a husband, one of Kate's daughters, Charlotte, plays her role well. She looks for the traits that would ensure a stable future for the family they would have together. She cares less about a prospect's "good looks or money" than about "strength and honor, and intelligence." As a result of prudent deliberation, Charlotte would marry "late, at twenty-five, for it took her a long time to find a man who met her standards . . . and her family's."[52]

For her part, Kate is pleased with Charlotte's choice, for already "he had made his reputation for stability" and "had everything she wanted in a son-in-law." Charlotte pursued and won the heart of Ralph Mc-Govern, whose attributes Charlotte locates in her mother-in-law to be,

Julia. In herself, Julia "demanded honor—virtue, good faith, loyalty and courage, and in everyone else she assumed it." After marriage and motherhood, Charlotte accepts her culturally determined task to indoctrinate in her own children the cultural values exemplified in her mother-in-law, including the "inflexibility of character" that Ralph and his brothers inherited from their parents. As Charlotte had learned, and as she teaches her children, their actions must remain above reproach or risk bringing shame on the family.[53]

Douglas's story of family life closes with the funeral of Kate Anderson. In the end the family members come "together because of her life, not her death," Douglas writes. "They all knew this, and knew that the others knew it, as clearly as if they had said it to each other." Even after Kate's death at eighty-five, the family takes her spirit as their moral compass and bond. In memory, her ideals, those of her society and culture, will be given continuity.[54]

Although prim and pure, yet anything but naive, Douglas's women are not helpless creatures of fragility and idleness. They indeed defy the mythic formulation of the southern lady. It is safe to assume that Kate Anderson and her fictional cohorts were conjured from Douglas's mental synthesis of historical and contemporary images. Yet their portrayal as the central, virtually unimpeachable executioners of moral authority and governesses of family honor and virtue does not reflect the errant fantasy of a fiction writer. These very character compositions affirm the value of *A Family's Affair* to the task of demystifying the garden club women of Natchez and their role as community historians. In their domestic responsibilities, social graces, as well as assertive posture, women of the Natchez elite were the real-life equivalent of Douglas's fictional characters.

More than sixty years earlier, Natchez historian Steve Power described a similar unreproachable woman of Natchez. He wrote that women were "trained in all that constitutes nobility of soul and sentiment, intelligence and purity, and their influence dominated the whole." Such paramount virtues also carried women through the crisis of war and destruction, according to Power and other local historians. "Reared in luxury from the cradle, every fine instinct carefully trained, . . . too sad to weep, too proud to complain, they stooped with dignity and took up the broken thread of life and like their divine prototype 'went about doing good.'" Prophetically, he continued: "This was the work of those great-hearted women who lived in those Natchez homes *after the war.*"[55]

Indeed, Power's complimentary prose places his work perhaps closer to the description of a pulp novel than of a serious history. But whether derived from historical truth or contemporary projection, or both, the image he invoked reveals a persistent pattern of female assertion when placed next to the fictional Kate Anderson and the factual Katherine Miller. The female descendants of "those great-hearted women who lived in those Natchez homes" founded the Pilgrimage on their own initiative for the sake of their houses, their families, and their history, and they revitalized an idyll that would have comforted Power. Their initiative was consistent with gender conventions of the day, or at least with a contemporary view of proper womanhood. Mississippian David Cohn wrote in a 1940 *Atlantic Monthly* article, "Natchez Was a Lady," that "Many a war-broken Southern family owed its resuscitation to the valor of its women, and this is largely true of the recent rise of Natchez."[56]

White women of Natchez found within the Pilgrimage a unique public repository for preserving history, heritage, and the culture. Southern society expected white women to be unblemished paragons of moral rectitude, and by example and nurturance they gave assurances to the perpetuation of the dominant culture's values. As late as 1947, the Natchez Garden Club reminded its members that they "[s]halt be an example in thy home." The Pilgrimage facilitated their labor. It was a veritable instructional aid that gave viable proof to the veracity of their lessons. It animated a way of life—the best of civilization—that whites could equate with their values and principles.[57]

It also enhanced the public life of women, even as it reinforced the social hierarchy. With the Pilgrimage, white women enlarged their circle of influence outside the family, developed and applied organizing and business skills, and in some instances expanded their political activities, especially on issues dealing with tourism or the community's appearance. To the standard texts that purged women from the historical record, the public history over which white women had control offered a correction that noted their involvement in celebrated historical events and activities, casting them as anything but passive objects. The Pilgrimage's impact on the lives of women was typical of historical pageants and festivals in other parts of the country, which middle-class women's clubs usually supported. One of the common qualities that the Pilgrimage shared with American pageants was the advancement of traditional patriarchal attitudes toward women, despite the enriching contributions to their contemporary lives. Whether at home teaching children the values of the culture or fostering the established social order through public history, white women were perpetuating their own second-class status. Repudiating what felt like the natural order of humanity and the sexes was rare. The southern white woman instead expected her pedestal, and she reached suppliantly for the supporting hand of her man as she took her place upon it.[58]

Just as public history fixed women in traditional roles, it fixed blacks in their prescribed social function and place. Unlike women, blacks were not decision makers in the production of history. They had little, if any, voice in public history, and there were no sympathetic whites advancing an objective perspective of black contributions. Quaint figures trimming the romantic image of the Old South, blacks were presented as abiding slaves engaged in the seemingly inconsequential activities of the wet nurse and the cotton picker. Presumably, their masters singlehandedly turned fortunes out of the land and built mansions with their fortunes, apart from the "inconsequential" labor of the enslaved.

Consistent with their designated place in southern society, blacks played only menial parts in the Pilgrimage, both behind the scenes and in the public eye. They manned the crews needed for cooking, cleaning, and preparation for a countless number of all-white private and public parties and to serve the month-long stream of visitors. One early source describing and promoting the Pilgrimage mentioned: "Perhaps a grizzled, bent, old ex-slave stands to bow you in, or a strapping, courteous young negro will direct the parking of your car and reply if you question him . . . that his people have been here since 'befo' de' War' in the service of the same family. . . . [Or] a little colored boy stoops and wipes your shoes lest you have the embarrassment of taking unnoticed souvenirs of park and garden."[59]

Blacks also played conspicuous roles in the animated scenes of the Pilgrimage. Guests were treated to landscapes of belles and beaux flanked by heavyset black "mammies," who wore traditional checked-gingham dresses with large aprons, colorful bandanas wrapped around their heads, and performed the servile duties of slave days. In one of the more popular tableaux, happy blacks, each with a canvas sack slung over a shoulder, stood behind a row of cotton bolls and entertained the audience with slave songs. The painted backdrop captured the world of the enslaved: a field high in cotton, a slave shack, and an outdoor privy. Completing the stereotype were two black children placed in the foreground eating watermelon.

Another favorite of locals and guests was a "chorus of 100 voices" performed at a local black church. The musical performances were variously called "Heaven Bound," "Straight and Narrow Path," and "The Evolution of the Negro Spiritual." Whichever name, the theme was always the same: the slave's journey was a continual ascent, beginning with heathenish Africa and concluding with the Promised Land. But it was God's inscrutable will, as in any biblical story, that there should be suffering along the way. For the African, it came with the cruel slave traders, who were implicitly northern and ruthlessly greedy. Redemption came with sale to the kindly white southerner, proof of the journey's upward direction. Southern civilization brought Christian conversion and earthly grace; it was the final stop and preparation for entering the gates of heaven.[60]

White minds turned the ethereal performances into an earthly validation of the righteousness of their system. In her scrapbook on the Pilgrimage, Miller pasted a *Natchez Democrat* clipping that described "Heaven Bound" as altogether "creditable," and as giving "an insight into the simple faith and possibilities of the colored race." A 1952 article in the journal of the Natchez Garden Club, *Over the Garden Wall*, revealed a self-deluding notion of the past when it noted, "A cherished testimonial to masters and slaves is the fact that the spirituals though born in slavery contain no note of bitterness. They voice the cardinal virtues of patience, forbearance, love, faith, and hope."[61]

To white ears, the crooning of a mournful spiritual was one of the few contributions of black culture to southern civilization. From slavery to the era of television, black performers had always pleased the senses and sensibilities of whites, in part because they exhibited the unthreatening, childlike qualities that whites considered the finest attributes of blacks.

The joyous singing in the Pilgrimage was a reassurance to whites that the "old timey darkey" was still around or reemerging in the contemporary black character. The *Natchez Democrat*'s editor wrote in 1934: "Nature has endowed members of the negro race with the great gift of music . . . and their melodies have brought happiness to millions." From the white perspective, the spiritual singer was little different from the "old time mammies." Both existed for the purpose of improving the quality of life of whites, and both fulfilled the wistful vision of the faithful servant. When ninety-six-year-old Aunt Alice, who had served six generations of families at Melrose, died in 1936, her obituary in the *Democrat* was almost nostalgic. It described her as "another of those typical old negro mammies of 'befo de war' . . . a trusted and valued *part* of the household" (emphasis added). Only typical old Negroes were honored with an obituary in Natchez's white newspaper.[62]

For blacks, the Pilgrimage was a conflicting experience with confounding consequences. While it subjected them to roles that strengthened racial stereotypes, it offered the opportunity to bring a few tourist dollars into the black community. In 1956, for instance, blacks who were part of the Confederate Pageant cast earned forty-five to fifty-four dollars for eighteen performances. The addition of the spirituals in 1933 in fact began as a black idea, sold to the garden club as a fund-raiser for a library for the black schools. Dolores George (pseudonym), who came from an established black family, participated in "Heaven Bound" from the time she was a young girl until she left for college in the 1940s. She earned a little money for her performance, while the church kept a portion for expenses. During the Pilgrimage, her brother made extra money by chauffeuring visitors around Natchez. A neighbor, Laura Davis, was engaged to make costumes for the Pilgrimage.[63]

But this kind of economic exploitation of the Pilgrimage came with social costs. During the 1941 Pilgrimage, a teacher from the all-black Natchez College complained that the singers in the cotton-picking tableaux were dressed "in costumes which were demeaning to the race." Apparently, some of the singers agreed. How and if the matter was resolved is unclear, but protestations of this nature were rare before the civil rights struggle of the 1960s. Until then, blacks continued to play the roles of affable servants. Similar to blacks who internalized the white image of blackness, those who participated in the Pilgrimage reinforced white reality by sending a false message, certainly unintentionally, to whites about the universal acceptance of the racial order.[64]

Voicing antipathy for the Pilgrimage publicly would have questioned the white sense of goodness. Whites believed that in allowing blacks to participate in the Pilgrimage and to share in white heritage they were doing a service to the black community. Writer and garden club member Ethel Fleming articulated this idea in a WPA project. According to her, "It was indeed fortunate for the negroes of Natchez and vicinity that the highest type of white people settled here. That culture and refinement of the Masters and Mistresses is still reflected in the lives of the descendants of their slaves as well as in the descendants of the free negroes who lived here." Natchezian Steve Power pronounced a similar historical gospel decades before when he asked whether the transformation of the "untutored savage" to the "trusted servant" was a "miracle wrought by magic." He found the answer in the "benign influences" of the "Southern matron" who undertook "the task of civilizing, training and protecting those who were dependent on her."[65]

White women, women of the Pilgrimage, committed themselves to the norm of racial superiority expressed in Power's words. Commonplace to that norm was the notion that there was nothing degrading about a system that allowed the best to rise above those, white and black, who were in need of oversight. Southern white women were certain of the goodness of the southern way of life, just as they raised their sons and daughters to believe in the righteousness of their class and race—sons and daughters who often grew up to be elitists themselves. Like their male counterparts, women feared the downfall of civilization in the absence of an enforced racial hierarchy. Southern civilization's very integrity reflected that of their own. If male authorities imposed this line of thinking upon them, women did not protest it. Instead, a persistent ideology of race and class bonded the two sexes.[66]

Favored by both men and women, segregation was the most salient expression of biracial society. No exception, Natchez had the usual physical duplication in public conveyances: restrooms, waiting rooms, water fountains, schools, movie theater seating, hospital wings, recreational areas, cemeteries, and neighborhoods—and even a separate "All Negro Fair," which featured livestock, crafts, and produce. The practice of segregation actually was somewhat less rigid than the ideal. But it was the idea of segregation that counted most. The locally owned retail shops, for instance, waited on customers in turn rather than by race, and white nurses cared for black patients at the municipal hospital. The county-operated poorhouse gave refuge to destitute elderly of both races before it closed its doors in the 1940s.[67]

At the other extreme were also outright exclusions. Until the 1960s, blacks could not use the municipal parks, and their only entry to white-owned restaurants that served blacks was through the back kitchen door. The most sacred forbiddance, of course, was black male sexual intimacy with white females. That restriction accommodated the white male privilege that, according to one school of thought, most completely defined the system of racial supremacy: access to women of both races.

Sexual boundaries were only one aspect of a larger, more complex problem. At bottom, segregation was a function of white perceptions about blacks and black culture. Searching for the reason for segregation, Robert Penn Warren in 1954 addressed the question to an anonymous Mississippi planter, "the very figure of Wade Hampton or Kirby Smith" (who could easily have been from Adams County). The planter articulated that reason in an unqualified single-word reply: "Character." To whites, blacks were culturally distinct, not only with respect to folk ways, but also in terms of their group code of conduct and behavior. The majority of blacks were regarded as emotionally and intellectually undeveloped, therefore lacking individual initiative and responsibilities. Whites located the origins of these presumed racial perversions in what they saw as a flawed value system and a deficient set of group norms. While holding up the historical figures of George Washington Carver and Booker T. Washington as cultural aberrations, the editor of the *Natchez Democrat* wrote, "the mass of the negroes show no inclination to self-advancement and achievements." The subordinate position of blacks was ascribed not to white self-interests nor to an oppressive social structure, but to an inherent inferiority of blacks themselves. Immutable conditions of culture, as whites saw it, were the chief impediment to black economic and social advancement. In its alleged state of arrested development and moral deficiency, black culture predetermined the plight of blacks as the South's lower caste and as the dominant among the poor.[68]

Based on these assumptions, segregation was necessary to retain racial and cultural integrity. Unchecked social interaction—even in circumstances not conducive to interracial sexual relationships—was tantamount to cultural commingling, and risked debasing white culture. Instead of blacks absorbing the traits of the "superior" white culture, the reverse might happen: whites would abandon the better attributes of their own culture for a diminished set of norms and values (as white poor had allegedly done). As one white Natchezian put it, blacks "have a carefree approach to so-called moral values, cultural standards, that whites would love to pick up." However imperfectly, institutional safeguards such as segregation were intended to stay the human impulse to moral depravity. At the same time, whites fancied themselves as stewards of humanity, morally and socially obliged to lift blacks from their cultural abyss. After all it had been whites, especially women, according to a local family biographer, who had exercised "that subtle, potent charm . . . which transformed the very nature of the colored race from the savage imported from the wilds of Africa to the faithful, well-trained servant."[69]

Women were indeed inseparable from the practice of racial separation. At the core of the ideology of segregation were opposing cultural images of the fair flower of white womanhood and the aggressive black buck of an oversexed race. No greater "unconscious tribute was paid to Southern women by the severest critics of the social order," wrote Steve Power, when Reconstruction regimes deemed former slaves "worthy to stand side by side with the Caucasian."[70]

Psychosexual fears and socioeconomic competition can only partially explain the religiouslike intensity behind the protected female and the lynched rapist. The link between white womanhood and culture better explains the motivation, not wholly chivalrous, driving that intensity and why women themselves were inclined to contribute to it. As was the case in the life and legacy of Kate Anderson, southern civilization was eternal in the white woman. Her unsullied body and soul were integral to not only the moral and spiritual integrity of the culture but also to its regeneration. She was the giver of life, and from her womb, the race and culture were reproduced. The system of segregation aided in securing her against her black pursuer and from what his behavior represented, the defilement of womanhood and the debasement of culture. Whites linked the preservation of the white southern way of life to that of feminine purity; without one or the other, the collapse of civilization was certain.[71]

A 1954 court case involving a Natchez women suggests just how deeply rooted in the culture was the fealty to protected white woman-hood. One Mary Dunigan, who was white, brought a suit of libel against the *Natchez Times* for inadvertently identifying her in a news article as black. Dunigan's attorney argued that the error had caused her signifi-cant public humiliation. The case followed the conventional route of ap-peal to the Supreme Court of Mississippi, where the justices sided with the plaintiff. "Under Mississippi law," the decision read in part, "to as-sert in print that a white woman is a Negro is libelous per se." The court apparently did not appreciate that a label that was considered demeaning to a white woman might also bring grief to those called Negro. For a brief moment in her life, Dunigan had been made into an "Artificial Nigger," to borrow a short-story title from Flannery O'Connor. She be-came the creation of the white mind, an inverted perception of fact. In both instances—libeled woman and "Negro"—the image attached was incomplete without a near opposite and artificially exalting image about whiteness.[72]

Nothing raised the historical concept of cultural dissimilarities to a higher level of public consciousness than did the Pilgrimage. It was a public-sanctioned affair for white self-indulgence. Its very existence depended on the collective notion of white cultural superiority and on identifying the white race positively within the context of favorable and unfavorable images. At the same time, the Pilgrimage spotlighted stereotyped images of blacks and sustained the perception of cultural deficiencies by recreat-ing the tone and tempo of the slave South.

In a sense, Natchezians, like other southerners, were prisoners of their history. It was a prison of which white women had been the architects and the builders and from whose walls neither male nor female cared to escape. History provided the cognitive basis for a two-tiered social order divided by race. Dismantling the caste system—changing attitudes and perceptions—would require not only rewriting history but overturning it, if not escaping it.

Until that day came, judgment day, whites embraced public history as a civil religion. The message of the Pilgrimage was delivered and received like the gospel of an evangelical minister: thrust into the open hearts of a willing flock. The worshiping of the past in Natchez was not so much a

calculated defense of a system—and the beliefs and behavior behind it—
as it was a search for and expression of cultural identity. Among those
who carried the past in their minds with the passionate devotion that an
evangelical carries the Bible, to quote Friedrich Nietzsche, "their cultivation of history [did] not serve pure knowledge but life." Ironically, life in
Natchez was, David Cohn noted, lived "with the dead." To the living,
the message of the Pilgrimage was clear—that white culture was endowed with the best of qualities from which all groups in southern society had benefited.[73]

CHAPTER THREE

THE HARMONIOUS SOCIETY

Jews, Gentiles, and Upper-Class Blacks

The horse-drawn carriage, jammed with Pilgrimage sightseers, lumbered along Commerce Street. As it passed the early twentieth-century synagogue, the driver/tour guide raised his voice above the clop of hooves. "Almost two hundred Jewish families lived in Natchez at one time," he said, exaggerating the number slightly. "Only a few Jews still live here now." One of them was waiting in his Lincoln Towncar in front of the synagogue for his 9:30 appointment.

The temple is an architectural symbol of Jewish acceptance and exception in Natchez society. Physically it does not look far different from the Christian churches, inside or out, except that it lacks the standard Christian symbols. Recessed in an Ionic-columned marble ark to the rear of the *bimah* are two Torahs. The Star of David hangs with the eternal light above a stout, carved mahogany pulpit. The interior's acoustics were sonorous and crisp as the Jewish host spoke. Even after living forty-seven years in the Deep South, he retained a noticeable New York accent.

The Jewish community was never very large in Natchez, the host explained, and in recent decades, emigration and assimilation had taken a heavy toll on the population. He was solemn about the changing community, but he also understood the logic in moving to places where better opportunities existed. The shopping mall and Wal-Mart on the outskirts of the city had bankrupted the once-thriving downtown retail trade, dominated until then by Jewish merchants. When the last rabbi died in 1976, he was never replaced. Worship continued with services led by individual members or by visiting student rabbis from the Hebrew Union College in Ohio.

The host emphasized that unlike some places in Mississippi, Natchez as a whole had always welcomed Jews. The host himself was an active member in the local Rotary Club, an organization, he lamented, that remained a foundation of racial segregation.

Directions to the home of the Natchez native led into a treeless neighborhood near sprawling, monstrous Atlanta. Clean asphalt streets and concrete sidewalks coiled through the neighborhood. Framed by sidewalk, house, and white driveway, winter-brown Bermuda grass blanketed front yards.

The black woman who answered the front door represented a new face in this upper-middle-class suburban living. Her skin was smooth and her hair black despite her age, which had bestowed upon her the use of a walking cane. She invited her guest in with a smile, turned and proceeded methodically around oversized living-room furniture, and steadily placed herself into a stuffed rocker, easier to get into, she said, than out. The spacious home was filled with furnishings of late and those accumulated over a long life and inherited from long-passed relatives. Shelves weighted with books—reflecting interests that ranged from history to literature to race relations—stretched the length of an interior wall. Scores of them were cookbooks, and the garage shelved hundreds more. Living alone now, she did not cook as much as she had before. She kept herself busy with water aerobics, writing workshops, and reading.

When asked to remember her early life in black Natchez, she was politely nostalgic. "I knew my husband when I knew myself," she said of the man with whom she spent more than fifty years of marriage before his death. "He told me he loved me when he was five years old." Together they raised a family in a loving home and nurtured it through the years of social transition, from Jim Crow to desegregation. As first the daughter and then the wife of hardworking black professionals, she had experienced the privileges and comfort of upper-class living and yet had felt the sting of racial discrimination.

T eighteen, Charlotte Mackel had flowered into a beautiful young woman. Shoulder-length black hair framed a silken, cinnamon face with luminous eyes and an even mouth that spread into a fetching smile. Her slender waist and preppie dress gave her a crisp schoolgirl look. Vital and bright, she caught the eye of many young men at Hampton Institute in Virginia, where she studied home economics. Despite many suitors, she would promise her hand to her childhood sweetheart, Robert Harrison, from back home in Natchez. He was attending Tougaloo College in Jackson, Mississippi, described years later by Anne Moody as a school for those with a "high yellow" complexion and a "rich-ass daddy." Robert would go on to study dentistry at Northwestern University before returning to Mississippi to practice his profession and to marry Charlotte.[1]

Like so many American blacks, young Charlotte had an assorted ancestry. White blood came to her through both parents, but her mother's line had the richer history. Here she found Robert H. Wood, her great-grandfather, a free mulatto of antebellum Natchez who later served as mayor during Reconstruction. The maternal line also included an Irish and a Native American connection. Charlotte's marriage to Robert Harrison then grafted the family tree with black Catholic, white Jewish, and white working-class stock. Charlotte and Robert also came from a line of black professionals, Natchez's black upper class in the twentieth century.[2]

When it came to one's social place, the state of Mississippi did not care about the professional status or complexity of the family trees of its nonwhite citizens. Even though by dint of ancestry Mackel was much more, by the laws of the state and by the social standards of 1930s Natchez, she was black. Anyone whose lineage was known to be at least one-eighth black, regardless of skin color, legally and otherwise fell into the lower racial caste of what in Natchez was a socially diverse society.[3]

Adding to that diversity was a small but discernible population of Jews, most of whom had earned a respectable position in the social order. Some, like Jerry Krouse, could not claim local roots as deep and as elab-

orately grafted as those of Charlotte Mackel, but Jews had been around
Natchez as long as the black upper class. All his life, Krouse had been
witnessing the Jewish population shrink rapidly, and Natchez society
grow less diverse, as Jewish sons and daughters intermarried with Christians or moved away for economic and romantic opportunities elsewhere. By the time he graduated from Natchez High School in 1958,
fewer than twenty Jewish youths lived in Natchez.[4]

As a second-generation Russian Jew, Krouse was no stranger to discrimination. Once he was asked to leave after he and a friend crashed a
party of a girl from an old elite family. Not being a member of the right
social clique had kept him off the party's invitation list, but being Jewish
may have played some incremental role in the rebuff. On another occasion, a non-Jewish white customer from the Louisiana side of the river
came into the Krouse family business where Jerry was working. A man
of considerable size and constitution, the customer said to Jerry, "We say
God bless America. What do you Jews say? 'God bless Israel.'" Jerry replied, "No, we say, 'God damn Rednecks.'" Impressed later that he lived
to tell this story, Krouse knew that overt expressions of anti-Semitism
typically came from outsiders rather than from Natchezians.[5]

Jews like the Krouses, who embraced their culture, encountered little
resistance from larger Natchez society. Jerry and his sister were brought
up in the temple, even though their mother was a Gentile. Attendance at
Friday-night Sabbath services, observances of the High Holy Days, and
participation in the Temple Youth Group were part of the routine of
growing up accepted by Jerry's non-Jewish friends, including one who
later became a Klansman. When Jerry went off to college, he attended
both the University of Mississippi in Oxford and the University of Alabama, which with its active Jewish fraternities offered the better social
life of the two. Oxford could be unbearable for anyone not from an old
and well-heeled Mississippi family, but few places in Mississippi were as
welcoming of Jews as was Natchez. Jerry had always expected to take a
Jewish wife but instead fell in love with and married an evangelical Christian. As an adult, Krouse was a barbecue-eating southern Jew, neither
kosher nor deeply religious.

By the 1970s, the vibrant Jewish community had declined to a few
families and the rabbi had died without a successor. In later years, the

local Jewish experience would regenerate itself, not through family lines, but through a museum of southern Jewish history.[6]

The caste system of southern life had passed by this time. In earlier times, though, Jews and upper-class blacks had their appointed places in the social hierarchy of Natchez. There were no half-castes blurring the racial divide between the upper and lower castes.[7] White Jews reaped the full privileges of the upper caste, including the supreme male indulgence of interracial sex. Upper-class blacks, even those with kinship ties to a white family, could make no effectual claims to white liberties. Prominent members of the community as they were, society conceded them the most latitude among blacks but less than that of working-class whites. Ironically, the white elite, the chief architects of the social order, often considered this last group, the blue-collar white folk, less disciplined and less desirable than upper-class blacks as neighbors.

Although complex, Natchez society was structured and orderly. It preserved the tenets of white supremacy, but it was not stonily rigid. The line between the races, in other words, was an undulating divide, flexing one way or the other, but never to the point of snapping. One might compare the structural nature of the racial order to that of a high-rise building. Its integrity depends on and is measured by its tensile strength, its ability to twist and bend, ever so slightly, under force of wind or with movements in the earth's crust. Without this built-in elasticity, the edifice would collapse. Fractures in the exterior surface are common, usually an aesthetic concern, though, rather than a structural problem. The architects of the southern racial order were as fastidious as their counterparts of the high-rise but not as premeditated in their design. Flexibility was built in as the social system evolved, and surface cracks were acceptable in the goal of systemic preservation. The social edifice's engineers included blacks along with whites, locked together in a continuing rivalry of challenge and adjustment, with whites bending to black pressure only enough to maintain the superstructure of white over black.

Within this dynamic, whites searched for social harmony. While they found semblances of it in daily life, they also exaggerated it in their minds. Whites could point to the peaceable ways of their black upper-class neighbors and Jewish neighbors and claim, with some accuracy, that Natchez was a harmonious society. Hardworking, law-abiding white

Jews benefited from the social arrangements in ways that white Protestants and Catholics benefited. It served their best interests and, therefore, gave them no reason not to support it.

This was not true for the black upper class, but they tended to go with the flow of the harmonious society anyway. They were aware of racial discrimination, joined and formed organizations that would address it, and took their concerns to white leaders, though always in the form of a respectful request. They knew their place and stayed in it. Segregation had allowed them to create a semiautonomous world of independent businesses, social institutions, and leadership. It was their own peaceable kingdom, with masses over which they too could lord. Those masses, the laboring black poor, gave status to the rest of society; that was their chief burden in life. Poor and powerless, they had not organized the means to challenge the racial order, and until that time, they had few other choices except to go about their business and accept their burden in silence.

Silence was the great deceiver in the harmonious society, which in itself was a fraud. Its continuous smooth-running operation required that all groups know their place and respect the racial hierarchy. Confinement of place was specific to one's racial caste, but it did not prohibit social advancement. Individual striving was tolerated, even encouraged, but only as long as one remained within one's specific racial caste. The key to harmony was mutual toleration: whites would tolerate the presence of blacks as long as blacks would tolerate subjugation. This biracial spirit of trust and cooperation preserved white racial hegemony at the price of democratic liberties, for criticism was forbidden.

Among those blacks whose individual striving did not disrupt social harmony were the black upper class, or the blue veins. A construct of social scientists, the term blue vein applies to blacks of mixed ancestry with skin light enough to expose the blue color of their veins. When discussing Natchez society during the period of this study, the term more appropriately fits blacks of established elite status, many of whom, but not all, were of biracial lineage. As in the white community, elevated social ranking in the black community was often delivered by birth, and attached with it in some cases was a recognizable family name, such as McCary, Fitzhugh, or Johnson in the early years, and Mazique, Mackel, Dumas,

Banks, or West in the later. Members of these families did not refer to themselves as blue veins. But if there were, ostensibly, blue bloods in the white community, there were inversely blue veins in the black. Very frequently, one might also imagine, the blood of an upper-class white family ran through the veins of an upper-class black.[8]

Like the white elite, the heritage of upper-class blacks was old and impressive. It dated back to antebellum Natchez's free-black community, which was proportionally larger than the regional free-black population. Roughly 280 Natchez men and women represented nearly half of the state's free-black population. If the census is to be trusted, 94 percent of Natchez's free blacks were mulattos, with many presumably bearing the anatomical markings of blue veins. Most, if not all, probably derived from the sexual privileges of the white male with the enslaved black female, undoubtedly a circumstance that had brought the gift of manumission to many Natchez free blacks.[9]

This group included many who were wealthy, entrepreneurial, land-owning, slaveholding, influential members of Natchez society. One's upper-class status depended on property accumulation (including slaves in some cases), continuing financial stability, and white patronage and endorsement. The best-known, best-connected, wealthiest, and most successful and socially prominent Natchez free black was William Johnson. Johnson owned three barbershops and a bathhouse and served a clientele that included Natchez's nabobs. Over the course of his life, he also held title to some thirty slaves. To win and preserve their freedom, and their status, blacks like Johnson had to first support slavery and hold service-related occupations acceptable to whites. Second, they had to disinherit the peculiarities of the "inferior" black culture, still noticeably and "offensively" African in many ways, while manifesting attributes of white American culture. Being exemplars of whiteness, in other words, helped upper-class blacks reach their station in southern society. At the same time, upholding the system of racial supremacy affirmed the white southerner's conception of social harmony.[10]

This changed to some degree, however, with the coming of the Prometheus of the North, cloaked first in the blue of the Yankee soldier and next in the tweeds of the carpetbagger, intolerable in either dress to white southerners. In southern white myth, the twin acts of northern aggression—the Civil War and Reconstruction—unfolded together into an era of shame and needless suffering. In truth, the era did disturb the harmonious universe in which slaves, free blacks, and whites had moved about. It upended the relationship between the races, blurred even more the division between black and mulatto, spawned autonomous black institutions, and opened the way for an expanded black elite. The group that scaled to the top of the social ladder was divided into a nonpolitical elite—large landholders—and a political elite—political officeholders. Very often, those who held political office also held sizable tracts of land.

Adams County blacks used their new freedom and votes in part to create what was arguably the state's most impressive delegation of black politicians serving at local, state, and national levels. Natchez was the only Mississippi town where local government was not dominated by whites. In 1870, the year of the ratification of the Fifteenth Amendment, some 1,198 of the approximately 1,600 registered voters in the courthouse district of Adams County were black. Empowered by this constituency, Natchez blacks were elected or appointed to the city board of aldermen, the county board of supervisors and the local board of education, to the state legislature and the U.S. Congress, and served in the offices of the justice of the peace, police chief, sheriff, tax collector, and secretary of state. Charlotte Mackel's great-grandfather Robert H. Wood was appointed by Governor James L. Alcorn in 1869 as Natchez's first black mayor, making Wood one of Alcorn's few black appointees, Mississippi's only black mayor during Reconstruction, and one of only five black mayors in the South. The next year, Wood served as justice of the peace, and in 1871, he was elected as mayor in his own right. He was joined on the board of aldermen by three other blacks, William McCary, Robert Fitzhugh, and William Lynch. The year before, Wood and Fitzhugh had managed the successful congressional campaign of John R. Lynch.[11]

Of the three blacks Mississippi sent to Congress during Reconstruction, two, Lynch and Hiram Revels, came from Natchez. Previously a free black from North Carolina, Revels embarked on a reluctant but ultimately laudable political career when he became a city alderman in 1868. He then went on to serve in the state legislature, where he accepted an appointment to the U.S. Senate to finish the unexpired term of Jefferson Davis. He was the first black to take a seat in Congress. His counterpart Lynch had been a slave and a house servant at Dunleith before entering Natchez Republican politics. He was appointed justice of the peace in 1869. A year later, after the ratification of the Fifteenth Amendment, he won election to the Mississippi House of Representatives, whose membership of 115 never included more than 40 blacks. As slim as the odds may have seemed, Lynch captured the speakership in 1872. He was only twenty-four years old. That same year he was elected to the U.S. House of Representatives and went to Washington as that body's youngest member. Before his death at age ninety-three, he would practice law in Mississippi, serve as auditor of the U.S. Treasury, write three books, and retire from the army with the rank of major.[12]

It is safe to conclude that the ascendant group of blacks preferred whiteness to blackness, suspended between the two though they were. Their social backgrounds were nearly as mixed as was their lineage. Nearly all, if not all, could claim a racially integrated bloodline, and some were blue vein in appearance. All were originally from a southern state, with less than half from Natchez. With their repudiation of the poor and rejection by whites, the black elite of Reconstruction, much like their free-black predecessors and their blue-blood counterparts, created a consolidated world, strengthened by endogamy and selective socializing. To be sure, when John Lynch's sister Catherine and William Johnson's son Clarence chose each other as mates, no one would have raised an eyebrow in concern of social incompatibility. Their union bore the fruit of economic prosperity. It also produced a son who became a physician and whose professional status alone would have preserved the family standing in the early twentieth century.[13]

But if the perpetuity of bloodlines and even prosperity were assured, political stature could not survive the rise of Jim Crow. The heyday for black politics in Natchez and Mississippi by the late 1870s had begun spiraling to an end. In 1875, the Democrats gained control of the legislature, in part because flocks of white Republicans were deserting the party of the black and tan, a party that they correctly surmised had a bleak future in the South. Black Republicans were left to fend for themselves. The changes further jaded many would-be black voters who were growing increasingly disenchanted with Republican politics. The odds piled even higher against black political participation when Mississippi adopted a disfranchising constitution in 1890. The state then proceeded to systematically purge blacks from the voter rolls through new requirements of poll taxes and literacy tests, as well as through old standby methods of intimidation and fraud. Black registration at the state level consequently dropped (as white registration climbed) from 86,973 in 1868 to 8,922 in 1892, the first year of the new suffrage provisions. Only 342 blacks of a possible 4,000 were registered in all of Adams County, where once the courthouse precinct poll book alone listed 1,200 black registerees. There were only 15 in 1902, and until the enactment of the Voting Rights Act of 1965, no more than 12 percent of the county's black voting-age population would find their names in the poll books. "Blacks felt very frustrated then," said George West Sr., a prominent funeral-home owner. "There was fear of whippings and reprisals on their jobs."[14]

By the early twentieth century, Natchez's black elite was moving through another transition. During slavery, the free-black elite had shown little leadership except among their own; then during the political days of Reconstruction an expanded elite tried to be leaders of a biracial constituency. Property, probity, and white patronage had been central to their status. That remained the case when a new black professional class emerged in the early twentieth century. Members of that group identified more closely with the larger black population than did the free-black elite of antebellum Natchez, but did not carry the political clout or exercise the assertiveness of the Reconstruction elite. Yet more than ever, they reached out a paternalistic hand to guide their sometimes darker, always poorer brothers and sisters through the age of Jim Crow. Each group buoyed the other in the unremitting ebb and flow of the white South's harmonious society.

As had historically been true with affluent blacks, those of twentieth-century Natchez constituted a small group. Of the 6,845 black men and women employed in Adams County in 1940, 108 were considered professionals—teachers, physicians, dentists, pharmacists, embalmers, and others. Sixty of these professionals were women; a few (probably fewer than 10) were nurses, while most were teachers. Education and law were the first professional fields Mississippi blacks entered after the Civil War. After the ascent of Jim Crow in the late nineteenth century, blacks continued to teach, albeit under conditions of increasing racial disparity. By contrast, black attorneys were a rapidly diminishing species. Favorable decisions from white juries and judges were rare. This, combined with constant harassment from the state's white bar association, turned lawyering into a near impossibility for blacks. As a result, only five blacks were practicing law in Mississippi in 1935. None was in Natchez.[15]

What Natchez did have was a modest but discernible group of black male professionals in health care and funerary services. In 1950, two black dentists, three black physicians, one black pharmacist, and four black funeral homes provided services to Adams County's approximately 16,000 blacks—a professional cadre similar in size to that which served the some 50,000 blacks of Montgomery, Alabama. (Of equal size to its racial counterpart, Natchez's white population had its choice of twenty-two physicians, forty-four attorneys, eleven drugstores, six dentists, and three funeral homes.) The black professionals were heads of families that composed the core of the local black upper class. Revels died in 1901, and Lynch had departed from Natchez by the early years of the twentieth century. As a practicing local physician, William Johnson's grandson William R. Johnston was a member of the new professional class. But with his death in 1938, the Johnson clan all but disappeared from Natchez. Dumas, Mackel, West, Banks, Harrison, and Rucker were among the new surnames connected with social prominence and community leadership, and all were professionals.[16]

The backgrounds of the black professional families were diverse. Unlike the white elite who could usually trace the family history as far back as Europe, black families could generally reconstruct only a generation or two of their lineage. Other families, like the Mackels, could follow their lineage to the slave and free-black populations of Adams County. Many of the families arrived in Natchez after slavery. Among the late arrivals were the Wests, who came from South Carolina and a family stock that included Choctaw and Scots-Irish blood. There was a white branch or two in most family trees of the black upper class, though the overall size of the Adams County mulatto population was uncertain at midcentury (the Census Bureau dropped the mulatto category after 1920). Regionwide, miscegenation was not as common as it had been in the antebellum years. Many white southerners, and those from Natchez notwithstanding, believed that miscegenation had been one of the great sins of the antebellum South. "To merge white and black," Joel Williamson explains, "would have been the ultimate holocaust, the absolute damnation of Southern civilization."[17]

Although mulattos were living symbols of the violation of the caste system, unions between blacks and whites in Natchez still existed. Allison Davis and the Gardners talked about the commonality of common-law marriages, or "permanent alliances," in 1930s Natchez. Charlotte Mackel Harrison's husband, Robert, grew up knowing a white Jewish grandfather, Charles Moritz. Harrison's grandmother Dorcas Walker had two daughters with Moritz, who took an active role in raising the girls. Both went to college and married dentists; Julie, Harrison's mother, was the creator and director of "Heaven Bound," and her sister, Lucille, became Mississippi's first black social worker. Under Mississippi state law, Moritz could not marry Harrison's grandmother. If the two had chosen to cohabit, which they did not, the social mores of Natchez society would have tolerated such an arrangement, even though many residents—black and white—would have objected. Not tolerated would have been a similar arrangement between a black male and a white female. Walker and Moritz never married anyone else, and fittingly they died in the same year. Long after Moritz's death, his grandchildren and great-grandchildren continued to visit his grave. "It was one of those things that was not discussed at the time in Natchez," said Charlotte Harrison, "but everyone knew who their father was."[18]

One local white tested the social acceptance of interracial cohabitation only to encounter family rejection. A merchant from an established upper-class family, he fell in love with a local woman who was as white as he. Because she was known to come from mixed racial stock, she carried the badge of the black caste. As rumor had it, the couple went to New York to marry.[19] Whatever the truth, they were estranged from his family after returning to Natchez and living as husband and wife. They resided in a substantial Queen Anne–style cottage near the black business district on Pine Street and raised two sons. Both bore physical characteristics betraying their father's Irish genes, as white and red-haired as their Caucasian cousins. Even so, there was never any confusion about their caste identity. They went to the black Catholic school, even though they lived across the street from the white Catholic school, played with black children, and adopted a black consciousness. Because their father was white, their social ranking in the black community was unclear. By adulthood, the brothers' lives had begun following diverging paths of consciousness that together suggested the competing egos in the fictitious Joe Christmas, William Faulkner's protagonist in *Light in August* who knew not whether to be black or white. One of the boys remained a part of the black community. The other moved to New York, passed into the white world, and married a Jewish woman.[20]

Collectively, the complexion of the professional black class displayed a spectrum of shades. Even within individual families, one found differences in skin and eye color and hair texture. A few among the black upper class could have passed as white and faded into the upper caste if family membership could have been concealed, difficult to do in a place the size of Natchez. Most of the black upper class were probably brown in skin color, neither dark nor fair, with brown eyes and wavy or tight black hair—on a whole darker than the Reconstruction generation of the black elite.[21]

Skin color as a determinant of status was even less important than it had been in the nineteenth century. The most valued attributes were family, education, and profession. Across the state, persons with Negroid features had been plucking their way into the upper echelon, turning the shade of the leadership class gradually darker. Nevertheless, Natchez women of the established upper class were probably more likely to reject a male suitor with charcoal skin and a broad nose than one of similar status but with moderately Caucasian features. The men bent toward similar preferences in their search for a mate. Ultimately, the black upper class tended to be an insular group, socializing and marrying among themselves, thus perpetuating their varied physical characteristics.[22]

Black upper-class families of the mid–twentieth century attained their station not only by strategic marriages but by personal initiative and hard work. Whites routinely pointed to Natchez's relatively large professional class of blacks as proof of white magnanimity, fair treatment, and ameliorating influence. Whites were apt, to be sure, to give themselves more credit than they deserved. By the mid–twentieth century no discernible familial connection existed between Natchez's blue veins and blue bloods that might have eased the prejudice blacks in general felt from the white community. Lighter skin color may have made black advancement into professional positions less threatening in white eyes. But light skin usually garnered nothing more than the lifting of an obstacle to advancement, not the provision of a means—such as a gift of land—for advancement.

Indeed, black upward mobility resulted more from black pushing than from white pulling. Personal initiative, often facilitated by family support, was needed for one to overcome the significant challenges to completing high school, graduating from college, and then succeeding in a professional school. If light skin color sometimes opened doors in the white community—even as the black upper class was growing darker— more than likely whites found it easier to identify their own "respect-able" values in persons who somewhat physically resembled them than in those who appeared considerably different. It is not inconceivable that whites were more able to accept the black commitment to education, hard work, and disciplined behavior as something more genuine in lighter-complexioned blacks than in darker blacks. Then, too, the long-time presence of a black elite, traditionally perceived as mulatto, would have reinforced this thinking. In the final sum, black achievements were more independent of white patronage in the mid–twentieth century than in antebellum and Reconstruction days.

The upward mobility of George West Sr. provides a case in point. A soft-spoken man of modest height and medium-light skin, West was most recognizable in later years by his shock of graying hair, fleshy face, black horn-rimmed glasses, and pencil-thin mustache. Born to local black educators in 1913, West grew up thinking he would pursue a med-ical degree, before circumstances dictated another course. By age sixteen, he had lost both of his parents, and as the oldest of six children, he went to work at a Natchez box manufacturer to support his siblings. Even-tually, he took a job in a funeral home and learned the embalmer's pro-fession. In the early 1950s, he opened his own funeral home and pros-pered, rising within the ranks of the black business community. He was a charter member of the Natchez Business and Civic League (NBCL), of which he served as president for several years. Affiliated with Booker T. Washington's National Negro Business League, the Natchez organization promoted black entrepreneurship, civic pride, community action, and voter registration. West also helped organize the Progressive Community Credit Union, which was funded by Natchez's black businessmen and professionals to extend loans to those people whose skin color disquali-fied them at white institutions. West's successes bore the fruit of a com-fortable life in a rambling two-story Queen Anne house for himself, his wife, and six children.[23]

The family's affluence was made possible by a semiautonomous black economy distinguished by a strong entrepreneurial spirit. Heading due east from the river bluff, Franklin Street was the aorta of the black professional community, lined by modest retail and professional buildings. It was the place to go if one needed a physician, dentist, or druggist. Franklin Street terminated near the former location of the old "Forks of the Road" slave market. From that point, Saint Catherine Street retreated back westward, peeling away from Franklin to run a parallel course a block away. Saint Catherine Street addresses included black barbershops and funeral homes, the homes of many past and present eminent black citizens, the black Brumfield High School and Holy Family Catholic Church, and the ill-fated Rhythm Club, where a catastrophic 1940 fire took 209 lives. In 1950, the larger black business community boomed with sixteen beauty shops, twelve barbershops, nineteen dressmakers, a score of beer markets, auto repair and upholstery shops, a drugstore, four retail confectioneries, two fish dealers, two interior decorators, twenty restaurants, four gas stations, two trucking companies, four midwives, and sixty-two grocers. Many of these businesses were in-home or neighborhood businesses, such as that of seamstress Laura Davis, who made costumes for the Confederate Pageant. One of the best-known and most enduring black enterprises was Nellie Jackson's bordello, which like many other black-operated businesses depended on both black and white patronage. It opened in 1930 a few blocks from city hall, operated openly and with the endorsement of city officials for six decades, and in later years advertised with T-shirts reading, "Follow me to Nellie's Place."[24]

At the top of this business community were the black professionals. To be a member of this group was to live in relative comfort. The Wests, the Dumases, the Mackels, and the others owned attractive houses, big late-model automobiles, and commercial real estate. They shopped in fine stores and sent their children to private schools and to college. Charlotte Mackel Harrison remembered never wanting for anything as a child and never envying the spoils of the wealthy white children. Her father, Robert Dunbar Mackel, was heir to a profitable funeral home and burial insurance business that his father had founded in 1898 after leaving a Louisiana cotton plantation. Upon Robert Dunbar Mackel's death, the operation of the family business passed to his children, then grandchildren. Harrison's parents were able to keep their six children well dressed, give them the option of attending private school, provide them with music lessons, and send them to college. It was always assumed that the Mackel children, as was true in other affluent black families, would continue their education after high school.[25]

The black upper class enjoyed privileges that other blacks associated with the white race, not their own. Most members of the upper class were active registered voters, generally welcomed at the polls after paying their poll taxes. The upper class had charge accounts at many of the white-owned, primarily Jewish, retail stores, where service was prompt and efficient and accompanied by a courtesy title such as "Mrs." and "Mr." It impressed blacks that they were even allowed to try on clothes, and as a result of this and other anomalies in the regional racial etiquette, many blacks believed that race relations were better in Natchez than "anywhere below the Mason-Dixon line." But this was how the harmonious society worked, how it deceived and placated, by honoring a legal right of a select few or by granting them a privilege or two.[26]

Life could be deceiving when all seemed pleasant and fulfilling. By her own admission, Harrison "lived a very sheltered life" as a child. When growing up, there was little need for contact with the community beyond her own sphere. She and the other children were aware of the separate black and white worlds. But they did not generally associate segregation with discrimination until later years, usually after reaching adulthood. Jim Crow "was a fact of life," said Duncan Morgan. But one did not dwell on that fact, nor usually challenge it. "It was the way our parents took care of us," said Harrison. "They protected us and provided alternatives so that we never had to think about" segregation.[27]

Even as it was open, the harmonious society was limiting. Before the 1950s, Natchez was a one-political-party city. It was not uncommon for a white polling official to ask a black voter about his or her affiliation to a local or state office. "The first thing they asked you," said Walter Nelson, "is if you were a Democrat and of course we would say, 'Yes.'"[28] Jury rolls included both races, but until the 1960s, juries consisted of only one race. The stores that waited on affluent blacks in turn with whites hired only white clerks. The black upper class sat in the colored balcony or section at Natchez's movie theaters. Henry Dumas's drugstore on Franklin Street served blacks and whites at its swank soda fountain, but the soda fountain at the white-owned Economy Drug Store, which employed black jerks, served only whites. Kaiser's Ice Cream Factory, a favorite place of Charlotte Mackel and her friends, had a horseshoe-shaped counter, one side for blacks and the other for whites. Before the city built a swimming pool on the property of black Natchez College, the kids of the black upper class swam with all the other black kids in the local creeks. There were no public recreational facilities for black children until the NBCL opened a youth center in 1962. City officials recognized that the center was "necessary to maintain good race relations," and the city provided eight acres of land for the site of the center. Ultimately, though, it left the NBCL and the black community scrambling for private donations for the construction of a facility.[29]

All the while that the black upper class tried to improve recreational opportunities for the black community, whites generally revealed a lack of enthusiasm for any ideas that required tax dollars. There were those who were more generous than others, such as Roane Byrnes, a wealthy Adams County planter who frequently spoke of race relations in the patrician terms of friendship and cooperation. In the mid-1960s, she built a baseball field on her 1,600-acre Beverly Plantation for her 220 or so black tenants and hosted baseball games between the Beverly Sports and teams organized on other plantations.[30]

Yet, even as exceptions existed, whites reasserted their commitment to racially separate and unequal conditions. The baseball diamond was no less a sacred venue than were the church and school. When in the early 1950s Audley Mackel Jr., along with the NBCL, decided to organize a baseball league for black youths, neither the city nor the county would allow the use of the public's ball field, reserved for white adult and youth baseball, or provide a separate one. Mackel and the NBCL were forced to turn to a local plantation family to acquire the use of an abandoned field, cow plops and all.[31]

Not even the breaking of the color barrier in major-league baseball could dismantle the local segregationist resolve.[32] In a remarkable feat of fund-raising on behalf of the Poor Colored Children's Christmas Fund, the NBCL in the fall of 1950 arranged to have Jackie Robinson, Larry Doby, Don Newcombe, and Roy Campanella, all black pioneers in the major leagues, compete in a benefit game with the Indianapolis Clowns of the American Negro League. As usual, whites had the last say about the conditions of public events. Advance tickets were bought at racially separate locations, and box seats and the grandstands along third base-line and left field were reserved for whites, leaving right field and first baseline for blacks. Sometimes such rigidity in segregation could be destructive. Four years later, Natchez's minor-league team, the Indians, a member of the Cotton States League, folded due to financial troubles. The Indians had refused to play against integrated ball clubs and to recruit black talent, as other minor league teams were doing by the 1950s.[33]

Segregation came with certain costs, financial and otherwise. But the benefits, found in the preservation of white culture, easily offset expenditures, particularly when unequal facilities reduced the economic burden of Jim Crow to a minimum. It made political and economic sense to keep all but a few token blacks politically powerless. Providing equal facilities would have been a heavy burden on the wallets of white taxpayers. For their part, black taxpayers helped finance a system that imposed upon them lesser facilities and consequently a lesser quality of life. Until the unrest of the civil rights struggle, Natchez whites gave little collective thought to the social impact of segregation on blacks. At midcentury, whites, like blacks, had known life no other way. Natchez was a universe with two worlds, and their separation seemed perfectly natural.

Even so, the discrimination inherent in a system of imposed separation did not go unnoticed by blacks. In the years before the civil rights movement, black professionals took the lead in dealing with issues of race. Their chief interest was in establishing full political, economic, and civil rights for blacks. Compared to the civil rights activists of later years, the black professional as race crusader was restrained. He approached the white power structure in the spirit of cooperation and good intentions. His concern was with equality, not with separation. He never challenged the system of segregation, only the disparity within it.

One of the early and most prominent leaders among the black professionals was Albert W. Dumas. In his private and public life, he was the prototypical black professional. Dumas was raised in Houma, Louisiana, the son of a free-black sugarcane boiler. According to family lore, the Louisiana Dumases were descendants of French novelist Alexandre Dumas, author of *The Three Musketeers*. After graduating from Illinois Medical School, Albert Dumas moved to Canton, Mississippi. Six months later in 1899 at the age of twenty-three, he was invited to open a general practice in Natchez by John B. Banks, the city's first black physician.

Black professionals did not require white sponsorship to practice in Natchez, as was the case in many other southern communities, but earning the endorsement of the white community was essential to one's longevity. Tall and trim with straight hair, light-brown skin, and the countenance of a sage, Dumas gained the respect of blacks and whites locally and nationally as both a physician and citizen. In 1939 and 1940, he served as president of the National Medical Association, the black equivalent of the white American Medical Association. With John Banks, he was one of the founders of Bluff City Savings, Natchez's only black financial institution. He also helped organize the Natchez Negro Business League, the predecessor to the NBCL. He bought property on Franklin Street, constructed six buildings, one a sanatorium for blacks, and hired a white Jew to manage his property. On Sundays, he devoted his afternoons to treating the white poor from Louisiana and Arkansas.[34]

Dumas led an active and busy life in Natchez for forty-six years. With his wife Cornelia Harrison, a sister of Robert Harrison Sr., a local dentist and father-in-law of Charlotte Mackel, Dumas was committed to raising the nine children in his household with a wholesome formal and practical education. Dumas ensured that his children and grandchildren were informed about their African American heritage. Whenever black entertainers, writers, and educators came to town, which lacked a decent black hotel before the 1960s, Dumas invited them to stay at his house. From this environment, seven of the Dumas children went on to complete college. A son became a pharmacist and drugstore and variety-store owner, another became an insurance executive, one daughter became a prominent Mississippi educator, and the other daughters married professional men. The oldest son, Albert Jr., wanted to go into mechanics, but his father was insistent that his namesake follow his footsteps into medicine. Although Dumas was Catholic and his wife Episcopalian, the family joined Rose Hill Baptist Church so Dumas could immerse himself in the community and build his practice. By the 1920s, he had emerged as a leading voice of the black community, a service he performed until his death in 1945.[35]

Dumas loved Natchez, but he hated discrimination. He was especially passionate about the importance of a quality education for blacks. He and other blacks, including his daughter Cecila Dumas, president of the black PTA, led a campaign in the mid-1920s for the construction of

Natchez's first black high school, Brumfield. In the 1940s, one of the local theaters, after changing ownership, erected a partition separating the black seating from the white, previously separated only by the aisle. Dumas could tolerate the separate seating, but he found the partition an unnecessary and insulting symbol of Jim Crow, and in response he organized a black boycott of the theater that resulted in the partition's removal. Like younger black professionals who would carry the torch after his death—Audley Mackel, Robert Mackel, and George West—Dumas was invited to black churches to give "motivational" talks about voting rights and self-sufficiency. Self-sufficiency in part meant doing business with black businesses, including physicians, dentists, and funeral-home operators.[36]

In giving up claims to public integration and equal political participation, the leadership approach of the black professionals in some ways resembled that of Booker T. Washington. That approach would begin to change in the mid-1950s and 1960s as the national civil rights movement was launched. Before then, blacks still remembered Washington's visit to Natchez in 1904, and the black leadership's dealings with the white power structure were earnest but cordial, revealing the supplicant's utmost respect for the patron. When in 1948 the Natchez Negro Business League approached the Natchez Board of Aldermen for a swimming pool for black children, its request contained the following words: "Here in the Southland is our home, we know no other—here our fathers lie dead and buried, here among our white friends, have we lived our lives and experienced our joys and sorrow, in time of need we know no where else to turn."[37]

Whites expected this kind of deference, behavior that in later years brought scorn from certain groups. In the 1960s, young civil rights activists showed little regard for the black professional and business leaders and their accommodationist ways. The established leaders were accused of being obstructionists, concerned less about the civil rights of the black masses than about protecting a cozy relationship with powerful whites to preserve their own economic self-interests. The bastion of professional and business leaders, the NBCL was dismissed as a den of accommodationists, even though the local police regarded the organization as a "front for the NAACP." If Dumas had lived, he would have most certainly been lumped with the accommodationists, for he operated by the dictates of his day. George West, who made the transition from the era of the professional black leader to the era of the civil rights leader and beyond, became the target of particularly harsh ridicule. West's natural soft-spokenness undoubtedly contributed to the Uncle Tom image he acquired.[38]

Being "one hundred percent with both races," as West was described, was an asset for both the individual and the black community. In any diplomatic arrangement, aggressive action, such as open demonstration and protest, usually follows as a last resort to failed negotiations. Dumas, West, and the others were negotiators who laid important groundwork for the activists who came later. While dealing with a white leadership entrenched in tradition, they had no national civil rights movement backing them or setting precedents. The NAACP was the only national civil rights organization that had made inroads into the South before the 1960s, but its efforts were crippled by objectives at the local level that were ambiguous and often at odds with national policy. As the later years would prove, support for aggressive action would not have been forthcoming from the larger black community in Natchez, where the prevailing belief was that race relations were "good." Because of the undertakings of the black professionals, life indeed was better in Natchez than in the many places that had no black swimming pool, no black high school, no common-law marriages, no thriving black economy.[39]

If black leaders were deferential, they were so, not by nature, but by instinct. They were practicing the rules on how to win friends and influence people before Dale Carnegie wrote the book. In 1933, Dumas told Allison Davis that blacks assumed a power position over whites by means of flattery. "That's what the white man wants—to feel that you consider him superior to you. Then you can get about anything out of him." George West was a "hard-fighting" man in his own way, said more than one local. His generation had "some of the best psychologists on earth," who, much like the trickster in black folktale, played upon white sensibilities to extract a promise or gift.[40]

Only to the white man of authority and wealth did the black leader humble himself. The white poor were generally worthy of his disdain, and the "country Negro" and the "uncultured black" were a class apart, his inferior. Although race maintained a real separation between the black upper class and whites of all status, the black professionals were wedded to the idea that a laissez-faire economic system favored the in-

dustrious and the frugal. To the professional, race was an artificial measure of power; class (as well as maleness) was a more legitimate signifier
of one's achievements and natural abilities and should thus, along with
deportment and education, be the determinant of one's status and power
in society.[41] Even as the barriers of race limited the wielding of their
power outside their race's community, black professionals assumed leadership roles with the attitude that they were in their positions by logic of
their proven abilities, abilities that would serve themselves and their
community.[42]

Those blacks committed to conservative marketplace values were
generally also committed to a community service ethic. If one were at the
top, one carried the social obligation to help the less fortunate and to
improve, if not uplift, black life generally. Fulfilling this obligation reinforced one's superior status. Although there was an elitist cast to the service ethic, it was not wholly disingenuous. Since Reconstruction, Natchez
middle- and upper-class blacks had overseen local charitable and civic
organizations, and they established various lending institutions to promote business development. In 1916, Dumas organized the Colored Christmas Tree, which was a community effort to distribute toys and groceries
to poor families at Christmas. It continued into the 1970s, when it
merged with the white community's Christmas Tree. With the help of
Works Progress Administration funding, the Athletic Club established
playgrounds for black children. Finally, the professionals served as the
black community's ambassadors to the white power structure, though
they never took their ambassadorship to the heights of restructuring the
racial order.[43]

Social obligations drew women of the professional families as well
into public life.[44] The income of their professional husbands afforded the
women freedom from employment and more time for voluntary and
community improvement work. They plunged into that work with imagination and enthusiasm and found self-fulfillment in bettering the quality
of life for children and the poor. One of the busiest of their organizations
was the Young Matrons Club. Organized during the depression, the
group engaged in charitable projects for the poor and contributed coal
and wood to heat the black schools. It also sponsored black Girl Scout
and Boy Scout troops. Another organized effort of women was the Art
Club, which made garments for the needy and distributed fruit, linen,

dishes, and infant wear during holidays. In addition to doing similar charitable work, the Flower Club concentrated its energies on landscape clean-up and beautification. Although men generally served as spokespersons in interracial affairs, the women were not politically silent. Of the 564 blacks registered to vote in the 1950s, 221 (39 percent) were women. A number of them, such as Artemese West, the wife of George West, and some of the Mackels, were also members of the NAACP.[45]

Whites would have taken notice of black political strength had it ever come to seem excessive, and they did notice the existence of the NAACP. But they welcomed and commended organized efforts of self-help. Those efforts affirmed their own paternalistic labors—as well as the white notion of black dependence—and ultimately complemented the function of the harmonious society. From the white perspective, black culture was still evolving, and the upper-class black was as much a creature of that culture as was the sharecropper. Although the black professional and his family exemplified the best of black culture, whites regarded that very culture as the obstacle holding exemplary blacks from rising to the full potential of civilization. Their professional success, their advanced education, their solid family life, their proper manners, and even their Christianity were to whites nothing more than an imperfect imitation of white culture. No matter how hard they tried, blacks could never be fully white as long as the black culture existed. Because it did exist, segregation was imperative, for in a fully open, commingling world, whites feared that they themselves could descend into blackness.[46]

There were not in Natchez society the same fears and beliefs about Jewishness. Even though blacks accepted the Christian messiah and Jews did not, Jews exercised the full rights and privileges of white society. They had been doing so since the late eighteenth century, when Mississippi became a U.S. territory. During the French occupation of the early 1700s, Catholicism was established as the official religion and Jewish immigration was restricted. The first Jews probably arrived in Natchez sometime during the Spanish settlement and remained during the British occupation after 1763, when their presence was tolerated but not their right to vote. Access to the political process was not a reality until the Mississippi territory passed from Spain to the United States in 1798.[47]

Since the first arrival of Jews in Savannah in the 1730s, the southern states and territories had generally been more welcoming than the North, though political rights in some places were delayed in coming. During the nineteenth century, two waves of Jewish immigration washed across the United States and into the South. The first, in the 1840s and 1850s, brought immigrants from France and the German and Austrian dominions, and the second, in the 1880s, from Russia and other parts of Eastern Europe. In virtually every case, the immigrants were fleeing oppressive anti-Semitism, and to them the American South represented a providential haven of religious and economic freedom.[48]

Although their numbers were never great, Jews were important participants in the social, political, and economic development of the communities in which they settled. Many Jewish immigrants of the nineteenth century began as itinerant peddlers, plying their trade from town to town and plantation to plantation. Typically, the peddler eventually settled into a retail store, prospered by hard work, sent his children to college, and left his business to be passed down through the generations. Ultimately, Jews branched out into dozens of vital businesses and professions, from mule sales to medicine. In Natchez, Jews operated nearly one-third of the city's retail businesses from the end of the Civil War to well into the twentieth century. During the postbellum years, an economic boom period for Natchez merchants, Jews owned more than half of the dry-goods stores and cotton-broker operations.[49]

This story of the southern Jewish rise from immigrant to middle-class American citizen defines the family history of the Krouse brothers. Mannie, Morris, and Alek Krouse arrived in Natchez with their parents in 1916, considered late by local standards, even for Jews. At sixteen, Mannie was the oldest, born in New York City. His brothers were born in Toronto in 1904 and 1906. Their parents emigrated to America from Russia in the late nineteenth century, when whole communities, not just individual families, were fleeing the pogroms there. Their father, Samuel, left to avoid conscription in the Russian army. In America, he found work as a wholesale men's tailor, met a seamstress named Dora, married her, and together they raised a family in a new land of opportunity.[50]

Stalking the American dream proved to be a tortuous and painstaking journey. The Krouses moved from New York City to Toronto, Montreal, Arkansas, and then to Greenwood, Mississippi, where they opened a scrap business. The business failed, and they returned to Arkansas before moving to Columbus, Mississippi, and back again to Arkansas. Finally, Samuel and his brother borrowed one thousand dollars from a relative, relocated to Natchez, rented a commercial building for ten dollars a month, and this time found success in the scrap business. The entrepreneurial Krouses were of an early generation of recyclers, prospering in a time when recycling was still recognized as a profitable economic endeavor, not disdained as an ecological inconvenience in a conveniently disposable society. They bought star roots, ginseng roots, bleached bones, and scrap metal from the public and resold all to wholesalers. They even collected grease from area restaurants to be purchased by soap factories. They learned to evaluate the pelts of possums, skunks, otters, and raccoons brought in by hunters and farmers, and they developed the largest fur business in the area. In 1929, their collective businesses were doing well enough to allow the Krouses to pay fourteen thousand dollars in cash for a comfortable brick house on Union Street. When Samuel eventually took ill, Dora assumed the responsibilities of the various enterprises.[51]

In their old age, the Krouse brothers would reflect on their hardworking parents as one of the most valuable of life's examples. None of the brothers had more than a tenth-grade education, but under the tutelage of their parents they learned the skills needed to become prosperous businessmen in their own right. The key to success, they understood, was the willingness to put in long hours and to put no task beneath oneself. In the evenings, for instance, they would park a truck overnight across the river in Louisiana, rise the next morning before the first scheduled ferry run, and hire a boat to row them to the other side where the truck waited. This gave them an early start on the road searching for scrap. During the depression, the brothers went into the pecan business, buying their product for cash and reselling on credit. Their father, who believed in dealing only in cash, wanted nothing to do with such a risky enterprise. Whatever odds were stacked against them, the brothers overcame. At its peak, the Natchez Pecan Shelling Company employed some three hundred women and fifty men. Eventually, it and the other Krouse family businesses were handed down to the present generation.[52]

When the Krouses first arrived in Natchez, Jewish life was vibrant. The temple congregation had dropped from its 1906 peak of 141 members, but it had an active Sabbath school, Sisterhood, and social club.

Natchez Jews claimed the state's oldest congregation, originally organized in 1843 as a burial society, or *Hevrah Kedusha,* that observed Orthodox traditions. By the 1860s, the expanding number of German Jews had exercised a concerted desire to adopt *Minhang America,* an outgrowth of the Reform movement that had begun in Germany before sweeping the United States. The Reform movement brought changes, which included opening religious services to women and children, that essentially modernized, or Americanized, observances and greatly muted the distinctions between Jewish and non-Jewish worship. Samuel Ullman, a German-born merchant recently from Port Gibson, led a group to organize a new congregation, B'nai Israel. In 1872, Natchez Jews dedicated their first temple, the state's first as well, which included a sanctuary that broke from Orthodox design. The next year, the congregation was invited to become a charter member of the new Union of American Hebrew Congregations, and thus one of the first Reform congregations in the country.[53]

Jews left their imprint on local architecture as well. In the 1890s, Isaac Lowenberg and Henry Frank, both temple members and merchants, developed Clifton Heights, a sidewalked subdivision of Tudor, Queen Anne, and Colonial Revival homes occupied primarily by Jews. Clifton Heights not only reflected the prominence and prosperity of the local Jewish citizenry, it expanded the local Victorian-era architecture, architecture of an order comparable to Natchez's distinctive antebellum mansions.[54]

The Reform synagogue and the elegant Clifton Heights were indicative of the successful assimilation of Natchez Jews into southern white society. Assimilation required an unspoken, reciprocal social agreement between Jews and the traditional white population. Jews had to be willing to absorb the ways of the white South and sacrifice some traditions. The traditional white population in turn had to temper its xenophobia and accept into its world a people who rejected the Christian savior. As was the story across the South, Natchez Jews walked farther down the road to accommodation than did non-Jews.

Except for their quiet retreat to temple on Friday nights and High Holy Days—and not all made that retreat—Jews were hardly distinguishable from their white Christian brothers and sisters. Sometimes only a surname could identify a Jewish family, but a name was often an unreliable determinant. Natchez, for instance, had Geisenberger Jews and non-Jews. A distinguishable Jewish surname by no means implied nonconformist behavior outside of worship. Jewish slaveholders in the nineteenth century, something of a proving period of assimilation, were as common as Jewish holidays. Natchez Jews also fought on the side of the Confederacy, doing so with more than three thousand other southern Jews. Said Jay Lehmann, a descendent of immigrants from Alsace: "My grandmother Jeanette told me that one of her grandfathers, a man named Moses, had been a matzoh baker and lived in New Orleans and had played the piccolo and led a band for the Confederacy." In Natchez, the four-foot-eight-inch Simon Mayer was affectionately and proudly known as the "Little Mississippi Major." His mother and Emma, his oldest sister who married Samuel Ullman after the war, smuggled supplies beneath their hoopskirts across enemy lines to Confederate troops. Seven-year-old Rosalie Beekman lost her life when the Union ironclad USS *Essex* shelled Natchez in September 1862. In later years, Beekman was extolled as the only civilian loss during the shelling, and her sacrifice came to symbolize the Jewish community's unmitigated loyalty to the white South. In one of the more profound gestures of assimilation related to the war, Jewish women identified with the Lost Cause. Two were founding members, one the founding vice-president, of the Natchez chapter of the United Daughters of the Confederacy.[55]

The Jewish integration into upper-caste society continued apace during the twentieth century. Through the course of generations, Yiddish inflections among the more recent immigrants gave way to a regional drawl, and Jews became full-fledged, not just honorary, southerners. Natchez Jews helped found the Prentiss Club, an interfaith social and literary organization; they joined the Masons, Knights of Pythias, and the Odd Fellows; they were active members of the Chamber of Commerce, the Rotary Club, the Natchez Country Club, and the Protestant Orphanage. Jewish women helped get the Pilgrimage off the ground, and their sons and daughters served on and reigned over royal courts. There were Natchez Jews who ate bacon and crawfish, not to mention black-eyed peas and fried chicken. For the synagogue's *seder* supper, Jay Lehmann's grandmother was famous for her matzoh balls served in turkey gravy. With the religious experience of Jews usually coming almost entirely from the temple, not from home, some Jewish families celebrated the Christmas tradition with a Christmas tree and the exchange of gifts. "We used to hunt Easter eggs every year, too," said Lehmann, who dated Catholic girls, and even took them to midnight mass.[56]

Not all Jews countenanced interfaith dating, and to many, putting up a Christmas tree was taking one's southerness to an extreme. While there were those who saw themselves as southerners who happened to be Jewish, there were those who saw themselves as Jews who happened to live in the South. This difference was played out, however subtly, in an old, stale history of discord between the German and Alsatian Jews on the one hand and the Russian and Polish Jews on the other. The latter were the newcomers. They were often darker in appearance, with black eyes, eyebrows, and hair. Some arrived cloaked in the dress and thick in the accent of the eastern European. They were the Jewish equivalent of "white trash" in the eyes of some of the established Jews who dwelled in middle- and upper-class southern comfort. With the growing prosperity of the newer group and the shrinking Jewish population, the need for solidarity gained importance. Old World prejudice eventually softened to recognized nuances in identity, with the newcomers more likely to retain a distinctive Jewish definition of life.[57]

Differences in identity were most sharply revealed over Zionism. While many Jews across the South shrank from Zionism, some felt comfortable enough to support the creation of a Jewish state.[58] The Natchez congregation was split over the question, and Temple B'nai Israel took no official position on Israel. Although their actions lacked the sanction of the synagogue, some members of the congregation launched in 1947 a relief drive for Jewish war refugees and the establishment of Israel. Divided though local Jews may have been over the Israel question, the *Natchez Democrat* encouraged its non-Jewish readers to support the fund-raising campaign of their Jewish neighbors.[59]

Beyond differences within the Jewish community, assimilation required acceptance of the host community, and Natchez had a long history of being a good host to Jews. After the Civil War, Isaac Lowenberg, a Jewish wholesale grocer, spent two terms in the mayor's office. Samuel Ullman and twelve other Jews served variously as city aldermen. The local sheriff in the 1880s was Cassius L. Tillman, who came from one of Natchez's early German Jewish families. In the early twentieth century he served as the county treasurer. Unlike the black upper class, Natchez

Jews continued to hold positions of social and political prominence after Reconstruction, even weathering the nativist storm of the 1920s. The local Klan of that era was obsessed with Catholics and blacks but not Jews. That same decade, Natchez elected its second Jewish mayor, S. B. Laub, who served two terms until 1936, when only a few hundred Jews resided among a citywide population approaching fifteen thousand. Two years later, the trustees of Adams County's ailing Jefferson College, a military institution of former prominence, pointedly rejected the offer of a $5-million endowment from George W. Armstrong, a wealthy Texas oil man and self-proclaimed anti-Semite. Armstrong's philanthropy required that blacks and Jews be barred from the school. While the exclusion of blacks would have been consistent with law and tradition, Jews had always been considered an integral part of intellectual, academic, and military life. In perhaps an equally illuminating example of acceptance, the congregation of B'nai Israel raffled off a new 1949 Chevrolet to raise funds for temple repairs. The drawing was scheduled to be held at Natchez's Liberty Park between innings of a game between the Natchez Indians and the Greenville Bucks.[60]

Beneath kindly southern manners and good deeds, some Jews said, lay a latent form of anti-Semitism. It was real even if it was as subtle as Protestant parents prohibiting their children from dating Jews. Sometimes it surfaced in the form of an omission from an invitation list to a socially important party, or in learning that one's Jewishness had been the subject of private conversations between friends. When the travel writer John Gunther attended a cocktail party of Natchez elite in the 1940s and mentioned that "there were two sides to the Negro question . . . several leading citizens of the town almost broke blood vessels to exclaim that I must be a 'Communist' or be 'influenced by Jews.'" Jews remembered that while their women had been among the organizers of the Natchez Garden Club, the later-formed Pilgrimage Garden Club initially behaved as if Jews were unwelcome. Beyond institutional prejudices, personal incidents served as an occasional reminder that southern hospitality sometimes had its limits.[61]

Usually, though, it required something like a skilled miner with a sharp pick to dig out the prejudice. Behavior that was nothing more than a social slight directed at an individual was sometimes confused with prejudice against a group. Jay Lehmann said white Gentiles always treated "me 99 percent the way they treat other people. I get some kidding, but they kid other people about other things." A fourth-generation Natchez Jew, Lehmann participated in the Pilgrimage "from the time I was old enough to walk" and played Babe Ruth and Little League baseball. The brothers Krouse remembered that the animosity of the older German Jewish immigrants for Russian and Polish Jews was greater than that of non-Jews for Jews. In general, non-Jews were less opposed to intermarriage than Jews, though the latter were dealing with the problem of a shrinking population and were concerned about the preservation of their culture. During the 1960s, when the Klan carried out a reign of terror against Jews in other parts of Mississippi, "there was intense concern" among local Jews, said Jerry Krouse, that anti-Semitic violence would creep into Natchez. It never did. The grand dragon of the local Klan announced that neither Catholics nor Jews, only blacks and outside agitators, were targets of his group.[62]

There was a significant theological difference between Jews and Gentiles that neither group ignored though. That difference was chiefly responsible for, to quote Jerry Krouse, "this thing that [was] lurking, nagging at the psyche" of non-Jewish whites. For many, it had begun nagging at them in childhood. In high school in the 1950s, Krouse was friends with L. C. Murray, who as an adult would serve as a high-ranking officer in a local Klan group. Without animus but with genuine concern for his friend's soul, Murray often said that hell awaited Krouse for his refusal to accept Jesus as his savior. Upon reflection of her own childhood, Katherine Blankenstein, who came from a Protestant family of long standing in Natchez, confirmed Krouse's suspicions:[63] "It disturbed us, I think, as children, perhaps maybe when we got a little older, that they were not Christians. But I don't ever remember trying to convert anybody. I remembered being shocked when our minister said to the effect that the Jews have never accepted Jesus as the messiah and we should try to explain that to them to save them. That had never occurred to me that they weren't going to be saved. And then it worried me after that."[64]

Blankenstein was not expressing pity. Natchez Jews never asked that from other whites, and the other whites in turn never felt the need to offer it. Southern whites and Jews were both peoples whose past included defeat and martyrdom, with Jews carrying the heavier historical load of both groups (which is not to discount the history of blacks). Most Natchez Jews never fully turned away from their heritage, but when faced with the choice between ethnic purity and potential alienation on the one hand and ethnic dilution and acceptance on the other, they clearly leaned toward the latter. Even in embracing their own culture, Jews were always too few in number and too much like white southerners to expect anything less than social acceptance. By the second half of the twentieth century, according to some locals, there were fewer Jews than non-Jews who had Jewish antecedents. Those few may not have been people of Jesus, but they were "People of the Book." As historian Stephen Whitfield notes, the neighbors of southern Jews "could not help but notice . . . their commitment to family cohesiveness and the loyalty to ancestry." They were nothing less than solid, law-abiding citizens of the community, successful in their ambitions of economic and education advancement—and they were whites who acted like southerners by conforming to the dominant cultural ethos.[65]

Acceptance and assimilation—cultural likeness—would not have been fulfilled without acquiescence to the existing racial order. Natchez Jewish merchants did not usually follow the more rigid racial etiquette of the larger South when it came to customer service, but neither did they hire black salesclerks. During the civil rights years of the 1960s, Jews did not rise up as outspoken defenders of segregation; their long-standing participation in the Pilgrimage alone was a form of acquiescence. Preferring segregated schools, Jews moved their children to the private academies that sprang up in the 1960s and 1970s in response to court-ordered integration. One can argue that Jewish dissent during the era of massive resistance would have led to alienation from the larger white society. But even conditional silence conveyed support, at the very least indifference, and allowed Jim Crow a healthier life. Perhaps because the sting of discrimination had not touched the majority of Natchez Jews, they avoided the side of the black struggle. While many surely felt conflicted over the treatment of southern blacks, though probably less so over what they believed to be a better treatment of Natchez blacks, they never in their collective political, social, or professional behavior showed favor for racial equality. Ultimately, Jews benefited from a system designed to separate black culture from white culture.[66]

*   *   *

On all levels, something approaching a true harmony existed between Jews and white non-Jews, unlike the artificial harmony, tainted with racial oppression, that existed between blacks and Gentile whites. Even as some blacks aspired toward whiteness, much in the way that some Jews ate bacon and grits and became Protestant-like, the upper caste rejected solicitations for membership by lower-caste people. By accepting Jews, Natchez whites unconsciously prevented a potential enemy from arising when the racial hierarchy was challenged in the 1960s. Before that time, black professionals managed to climb the class ladder to the top, where they could enjoy whatever money could buy. At the top, though, was the realization that money alone could not buy passage into that elusive world of full political and social equality. White southerners accepted Jewish culture, sans Jesus, but not black culture, Christian and southern to the core. Not even black professionals could transcend the stigma of inferiority attached to black culture.

This story of discrimination was well known by the majority of blacks, those without the money or the class privileges of the professionals. During much of the twentieth century, working-class blacks found themselves entangled in a cultural struggle with working-class whites as both groups attempted to improve their economic lot.

CHAPTER FOUR

"THEY WENT ALONG WITH THE SEGREGATION PART OF IT"

Industrialization

Directions to the home of the black retiree were uncomplicated. "The brick house down the road," said two black men, probably in their early thirties and unemployed, as they pointed ahead from underneath their shade tree (theirs, because they sat underneath the same tree two weeks later and waved).

With the exception of the community Baptist church, the retiree's house was the only brick structure along the rural Adams County road slicing through the thick, green landscape. All the others were cottages, shacks, many shading a scruffy dog lying in the dirt, or house trailers settling on cinder blocks, a junk car or two crowding the front yard.

Along this stretch, a sign by the edge of the road read, "Flower Shop"; this business was owned by the retiree's wife. Their paved driveway (another distinction) led to the two-car garage of an attractive ranch-style home with burglar bars on the windows. There were no neglected canines or cars occupying the yard. A career at Armstrong Tire and Rubber Company—and the flower business—had apparently been good to the couple.

The retiree agreed. He was a tall, angular man with long hands and feet. Sitting in his recliner, he was mere inches from an oversized color television console tuned to an afternoon soap opera. His wife was outside working in the greenhouse. "I have five children," he said, "and I give all five of them a college education. I think I done nice."

The white couple had been married for more than twenty years. All but one of their children went to college, and they were at peace with the knowledge that they had given their children opportunities they as children had not imagined. "It was a hard life," said the wife of her childhood, one not unlike her husband's— enmeshed in poverty.

In a house with nearly three thousand square feet of living space, flames snapped in the fireplace of the couple's large sunken den. Situated on three and a half acres in a quiet, wooded neighborhood outside of Natchez, the modern brick house had few windows. Most rooms instead had French doors leading outside to a porch or patio.

Both the husband and wife had retired from Armstrong, though not from work, and lived comfortably. The wife owned a used-car lot in town and operated a beauty consulting business on the side. When not overseeing operations at the car lot, the husband enjoyed growing and cultivating roses.

They were quick to thank Armstrong for their success. "They talk about the good ole days," said the wife. "I don't want to go back to the good ole days."

ARMSTRONG Tire and Rubber Company was like a fine, upstanding citizen in the Natchez community. No one who gathered that October day in 1949 to celebrate the plant's tenth anniversary would have said otherwise. It was a day of celebration for the Chamber of Commerce, business boosters, and working people. Corporate chiefs flew from Connecticut to thank the citizens of Natchez for a decade of profitable partnership. The mayor came, too, as the city's ambassador, to give a speech and to shake a few hands. Representatives from the Chamber of Commerce attended the ceremony as well, calling Natchez a fine city, a good place to live and to do business. It was clear from all the speeches, the handshaking, and the genial backslapping that day that Armstrong was the city's prized employer, an economic jewel in a place that could no longer put its economic faith solely in agriculture.[1]

Not everyone in Natchez was willing to accept Armstrong as the city's crowning symbol of progress. The garden club women, for instance, were not sure what to make of the tire plant and all the "common" folk it employed. Many members from the old-family elite had objected to Armstrong's construction ten years before. Some opposed industry all together. It did not fit, they said, with Natchez's Old South image. But there sat Armstrong smack within the city limits, not even on the outskirts, an ugly, sprawling, belching factory, three stories high and the length of two and a half football fields. Even worse, local tax dollars had helped put it there.[2]

Industry's boosters were eager to come to the defense of Armstrong. The city needed both the tire plant and tourism, they said, and there was no reason why the two could not coexist. Like the Pilgrimage, Armstrong brought outside dollars into the community. Its million-dollar annual payroll—the largest in the area of any single employer—circulated widely and deeply through the local and surrounding communities. Boosters talked about how Natchez had successfully brought together "the spirit of progress" and "the mellowness of history." Natchez was a shining example of Henry Grady's vision of the New South, said the *Natchez Democrat* editor. "In only this American city can the outsider[,] or the resident for that matter, find a skillful blending of the new and the old."[3]

No one at the tenth-anniversary celebration valued Armstrong more than did the employees. When Armstrong rolled the first tire off its production line in 1939, it employed a workforce of fewer than two hundred. Ten years later, nearly a thousand workers drew regular paychecks. They saw themselves as hardworking people who asked only for a simple chance to earn a fair wage and to make a decent living. They joined the union and occasionally walked the picket line, but they did so knowing that they would not want to work anyplace else. Armstrong was the font of economic opportunity to the working class of southwest Mississippi and eastern Louisiana. The plant meant the difference between sharecropping and working for a company with benefits, between poverty and comfort. No generation before or after had been, or would be, so attuned to the contrast between opportunity and privation. For many at the celebration, Armstrong was one of the best things that ever came along in their lives.

Black workers and white workers shared this belief, just as they shared the payroll and belonged to the same union. They went to the anniversary celebration together, too, though they tended to keep to themselves as they virtually always had. When the speeches were done and the ceremony was over, they went back to their shifts, whites to the better jobs and blacks to the lesser jobs. From management on down to the lowliest worker, a passive acceptance of racial division of labor prevailed. White workers took their privileges for granted. In later years, long after segregation had passed, some even said separate jobs for blacks and whites had never existed. They had though. Blacks thought about the segregation if whites did not. Yet blacks said nothing about it, not in the 1940s or the 1950s. Life and living had always been defined by race, and blacks expected nothing different from southern society. As long as any kind of mill or factory operated near Natchez, separate jobs and separate pay had been the standard.

Natchez was no Chicago of the South, but at any one time in the 1930s, the city of fewer than fourteen thousand had several hundred factory jobs for blacks and whites. Along with the usual sawmills and cotton mills, it had a cannery, meatpacking plant, coffee roasting and grinding company, brickyards, foundry, and match factory.

As elsewhere in the South, industry in Natchez was the crucible of the color line, shifting it, blurring it, but never obliterating it. Blacks and whites constantly negotiated the color line for possession of factory jobs and sometimes whole industries. One typically pursued employment where his or her neighbors, friends, or relatives worked. There was greater comfort among those with whom a group identity was shared and where social formalities and etiquette could be relaxed and new friendships could thrive.[4]

Timber mills, which migrated to the area in the early nineteenth century, provided the first local meeting ground for white and black workers. By the early twentieth century, timber had become a mainstay in the Natchez economy, making its most important contribution at the processing stage. A highly competitive business, timber required efficient use of local raw materials and the labor force, which meant employing the cheapest wageworkers. Timber companies in the rural, wooded counties east and west of Natchez kept a predominantly white workforce on the payroll. This was consistent with the South's largest industry, textiles.

The timber mills in Adams County were different. During the late nineteenth century, blacks had begun replacing white workers in the mills. By the 1930s, timber-related industry employed more blacks than did any other type of work except farming.[5]

Whites did not feel that mill work itself was unfitting. But the mill had been reduced to an inferior place and the work into "nigger work," if only because blacks dominated the mill workforce. Employment in a predominantly black establishment as a laboring equal was considered beneath white culture, much like living in an all-black neighborhood. Most whites preferred to keep their interaction with black culture to a minimum, and they withdrew into the familiarity of their own world. With few exceptions, when whites did work in mills they worked either in supervisory positions or where they maintained a significant group size. The white worker and the white boss both understood that in a biracial world one white man's dignity depended on the others' and that whites should never work under blacks. On this level, the racial division of labor corresponded to a personal division of associations that originated in the private and communal lives of the workers.[6]

Perhaps the most important party in the negotiating process between white worker and black worker was the employer. Mill owners preferred black to white for three principal reasons. Black workers were more plentiful in numbers, they were willing to work for less compensation, and Natchez employers regarded them as generally dependable and capable, despite prevailing white preconceptions about black indolence and capriciousness. During his discussion with one of the Davis researchers, the office manager of National Box Company conceded that skin color did not predetermine worker performance. "It's just an individual thing," he said. At the same time, he knew that blacks as a whole tolerated extreme working conditions that whites would have protested. Politically empowered and culturally linked to their bosses, whites were in a better position to disrupt the relationship between management and labor that kept the engine of a business in tune. The office manager said: "The thing about it here is that there aren't enough white laborers here to run our plant without Negroes, so if any of them [whites] object they can just get off the job, and we can get plenty of others [blacks]."[7]

Black workers in Natchez never seemed to be in short supply. Demographic and economic trends by the 1940s had begun working in the mill owner's favor. During the war, hundreds of Adams County blacks joined the Great Migration to northern and western cities seeking employment in the defense industry. Yet the tractor, the mechanical cotton picker, and herbicides were dismantling the share-tenant system family by family and assuring local employers a growing stock of male and female workers. From 1940 to 1950, the number of farms in Adams County dropped by nearly 35 percent, which translated into a decline of 41 percent in the number of black farm operators. Most of those blacks were tenants or sharecroppers, and by 1950 more than half had vacated the land. With many losing their property to whites who paid their delinquent taxes, blacks learned that land never evolved into the great social leveler that Thomas Jefferson and others had once nobly envisioned. Whites, especially wealthy planters, had seen to that. Yet the land had at least once given sustenance, even if on economic scales subsistence sometimes factored into poverty. But by the end of World War II, land no longer held that meager promise. Even while contracting with an honest landlord, a man or woman could hardly support a family on a workable piece of soil.[8]

To offset declining farm incomes, many blacks sought temporary work in the timber industry. They came and went with the seasons, working at the mills during the slack winter months and in the summer, when the crops required minimal attention. They followed the pattern of an unsteady worker—a pattern that could leave white employers with a false impression about black work ethics. In reality, these part-time mill workers were steady workers in their own right, toiling at two jobs to earn the income necessary to provide for their families. The black farmer/ mill worker adapted to the changing economy of the early and mid– twentieth century, when small-scale farming was growing less financially suitable and Natchez was converting to an industrial economy. Many who had farmed all their lives felt insecure about detaching themselves from the land altogether. Presented with few alternatives, they learned to balance a working life between the farm and the mill.[9]

Sargent Butler was one of many of his friends and neighbors who combined the incomes of farm and factory to make a living. Butler was a descendent of Adams County slaves. For five generations, from 1870 to 1971, members of the Butler clan tenant-farmed on Aventine Plantation for the same white family, the various descendants of Pierre Surget. Butler left Aventine in 1927 at age fifteen, taking his mother and younger sister with him, a boy thrust into the role of the man. They went to one plantation, stayed a year, and then to another where Butler worked shares for most of the thirty-three years he lived there.[10]

It was not enough. Between the increasing difficulty in cultivating a living from the land and his landlord's questionable accounting practices at the year-end settle ("Everybody was cheated, man"), Butler was forced to find ways to earn extra money: wage work on the plantation, grunt work on the levees, and ditch digging on public relief. Of all of them, the job he took at Natchez Hardwood Company in 1945 was the best. "I was there when they were building that mill," said Butler. "I went to work [there] for a while, and after that I went back to work on the farm. Then after a few more years, I went back [to the mill]. I stayed there till 19 and 68. The big boss died then, and the mill closed down, in 19 and 68, if I'm not mistaken. I didn't quit farming. I was farming and working down there, too. My spare time I'd go down there and go to work. When my crop was needed, I'd work my crop."[11]

Butler never earned more than minimum wage at the mill. The local labor market gave the advantage to the employer. If not for the permanent implementation of federal minimum-wage standards, unpopular in Mississippi, mill workers would not have been making even that. Before unions were organized locally, mill workers could expect no guarantees beyond minimum wage. There were no benefits such as medical insurance or vacation pay. "In '45 I was getting $.45 an hour," said Butler. "I worked there [at the mill] about twenty years straight. For twenty years straight. When I left there I was getting $1.30 an hour. That was in 19 and 68. I closed it, and built it."[12]

In Butler's day, company benefits were as rare as miserable working conditions were common. Amidst the deafening wail of the power saws, the work was dirty, laborious, and mind-numbingly repetitive. "It was harder than farming in a way, because you had to steady go at it," said Robert Carroll, who worked at Natchez Hardwood Company after being discharged from the Navy in 1946. "Farming, if you get too hot or something, you could go under a tree or something." A worker with a grievance about working conditions or benefits had no recourse besides quitting. For the employer, there was always another black ready to step in to take a vacated job.[13]

Blacks both lost and gained in the shift from plantation to factory. In some respects, employment practices at mills represented an extension and continuation of the principles of plantation management: whites assumed the role of plantation landlord and lumber-mill proprietor; black labor was preferred over white; blacks worked for the lowest wages and under poor conditions; and whites filled most (all upper) managerial positions. Despite resembling an old and familiar system, the mill offered an alternative to less dignifying and lower-paying work. Even minimum wage was as much as five times more than farm wages. Mill workers as a result enjoyed a higher economic status than their agricultural counterparts. At the mill, blacks were treated less like property and more like workers, and mill owners exercised less control over the private and family lives of their workers than landlords did over those of their tenants.[14]

The paternalistic arrangement common to the plantation existed in diminished form at the mill, while the standards of modern society increasingly defined management-worker relationships. A few blacks and whites did try to perpetuate old habits of the plantation, and some blacks did regard the "big boss" of the mill as their caretaker in times of need. But black mill workers turned with decreasing frequency to mill owners for cash advances, assistance with medical bills, or sponsorship when difficulties arose with the law or otherwise. They willingly relinquished one of the few benefits of the old plantation system, in part because they had become more financially independent. A paycheck, not debt, became the incentive to work. The reductions in paternalism, nonetheless, did not necessarily reduce the worker's relationship with the employer to an impersonal or abstract level. A basic understanding of mutual obligations still stood between the two. In return for hard work and dependability, workers expected fair treatment and a modicum of respect.[15]

Regardless of one's dependability, the steady availability of work at the mill was always an uncertainty. Much like their workers who lived from payday to payday, mills existed from sales order to sales order and generally operated on a shoestring budget. If orders were down, layoffs, and sometimes closings, were necessary to keep the business solvent. If mill owners felt the economic crunch during these times, the workers suffered it, too. For them, interruption in production meant no work and no pay. In the economic ebb and flow, the mill business amounted to a sort of adjustable partnership between owners and workers that favored the former. During hard times, the two groups shared the suffering together, though not equally. During boom times, profits trickled down from the pockets of owners to workers in the form of a minimum wage.[16]

Greed was not the mill owner's sole incentive. In the case of a mostly black workforce, economic considerations mingled with traditional racial beliefs to determine pay and work conditions. Any businessman interested in containing overhead costs, staying competitive, and making a profit was apt to seek cheap labor. At the same time, the white mind assumed high wages would be wasted on a group that seemed to have no more sense than to squander its money on liquor, gambling, prostitutes, and funerals. The integrated logic of race and economics figured into work conditions as well, and in a highly competitive and low-profit business, inferior work conditions were as certain as unsteady work. Improvements added to overhead costs and, to all appearances, made little sense when blacks were naturally accustomed to less in the fields or at home, where they presumably created their own squalor.[17]

Blacks had learned long before to work with and around these kinds of attitudes and to squeeze whatever benefits they could out of new opportunities, however limited. Even if the white mill boss thought blacks chose to live in a repulsive way, many gained for themselves a sense of dignity at the mill that working some else's land had denied them. Mainly, the black mill worker no longer answered to an imperious landlord or plantation manager. "At the mill down there, my work was my boss," Sargent Butler said. "As long as I kept up with my work, I didn't have no boss. My work was my boss (I was over there where the green lumber come down) as long as I kept that going, working on the slip, me and another boy. I did that about fifteen, twenty years. It was all the work we ever did. But it was pretty good because I worked and got my money."[18]

And he did. As a mill worker, Butler was liberated from the worry of being cheated at the year-end settle or out of his plantation day-work wage. Whatever the drawbacks to mill work—the brutal conditions, the repetitive nature of the labor—the assurance of a regular paycheck, when work was steady, at a guaranteed minimum wage outweighed them all. Although mill owners feared federal wage standards threatened their autonomy as private employers, workers welcomed those standards as protection for their labor.[19]

123

Though modest, the income from the mill afforded many workers a life and freedom they had never experienced, or imagined. "I was just getting some money then," Butler said. "Not a whole lot of money. But I could tend to my own business and everything." In 1963, Butler bought a new house in a quiet, tree-shaded residential area on the outskirts of town. Before then, he had never lived in a place with indoor plumbing or electricity. Partly by habit and partly by necessity, he continued to raise hogs and chickens and plant a vegetable garden. He supported his common-law wife, Beatrice, and raised her grandson, eventually sending him through four years of college before the young man became a schoolteacher.[20]

Predictably, black women valued the mills for the same reasons men did. In a continuous current that began in slavery, black southern women had always augmented family income by working outside the home. Circumstances were no different in Adams County. Proportionally, the number of black men to black women had been shrinking since slavery, and not enough men were available or willing to support all the women and their families. Even if a woman could find a man, that man could not always find steady work. She, by contrast, always had domestic service, work that tradition set aside almost exclusively for black women. Life granted them few choices. More black women assumed the tasks of a domestic than of any other occupation. Like farm work, domestic service did not come under the protective umbrella of social security and minimum-wage laws, and the women who worked in the white homes did so for exploitative wages. Even during the depression, white families on relief could still afford a maid coming in once a week. The hours were long, and the work anything but dignifying. To some black women, the mills were a godsend. "That is so true. That is so true," proclaimed Lillian Carter, who said she loved her job at River City Mill (fictitious name), where she worked twenty years.[21]

Born in 1928, Carter was conceived in circumstances familiar to so many southern blacks. Her parents were rural Adams County sharecroppers who raised nine children on a small place near Washington, in the lush hinterland east of Natchez. The Carters planted cotton, grew beans, greens, peas, corn, sugarcane, and raised hogs and chickens. Even with that, Carter's mother took in washing and ironing. As soon as Carter's brothers were tall enough, they went to work on plantations as day laborers. Childhood and work were one and the same. Through the summer and fall, young Lillian gathered crops, and every morning before school, she milked the cow. Tasks at home recurrently interrupted her eight school years, the most public education available to blacks in Washington. Still, she graduated, and afterward she took a job as a cook at a Washington café. The café's Jim Crow policies bothered her, but she could tolerate them more than she could tolerate cleaning for a white lady, and she needed the job. Carter had learned at an early age that bringing in extra money was essential to the family's welfare. "I would buy my younger sisters and brothers all their school things, then would give my mother something. I sure did."[22]

Carter worked at the café for a couple years before it went out of business. She then moved to Natchez and looked for a job, all the time hoping she could avoid cleaning houses for a living. The job market presented few other alternatives for black women, but Carter managed to find work at a succession of places, including Excelsior Laundry, Natchez Steam Laundry, and Wilson Box Company. At times, depending on the place and the employer, she worked alongside white women assigned to the same task. But employers characteristically categorized workers by race and sex and put black women at the bottom. When the Natchez Fabricating Institute opened in 1937, for instance, it advertised for "350 White Women" to apply for minimum-wage jobs. The shirt manufacturer did hire black women, but assigned them to the pressing department and reserved the skilled positions on the sewing line for white women.[23]

Following this string of jobs, Carter found an occupational home at River City Mill. Thomas Osgoode (pseudonym) started the company in 1946 in Washington, Mississippi, before moving it to a vacated mill in Natchez four years later. By that time, his two sons were overseeing the mill's daily operations, which entailed the reduction of logs to thin strips of veneer for crate manufacturers. River City Mill's customers were as close by as the National Box Company and as far away as Canada and California. Raw timber came mostly from Adams County and nearby Concordia Parish in Louisiana. The cotton allotment system that began during the depression encouraged local planters to clear extra tracts of land, sell off the timber at a low price, and collect a larger government subsidy. "And when the soybean got to be the thing [in the late 1960s

and 1970s]," said Frank Osgoode (pseudonym), son of Thomas Osgoode, "man, there was just thousands and thousands and thousands of
acres just cleaned up." At its peak, the Osgoode mill ran three shifts and
employed more than one hundred workers, all of them locals.[24]

Carter went to work at River City Mill in the early 1950s with her
sister Amelia. Nearly all their new coworkers were black. They were the
least expensive to hire and the most readily available. "We'd just call up
the employment agency when we needed somebody," said Osgoode,
"and they'd come within the hour." The mill workforce included no
white women and only a few white men. When local blacks first learned
that River City Mill was moving to town, the Carter sisters heard that
the senior Osgoode preferred to hire black women, regarding them as
more dependable than black men. "Women were good steady workers,"
said Frank Osgoode, "the best for handling veneer." At the same time,
Osgoode believed that the domestic arrangement of many women undermined the work ethics of men, rendering them inaccessible to the white
employer. "They would either have a kept man or something," said
Osgoode of many of the women who worked for him. "Those men won't
work because their women are supporting them. That's just the way it is
with them."[25]

The Carter sisters went to work for seventy-five cents an hour, minimum wage. Carter learned that most of the black laborers made the
same pay. Some of the men she knew who operated the veneer lathes, a
skilled position that also employed whites, earned slightly more than
minimum wage. The Osgoode brothers supervised operations during the
day; they put the night shift under the responsibility of a white supervisor as well as a black supervisor who oversaw only black workers. Carter
was assigned to the dry kiln. It was monotonous work, and the pay was
low, but it was better than farming or cleaning. "When I was on the back
of that kiln," said Carter, "I'd just pick them boards up and put it in the
dry kiln. When I was working on the front, take them off the dry kiln,
count them, on that table. I loved it." Twenty years later when the mill
closed, she was doing the same job and still making minimum wage.[26]

Carter anguished less over the pay than the working conditions at the
mill. "When I first started working out there," Carter said, "the place
was just so ragged. So much exposure." Although the mill had running
water for production, it never provided anything better than outdoor pit

toilets for the workers. For lack of a cafeteria, they warmed their lunches and dinners on the kiln and ate at their work stations. The winter months were the toughest. Nothing more than a metal roof over the open production area protected the workers from the elements. The dirt floor often turned to mud, and gas spot heaters gave minimal relief against the penetrating cold air. The workers would get "a barrel fire going" out in the lumber yard and warm their hands and feet before returning to the mud. "Just looking at that fire kept you warm," said Osgoode. Carter had a different memory. "It was something, I tell you, we just had to go through. By the grace of God, I tell you the truth, He brought us through it."[27]

Carter loved her work too much to speak out against the unsuitable conditions and low pay, and she appreciated not having to cook or clean for a living. The day that River City Mill closed down in the early 1970s Carter counted as one of the saddest in her life. "I was so sorry when that plant closed down," she said, "I didn't know what to do. In fact, all of us womens was sorry when it closed down because we loved that work. We loved that factory work. Yes. That's right. We sure did." The mill to Carter and others represented a rare kind of security for black women: security from financial privation and from domestic service. For more than twenty years, Carter had avoided the indignity of cleaning a white woman's home. But like most of the other women at River City Mill, she had no marketable skills outside of mill work, farming, and domestic service. When the mill shut down operations, she and many of her former coworkers swallowed their pride, as black people of her generation and generations before had learned to do in the interest of survival, and put on aprons. "I didn't want to do it," said Carter. "That's right, because there wasn't nothing else to do. I had more work to do—Yeah, it was more work to do"—with less pay.[28]

Mill owners failed to see their practices as exploitative. From their point of view, the mills were an acknowledged community asset that extended employment to hundreds of blacks and whites, raising their standard of living. Still, like many whites, mill owners felt that black labor was at their disposal. Southerners of both races had known life and work no other way than that in which blacks served the needs of whites. Blacks had always done the lifting, chopping, picking, cleaning, and cooking—tasks that were perfected through repetition more than through thought.

An employee's protracted relegation to a similar repetitive-type job at minimum wage was the consequence of such perceptions, and a black workforce's dedication to that job seemed—to whites—a fair testimony to the correctness of those perceptions. According to white understanding, blacks had not been endowed with the abilities or acquired the experience to deal with anything more complex. The black community in Natchez could hold up a surplus of exceptions. But to whites, the vertical relationship of white worker over black worker followed the natural order of the races and their respective and distinctive cultures. Not white oppression, but a lack of character and ambition, rooted in cultural values, determined the lowly status of blacks. Whites believed this, and they believed that blacks believed this.

Those attitudes prevailed when Armstrong Tire and Rubber Company introduced modern manufacturing to Natchez in 1939. When the Davises and Gardners took residence in Natchez in the 1930s, they noted the unfolding economic transition evident at the time, and they wondered about the potential of industry to usher in social change. They made the bold prediction that modern industry would impose pressures that would modify caste customs. But after the anthropologists left for the North to write their book about Natchez, and after Armstrong materialized into reality from a Chamber of Commerce dream, the prospects for racial change looked grim.[29]

Armstrong began operations in Mississippi as one of the first and finest examples of the state's controversial Balance Agriculture with Industry (BAWI) program. The brainchild of Governor Hugh White (1936–1940), BAWI was designed to combat the economic depression by expanding the state's industrial base and by offsetting the economic dependence on agriculture. BAWI was unprecedented in the South. Under the plan, the state and municipalities joined forces to attract new industry with public subsidies allocated for the construction of manufacturing facilities. It was a bold initiative for a state where cotton had always been sovereign and the taxpayers conservative. Not surprisingly, BAWI had its many vocal critics, primarily Delta planters who believed higher-wage industry would siphon their monopolized supply of cheap labor.[30]

It was easy, though, to sell the governor's economic panacea to Natchez business and city leaders, who professed a heritage of and commitment to progress. In 1937, the editor of the *Natchez Democrat* proclaimed in reference to BAWI: "Natchez must go forward" and not "dissolve into a village." When Armstrong's executives were scouting for a new plant location, they carried a promise from Sears, Roebuck to buy tires for ten years; they also projected employment numbers in the several hundreds. Natchez officials took notice. Their city was struggling with the Great Depression, as was the rest of the country. Natchez's oldest and largest bank liquidated its assets and folded in 1933; and more businesses were closing than opening, sending a perilous ripple through the working population. Rural landowners reduced cotton acreage; yet the number of sharecroppers peaked in the middle of the decade, indicating that workers laid off from jobs in town returned to the false security of the land. Adams County reported that 5,400 citizens were out of work and forced to apply for public relief in 1932. Throughout the decade, the unemployment rate in Adams County hovered around 9 percent, lower than the national average. In Natchez, where the destitute gathered, the rate was usually well above 10 percent.[31]

Unlike other Mississippians, Natchezians were not blindly attached to cotton, and city leaders were willing to reach beyond the South's agrarian tradition. Responding to the economic crisis, they actively looked at expanding the industrial payroll, and in the process, they launched an aggressive campaign to recruit new manufacturing plants. Natchezians had always believed their city was special, somewhat above the rest in many ways, including in economic outlook. From her office of the local Federal Writers Project, Edith Wyatt Moore observed that although Natchez to date had "made no great industrial strides she has all the potential wealth, water-power and climate necessary for a great development." The editor of the *Natchez Democrat* offered a long list of attributes that were conducive to industrial growth, from "favorable operating sites" to "good churches" to "splendid labor conditions."[32]

Voters showed they were equally enthusiastic about industrial development. By a wide margin (1,347 to 56), they approved a $300,000 bond issue to construct a manufacturing facility for Armstrong, the largest bond floated for a BAWI plant. Under the agreement, Armstrong paid no rent for the first five years and after that paid a $3,600 yearly rent on a fifty-year lease. Armstrong was also granted total exemption from local taxes, and city officials offered to work with the company to obtain exemption from state taxes as well. Before finalizing the deal, the city agreed to provide pavement and grading to the plant site at an expected cost of between $35,000 and $50,000.[33]

To attract the tire manufacturer to the area, local officials had to offer more than a generous package of benefits. One of the South's greatest appeals to Armstrong was the prospect of plentiful, inexpensive, and unorganized labor. City officials had to demonstrate that Natchez and its environs could deliver such a workforce, and to win bond approval from the state industrial commission, labor could not come out of the cotton fields. At the time, the existing industries—the box companies, the mills, and the garment factory—employed a disproportionately large number of white women and blacks of both sexes. This was common in a region where low wages forced women to work to help the family and where white men refused to work for wages regarded as suitable only for women and blacks. To offset that imbalance, the local industrial recruitment efforts targeted industry that would employ mostly white men. Natchez officials assured Armstrong executives that Adams County and the surrounding area contained one thousand eager, able-bodied male workers outside of farm hands. The attorney for the city, S. B. Laub (the mayor of late), relayed the same information to the industrial commission with the additional promises that Armstrong's workforce will "be 95% men and will be better than 95% white labor, using only a few colored hands for certain porter work and possibly for mixing of carbon black."[34]

BAWI recruitment strategies in other Mississippi communities put the needs of white males ahead of those of white women and blacks. These efforts complied with New Deal policies to reemploy family "breadwinners" (fathers and husbands) before all others and to restore the male workforce. Half the male breadwinners in Mississippi were black, but restoration of the labor force meant also keeping black labor in its "proper" place. According to a study published in 1967, officials throughout the state historically sought industries that would employ whites and exclude blacks. The authors of the study acknowledged the lack of evidence proving that BAWI was used intentionally to deprive blacks of jobs or to restrict their movement off the land (or later, after farm mechanization, to induce their migration out of the state). "On the other hand," the researchers wrote, "it is equally difficult to find an instance where a benefit accruing to the Negro worker is anything but incidental to the plant placement."[35]

Despite its elevated stature in the community and its external corporate ownership, Armstrong's employment policies followed the routines of biracial society. When the plant opened, company officials kept their original promise to hire a mostly white male workforce and to leave the menial positions for blacks. White men indeed quickly snagged a foothold at Armstrong. The permanent implementation of the federal minimum wage, signed into law the year before, removed the economic incentive to hire blacks or women. Unlike the local timber industry with its established black workforce, tire manufacturing came to the area with a history of employing mostly whites. During its first year of operation, Armstrong supported a total workforce of two to five hundred, but hired no more than twenty-five black men. A few white women worked in the inner-tube department, as inspectors and packers, and in administration; a single black woman was hired to clean the offices and restrooms. White men earned from forty to seventy-two cents an hour as production workers. Blacks earned thirty cents an hour, minimum wage, as janitors, equipment clean-up men, and carbon-black mixers—black jobs for black pay.[36]

The war economy that soon followed Armstrong's opening forced minor shifts, though not a full collapse, in the racial underpinnings of the workplace. The plant stepped up production to meet new orders for military tires and expanded into munitions production for the army. The payroll added more women and blacks to offset the armed forces' drain on local labor. Still, jobs remained quietly and unofficially categorized as either black or white. Ruth Tiffee Jordan, who worked most of her twenty-five years at Armstrong in the personnel office, said that black workers were excluded from better-paying jobs as tire builders, bias cutters, mill operators, and cure men. "They were janitors. They had them in shipping. They had to move the tires out to the dock. They worked in the receiving department."[37]

With some ambivalence, blacks accepted the new employment opportunities in an old Jim Crow environment. They reluctantly continued in the late 1940s and 1950s to observe the imposed racial boundaries at Armstrong and the other modern manufacturing plants. A black worker could go from Armstrong to either of the other two major industrial employers, Johns-Manville or International Paper Company, both post–World War II companies (and BAWI subsidized), and encounter identical racial indignities. "They did misuse you in several short little ways," said Albert Harris, who went to work at International Paper Company in 1950. "If you black, you just as black as a paper mill [sic]."[38]

Robert Latham, who devoted a career to the tire plant, remembered it that same way. "I was at Armstrong from 19 and 44, the second day of January, to the thirtieth of August in '85. That's when I retired," he said. "I put up the best portion of my life at Armstrong." Like many of his coworkers, Latham hailed from local farming stock. His father owned four mules, a wagon, and a 136-acre spread of land, from which Latham never moved after his birth. As with every other farmer in Adams County, cotton was his father's main cash crop. He also raised cattle, hogs, and chickens: "Name it; he had it." As a youngster, Latham attended school at Milford Baptist Church, a few hundred yards down the road from where he lived. He finished all eight grades offered, though each school year was interrupted by responsibilities on the family farm. In 1942, he entered military service and fought for his country. Within three weeks of returning from soldiering, he went to work for Armstrong. Latham had not wanted it any other way. "Some people worked the sawmill jobs," he said, "but I never wanted a sawmill job. I wanted a job with a company."[39]

Although blacks were limited to certain jobs at Armstrong, the tire plant was a powerful draw with its incomparable opportunities in steady employment, decent pay, and company benefits. Throughout the years, blacks like Latham came off the farms—their own or someone else's—from Adams County and, across the river, out of the Louisiana Delta. They came from sawmills, lumber camps, quarterboats, and levees from town, where they had been porters, draymen, doormen, gas-station attendants, and even preachers. When in other parts of Mississippi mechanized cotton farming turned once bustling agricultural communities into decaying hamlets of the unemployed, the timing of Armstrong's opening seemed almost providential. "Yes, indeed," said Gerard Stanton, who set aside his plow to work at the tire plant. "Armstrong was a life saver. It helped many [a] man, white and black."[40]

Latham agreed. "I was raised up poor, wasn't never used to no whole lot," he said of his days before Armstrong. "You see back when I was raised up here on the farm, my daddy used to make eighteen or twenty bales of cotton, and as high as cotton was then was 5 to 6 cents a pound. One week's work at Armstrong, when they was paying 47½ cents an hour, would bring as much as a bale of cotton. I was hired in for 47½ cents an hour. I have made a many hundred and something hours out at the plant by working over during the week, working on Saturdays and Sundays, seven days."[41]

The pay was favorable to farming, but the work was still laborious and lowly compared to the white jobs. "My first job was cleaning the [tire] molds," Latham said. "They had some jobs then that a black man couldn't work, such as a tire builder, such as laying tires." Tire builder was among the most coveted of the production-line jobs. But it was a white job. Officially, Armstrong and the union maintained that blacks possessed neither the education nor the experience needed for the better-paying positions. Those jobs required the skills to read a ruler, specifications, and formulas. "They just didn't qualify," said a former union official in reference to the black workers.[42]

But Latham and the other blacks knew better. Latham himself had as much education and industrial experience as many of the tire builders. Blacks regularly substituted in the skilled positions that whites were assigned to permanently. "You couldn't get them jobs like tire builder," said Samuel Stewart, a longtime Armstrong employee who in various stages of his life had been a sharecropper, a pecan sheller, and a pulp-wood hauler. "Now black people knew how to do it. They released the white man. But they didn't hold the job eight hours. They'd work there twenty minutes or thirty minutes. And then when the man come back, they go back on their regular job picking up scrap, or cleaning up, or whatever. But yeh, them fellows could do it just as well as [whites] could."[43]

The majority of people, black and white, who went to work at Armstrong were unprepared for modern factory work. The average industrial worker in Natchez developed the skills for his or her job within the plant itself. Since mostly blacks worked in the local timber mills, blacks arguably had more experience at factory work than did whites.

The closest tire manufacturer was in north Alabama; outside of Armstrong, no comparable industrial plant existed in southwest Mississippi or northeast Louisiana before the late 1940s.[44]

Armstrong's employment practices may have in part reflected "profit motives," as some historians have interpreted policies in other southern plants. But at Armstrong, racial prejudice in turn affected those motives. Uninterrupted production and market competitiveness depended on good worker relations, which meant, as always, blacks sacrificing advancement while quietly submitting to white authority and privilege. The modern employer in turn deferred to tradition. Assigning a black to a traditionally white job would have challenged the racial norm and jeopardized a "harmonious" work environment. Based upon the historical experience of blacks and whites working together, employers knew that white workers would not placidly accept blacks as equal coworkers. One employer told the Davis research team that when blacks and whites worked together in equal capacity, whites instinctively assumed the role of supervisor. Albert Harris remembered an incident at International Paper Company in the 1950s in which a young white worker began barking orders to a veteran black employee, who neither knew nor worked in the same department as the white worker. When the black man complained to his supervisor, he was told (in Harris's words): "Every white out here's your boss. You do what he tell you to do if you want to stay here." In an equally abrupt response, the black man said, "Ya'll got my address. Mail my check. I won't be back."[45]

Each day that Latham and his black coworkers went back to Armstrong, they encountered within the factory walls the usual physical reminders of larger society's racial divide. Financed with local taxpayer money, the modern production plant had been designed and built to accommodate local segregation standards. "Yes, indeed, they had separate bathrooms," said Latham. "They had separate water fountains. They had all of that." It was the same way at the two other big industrial employers in town, International Paper Company and Johns-Manville, which hosted segregated Christmas parties every year. At the end of the work shift at the three plants, blacks and whites showered in separate restrooms. There were also separate cafeterias, a full-service facility for whites and something less for blacks. Armstrong had a cramped room with tables and chairs located next to the carbon-black spray booth.

"You'd go in there and everything in there was black," said Samuel Stewart. "That was where we ate at, in that little area." The full-service cafeteria, the white cafeteria, was located at the other end of the plant in a different, cleaner building. At mealtime every day, food-service workers wheeled a cart of food across the plant to black workers waiting in the darkened room. Stewart wanted no part of it. "I would bring my own and eat out there on the dock where they load the train."[46]

Sitting out on that loading dock day after day, Stewart knew that for generations segregation had been an unspoken assumption among both races. He had acquiesced to it all his life, just as his father and grandfather had. And they had done so exercising good manners, asking the white man when and where they could tread; and whenever they asked, they unintentionally sent the white man the message that his system was fair. Stewart's contemporary, James Anderson, followed the ritual when he worked on the construction crew that built a new plant for Mississippi Power and Light. After construction was completed, Anderson wanted to go to work for the power company itself. But before he could apply, he knew he would have to ask the question that whites never had to ask. He queried a supervisor, "When they complete this job, do they have black folks working here?"[47]

In Anderson's mind, he was showing less obeisance to the white supervisor than to tradition. He, Latham, Stewart, and the other blacks felt the real and forceful presence of history; its boundaries confined them. At the same time, comprehending history's role in shaping society helped them face its consequences. "That's just the way they [whites] was raised up," said Samuel Stewart. "That's always the way it was. We all know it." James C. Anderson, another local black who went to work at Johns-Manville when it opened in 1948, made a similar observation: "That was just the way of life, as far as black and white jobs. I feel that when something is in you, when you've been taught something, people believe in what they are being taught. I felt that people thought that they were right. I always said people grew up in that, and they feel they right. You just got to convince people that they are wrong."[48]

Convincing the whites who worked at those factories was difficult, especially when they believed that they knew the depths of poverty as well as anyone. "We grew up just like the blacks did," said Anna Nethers (pseudonym). "They can't tell me they were poorer than I was." If not most, many of the whites who took jobs at the tire plant in the early years indeed came from backgrounds that matched the economic privation of their fellow black workers. Whites too had been waiting for an employer such as Armstrong to extend an economic ladder upon which they could climb out of their misery.[49]

"The first industry worth anything was Armstrong," said Mary Jane Beltzhoover, who moved from McComb, Mississippi, seventy miles from Natchez, to take a job at the tire plant in the 1940s. Armstrong lured whites out of the Homochitto National Forest, from company logging towns such as Bude, Meadville, and Roxie. They came from Lincoln County to the east, Wilkinson to the south, and from parishes in Louisiana; from an unpromising life of farming—on shares or on their own piece of scrappy land—barely making it on what their cotton and produce got at the market. "It was just like a magnet," Malcolm Graves said of Armstrong. Born in Roxie, where his father supported a family on a public-works salary, Graves said, "I wanted a better job. That's the whole thing." So when Armstrong opened its doors, whites like Graves and Beltzhoover and Nethers went to Natchez for a chance to better their lives and that of their families.[50]

The opening of Armstrong and the influx of the working-class population in Natchez troubled many other native whites. "Those people were reluctant," said Robert Fly, a former local labor union president, in reference to old family and middle-class opponents of industry. "You could feel it sometimes. You could tell it. They thought working people were a necessary evil." It was to the disadvantage of the working poor that Natchez entered into its new stage of industrialization about the time the garden club was launching the Pilgrimage. Just as the romance with the Old South reinforced racial stereotypes, it sharpened class differences, particularly when one chose a friend or a mate.[51]

Coming from the hinterland, Malcolm Graves and others were regarded much like the hordes of Eastern European immigrants who boated to America in the late nineteenth century. They were desired for their labor and repulsed for their religion, language, and habits. The local vernacular provided stigmatizing labels for the country-to-city white migrant. They were "common" folk, "hicks," and "rednecks," whose hayseed ways and improper grammar threatened to change the genteel image of Natchez. They practiced the Baptist faith, which was branded a backwoods religion that discouraged progress of any sort by damning to hell virtually every earthly act, from dancing to drinking, except the act of loving Jesus Christ. Nearly everyone believed that it was the Baptists who were responsible for Mississippi being the next-to-last state to lift prohibition, which lasted until 1966. Even so, according to the stereotype, many among the Baptists' self-righteous sort were hypocritically given to hard drinking and gratuitous violence. They minimized the importance of education, lacked discipline in their industry, showed no interest in civic responsibilities, and chose not to sacrifice for their children's future.[52]

Seen through the lens of white middle-class vision, these were largely inescapable images that shaped class prejudices. Davis and the Gardners noted during this time that within the class hierarchy "the lowest group symbolizes all the negative values, all the wrong sins, of the society." The plight of the white poor was considered the fault of individual shortcomings. The poor had failed to live up to the expectations of their racial group by their dereliction of commitment to the white cultural ethos. The white poor were not, in other words, honest representatives of the white culture, as were their upper- and middle-class counterparts. They were instead cultural infidels, "white trash," often disliked more than blacks, whose culture more than the individual self was regarded as the source of black social ills.[53]

The prejudice was sometimes difficult to endure. But even as blue-collar whites encountered the disdain of other whites and even as they sometimes felt underpaid for their labor, they worked within the system and successfully sought opportunity and aimed for a better life. Perhaps only subconsciously at times, they always knew that they had something more than any black. Their whiteness provided a sense of belonging to the dominant group, and the racial structure provided a sense of status and privilege. They had, or they believed they were guaranteed, equality of opportunity. Since the founding of the country, it was the recognized democratic right of every white male American to go as far and as high as he aspired, and with him, he would take "his woman."

Among the first generation of white Armstrong workers who had such a determination were Thomas and Anna Nethers. Both children of the depression, they shared similar memories of their respectively destitute childhoods. "We were poor, but we didn't know it because everybody else was poor," explained Anna. "And you just didn't think about it." During the nadir of the depression, the Federal Land Bank in New Orleans repossessed the farmland of their fathers. "Daddy lost his farm, mules, cows, everything," said Thomas. Anna's father lost his property in Hazelhurst in 1937 with similar results. The family then left Mississippi altogether and repaired to the Louisiana Delta. The former landowner turned to working shares on someone else's property, as Thomas's father had done. Eventually securing a federal Farm Security Administration loan, which made low-interest loans available to farmers, Anna's father acquired forty acres of uncleared land in Tallulah, Louisiana. Using mostly scrap lumber, he built a house with a low, sloping metal roof, three rooms—beds in every room—and a kitchen. It had no indoor plumbing, only a pitcher pump on the back porch. "Back then we didn't have electricity, either," said Anna. "We thought we was in really big times when we finally did." The nine children helped their father clear the land for cultivation. With axes and crosscut saws they felled trees, then burned the stumps. They managed to plant a crop of cotton and corn that first year.[54]

As with black rural dwellers, life for the white poor smacked of a spartan existence, with imperatives of self-sufficiency, industry, and frugality. Davis and the Gardners blamed a dysfunctional value system of an improvident and lazy people for the economic instability of lower-class whites. But the conclusions of the scholars contradicted the attitudes of the whites who would eventually seek work in Natchez industry. At precisely the same time that the anthropologists were formulating their conclusions, the families of Anna and Thomas were looking for ways to keep food on the table. For them, laziness was the friend of starvation. They raised, grew, shot, or caught most of what they ate—deer, squirrels, raccoons, and fish—and made much of what they used and wore. Survival depended on the integrity of the family and on each member sharing the heavy burdens of work. Thomas's father sought relief work only when the family needed temporary assistance. Anna's father managed to avoid government aid: "My daddy was, shall I say, too proud to ask."[55]

Growing up poor offered little time for play and relaxation. Hard work generally consumed life's pleasures, and youthful energy drained away into daily chores and tasks. "You didn't have any leisure," said Thomas. As a child and later as a young man, he rose before the sun every day and labored until dark. In addition to tending to the family's farm, he also worked on someone else's to bring extra money into the household. "The only time you got a rest was when it was pouring down rain," said Anna, "and then you were doing something in the house. You were having to iron, do something inside. Can or shell corn." She described the daily routine on dry days: "I picked cotton, gathered corn, did it all. We worked. Got up at four o'clock in the morning, milked cows, slopped pigs, and cooked on a woodstove and all that. Then you walked three miles to catch a school bus. Only it wasn't a bus. It was a truck."[56]

Like the children of black sharecroppers, white farm children were slaves to the seasons, with the result that formal education often eluded them. True, white schoolhouses were nicer than black ones and better equipped; whites had smaller class sizes; the teachers were better trained and better paid; and the white students' books were newer, not hand-me-downs from someone else's school. But these advantages were often extraneous in the overwhelmed lives of white farm children, who had to answer to the needs of their families before answering the school bell. Although the school year started in September, October brought the start of harvest season. "We always had to pick cotton before we'd [start] school," Anna said. "We went and got registered for school and got our books and all. But we had to stay out until we got through. On rainy days you got to go to school. Otherwise, you didn't. It was hard, too, to catch up or know what was going on. You had to be determined."[57]

As youths, Anna and Thomas did not complain about the austerity in their lives. They instead latched on to the attributes of their environment and transformed shortcomings into virtues, much like their black counterparts. By necessity, poverty taught them the value of hard work and family. The latter was the nucleus of individual strength. The family furnished necessary coping mechanisms and the experiential and didactic structure for learned values. "We had loving parents," said Anna. "And we all knew we had to help. And they didn't have to ask us to do it. You got up and did it. You knew you had that to do, and you did it to survive." Thomas agreed: "You didn't know anything else."[58]

Later as adults, the Netherses turned the lessons of their youth into resources of self-motivation. "I was determined to finish school and better myself," she said, "and that I did." After graduating from high school, she went to live with an aunt in Natchez, and in 1944 she signed on for a job in the munitions department at Armstrong. When the war ended, she transferred to the tube department. Thomas quit school in the ninth grade, and after trying his hand at a number of jobs, he moved to Natchez in 1949 and took a job driving a bread truck. One morning, a customer on his route made a phone call to the personnel manager at Armstrong, and Thomas went to work that afternoon.[59]

"It was a wonderful place," Anna said of Armstrong. "I couldn't wait to go to work every day. I loved it. I loved it. We had some good times. Everybody worked together, cooperated, were proud to have a job. It was great." The Netherses and their workmates were radiant with appreciation for Armstrong's presence. It had raised many southwest Mississippi whites to the level of their true ambition and gave them a solid foundation for membership in the blue-collar middle class. Since the first cotton-picking days in their youth, the white poor had been instilled with the idea that hard work would one day bring their passage out of poverty. All they needed was an opportunity that was equal to their abilities. Industry gave it to them, filling not simply an economic void but also a cultural one. It provided the vehicle that set their work ethic into motion and helped them fulfill their life expectations. "I knew I could handle anything," said Anna.[60]

Black workers came to Armstrong with the same solid values, but whites put theirs to work in the better jobs. It followed without question that in addition to hard work and self-motivation, their whiteness would give them the edge over their black coworkers. History and tradition had taught whites that they could expect the best jobs, while blacks would be given the pickings of the leftovers. Blacks had always been accepted in certain skilled jobs, such as carpentry and masonry, because these had once been slave occupations. But industry ushered in a new kind of skilled employment and a fresh opportunity for the white poor, while tradition as a guideline for social behavior and habit dictated the appointment of jobs. The generation of workers of the mid–twentieth century had known the racial order as their grandparents had known it, and no more than their grandparents could they fathom a racially open society. "It was a southern tradition," Russell Parsons said in reference to the racial division of labor. "They didn't know any difference," said Ruth Tiffee Jordan. "People live with something they're accustomed to better than with something new." Ultimately, when accepting and insisting on the better jobs, whites were moved by a competitive spirit, by historical and personal experience, and perhaps most importantly, by a sense of cultural separateness from blacks.[61]

Even without the provisions of tradition assuring their work status, whites regarded themselves by cultural qualification the logical recipients of the better jobs. Poor, they felt deserving of any new opportunities for economic uplift. White, they considered themselves the primary possessors of the moral and attitudinal prequalifications of social advancement, lacking only the necessary economic opportunities to pursue a better life. Purportedly embodied within their culture were traits conducive to success, traits whites did not regard as universally evident in black culture. By upbringing, whites were supposedly better equipped to overcome the obstacles of poverty and the best qualified to make the most of economic opportunities. From their perspective, they made better citizens in terms of morality and social behavior. They believed that their uplift from the ranks of the poor would in turn best benefit the community.[62]

Whites did not deny that the assembly of good workers at Armstrong included many blacks. Workers and supervisors alike acknowledged that among the indolent and incompetent were whites as well as blacks; among the intelligent and capable were members of both races; and blacks were as dependable and hardworking as whites. But exceptions did not transform attitudes. Lodged in the consciousness of even the most enlightened whites were convictions about cultural differences. In truth, whites and blacks punched the time clock at Armstrong with the same attitudes about work and the same ambitions for personal advancement. But as blacks well knew, the racial etiquette of southern society imposed unequal limits on the aspirations of the two races. For a relaxation of those limits, blacks had nowhere to turn, not to local authorities, not to company management, not even to the unions.[63]

"The law was just the law in the South," said Gerard Stanton. He was reflecting on the caste-bound rules that affected most of his four decades at Armstrong and with Local 303 of the United Rubber, Cork, Linoleum, and Plastic Workers of America. The union "would help you if they could. But they couldn't go over the law." The unions at International Paper and Johns-Manville operated under similar legal and social premises. "They went along with the segregation part of it," said James C. Anderson in reference to Local 440, Woodworkers of America, at Johns-Manville. "But if you was misused on the job that you was on, they'd speak up for you like that. They'd see that you wasn't misused on the job that you was on."[64]

Since the 1930s, modern industry had brought to Natchez new jobs, capital expansion, a revived economy—and ultimately labor unions. As former Natchez mayor Troy B. Watkins put it: "If you wanted industry, you were going to take the unions. There was no way around it." To some local observers, the word labor, which once meant "working your hardest at any job," took on a new connotation that included portentous words such as "negotiations," "demands," and "unions." In the middle decades of the twentieth century, one of the South's most seductive drawing cards for new industry was the absence of organized labor and widespread antiunion sentiment. Mississippi was one of the most antiunion states in the country, in a region where less than 11 percent of the nonagricultural workforce was organized. Vitriolic charges of union alliances with communists and integrationists frustrated many early attempts to organize labor. In 1954, state lawmakers passed a right-to-work law (three months before the *Brown* decision) in a resolute show of opposition to union activity. Claude Ramsey, one of the most effective labor leaders in Mississippi, personified ideals that were antithetical to the sensibilities of reactionary southerners. "I was an integrationist and I was a labor leader," he said upon reflecting on his labor activities in the 1950s and 1960s, "and if there is anything that the rabid element in Mississippi hated any worse, I don't know what it is."[65]

Local hostility to organized labor in Natchez remained suppressed beneath a quiet intolerance, with one exception, which was related to race. In 1939, L. H. "Lib" Jones, district representative of the International Hod Carriers, Building, and Common Laborers Union, tried organizing unskilled labor in Natchez. Operating out of Jackson as the state president of the American Federation of Labor, Jones provoked the contempt of Natchez officials once it became evident that his recruiting efforts included the black workforce at the local mills. The *Natchez Democrat* declared in an editorial headline, "Natchez Is No Place For Agitators To

Disturb Racial Relations." Behind the newspaper's rhetoric, disturbance meant fomenting discontent in the suppliant and peaceful black community. Craft unions of skilled workers were welcome in Natchez but not "such communistic organizations as Jones proposes." Nor would "Natchez permit her negro citizens to be exploited by agitators and organizers." Local officials met with Jones and demanded that he stop his activities. Mayor W. J. Byrne, along with the chief of police, the county sheriff, and the Chamber of Commerce president, fired off a letter to AFL headquarters in Atlanta requesting that Jones be reined in. Working-class members of both races were "absolutely satisfied and happy with present conditions," the letter writers claimed, and Jones's organizing efforts had "drawn the united protests of white and colored citizens." Seeing the matter differently, Jones defended his organization's own anticommunist position and maintained that his pronouncements had not stirred animosity, but won favor "from practically all types of workers in Natchez."[66]

By the late 1940s, workers of nearly every industrial employer in Natchez had organized, validating Jones's claims about widespread interest in union membership. New Deal labor legislation and the return of prosperity helped secure a relatively clear path for union efforts in the South, where membership was highest among steel and rubber workers, affiliates of the Congress of Industrial Organizations. Joining the initiative of Clyde Mullins, a former schoolteacher from Franklin County and a laboratory worker at Armstrong, workers organized Local 303 of the United Rubber, Cork, Linoleum, and Plastic Workers of America (CIO) in late 1945. The employees voted the union in for the immediate purpose of raising pay scales to the level of those at the Armstrong plants in New Haven, Connecticut, and Des Moines, Iowa, and to abolish nepotism by establishing a seniority system.[67]

"You know the union should have never been born if people would've done right," said Robert Fly, who began working at Armstrong in 1940 and went on to preside over Local 303 for more than a decade. Fly said that when he and other Armstrong workers served in the military during the war, they were awakened to the benefits of collective bargaining. They were unaware that industry in the South consistently paid the lowest wages in the country. "Then we found out what everyone else was making," Fly continued. "We was working for nothing, and that's the reason they [Armstrong] is down here. We made up our minds that we were going to make the same thing they were making in Jackson, Michigan; Akron, Ohio; New Haven, Connecticut. So we made some real Donnybrooks."[68]

Accustomed to dealing with unions, Armstrong corporate management resisted the new local. In an attempt to frustrate union efforts, the police raided secretly held organizing meetings (which were integrated). Mullins was labeled an agitator, and some among Armstrong management questioned the legitimacy of the union. "A bunch of pea pickers," was reportedly the personnel manager's opinion of labor organizers. Even a few workers were initially skeptical about rules and policy being "dictated" from yet another higher and external body of authority. In the end, all but one worker joined, and most foresaw the benefits of union representation.[69]

As standard policy, the CIO prohibited segregated unions and locals in its federation. But the federation recognized that southern whites would not accept class unity at the expense of racial custom, and it refrained from insisting that southern locals "follow national policy to the letter." Local 303 had three blacks sitting on its twelve-member executive committee, and its meetings were integrated. Yet the union and the workplace were separate venues. The whites who sat in the union hall with blacks, though on separate sides of the room, would not eat in the same plant cafeteria with blacks or use the same restrooms or showers as them. As union members, blacks and whites walked picket lines together and harassed scabs and turncoats. The seniority system that the union had won through collective bargaining applied to all workers. But blacks knew better than to bid for traditionally white jobs or bump a junior white employee from a better position. The union assured blacks equal pay for equal work, but would not open skilled positions to blacks on a permanent basis. After hours, white union members occasionally hunted turkey and deer and squirrel with black union members. Still, only whites could play on the softball team Armstrong sponsored in a city league. Until 1967, the discrimination clause in labor contracts between Armstrong and Local 303 referred to mistreatment of union workers but made no mention of discrimination by race (or gender).[70]

Robert Latham put it best when he said that the unions were segregated "to a certain extent." The final implementation of international decrees was the responsibility of local leaders, leaders elected by the local's predominantly white membership. Union halls served as a convenient bureaucratic filter for removing or reshaping objectionable policies coming out of northern headquarters, and until the mid-1960s, locals generally exercised unchallenged authority on matters of race. Benefits accrued to blacks from collective bargaining were incidental to the gains of the entire workforce. Despite the discrimination, southern blacks were among the most loyal and disciplined members, and the unions therefore benefited from biracial locals. "Some of the best union members we had were black people," said Robert Fly, "They never had anything. This was a chance for them to advance and acquire things that they had never had before."[71]

Beyond higher financial prospects, unions raised new expectations in the minds of black workers. They learned from union activity, for example, that the system would tolerate more than resigned acquiescence (a lesson that was an influential precursor to the local civil rights struggle). During the late 1940s, black employees from at least three mills staged walkouts. At the Natchez Stave Company, fifty-five black women of Local 440, which had organized a year before, walked off the job in early summer 1947 seeking higher wages.[72] Across town, Natchez Hardwood Company's black workforce (which included Sargent Butler) stopped the production line for one day to win union recognition and a nickel pay raise. The owner of Natchez Hardwood had mills spread across southern Mississippi, and his conspicuous wealth annoyed the minimum-wage labor force. "He had nothing but money," as James Anderson, who divided his labor between the farm and the mill, saw it. "That's what we was wondering about, how come he didn't pay us no more." The practice of local blacks withholding their labor to air their demands had roots in Reconstruction, when freedmen engineered a shift away from contract labor to sharecropping. As in the late 1860s, the black challenge to white authority in the 1940s was bold, but necessarily cautious. "We didn't press too hard because at that time they could get labor anywhere," said James Anderson of the first and only walkout staged at Natchez Hardwood.[73]

The success of black-initiated strikes is irrelevant to the underlying meaning of the strikes. In walking out against white objections, blacks demonstrated that they, like whites, wanted more return for their labor than the bare necessities of living. Unable to cultivate a reasonable livelihood out of the land and no longer satisfied with simple existence, they turned away from the farm to the opportunities of the mills and factories. On the farms, they had worked in virtual racial solitude, isolated from direct encounters with white labor. In the factories, hardworking blacks watched while white coworkers were promoted to better jobs.

With its capital investments and gainful payroll, industry of external origins raised the standard of living for hundreds of working people. At the same time, northern-owned factories expanded the institutionalization of southern customs by upholding a racial division of labor that limited competition. Racial attitudes that made sharp distinctions between the two cultures remained strong even as the forces of modernization tugged at the traditional economic underpinnings of white supremacy (i.e., the plantation system). When an evolving class consciousness should have been pushing the races together, the political economy, as well as the perception of cultural difference, pulled them apart. In their close encounters with blacks in the workplace, white workers retained their sense of cultural and social superiority, which in turn informed their expectations of hiring and job preference.[74]

Blacks who worked at Armstrong in the early years tolerated segregation for so long in part because they had adjusted to its impediments. Primarily, they wanted a chance to work. They never knew life without discrimination and knew to expect disappointment. "It was something that we had never been used to doing," said Latham of the local black experience working in the factory. "And I don't reckon you ever thought you would have done it. So you never did fight for it." When reflecting on their lives before the coming of the factories, Armstrong's first generation of black workers saw little benefit in defying the racial division of labor and jeopardizing their relationship with the best employer they had ever known. After rising above suffering of one sort, it seemed illogical to bring upon themselves suffering of another. Unfortunately for them, their apparent contentment gave another nod of assent to white supremacy. In and of itself, though, black toleration of discrimination in the modern workplace was a testimony to the desire to work and the commitment to family.[75]

That very work ethic would eventually buck the system. "I thought about it like this," said Robert Carroll, who had made the transition from farm to factory in the late 1940s. "If I can do the job a white can do, I should get the pay." James C. Anderson, a former sharecropper who spent a career at Johns-Manville, was equally sensitive to the indignities at the factory, in spite of the economic advantages over farming. "The jobs that [blacks] had were such hard work. You just kind of wished you had one of those good jobs, and those jobs paid more money. Where I was working at, that was suppose to have been on one of the high-paid black jobs, and that was just a dime more than a sweeper—I mean the guys that were picking up the trash!"[76]

"Oh, it was some considerable time," said Robert Latham, "before they broke up the segregation." In the meantime, the racial division of labor was raising the consciousness of blacks—even that of the traditionally silent. They had long recognized that whites and the system that whites created kept blacks mostly down and out. They attributed their comparatively high wages as factory workers to federal law and, to some extent, to unions, not to the benevolence of the employer. Said James C. Anderson: "I could see what was going on where I was working, and I knew there'd be a change, needed a change. That's what caused me to get out to try to make the change." Unprecedented economic opportunities and sustained discrimination, two fundamental facts of the factory workplace, made a volatile combination that eventually transformed black expectations. That transformation in turn prompted a black challenge to white cultural assumptions about race.[77]

Natchez is home to a stunning collection of antebellum mansions, such as Dunlieth, that survived the Civil War. Most of these homes are privately owned and opened to tourists in the spring and fall during the Natchez Pilgrimage.
Mississippi Department of Archives and History

Despite the architectural grandeur that has come to symbolize Natchez, adequate housing was still a problem as late as the 1980s. Sharecropper shacks much like the one shown can still be seen in parts of Adams County.
Mississippi Department of Archives and History

Founders of the Natchez Spring Pilgrimage 1932.
Collection of Thomas H. Gandy and Joan W. Gandy.

Belles and beaux of the Natchez Pilgrimage on the portico of the Melrose Plantation house.
Historic Natchez Foundation

Participants of one of the Confederate Pageant tableaux depicting a popular pastime of the Natchez elite. Fox hunting remained a sport in Adams County well into the twentieth century.
Historic Natchez Foundation

The king and queen of the Confederate Pageant lead their royal court onto the dance floor in one of the scenes performed before an audience of tourists and locals.
Historic Natchez Foundation

One of the favorite tableaux at the Confederate Pageant featured blacks performing slave songs. During the civil rights struggles of the 1960s, blacks stopped participating in the program.
Historic Natchez Foundation

As late as 1960, one-room schoolhouses with woodstove heating and outdoor privies were typical of the education system offered to blacks living in Adams County outside of Natchez.
Mississippi Department of Archives and History

Production worker at Armstrong Tire and Rubber Company, which was the hub of the industrial economy in Natchez and during the civil rights struggle a major venue of strife between white and black workers, the latter of whom were restricted to low-paying jobs in a segregated workplace.
Mississippi Department of Archives and History

Katherine Miller stands with two belles in front of the Mississippi Republican campaign headquarters in Natchez during the 1952 presidential election. Miller led the campaign and was one of the first white Mississippians to vacate a generations-long loyalty to the Democratic Party.
Historic Natchez Foundation

The Dumas Drug Store, located on Franklin Street in Natchez, was the anchor of the black business community for three decades. Albert W. Dumas Sr. and Albert W. Dumas Jr. located their medical offices above the drugstore, which was operated by Michele Dumas.
Jack E. Davis

CHAPTER FIVE

THE END OF SOCIAL HARMONY

A friendly yellow Labrador retriever sidled across the driveway to greet the approaching visitor. She had been enjoying the shade beneath the carport and moved slowly in the sweltering September heat. Her welcome provided a comforting reassurance of what could be expected in the disposition of her owner, a onetime president and longtime member of the now defunct Citizens' Council.

His house, sitting on five wooded acres in the city limits of Natchez, was small and unprepossessing, not what one would expect of a self-made, successful businessman and former city alderman. The architecture had the nondescript look of public housing. Inside, enclosed by dark paneled walls, the living room was cramped, the furniture worn. Burglar bars on every window heightened the feeling of closeness.

This security precaution was not necessarily the sign of a fearful elderly widower who lived alone, but that of a city that had become besieged by drug-related crime. "They'd have to tear in through those bars," he said of intruders, "and I could get my gun and get a few of them by that time." Twenty-five years ago, he said, he would have kept the front door unlocked. He admitted, nonetheless, that overall the quality of life in Natchez had improved somewhat, especially for the "colored people."

Still, he saw serious problems. They began with New Deal reform and escalated with forced integration. He blamed the "damn liberals." The former Demo-crat-turned-Republican summoned a seemingly ancient diatribe as he leaned back in his aged recliner: "Mississippi is the only state in the union that's worth a tinker's hoot. We've got the right ideas. But you've got all the old ones [white leaders] that's died off. I'm seventy-five years old, and I can remember when Bilbo, he lacked one vote of sending all the blacks back to Africa. That's where they belong." As he continued a discussion linking black rights with social de-cline, his tone was never hostile, but his views were driven by a timeworn philos-ophy.

More than an hour later, serious conversation ended with an admonition: "We've all died out, and if you younger generations don't take over and get the proper people elected, God help you. God help you. You gonna be slaves. Just like they were at one time."

ARCH was always a busy and exciting time in Natchez. As throughout the rest of the lower South, nature began to re-generate with pronounced colors and perfumes. In Natchez, that meant the azaleas were in bloom, nature's trademark for the spring Pilgrimage. The city was filled with tourists milling the sidewalks, snapping pho-tographs of mansions and hoopskirted belles, shopping at local retail stores, and eating at restaurants. Sometimes the Pilgrimage would bring famous people to Natchez, a movie star, a foreign dignitary, or an impor-tant politician. In 1948, Mississippi Governor Fielding Wright came to Natchez in late March.

Something more than pleasure brought the governor to Natchez though. Much was astir in national politics that demanded the attention of the white South. Several weeks before, on February 2, President Tru-man delivered a foreboding message on civil rights to Congress. He called for the abolition of the poll tax, establishment of a permanent Fair Employment Practices Committee (FEPC), passage of antilynching legis-lation, and outlawing segregation in interstate transportation. Although the president's so-called civil rights platform had occasioned no surprise, it horrified white southerners, and the southern wing of the Democratic Party scrambled for a unified response.[1]

Governor Wright's star within that wing was rising quickly. A native of Rolling Fork, a rural Delta community, Wright was in Natchez to reaffirm the commitment of southern leaders to protecting the values of their constituency. Natchez in March offered the perfect backdrop for such an occasion. Nothing celebrated the values of the white South more eloquently than did the Pilgrimage. Wright spoke of these matters—the threat coming out of Washington and the need to respond—one afternoon from the steps of the county courthouse. Eighteen radio stations around the state carried the event. It was a passionate speech, but the airwaves could not transmit the poignancy of the setting—the century-old courthouse before which Wright stood and the ancient live oaks that flanked him, nostalgic evocations of what had been lost once before and what was at stake once again. That evening, the governor attended the Confederate Pageant, where scenes and music of the Old South reinforced the importance of the mission of the present.

The next day, Wright addressed attendees at the Natchez Democratic caucus meeting. The Reverend W. A. Sullivan of the First Baptist Church gave the invocation. Mary Louise Kendall, Natchez resident and chairperson of the women's division of the state Democratic Party, introduced the honored guest speaker. Natchez Democrats, by now calling themselves Jeffersonian Democrats, held up Wright as the answer to putting the party back on track and preserving the cherished doctrine of states' rights. They had recently drafted a resolution to nominate him for president, but Wright had gracefully bowed away from the offer.[2]

Still in their political camp, he did not entirely disappoint his Natchez supporters that day. Wright, who looked more like a banker than a hardcore politician, rose to the lectern—again, his speech was broadcast across the state—and he unleashed his vitriol against the evils of federal control and integration, whipping the audience into a frenzy of "Rebel yells and loud applause." In words that resonated with political rhetoric of the past and that commingled with anticommunist diatribe of the present, he warned that "our open and present enemies" are "pledged to invade our State and others, and destroy those privileges and rights reserved to the state under the constitution." He assured the crowd of the southern white resolve to stand before the dangers of federal power. Driving home his point, he appealed to the white southerner's keen sense of history. He compared Truman's civil rights platform to the ideals of "the carpetbaggers and scalawags that swarmed into the South to prey upon her people when she lay bleeding and helpless at the close of the Civil War." The FEPC would violate "the private right to hire and fire and [would] compel intimate association of one person with another in private employment irrespective of desires."[3]

It was inevitable that he would turn to the subject of race, one subject no southern politician of his day could avoid. With "anti-segregation laws," he said, "the freedom to choose one's own company is completely and utterly destroyed." Federal voting laws would subvert local jurisdiction over the political process and open the ballot to unqualified people. He described the intermingling of the races as a "fatal mistake" that "would destroy in a moment the harmonious and peaceful progress of our race relations which we have so studiously and so long encouraged and maintained." Finally, Wright closed with an appeal to civic virtue. The fight against enemies within was no less a patriotic duty than fighting those from afar. He urged Mississippians to take the required measures to "preserve those things necessary to our very existence," and "declare their freedom from the dictates of their enemies."[4]

As white southerners were coming to realize, more than the actions of the president and the federal government threatened their "very existence." National organizations for black civil rights had gained a new momentum during World War II, and they were beginning to change American society. To the way of life and thinking of white Natchezians listening to Wright's admonitions, Truman and the fledgling black movement for freedom symbolized so much that was dangerous: federal intrusion, racial equality, and physical and cultural integration. It all boiled down to a struggle between the forces of continuity and change, white reactionaryism against black progress. The latter had been manifesting itself in legal decisions that challenged racial segregation in higher education and interstate transportation and that outlawed the white primary; in federal legislation and public policy that protected the wages of black labor; and in an increasingly aggressive black reform movement that was threatening to spread from the North to the South.

The struggle unfolding across the region and the nation infected black Natchez both in spirit and with activism. In the mid-1950s, a handful of black citizens momentarily stepped forward with unprecedented demands for racial equality, and in the early 1960s, activists with national civil rights groups converged on the community in an assault on the white southern way of life. With the threat of a second Reconstruction looming, reactionary groups formed to contain indigenous civil rights initiatives and nationally organized activists, derided as outside agitators. Beyond the community level, the ominous, forward drift of history, which for nearly a century had left the alabaster South alone to do what it pleased, was changing the country, and it was pulling Natchez into its treacherous current.

As in virtually every other southern community, local whites in Natchez tried swimming upstream. The resistance to change reflected a conservative ideological concern about expanding centralized power on the one hand and a white-supremacist ideological fear of a disrupted social order on the other. The dual ideologies merged into a single and inseparable defense once the federal government and black activists seemingly joined in an equally inseparable offensive alliance. The means for staying the course of white supremacy began peacefully enough, with a rhetorical and political campaign. But when means seemed no longer to effect adequately the desired end, they degenerated into white violence against black citizens. Even whites who denounced the hardcore tactics of vigilante groups shared their vision of caste society and contributed indirectly to the syndrome of violence.

Although a seeming contradiction, the defensive attachment to liberties by the same group that denied liberties to another bore no philosophical contradiction in the white segregationist mind. In a society where whites embraced the idea of cultural hegemony, blacks were deemed unqualified for liberties equal to those of whites. The latter argued that good government required an intelligent and responsible citizenship, a criterion blacks presumably did not fit. The *Natchez Democrat* was particularly active in promoting this position on civil rights, printing editorial after editorial denouncing Truman. The newspaper's editor, Elliot Trimble, a descendant of old Natchez stock and a self-proclaimed aristocrat, supported fair treatment under the law for blacks in their "daily pursuits" of livelihood, but he opposed giving blacks political rights. They "are not fit, mentally, morally, or physically, for this new kind of emancipation," the editor wrote. That attitude manifested itself in the systematic disfranchisement of eligible black voters in Adams County; less than 12 percent were registered. Participating in the political process, the newspaper claimed years later, was a "privilege," not an "inherent right."[5]

At odds with this kind of thinking, President Truman offended southern white sensibilities with two intolerable initiatives. First, he tried to elevate what whites believed to be strictly a local matter, in this case race relations, to a national level. He also instituted civil rights policy. In July 1948, he signed executive orders to end discrimination in the defense industry and in the military. The *Natchez Democrat* called the orders a mandate of "equality of treatment among unequals." Then in August, Truman rolled over his congressional proposals from earlier that year into a civil rights platform at the Democratic National Convention. With this platform, the South for the first time since the nineteenth century faced what whites saw as the possibility of two distinct evils—federal intrusion and black equality—merging into a single destructive force threatening individual liberty and community peace. Unable to tolerate Truman's liberalism any longer, the entire Mississippi delegation walked out of the convention. Days later, southern Democrats held their own convention, nominated South Carolina governor J. Strom Thurmond for president and Mississippi governor Wright for vice-president and styled themselves as States Rights Democrats. The press and others called them, appropriately, Dixiecrats.[6]

The Dixiecrats won less than one-fifth of the southern vote in the November presidential election, but they carried Mississippi and Natchez. In a record general election turnout, Adams County voter support for Thurmond and Wright topped 80 percent (as did support at the state level); Truman and Republican candidate Thomas Dewey evenly divided the rest of the vote. To Natchez Democrats, the party of their forebears had abandoned the Jeffersonian doctrine of government by consent of the governed for a perverse principle of executive control. In reality, the grievance was not so much with executive control as with the president and the liberal ideals associated with his administration. As white southerners saw it, the actual bolters from the party line had been the regular Democrats and not the ideologically pure southern delegates.[7]

Four years later, states' rights and civil rights remained conjoined issues of principal concern. Skeptical about the success of a third party, Natchez voters began giving serious consideration to supporting the party of their ancestors' oppressors, even though support meant abandoning one of the most sacred of southern institutions. Leading the party shift in Natchez was Katherine Miller, matriarch of the Natchez Pilgrimage. She entered politics with the same verve she displayed in historical tourism. In the spring of 1952, Miller was named national committeewoman of the "all-white" Mississippi Republican Party. She described her conversion in political alliance as a trying and gradual conversion. "The superstition of being a Southern Democrat for generations had me in its grip," she wrote a friend in August 1952, "as it has many others." Miller had become disillusioned with government expansion under the Democrats. The party's leftward swing on civil rights equally disturbed her. She labeled herself a "new Republican," which to her detractors was a smokescreen for a lily-white initiative designed to oust Mississippi's traditional black-and-tan delegation. The delegation chairman said with some accuracy that Miller represented "the silk stocking district of the Old South." Miller denied having any racial motives. But at the 1956 Republican National Convention in San Francisco, she created a national scene after refusing to sit with Mississippi's regular delegation, which included several black members and a controversial chairman, who also was black.[8]

Four years earlier in Natchez, where she did not have to defend her racial views, Miller opened a Republican campaign office. She personified the merging of powerful ideals: Old South, New South tourism, segregation, upper-class leadership, and new conservative Republicanism. She brought into her new political role the skills and intensity used to promote the Pilgrimage. She also incorporated familiar concepts. In one publicity photograph, which would have given credence to the "silk stocking" claim, Miller had two hoopskirted women stand before the Natchez Republican headquarters, cradling its new sign. With wonted fortitude and the experience of a tourism promoter, Miller also tackled the local campaign circuit. In her first political speech, delivered at the Natchez Lions Club, she assured her audience that presidential candidate Dwight Eisenhower opposed the FEPC and "thinks like we do." The Republican platform, she said, was acceptable to the South "in every way."[9]

Others thought so, as well. Following Miller's persuasive lead, the two local garden clubs openly supported the Republican candidate. At the *Democrat,* editor Elliot Trimble advanced Eisenhower an implicit endorsement and predicted that the candidate would reinstate a commitment to individual liberty and conservative government.[10]

Ultimately, the Democrats, with Illinois governor Adlai E. Stevenson and Alabama senator John J. Sparkman heading the 1952 ticket, carried the South, including Mississippi. But Miller's campaign, the new Democratic liberalism, and Eisenhower's popularity as a war hero moved Adams County voters enough to put aside old loyalties and endorse the Republican ticket. One among thirteen of Mississippi's eighty-two counties to support the Republicans, Adams County gave Eisenhower a 675-vote victory in a record turnout that November of 4,069 voters. The general-turned-freshman-politician took 39.6 percent of the state aggregate, a remarkable development, writes Stephen Whitfield, that "threatened to falsify the Magnolia State maxim that local Republicans were being preserved from extinction only by game laws." It was a "Smashing Vote," read the headline of the *Democrat.* Eisenhower captured the greatest number of Adams County votes of any Republican since "carpetbag days."[11]

If white southerners had hoped that a Republican in the White House would reverse the growing trend of federal activism, they were soon disappointed. Two years into the new president's administration, the Supreme Court, under the leadership of Eisenhower appointee Chief Justice Earl Warren, handed down the *Brown v. Board of Education* decision, which outlawed segregated public schools. Initially, there had been wishful thinking about Warren's judicial conservatism. But the Court's decision came as no surprise to Elliot Trimble and his editorial counterpart at the *Natchez Times.* Both regarded the Court's action as another example of federal contempt for constitutional law. In a series of editorials, the two newspapers said the Court had ignored legal precedent and original intent for a social philosophy that espoused the incredible idea that separation of the races would retard the mental development of black children. By "caesarean method," wrote Trimble, the Court had "pave[d] the way for judicial decisions, in all aspects of life, which do not depend upon the law for guidance."[12]

In support of their position, the editors themselves resorted to social philosophy. Instinctively, stated the *Natchez Democrat,* southern whites could not peacefully accept "mingling in the classroom." Mixing contradicted everything whites believed and understood about racial separation, and it would mean the ultimate destruction of society. Not only were whites opposed to it, the newspapers argued, blacks hated the idea as well. The children of neither race would be able to cope with integration. Trimble reminded readers that Lincoln himself had been a segregationist who recognized the dangers of mixing the races. From Trimble's perspective, the "decision impose[d] a Second Reconstruction on the South." The ghost of federal tyranny of ninety years before had returned to haunt white southerners, whose historical vision of the first Reconstruction conformed to the teachings of Pearl Guyton. Like their ancestors, white citizens would not "lie prostrate" in these times of danger.[13]

Brown's federal mandate to desegregate the public schools did indeed excite the ire of white southerners. In Mississippi, whites in the Delta formed the Citizens' Council in July 1954 to lead an organized resistance at the community level. Mustering a membership of mostly middle-class businessmen and professionals—not limited to Christians—the council presented itself as law-abiding and nonviolent. Despite such pretensions, it openly engaged in intimidation—usually economic—to frustrate desegregation and voter registration efforts. When questioned, the council used both history and religion to justify its existence. One council tract read: "If we are bigoted, prejudiced, un-American, etc., so were George Washington, Thomas Jefferson, Abraham Lincoln, and other illustrious forebears who believed in segregation." According to other council material, segregation was "God's own plan for the races." At the bottom line of council philosophy, blacks were culturally unsuitable for free association with white society.[14]

White Natchez did not feel the Deltans' urgency until a year later. It was then that the local NAACP began sowing the seeds that, though cast upon fallow soil, would eventually grow roots mighty enough to crack the foundation of white supremacy. Joining a regionwide initiative originating from NAACP national headquarters, the Natchez branch petitioned the local school board to begin desegregation in accordance with the Supreme Court's May 31, 1955, implementation decision in *Brown* II. Branches in Jackson, Vicksburg, Clarksdale, and Yazoo City also followed the national NAACP's initiative. The petition was the Natchez NAACP's second boldest act.[15]

The boldest had been the branch's resurrection in 1940. Barely one hundred Mississippians throughout the state at that time held membership in the NAACP, the type of black civic organization not welcomed in Mississippi. A chapter existed in Natchez briefly during the 1920s, and its short life apparently had as much to do with economics and local black indifference as with white resistance. There were a number of attempts in the 1930s, led by different individuals, working-class and professional, to recruit the fifty members required to charter a new branch. But in the midst of the depression, many Natchez blacks could not afford the one-dollar annual membership fee. Dillard University sociologist Saint Clair Drake, who in 1937 was assisting Allison Davis with Natchez research, had a different take on Natchez's inability to organize a local branch. As a devoted NAACP member who was active in many capacities, Drake showed little patience for black Natchez. He reported in a letter to the national office, "Why even the 'big Negroes' here wont [sic] have anything to do with the NAACP; they're so scared and uncle Tommish. I just finished talking to a young Negro who tried to start a chapter and couldn't get any support." Three years later, Audley Maurice Mackel, a dentist and uncle of Charlotte Mackel Harrison, generated enough local support to reopen a Natchez chapter of the NAACP.[16]

Mackel was an activist of some experience. Like so many other southern black professionals of his day, he had followed a higher-education route through black institutions: first Natchez College, then Atlanta University, and finally Meharry Medical College. After graduating from Meharry in 1927, he returned to Natchez briefly before moving to Monroe, Louisiana, in 1931 to practice his profession. Remembered as an "impressive" individual with a "ranging intellect," he fit the image of the contemporary black leader: professionally educated, always well groomed, and dignified. Yet, he was also different.[17]

Mackel was more demanding of change in the racial status quo than were perhaps most other black leaders of his generation. His appreciation for a decent education stoked an overt distaste for Jim Crow, and in 1934, he organized the Monroe Civic League to prod an indifferent white leadership into fixing Monroe's deteriorating and overcrowded black schools. After seven years in Louisiana, he moved his family and practice to Natchez to be close to his ailing mother. Mackel brought his activist spirit with him and immediately immersed himself in community affairs. He first tried to organize an NAACP branch in 1938 and failed, but his efforts succeeded nearly two years later in the spring of 1940. In addition to resurrecting Natchez's long-defunct NAACP chapter, Mackel spent many exhausting evenings traveling to black churches, drumming up dental business and delivering "motivational" speeches that exhorted the masses to register to vote. A man could only be a man, he told them in his most recited speech, when he loved his God, supported his family, and exercised his constitutional rights; southern society had no legal cause to steal his manhood. The black community quickly came to know Mackel as indeed a man, one of principle and conviction, assertive in his beliefs and nothing short of honorable.[18]

Many in the white community undoubtedly saw the broad-shouldered, barrel-chested black dentist as a danger to the established racial hierarchy. Being an NAACP activist was enough alone to ruffle the dander of whites. Mississippi segregationists spared no malice for the country's oldest existing civil rights organization, labeled as subversive and communist inspired. The Natchez NAACP obligingly gave whites reason for their hatred and fear. In the summer following the Brown II decision, Mackel attended a meeting in Atlanta with national and regional NAACP leaders, including Medgar Evers, Mississippi field secretary, and Aaron Henry, state president, to draft the school desegregation petition. It was eventually filed in some sixty southern school districts. In the capacity of branch secretary, Mackel and the chapter president, David Bacon, who worked as a porter at a white-owned clothing store, presented the petition to the Natchez school-board president, R. Brent Forman. It contained the signatures of eighty-six black residents; among them were farmers, factory workers (including James Anderson), and professionals. In essence, the petitioners were telling the school board, "In the past, school plans have been made for us rather than with us."[19]

Natchez whites responded swiftly to the petition by organizing a Citizens' Council. According to a Jackson Daily News article: "Scores of Natchez citizens entered the fight to maintain segregation in the public schools by enrolling in the Adams County Citizens Council." The mass matriculation came at an August 4 rally held at the city auditorium. The rally included local political stump speakers and many council luminaries, such as the founder, Robert Patterson. The featured speaker was Mississippi circuit court judge Thomas P. Brady, "intellectual godfather" of the council and author of segregationist-acclaimed *Black Monday*. Brady told a spirited audience that segregation was God's law and anyone who thought otherwise was "ignorant or brainwashed." He said the NAACP had misled innocent blacks into believing that the Supreme Court ruling had followed the rule of law, secular and Christian. The best way for whites to fight the communist-led group of black extremists, as Brady portrayed the NAACP, was with an organization of their own. The main objective adopted by the new chapter, which materialized from the meeting, was in keeping with council principles: "to keep our schools and our churches and everything like it was then," said a former chapter president, "to maintain segregation."[20]

The first order of business of the Natchez council was to turn back the petitioners. In a gesture of cooperation, School Superintendent D. Gilmer McLaurin, who once said he would fire a black teacher associated with the NAACP, forwarded lists of the petition signers to the state attorney general's office and later to the Mississippi State Sovereignty Commission. Also aiding in the effort, the two local newspapers published the names and addresses of the petition signers. It was no secret that the newspapers intended "to let the people in the community know who had signed the petition so they could take whatever action they wanted," Elliot Trimble said in later years. "That was an effort to beat integration."[21]

In this instance, it worked. Most black families were directly beholden to a white employer for their livelihood. In a small town such as Natchez, word about an "uppity" black spread easily and quickly, and incipient sparks of black discontent were summarily and effectively extinguished. The council, white employers, police, and others pressured the petition signers. Some, like Harden Wallace, an Armstrong employee and future president of the Natchez Business and Civic League, stood their ground. Wallace received numerous threatening phone calls. At one point, his antagonists called the Mackel funeral home with instructions to pick up Wallace's body at his house. This scare tactic failed to work as well, and Wallace refused to remove his name from the petition. His

Race against Time

stubbornness, matched by that of Mackel and George West, proved to be the exception though. On the advice of the state attorney's office, the school board rejected the NAACP's petition; by that time, roughly three-fifths of the petitioners had withdrawn their signatures. Even David Bacon, apparently feeling pressure from his employer, withdrew his name and resigned as chapter president. The council enjoyed equal success in the other petitioning cities.[22]

The NAACP's defeat was the Natchez Citizens' Council's first and greatest victory. The council remained active for two decades more, mostly by way of sponsoring free public films, distributing literature extolling the virtues of segregation, and holding public meetings to discuss the need to preserve peace and the status quo. Its membership peaked at about 750 and reached all corners of the white community to include a number of prominent citizens, many of whom preferred to keep their affiliation secret. Despite its sizable membership, the council mostly engaged in rhetoric rather than action.[23]

Unlike other southern cities where the NAACP was well organized and stable, the Natchez branch disbanded after the petition defeat. Constant death threats made life in Natchez too hazardous for Audley Mackel and his family, and a year later they left Natchez "secretly and swiftly" and permanently for Chicago, leaving segregationists without a chief adversary. It was the same year that Governor James P. Coleman set up the Mississippi State Sovereignty Commission for the purpose of destroying the NAACP and its desegregation efforts. The commission, with the help of local officials including the police and sheriff's departments and the school superintendent, maintained an almost phobic vigil on revived NAACP activity in Natchez and elsewhere. Beneath the circumspect eye of a state agency, black and white citizens of Natchez continued to function by the enforced rituals of caste society. The council had temporarily restored the white prescription of racial harmony; even so, the council would never be as powerful a force locally as were the ideals that the segregationist group endorsed.[24]

With the local NAACP neutralized, white Natchezians continued to work mainly through the political process to preserve those ideals. By the late 1950s, Eisenhower and the Republicans had proven to be disappointingly irresponsible with the Warren appointment, the *Brown* decision, and the 1957 and 1960 civil rights acts, which empowered the U.S.

Justice Department to take action in incidences involving voting rights abuses. The *Democrat* warned readers that if they voted Republican in the 1960 presidential election they would be supporting a party that enforced "the school decision with bayonets at Little Rock" and a candidate, Richard Nixon, who was a member of the NAACP.[25] White Natchezians liked John Kennedy and his "Ivy Tower" liberals even less. Ideologically stranded between the "ultra Socialistic" agenda of the Democrats and the conservative ambiguity of Nixon and the Republicans, Adams County whites followed the trend at the state level and gave a plurality of their votes to electors unpledged to either party before the November election. For the fourth consecutive time in a dozen years, Natchez whites deserted the presidential candidate of the party of their ancestors. Kennedy's victory was more frightening to white southerners than would have been the resurrection of the Great Emancipator himself (who, after all, had been a segregationist). White Natchezians watched with concern as the world continued to erupt around them. Most remained convinced of the need to keep the federal government and the emerging civil rights movement at bay.[26]

In the white mind, the culprit in the breach of the domestic tranquility was not an iniquitous social order, rather it was the civil rights movement, whose intrusive workers whipped up the emotions of peaceable blacks with spurious ideas of racial injustice. Social advancement came through perseverance in education and work, whites repeatedly contended, not through sit-ins, protests, and marches led by outside troublemakers. "The colored people agreed with us until the NAACP come in," said a former Natchez Citizens' Council president. Natchez is a "victim," wrote Adams County resident Roane Byrnes in a letter to Mississippi senator John Stennis in 1966, "of paid professional agitators, both white and colored."[27]

With its mostly disfranchised black population and Jim Crow manufacturing plants, Natchez had become the target of "outside agitators" beginning in the summer of 1963. Local whites gave a chilly reception to Bill Ware, George Greene, and Bruce Payne, all young Student Non-Violent Coordinating Committee (SNCC) workers who were organizing polling places for a statewide mock election. The election was intended to demonstrate the interest of disfranchised blacks in voting. In August, after Ware tried to use a white restroom at a filling station, the Natchez police detained him and then proceeded to reconstruct his face with a billy club. The police charged Ware with "assault and battery of a police officer." The white physician who sewed thirty stitches into Ware's face called him a "brainwashed" agent of Attorney General Robert Kennedy, with a "martyr complex" and an unhealthy disrespect for the southern way of life. In another incident, four white thugs assaulted Bruce Payne, a twenty-one-year-old Yale graduate student, at a gas station in Port Gibson, thirty-five miles north of Natchez. Two days later, the same quartet was hot on the trail of the "votemobile" of Payne and Greene, who were working near Natchez. By way of a 100-plus-mile-an-hour car chase, Greene's intrepid driving skills, and sheer luck, the SNCC activists dodged the bullets and escaped the clutches of their pursuers. The FBI pressured local law officials to arrest the thugs and charge them with assault with intent to kill, but the charges were later dismissed. That September, a black church in rural Adams County went up in flames. It would not be the last.[28]

In each case the violence and harassment that summer was likely the work of the Ku Klux Klan. With an aggregate Klan membership estimated at four hundred, reportedly one of the highest per capita memberships in the entire South, southwestern Mississippi gave civil rights workers good reason to describe the region as the most dangerous Klan stronghold in the state. It was also, consequently, the most successful in limiting civil rights activity.[29]

Chief among the hooded who claimed to be fighting for *white* freedom was Edward L. McDaniel. A former oil field worker and truck driver, the twenty-nine-year-old E. L. McDaniel organized and led one of the four Klan terrorist groups operating in southwest Mississippi. Born and raised in Natchez, the oldest of seven children, McDaniel had known the life of Adams County's many working poor families. His mother labored at a garment factory and his father in "public work." The two incomes kept the family of nine fed, clothed, and sheltered, but the McDaniels could never afford an amenity such as an automobile. Within the family means though, and bespeaking the economic distance between the black poor and white poor, was Aunt Mary, "an old colored lady" who cared for the McDaniel children. "She was like a mother to us," recalled McDaniel. He and his siblings grew up in a racially mixed neighborhood, where they played and swam with black children and where a black family lived behind them. "I can't recall a time in my boyhood days," said McDaniel, "of even thinking about the racial overtones."[30]

But integration in young McDaniel's day ended with child's play, and segregation defined schooling, dating, and cultural values. Separation and cooperation existed like a code of honor between the races, and there was no need for enforcement by groups such as the Klan. McDaniel, in fact, feared the Klan, as many whites did then, until one day his grandfather offered sober advice. The precise moment of that advice remained imprinted on McDaniel's mind in sentimental images of an evening at sundown, a back-alley chance meeting, and an elder passing on his wisdom to a young man coming of age. "Son," said the grandfather, "if you ever have a chance to join the Klan, join the Klan."[31]

By the 1960s, the federal government's activism in southern affairs had strengthened the logic of that advice in McDaniel's mind. He had objected to the presence of federal troops in Little Rock in 1957 and to federal marshals overseeing James Meredith's matriculation at Ole Miss in 1962. On matters of race, he ignored state violations of the laws of the land but could not stomach the federal government enforcing those laws. He joined the Original Knights of the Ku Klux Klan sometime in 1961 and organized Klaverns across Mississippi. The Originals expelled him for alleged financial improprieties, and after joining the White Knights of the Ku Klux Klans, he experienced the same difficulties and was again expelled. He then turned to Robert Shelton, imperial wizard of the United Klan of America (UKA), headquartered in Alabama. Shelton appointed McDaniel grand dragon of Mississippi in September 1964.[32]

Under the incorporated name of the Adams County Civic and Betterment Association, the Mississippi UKA opened its headquarters at 114 Main Street in Natchez. Membership was primarily working class, and it penetrated local law-enforcement agencies, county and city government offices, and the major manufacturing plants. McDaniel described his Klan group as "100 percent Pro-American," nonviolent soldiers of Christian civilization who mobilized against communism and civil rights. At cross-burning rallies in city parks, McDaniel vowed that the Klan would "fight to our last breath" to defend the white southern and American way of life.[33]

McDaniel's commitment to nonviolence was, of course, suspect. People on both sides of the struggle said that nonviolence and the Klan were unnatural allies. Hardcore Klansmen believed that preaching nonviolence was a bad way to defend the cause. Such ideas were in part responsible for the development of so many Klan organizations and renegade factions. "Eddie Mac," some believed, was disingenuous. He was in the Klan business simply for self-enrichment. He would "hold a rally, burn a cross, and take the money," someone once said. Whatever his true motivation, McDaniel helped charge an atmosphere in which intimidation, threats, burning, torture, and even murder were justified to accomplish certain ends.[34]

The early violence and harassment in 1963 served as a warning to civil rights workers and to local blacks that any challenge to the existing racial status quo would not be tolerated. The response of most Natchez blacks did not disappoint the white supremacists. The daily struggle to make a living kept many blacks too busy to get involved. Nearly all worked for a white employer and "knew better" than to support the cause of civil rights. The leadership in the Natchez Business and Civic League continued to believe that working in concert with the traditions of social harmony was the best means to protect the community's interests as well as their own economic well being. So unthreatening was the group's presence, the *Natchez Democrat* routinely published the dates of its meetings for the benefit of the membership. The civil rights workers labeled them the mayor's "black boys." There were some activist-minded members among them, including in earlier years Audley Mackel, who also held memberships in the NAACP and who, like NAACP lifetime member George West, helped underwrite the movement. It was perhaps under their influence that the league recognized that fewer than one thousand local blacks possessed the ballot and encouraged qualified and "intelligent" black citizens to register to vote. Somehow, though, the league still maintained that black entitlement to the ballot was "an accepted fact" in Natchez and that "Negroes do not find an unfriendly climate at the Registrar of Voters Office nor at the polling booths."[35]

Particularly deferential to the established power structure were local black ministers. Many black churches were dependent on the goodwill of white benefactors and the lay ministers who preached on Sunday and labored on Monday for a white boss. In a practice common across the

South since slavery, ministers dutifully preached to their flocks about accepting their worldly troubles in return for heavenly bliss. With few exceptions, black churches closed their doors to local civil rights efforts and condemned protests of virtually any sort by either blacks or whites. "A lot of people were afraid back in those days," said Joseph Hall, a local participant in the struggle, "and those young [SNCC] people weren't afraid, and they could have brought death and destruction on top of you."[36]

But while the Klan's message of fear held most local blacks in subjection, it moved a small group to revive the old Natchez branch of the NAACP. Among the new members were the Reverend William J. Morrisey, white priest of the black Holy Family Catholic Church; George Metcalfe and Wharlest Jackson, employees at Armstrong Tire and Rubber Company; and the Reverend Shead Baldwin. The new membership also included women, such as Lillian Carter, a planing mill laborer; Mamie Mazique, whose late husband left her several mortgage-free rental houses that would aid the movement; and Mary Lee Toles, who would later serve as president of the Natchez NAACP. Although the chapter officially received its new charter in January 1965, the organizing effort started much earlier.[37]

Individual circumstances and experiences inspired the revival of the chapter. For Baldwin, a stocky bulldog of a man who resembled a prizefighter more than a preacher, it was the September burning of his church, which was randomly selected to set an example to those who might challenge the established social order. Metcalfe and Jackson were busy trying to break down segregation barriers at Armstrong, where the connection between Jim Crow and economic disparity was immediately apparent. The June 1963 killing of Medgar Evers sparked a change in the attitude of chapter secretary Mamie Lee Mazique, and the fortitude of Rosa Parks in Montgomery in 1965 encouraged Carter to do something for her community. For Toles, it was one too many in a long list of racial insults. The last came in 1962 when a white man in line behind her at a fast-food restaurant told her: "Get out of line, nigger."[38]

With Metcalfe as president, the new membership represented a fresh generation in local black leadership. They came, not from the professional class, but primarily from working-class stock. They refused to humble themselves before whites and instead expected equal respect.

Along with the rest of the NAACP's tiny membership, these individuals initially stood alone among local blacks in publicly condemning Jim Crow and its violent stewards, the Klan.

The reorganization of the NAACP and the arrival of SNCC activists seemed to provoke the worst in the Klan. White terror escalated through the late fall of 1963 and on into the next summer during the campaign known as the Summer Project, a statewide voter-registration campaign launched by national civil rights organizations. Much of the violence could be traced to the factory workplace, the common meeting ground of white worker and black worker, Klansmen and NAACP members. Leonard Russell in 1963 was a shop steward for one of the segregated unions at International Paper Company in Natchez. As a black labor organizer, Russell's greatest antagonists were not union busters or strikebreakers, but white coworkers. One night in November, a group of white men approached Russell near his home in rural Franklin County, southeast of Natchez. Russell sensed danger and quickly sought refuge in his house, behind a shotgun that he discharged at will, barely escaping injury and an attempted kidnaping. He later associated his would-be kidnappers' actions with the recent desegregation of the water fountains at the paper mill and a grievance his union filed three weeks earlier against the plant's remaining Jim Crow conditions, including racially designated jobs.[39]

The Klan made its message clear to others besides Russell. In February, James Carter Wilson, a black cafeteria employee at International Paper, was abducted at gunpoint one night while hitching a ride home from work. Three men wearing Halloween masks placed a hood over his head before driving south on Highway 61. Forced down onto the backseat floor, gun at his head, he was asked if he belonged to the NAACP. He said no. He was then asked whether he was married. Again he said no. Was he in favor of sending his children to school with white children? Wilson had no children but said he probably would be if he did. A rumored homosexual, Wilson was then asked if he had ever had sex with a white person. Wilson said yes, when he was a younger man. Somewhere en route, the car turned off the highway and motored down a gravel road to a secluded spot deep in the woods where other men waited. Pulling Wilson from the car, they stripped his clothes and whipped him like a slave before emptying a bottle of castor oil down his throat. At one point, the beating stopped while his abductors inspected his "private parts." Wilson heard a voice say, "Not as big as I thought it would be." Wilson was then released. Still naked, he forged his way through a marsh in the February cold before finding help at the house of a black tenant farmer.[40]

A coworker of Wilson, Clifton Walker met a worse fate. One evening in March, Walker never returned home from the paper mill. The next day, someone found his body; a shotgun blast had ripped away much of his head. No arrests were made. Sadly, most whites put little value on the life of a black man. Regret over a death the like of Walker's was limited to the burden of explanation it left for officials, if explanation was demanded, and the unseemly blotch it left on the community's race-relations record. That record was never outstanding—though local whites believed otherwise.[41]

As if to test that belief, violence continued to leave its mark in 1964. Across town from International Paper at the Armstrong Tire plant, Alfred Whitley left work one evening for his home in the hinterland surrounding Natchez. The twenty-minute commute turned into a nightlong terror after several men in hoods intercepted Whitley and took him to a swampy area. The ghostly assembly accused Whitley of active participation in the NAACP, and it threatened to shoot him unless he summoned up the name of a white man who was allegedly a member of the local organization. The tire plant janitor had no affiliation with the NAACP and could offer no names. Then in a scenario similar to previous kidnapings, the hooded men stripped Whitley's clothes, beat him with a bullwhip, and forced him to drink a bottle of castor oil. They next ordered the naked Whitley to run, firing shots his direction as he somehow fled to safety. Although Whitley later identified one of the abductors to investigators, no arrest was made.[42]

The list of Klan victims did not end with factory workers. Also in February, black funeral-home director Archie Curtis, a registered voter as well as a past president of the Natchez NAACP, and his assistant were lured away from the business one night to a rural area in the county. There, three armed and hooded men apprehended them, had them strip before whipping them, and talked about killing the two before letting them go. That spring, two farm workers (one was Adolph Butler, cousin of Sargent Butler) in separate incidents were shot and beaten, one by the Klan, the other by police (possibly Klan members as well). In midsummer, two more black churches were burned, again one of Shead Baldwin's. During the massive search in June to recover the bodies of the three civil rights workers slain in Neshoba County, authorities fished two badly decomposed bodies out of the Mississippi River. They were those of twenty-year-old Charles Eddie Moore and nineteen-year-old Henry Hezekiah Dee. The FBI turned over evidence to state prosecutors, including a signed confession, pinning the murders on James Ford Seale and Charles Marcus Edwards, both members of the White Knights. Edwards was also an employee at International Paper in Natchez. The accused were never indicted. As usual, the southern justice system failed to work for blacks in any of these cases. In only one did police make arrests, but the charges were dropped because only the black victim could identify the assailants.[43]

This was the state of "social harmony" when SNCC workers returned to Natchez in July 1964. With the assistance of George Metcalfe and the local NAACP, Dorie Ladner, Chuck McDew, and Charles "Chico" Neblett established a base of operations under the auspices of the Council of Federated Organizations (COFO) and its Summer Project (also known as Freedom Summer), whose members blanketed Mississippi. Joining them was George Greene—the Greenwood, Mississippi, native who by this time had earned a reputation for his driving brilliance—and Bill Ware and Burt Watkins. Waiting with a dubious welcome were Chief J. T. Robinson's police, who in May had prepared for the invaders by enrolling in a special three-day riot-control course. Within less than an hour of his arrival, McDew was fined for running a stop sign, one that did not exist, and given the promise that the police would be monitoring the movements of the activists "every minute of the day." Robinson reportedly warned, "If you people make trouble, I'll guarantee you there is going to be some slow walking and some sad singing."[44]

Harassment came from other quarters as well. The activists endured an endless barrage of threatening phone calls; their headquarters, automobiles, and places of residence were frequent targets of rocks and gunfire. Five days after their arrival, George Metcalfe received a bomb threat at his home, where some of the COFO workers slept. Then in the late hours of August 14, a bomb destroyed the juke joint next to a house George Greene had rented. In the crowd watching the blaze, a fireman remarked to Ladner, mistaken for a local, that "the wrong place" had been bombed. He added that "these outside agitators are in that house.

The bomb was set for that house. They're here to stir up trouble." A few days later, Greene's landlord asked him to leave, and Metcalfe's insurance company threatened to cancel his homeowner's policy.[45]

From the perspective of whites, the invaders from the North were the salt in the wound of federal civil rights legislation. The passage of the "iniquitous" 1964 Civil Rights Act, which outlawed segregated public facilities and job discrimination, presented Americans with their "New Slavery," proclaimed a *Democrat* editorial. Before the bill's enactment in July, the Natchez Lions Club led a grassroots letter-writing campaign to urge southern congressmen to defeat the bill, which in the reckoning of local whites was "dangerous legislation." Adams County voters also expressed their discontent at the polls by giving ultraconservative Barry Goldwater 84 percent of the vote in the 1964 presidential election. (Goldwater took 95 percent of the vote in a mock election at Natchez High School.) The Voting Rights Act of 1965, which banned literacy tests in federal elections, was considered equally "obnoxious." It threatened to inundate the polls with "illiterates and other unqualified persons who are not competent to vote intelligently."[46]

There was no question among many whites that the federal government had woven centralized power and civil rights into a conspiracy against local autonomy and white supremacy. Whites were convinced that the "Civil Wrongs" legislation granted blacks not only equal rights but special rights that "seriously impair[ed]" the liberties of others. The "government has gone overboard," as one Natchezian put it. Whites believed that the federal government had forged a paternalistic relationship with blacks that supplanted that between white "superior" and black "inferior," completing a process that had begun sixteen years earlier with Truman's 1948 civil rights platform. Whites took the view that liberals in Washington had created a central authority that embodied tyrannous forces from above, and that civil rights legislation began a "destructive leveling process" that could spark a revolution from below. As one white election official in Natchez said, "We're caught between the devil and the deep blue sea on this one."[47]

White supremacy meant more than political and economic dominance. Equally important, if not more so, was cultural supremacy, which imposed upon society so-called white values of honesty, intelligence, diligence, goodwill, morality, and citizenship. Whites concluded that their culture provided the structural framework for these values, many of which they believed were absent from black culture, and that the federal government was trying to create equality where equality did not exist. Doubting the capacity of black culture, whites took the posture that in the century since the end of slavery, blacks had failed to rise to the heights of white culture. Proof was there in the persistence of character-istics originally exhibited in slave life: corruptibility, licentiousness, irre-sponsibleness, vengefulness, thievery, and general ineptness. Federal leg-islation threatened to open society to the corrupted ways of black life and effect an unnatural leveling of the races, with blacks elevated upon artificial props while whites fell back under the heavy weight of new and reinterpreted public policy. "Some whites believed that blacks would pull society down," said a former city alderman.[48]

This view was shared by all classes of whites; it permeated the think-ing found in the Klan, Citizens' Council, garden clubs, civic groups, churches, law-enforcement agencies, local governments, and among Prot-estants, Catholics, Jews—all levels and all enclaves of white society. The old fear of biological "mongrelization" at the hands of the lecherous "black buck" had not disappeared. But the fear of cultural mongreliza-tion was equally potent. A group of Natchez aristocrats told one visitor: "We can't have our civilization *overwhelmed*!"[49]

Maintaining white cultural dominance required keeping blacks polit-ically powerless. Excluding their names from the voter rolls was one of the best ways to ensure that political impotence. The COFO workers es-timated that 90 percent of the registered voters in Natchez were white, and the workers gathered testimony after testimony of incidents of vot-ing discrimination. Aided by the *Democrat,* which published the names and addresses of those who applied to register, many employers and landlords threatened to discharge blacks if they tried to vote. Mississippi was the first southern state to implement the poll tax and literacy test re-quirements and one of the last to eliminate them. In Adams County, whites generally had no trouble with the test, but blacks had to interpret a section of the state constitution, write a paragraph on the "duties and obligations of citizenship," and wait two weeks or more before learn-ing—in most cases—that they had failed. For decades, the registrars in Adams County and Natchez disappointed even college-educated blacks.

In later years, COFO workers uncovered evidence of an unwritten policy of qualifying only 10 percent of those blacks who tried to register. According to Shead Baldwin, when he took the test sometime in the 1950s at the same time as his wife, who passed while he failed, the registrar in an uncustomary gesture took him aside and explained: "Got a lot of women [working] in here that are members of the Citizens' Council. I can't register two out of the same family. Now, I could do it but I'd have to figure out how I am going to drink up all that water down at the Mississippi River."[50]

Baldwin's contemporary James C. Anderson recalled the frustration blacks typically felt when trying to register.

> They gave me the Constitution to interpret it, and I couldn't interpret it. I had a friend going to Ole Miss, and I was going to get him to interpret the Constitution for me. So he did it the best he could, and I carried it down there, and I showed it to them, and they said, "You'll have to try it again." I finally gave up. They wasn't going to let me pass it. I always felt that I should be a registered voter. I paid tax and what not. You felt like you was a citizen, and you felt like you just had a right to do it. But there wasn't anything you could do about it.[51]

COFO activists hoped to do something about it. COFO's main objective was threefold: instruct disfranchised blacks on the importance and procedures of voting, register them, and challenge violations of the 1964 Civil Rights Act. The Summer Project workers compiled a list of sometimes shocking inequalities that reflected the political powerlessness of Natchez blacks. The median income of black families was less than half that of whites; 75 percent of working black women were employed as domestics or as service workers; public-school expenditures per white students were 65 percent greater than that per black student; and the median number of school years for blacks was 6.4, compared to 9.2 for whites. Under these conditions, COFO activists had to work on more than hope.[52]

White city officials did not cite such statistics when speaking the language of racial harmony and community progress. One of the city's most implacable boosters was Mayor John Nosser. Nosser was a popular mayor in part because of his love for Natchez, but also because he spread his pallet in the segregationist camp. He wanted the best for Natchez, and he believed that community progress was possible in a racially separate society. There was no contradiction in this thinking in his day and among his people: whites tended to believe that progress was only possible with the dominance of their culture; failing that, society would surely go the other way.

A native of Lebanon, Nosser embodied both the cosmopolitan nature of Natchez society and the local caste system's accommodation to ethnic differences. He moved to Natchez in 1939 and opened the area's first supermarket. Before long, he became active in community affairs, and locals respected him as a gentleman and a highly successful businessman. He owned a shopping center (Nosser City), two Jitney Jungle supermarkets, and a sundries store. In 1960, he handed over the bulk of the business operations to his sons so he could run for mayor, a longtime dream; locals said that no one had a mind to be mayor more than John Nosser. His understanding of the black plight reflected at best a naiveté, ill-gotten and informed by the southern white point of view. In a January 1966 statement, for instance, he maintained that when he was elected mayor in 1962, he had been a dedicated proponent of police escorts for black funeral processions. Had other city officials supported this simple consideration, he later contended, the racial problems his administration subsequently faced would have been "averted."[53]

Racial unrest was indeed Nosser's greatest problem. When it struck before the end of his first term, his opponents during his reelection bid questioned his ability to understand the traditions of the white South. The Lebanese native had, in fact, absorbed the white South's ways. He had been a leader in the local states' rights campaign in the 1950s, and he was a devoted white supremacist. "I Am for Segregation," he announced in the bold headline of a newspaper reelection advertisement intended to put to rest any questions about his stand on the race issue.[54]

Nosser was reelected to a second term, but doubts about his leadership persisted in the minds of some people. In his effort to seek some muddled middle ground, Nosser displeased whites who thought he should take a stronger stand against the white zealots terrorizing the city. Others thought he was too soft on the civil rights workers who had recently descended from the North. Right-wing extremists regarded him as an accommodationist for agreeing to talk with black leaders (though he did not listen well) and for employing too many blacks at his supermarkets. They also denounced him for blaming the city's racial problems on maniacal white vigilantes (though he would never identify the Klan by name). For over a month, leaflets circulated the city with a *Chicago Daily News* reprint that credited Nosser with accusing white radicals for turning Natchez into a vortex of terrorism. In mid-September 1964, someone threw stink bombs into his two Jitney Jungle stores, causing several thousand dollars of damage. Mayor Nosser and the board of aldermen offered a five-thousand-dollar reward for information leading to the arrest of those responsible. Ten days later, two dynamite bombs exploded in close sequence.[55]

Both came in the evening. The first exploded in front of Nosser's colonial-revival home, located on a manicured street in the old Jewish suburb. At the Blankenstein house next door, Rodney and Katherine Blankenstein had been enjoying a quiet evening. Katherine had put their three children to sleep and gone to bed. Rodney stayed up to watch a war movie on television. At the precise moment an American bomber released its explosive cargo on television, the house erupted with the force of real dynamite. Glass shattered from all the windows facing the Nosser house. Katherine bolted from bed and safely retrieved the children from beneath blankets of glass shards. Momentarily stunned by what he had seen and felt, Rodney then thought of the Klan, grabbed a gun, and made for the alley behind the house. There, he was met by the headlights of an approaching police patrol car. Nosser's wife, home with her daughter-in-law and grandchildren, had the same agitated thought and stood at the back step next door. The culprits had disappeared by the time police and a bevy of neighbors gathered about the crater in the Nossers' front yard. There were expressions of relief that no one had been hurt, speculations about how the bombers had carried out their task, and unreserved comments about the Klan's ruthlessness. The commotion was suddenly stilled when a second bomb exploded a few blocks away in the yard of Willie Washington, a black contractor, who on occasion did work for Nosser.[56]

For the first time since the violence began a year before, a public chorus of outrage materialized. Whiskey sales and gambling, though already illegal, were suspended indefinitely, and the city doubled the reward money. Governor Paul B. Johnson Jr. pleaded for peace over the radio and sent in officers of the "Cattle Theft Division" of the highway patrol to assist with the bomb investigation. Local civic groups publicly condemned the attacks on the "highly respected and widely known image of this great southern city." The *Democrat* in a page-one editorial also denounced the recent violence, and a letter writer proclaimed, "Our police have become outnumbered, outgunned, and outsmarted by the organized terrorists." The response and outcry was unprecedented, but the beatings and kidnapings of blacks, as well as the church burnings, had failed to move the white community in the same way. As was the policy with most southern newspapers, the *Democrat* refused to devote space to local civil rights activity and the related crimes committed against the black community. Not even the brutal killing of Clifton Walker the previous March made the local newspaper. March was Pilgrimage month.[57]

The work of the "disreputable" and "disgusting" and "anti-American" Freedom Summer workers, as the *Democrat* called them, pushed on through the fall, winter, and spring. Their presence in Natchez encouraged some local black high-school students to inaugurate their own campaign against segregated public facilities. By November 1964, they had successfully desegregated the lunch counter at the S. S. Kress department store. Joined by COFO workers, they then found resistance at Fisk Public Library and the coffee shop of the Eola Hotel, the flagship hotel of the local tourist trade. They expanded their targets to include the local YMCA and the city's Duncan Park, where the only blacks allowed were women minding white people's children.[58]

By year's end, the students had organized into a chapter of the Mississippi Student Union, a COFO creation. Chief Robinson's police arrested and harassed them with regularity, even as the local businesses failed to comply with the 1964 Civil Rights Act. At the city jail, the police manhandled freedom workers and beat at least one. Jailers removed mattresses and blankets from the bunks, leaving only bare steel springs; and they turned off the heat and opened the cell windows to let in the cold air. Following months of picketing and boycotting, the students' first victory of the new year came at the Clarke movie theater. It had been a favorite target with its separate ticket windows for blacks and whites, segregated seating, and a female employee who assured worried telephone callers that the "ignorant niggers" would not be allowed admission. Klansmen dressed in robes and sometimes in street clothes (sometimes in police uniforms) made appearances at many of the demonstrations but failed to leave a daunting impression on the young activists, who by spring had succeeded in desegregating most public places. Some proved impenetrable though. The municipal swimming pool at Duncan Park was closed indefinitely for "repairs," and the directors of the YMCA chose to shut down the facility rather than permit black and white children to play together.[59]

That March, the civil rights activists shifted their energies to white Natchez's most sacred institution next to its churches: the Pilgrimage. During Pilgrimage month, freedom workers were denied access to home tours on grounds that they were "agitators." A white freedom worker who tried to buy tickets to the Confederate Pageant was turned away for not being "a legitimate tourist," and six demonstrators who tried to picket the pageant were quickly arrested.[60]

The integration attempts had been expected. The passage of the Civil Rights Act had heightened concerns among the members of the Pilgrimage board of directors. They called in a team of five attorneys for a special meeting. The Pilgrimage Garden Club's restaurant, guest rooms, and the Confederate Pageant were subject to the new law, the lawyers advised them, but the tours of private homes were exempt. Some members suggested that advertising specify that the Pilgrimage was a private entity and that under regional "customs and traditions people of Negroid blood are not welcome." This restriction would violate the law, the attorneys said. At one meeting, a board member asked whether the election of archconservative Barry Goldwater in November would ease enforcement of the law. Ultimately, the members agreed to "stand together not to accept Negroes"; Katherine Miller herself favored keeping "COFO people" out. Letters sent to travel agents requested that they book only white tour groups, and "trained men" who could "meet any emergency" stood post at the gates of the houses.[61]

The civil rights activists were never able to penetrate these defenses before Pilgrimage officials finally decided in 1967 to open the home tours to blacks. By this time, Natchez blacks recognized history as an instrument of social power. In the decades that followed, history would become disputed territory between the races as blacks attempted to recapture their past. Meanwhile, black performers, encouraged by the civil rights activists and offended by the garden clubs' recalcitrance on the integration question, pulled out of the Pilgrimage permanently and walked away from the demeaning roles of servant and slave singer.[62]

COFO and the local students continued their demonstrations into the summer of 1965. Following the August enactment of the Voting Rights Act, SNCC and the local NAACP intensified their registration efforts in Natchez. Black funeral-home operator George F. West Sr., accused by COFO of being an Uncle Tom, set up voting booths in his flower shop for recently franchised blacks to practice their newly exercised right. Black registration numbers pushed higher despite Mississippi and Adams County retaining a poll tax until the federal courts ordered its abrogation in April 1966. In a similar act of resistance to black franchisement, county voters turned down a state amendment abolishing literacy tests. In a hopeful attempt to challenge the November election of regular Democrats and as evidence in support of the need for protective legislation, lawyers representing the Freedom Democratic Party collected depositions in the winter of 1965 from local blacks who described a "general pattern of harassment." Once federal law was behind them, blacks pursued the ballot, raising their percentage of eligible voters in Adams County from 6.7 to 59.8 by 1967. Whites reacted in kind, elevating their percentage to 91.5 from 69.9. A *Democrat* editorial in August 1965 warned its white audience, "From here on out, for those really qualified, voting is a stern duty."[63]

As before, some Natchez whites thought their duty went beyond voting, and they chose less civil responses to the mounting wave of black civil rights. Bloodshed lay in that abstract beyond, predicted a Natchez man in the summer of 1964, the high point of civil rights activity in Mississippi. Sitting in a white coffee shop in Hattiesburg, he told other patrons that "Natchez is ready. . . . And the people there aren't going to put up with one single bit of outside interference . . . they're not going to have one single thing shoved down their throats. And they won't!" He explained that most of Natchezians, including himself, were not willing to resort to violence to protect their traditions. "But all you need is a handful of men, so what does it matter." In fact, a handful had "organized like a combat infantry company," he said. "They've got all kinds of rifles, automatic weapons, grenades, sniperscopes and the rest." He added, "They've got enough scrap iron ready to sink a dozen bodies in the Mississippi." The man from Natchez did not agree with these tactics, but as a white southerner, he said he understood the anger behind them. His observations were, so to speak, deadly accurate. In August, a retail store reported a run on weapons and ammunition. Two months later, the FBI seized a small arsenal—which included high-powered rifles, hand-guns, hunting knives, and a shotgun—at the home of Jack Seale, King Kleagle of the Original Knights of the Ku Klux Klan.[64]

Later that year, a handful of Klansmen, impatient with the timidity of the Original Knights and other groups operating in Louisiana and Mississippi, formed the so-called Silver Dollar Group. Members of the group identified themselves by revealing a silver dollar minted in the year of their birth. The rogue Klansmen showed a fondness for dynamite, per-fecting the technique of using the electrical system to detonate an auto-mobile. On one occasion, according to author Don Whitehead, they practiced their craft during a picnic on a Louisiana farm, blowing up tree stumps while their wives fried catfish. More than likely, these were the parties responsible for the Nosser bombing, which some said, and others worried, was only a warm-up for more terror to come.[65]

Inextricably tied to the violence was the racial division of labor. One SNCC report described Armstrong, where some four hundred blacks were employed, as "one of the keys in this system of terror here." From George Metcalfe, Wharlest Jackson, and others, the COFO people learned about the racial discrimination and the Klan presence at Natchez's man-ufacturing plants and the union locals—already manifested in violence perpetrated against Armstrong and IP employees after hours. During the workday, Klan literature constantly circulated the plants. One pamphlet claimed that the NAACP and the AFL-CIO through "the use of the Negro have become the greatest enemies [of] our country." Three weeks after President Johnson signed the Voting Rights Act, a bomb of the Silver Dollar Group's stamp exploded at Armstrong, launching Natchez into a belated era of collective black activism that exposed the lie of the harmonious society and forever changed local race relations.[66]

CHAPTER SIX

CIVIL RIGHTS AND UNCIVIL RESPONSES

"You just missed him," the woman said evenly as a pickup pulled away from her yard and down the dirt road fronting it, plumes of dust trailing behind. "He's gone to Texas to bring back a truck." The man she talked about was her husband, sixty-seven years old and thirty-two years her senior. On her left hip, she cradled their twenty-one-month-old daughter. There was a guarded politeness to her manner as she stood before two strangers wanting to pry into her husband's past. She was clearly capable of handling this intrusion. Parked behind her along the front yard was a logging truck with a full load of loblolly pine. Her name was painted on the door. The rig was hers, and she clarified as much.

In the other direction across the yard, spare in grass and shade, were the exiled remains of another pickup, now a hulk of rusting metal and glass resting on cement blocks. It faced the side of a two-tone, otherwise nondescript, single-wide mobile home. There were many homes like it in the area. Just across the dirt road in front of the single-wide, railroad tracks bore an Amtrak train between New Orleans and Jackson, Mississippi, several times a day. "He'll be back tomorrow afternoon," she offered. "He doesn't remember too much that long ago. His memory's getting kinda bad."

Coming back the next day would mean returning to a no-traffic-light, backwater community, described by blacks an hour's drive west in Natchez as a mean, uninviting place. This was rugged timber country, a land whose people, mostly white, exhibited a kinship of values in their born-again Christian devotion, flag-waving patriotism, and their racial orthodoxy.

The man retrieving the truck from Texas was an alleged member three decades earlier of the most militant of the three Klan groups operating in Mississippi in the 1960s. He and two other men had been arrested on the charge of killing a local black man. As was true to those days, the white man was never convicted. People who remembered him said he had always been a little crazy, that he had even been committed to an institution once. Some people said that trying to interview him was also crazy.

The next afternoon, he obligingly stepped through the open front door of his trailer, lit a cigarette, and stood and talked for the next two-and-a-half hours. Perhaps six feet tall, he still bore a full head of shortly cropped graying hair. Though not a large-framed man, he apparently stood sturdy and solid in his younger days. Shirtless beneath his overalls, he wore jacketlike on top an open denim shirt with cut-off sleeves. Pale blue eyes peered from the depths of his leathery face, empty and distant even when he was fully engaged in conversation.

When he responded to a question about the murder, his voice grew solemn, but his eyes never changed. He denied killing anyone, claiming he had been set up by either the FBI or the Klan. A jury of "three niggers, eight whites, and a Jew," he said, declared his innocence.

While also denying any affiliation with the Klan, he said, "I know more about the nigger than the nigger knows himself because I have studied him." He talked about the *Brown* decision, the Little Rock incident, and the Medgar Evers murder. He also knew the year of the founding of the NAACP, 1909. When asked what he as a working-class man thought of the wealthy families in Natchez, he responded with a description offered to him by an acquaintance: "The Jews owned it, the Catholics ran it, and the niggers enjoyed it."

Before the interview ended, his son, an oil rig worker who spent every other month of his job in Nigeria, walked over from the trailer next door. He had only a high-school education, his father said, but he was in charge of a crew of college-educated "African niggers." The father then told the story of how a few weeks earlier his son witnessed one of the crewmen killed in a gruesome accident on the rig. It sickened his son, the father laughed. "He couldn't take it when that nigger's brain rolled out of his head."

GEORGE Metcalfe knew all the white-supremacist groups in Natchez: the Citizens' Council, the Americans for the Preservation of the White Race, the Adams County Committee for Constitutional Government, the Adams County Committee for Religious Integrity, and the Ku Klux Klan. As president of the local chapter of the NAACP, he had had dealings with each in some form or other. If his employer, Armstrong Tire and Rubber, had been locally rather than corporately owned, the Citizens' Council, in its silent and secret manner, probably would have arranged to have the twenty-year tire plant employee fired. Yet, a groundless dismissal might have ultimately unfixed the terrible fate that awaited Metcalfe on August 27, 1965, when the Klan loomed as his most immediate and malicious antagonist. There had already been beatings, church burnings, and at least one killing. Some said that these were cowardly acts of the Klan. But they had their intended effect. Neither Metcalfe's NAACP chapter nor any other civil rights group had been able to coax black Natchez into mass protest.

That pleased the Klan and others, but did not give them reason to rest. By its very existence, the NAACP gave immediate urgency to the segregationist cause, and Metcalfe knew that as chapter president he sat in the crosshairs of the Klan. Threatening phone calls had become part of life's routine, as had the gunshots fired at Metcalfe's Saint Catherine Street house and the threats vocalized by local law-enforcement authorities. Nine days before that fateful August day when the Klan hoped to send Metcalfe to his maker, he had delivered a petition to the school board requesting the desegregation of the public schools. To some, the petition was the crucible of white resolve. The local newspapers obligingly printed the petitioners' names and described Metcalfe as the man who demanded immediate change in the way things had always been done. That morning of the 27th while Metcalfe was working the graveyard shift at the tire plant, someone discreetly wired dynamite to the electrical system of his car.[1]

To racists who believed in violence, the bomb was Metcalfe's due. He acted as his own man in ways that white-controlled society forbade a black man to do. If he had been white, he might have been regarded as a

180

good American who challenged a democratic society to live up to its principles. Since 1954, he had participated in the political process as a registered voter. He was also a hardworking man who, besides his job at the tire plant, sold burial insurance and earned extra income from rental property he owned. He loved baseball, loved to talk about it, especially the Negro Leagues, with friends and acquaintances at the barbershop or on someone's front porch. A tall, robust man with sleek, wavy black hair, he always dressed nattily. Locals knew him to favor a straw hat, two-tone shoes, and a white shirt and tie. Joe Frazier recalled, "He was a man that a lot of kids liked to emulate." This was the rub with white society, for Metcalfe exercised his constitutional rights in defiance of a racial system that thwarted those rights.[2]

Metcalfe and a few other black workers had long been testing the Klan's patience. Before submitting the school-board petition, Metcalfe and the others had successfully pressured Armstrong to put an end to the Jim Crow conditions at the plant and to begin awarding promotions according to seniority and qualifications regardless of race. The Natchez activists were as much interested in improving economic opportunities as they were in ending segregation; the former could not happen without the latter. They took their struggle to the larger community, spearheading voter registration drives and a boycott against stores, including the mayor's, retaining discriminatory hiring practices. They were doing so a full year after passage of the Civil Rights Act. The white power structure had made only token gestures toward compliance with the federal law, while the Klan stood as implacable sentinels against it.

If Metcalfe had known about the explosive strapped to his car, he undoubtedly would have believed it to be the work of that malevolent fraternity. For each step he took toward his car after punching the time clock, he could have counted a worker at International Paper Company, at Johns-Manville, and at Armstrong who belonged to the Klan. Behind the want-to-believe world of white-columned serenity, four Klan groups operated without hindrance from local authorities. A House Committee on Un-American Activities report released the next year included a list of fifty-five suspected Klan members at International Paper Company alone. Also identified as a Klansman was Adams County sheriff Odell Anders. Handbills announcing Klan rallies and affirming the group's local presence were routinely sprinkled about the paper mill and the tire plant.

Some workers at Armstrong left their white robes and hoods lying in their cars and pickups, where all could see. Whether brazen or careless, these acts revealed the Klan's open license for intimidation and terror.[3]

Armstrong management steadfastly denied the existence of Klan activity at the tire plant. But Metcalfe knew better as he walked across the plant compound past the unoccupied automobiles of his coworkers. He had been requested to work overtime that morning, and he was leaving at noon in the middle of the day shift. He was alone, and the parking lot was quiet as he approached his car, parked on an adjacent street. He opened the door of the nine-year-old Chevrolet Belair, climbed in, positioned himself behind the steering wheel, and turned the key. In an instant, Metcalfe's world flashed white before it went dark.[4]

The detonation thundered across town. A mile or more away, the walls of the NAACP headquarters quaked, like the skin of a bass speaker, with an unhalting, earthy rumble. Civil rights workers at the headquarters thought that "all of Natchez [had] been blown apart." They had felt this kind of percussion before; it had the feel of terrorism and hatred. A scream of sirens then broke the quiet that tends to follow isolated explosions. When rescuers reached Metcalfe, they pulled him from the mangled shell of the automobile. His shoes were left behind, smoldering on the floorboard. The rescuers rushed him to Natchez's Jefferson Davis Memorial Hospital, where after surgery he was admitted to the hospital's segregated black ward. The fifty-three-year-old Natchez NAACP president somehow cheated death, surviving the blast with a broken leg and arm and a permanently damaged eye, obviously not what the bomber or bombers had expected.[5]

Rumors about the identity of the bombers circulated among the townspeople. The Klan, which caught blame for any racial violence, was indeed the likely source of the bombing, but justice would require identifying which members of which group were involved. The FBI conducted an investigation and apparently identified those individuals responsible but could drum up nothing more sound than hearsay evidence. In a front-page editorial, the *Democrat* condemned the bombing, blaming it on "minority elements—hoodlums, renegades and criminals." This vague conclusion constituted the best offered by city and law-enforcement officials, who never brought the bombers to justice.[6]

The Metcalfe incident was just another in a series of terrorist acts intended to discourage organized protest. But it backfired, so to speak, and ignited the black community. Before the incident, the NAACP, COFO, and a handful of local students had led virtually a solitary crusade in Natchez. Civil rights workers found local blacks forthcoming about individual experiences with discrimination but unwilling to take part in the demonstrations. The NAACP's business boycott had failed to take hold; on the whole, black Natchez moved in cautious steps rather than aggressive strides and continued to buy the white man's goods. But the bomb that shook the earth below Metcalfe's Chevrolet shook the black community out of its dormancy. "Everybody was stirred up then," said Baldwin, who accurately estimated that local membership in the NAACP increased tenfold almost overnight to approximately thirteen hundred. Robert Coles observed of black Natchez at the time, "A thousand psychological and sociological truths [were] shattered, turned into splinters by the fact that violence can sometimes generate a new relationship between victim and oppressor."[7]

Metcalfe's forced departure (though temporary) from the scene left a void in the leadership needed to generate that new relationship and to manage the mushrooming energy in the black community. NAACP vice-president Archie Jones initially stepped in to serve as acting president, but then deferred authority when Mississippi field secretary Charles Evers arrived in Natchez the night after the bombing.

A native of Decatur, Mississippi, the forty-three-year-old Evers was the older brother of slain civil rights leader Medgar Evers. Compared to his brother, Charles was something of an enigma. He had been a numbers runner in Chicago before returning to Mississippi in 1963 to claim, somewhat presumptuously, inheritance of his late brother's position as field secretary. As Mississippi activists and the NAACP national office quickly came to learn, Evers was nobody's man except his own, as he liked to say. He was wont to carry out tasks and pursue goals in his own way, sometimes seemingly in spite of the ideas of others. From the beginning, his authoritative manner caused a rift in the already rocky relationship between the NAACP and COFO. The national office seemed less bothered by the rift he exacerbated than by his aloofness toward his superiors. In memos and in hallways and offices in New York, including the office of Executive Director Roy Wilkins, he was assailed as an undisciplined maverick. The national office had set the machinery in motion to fire Evers when the Metcalfe bombing saved his job.[8]

Natchez blacks embraced Evers. He had helped revive the local NAACP in 1965, and the people of Natchez recognized the need for his style. He was a child of Mississippi Jim Crow and an adult of the big-city hustle, wise to the ways of the rural South and the urban North, the possessor of calculating street smarts developed in both environments. He was the natural and logical leader of the Natchez campaign's newly invigorated constituency.[9]

His was clearly the dominant voice at a mass meeting called in response to the bombing. He tried at first to channel the evident rage of the gathered citizens into productive energy. But the man who had lost a brother to the struggle surrendered to the collective anger, his mind to his emotion, and in the end he told his listeners to do whatever was necessary to keep their own brothers and sisters safe from the white menace. Hundreds of normally peaceable black citizens ranged through the city, many of them armed and all of them ready for action. White Natchez had never seen anything like it before. One visiting journalist observed that "with the exception of military posts and hunting resorts, this city probably has been more heavily armed, man for man, than almost any city in the country during recent weeks." Natchez was seething, but it experienced nothing more violent than rock throwing, the worst of which took out the window of a patrol car.[10]

The next day, the NAACP presented a list of demands to the mayor and board of aldermen. Still trying to recover from the shock of the previous two days, city officials were caught off guard. The NAACP leaders prefaced their written demands with a verbal one requesting that the mayor and aldermen address the presenters, Evers and Baldwin, by proper courtesy titles rather than as "boy." Their list included the same demand for all black city employees and blacks who conducted business with the city. The NAACP negotiators requested that six black police officers be hired and given full arrest authority, meaning outside the black community; that all public facilities be desegregated; that city employees be hired on the basis of merit; that blacks be appointed to public boards; that equal protection be provided for blacks under local law and law enforcement; that a $2.5-million bond for improvements in poor neighborhoods be scheduled for public vote; that local merchants hire black cashiers and sales people; and that the Klan be officially denounced. If their demands were not met, the negotiators warned, the boycott launched in July would continue and a united black community would march on city hall.[11]

The answer from the mayor and aldermen to the list of requests was, as Baldwin phrased it, "650 National Guardsmen." City officials rejected the entire list, saying they refused to make concessions "under duress or intimidation." Before announcing their decision, they asked the governor to activate the National Guard, citing the city's "imminent danger." It was the first time since James Meredith enrolled at the University of Mississippi in 1962 that the Mississippi National Guard had been dispatched to keep peace in a local community. At the same time, the board of aldermen convened a special meeting to adopt an ordinance imposing a 10 P.M. to 5 A.M. curfew and to suspend the sale of whiskey. The presence of the guard thwarted a march, but the day after the soldiers' arrival, Evers reiterated the call for a full-scale boycott.[12]

Evers set in motion the local movement's most effective strategy, and each time he defended the boycott, its deepening impact was reaffirmed. When whites complained that boycotts unfairly singled out innocent business owners, Evers pointed out that blacks had learned the boycott from its originators, whites; ever since Lincoln freed the slaves, whites had been boycotting skilled black labor. "Natchez deserved a boycott," he said, "as much as any town that ever was." The *Democrat* derided Evers's leadership, saying the boycott never materialized. But local merchants could not ignore their shrinking sales and profits. Boycott organizers formed car pools to transport black shoppers out of Natchez, reminded local black shoppers to trade elsewhere, read at mass meetings the names of those who refused to cooperate, and brought school supplies in from out of town, leaving local merchants overstocked. Nosser believed that his own businesses had been unfairly singled out, and in a September 10 newspaper advertisement asking for an end to the boycott, he announced that he had laid off 62 of 147 employees. The boycott leaders, he said, "mislead and beguile their race for their selfish reasons." Other merchants reported sales declines as much as 50 percent.[13]

Within two weeks, Governor Johnson withdrew the guardsmen, leaving behind a complement of highway patrolmen to enforce the continued curfew. Almost immediately, another black church burned. On September 30, the city obtained an injunction against demonstrations and marches, aimed at both the NAACP and the Klan. Blacks ignored the court order. Over the next several days, hundreds of marchers led by Evers and the local NAACP poured into downtown streets around city hall. More than five hundred demonstrators were arrested, forcing the board of aldermen to convert the city auditorium—the locus of the Confederate Pageant—into a temporary detention center. To relieve the swelling local jail facilities, more than half were taken to the state prison farm at Parchman, where they were subjected to the same brutal treatment COFO activists encountered the previous winter in the Natchez jail.[14]

Relief soon came for the demonstrators in Natchez. On October 6, U.S. district court judge Harold Cox, "of all people," said an NAACP official, upheld an NAACP petition to lift the injunction against peaceful marches. Reared in Sunflower County and in the native sensibilities of white superiority, Cox distinguished his career on the district court by ultimately having three-fourths of his civil rights cases overturned. That night after Cox's ruling, some twelve hundred supporters of the movement in the largest march to date quietly filed through downtown streets in orderly fashion to the courthouse. In an apparent attempt to intimidate the marchers, Grand Dragon E. L. McDaniel positioned his Klansmen, wearing paramilitary clothing and flashing walkie-talkies and heavy "nigger-knocker" flashlights, on street corners. McDaniel's chief deputy, Lane C. Murray, a 1958 graduate of Natchez High School and former president of the student body, prowled the streets in a sound truck, broadcasting a favorite Klan song: "Move Them Niggers North." On subsequent nights, McDaniel led his robed followers in countermarches, and with Imperial Wizard Robert Shelton in attendance, they staged nighttime rallies in city parks and burned crosses. The marches and rallies and countermarches and counterrallies continued into December. White Natchezians believed extremists on both sides had besieged their city. Many complained that Evers had imposed the boycott for his own gain after purchasing a small Natchez grocery, and they encouraged the state leadership to pressure the national NAACP to oust the controversial field secretary.[15]

* * *

Complaints about Evers surfaced from the ranks and leadership of the civil rights movement, as well. After the board of aldermen rejected the NAACP petition, Evers invited the Delta Ministry, a group of activist clergymen with the National Council of Churches, to Natchez. He also telegraphed Martin Luther King, asking him to lend his support and prestige with a speech. Andrew Young came in King's stead, and a team of five Southern Christian Leadership Conference organizers followed. They saw in Natchez the possibility for securing federal legislation outlawing violence against civil rights activists. Four civil rights groups were now crowding Natchez. With the exception of the Delta Ministry, each had a reputation for an unwillingness to submit to the leadership of another. It was inevitable that a power struggle developed between them. On their view of Evers, however, three of the groups stood on common ground: he was a reckless, power-hungry opportunist. By late October, the SCLC had stomached enough of him and pulled out of Natchez.[16]

Some female activists were critical of Evers, too, but more so of male civil rights leaders in general. From the beginning, before the Metcalfe bombing, local women had assumed a central role in the Natchez movement. Black women throughout the South were among the most eager to organize, march, picket, and challenge a surly white voting registrar, in part because they were generally the least vulnerable to white reprisal (though sometimes that invulnerability is overstated). The organizing and activist fervor of women had a long history traceable to roots in civic organizations, church work, and the family. Many women, perhaps the majority, were mothers, and many were single parents, summoned to political action by concerns of family and their children's future. They sought better jobs and voting rights in the hope of alleviating the structural barriers black families faced in caste society.[17]

Natchez women had been among the original members of the local NAACP. They revived it in 1952 after Audley Mackel's rechartered 1940 chapter foundered, and two women served terms as president that year and the next. During the 1960s campaign, men were the strategists and negotiators, but the women through their numbers and infectious determination gave the movement its backbone. Mamie Mazique provided housing for visiting activists, and on more than one occasion, she hid Charles Evers from danger; Mary Toles moderated the mass meetings; and

Jessie Bernard served as secretary of the NAACP and assisted Charles Evers as a lieutenant would a general. There were complaints that male leaders were self-serving and that they subordinated the ideas and direct-action initiatives of women, bogging down the local effort with meetings and negotiations while jealously guarding the leadership. Yet, for the good of the cause, the female activists in Natchez generally put the struggle above concerns about male chauvinism, though not always without complaint.[18]

The deepest conflict in the local movement developed between Evers and the COFO workers, now identifying themselves as members of the Freedom Democratic Party (FDP), black and white Mississippians who challenged the all-white delegation of the state's regular Democrats. Borrowing from the language and tactics of white segregationists, Evers referred to the FDP workers as "outside agitators." He excluded them from some of the mass meetings and on at least one occasion publicly called them communists. They were "a little too radical for us," said Shead Baldwin, "almost as bad as the Klansmen, in our estimation." Echoing complaints sounded in campaigns in other cities, the FDP workers criticized the NAACP, with its relatively older leadership, for being too timid. Rumors had Evers mishandling campaign contributions and maintaining a secret relationship with some of the white leaders, and his dictatorial ways were legendary. Part of the enmity toward Evers may have stemmed from leadership envy. Evers was the clear favorite of the national media and the popular son of black Mississippi. He worked closely and well with local black leaders, generally sharing power and credit. Most of all, he had been successful where the FDP had not: he had galvanized the black community. Even his bosses in New York were beginning to change their "evaluation" of their self-willed field secretary.[19]

Under Evers's leadership, the boycott continued to take its toll on the local economy. On October 8, a complement of NAACP leaders met with white officials and submitted a less offensive "petition of relief," which actually contained the same requests as before. The mayor, board of aldermen, board of county supervisors, board of education, and Chamber of Commerce reviewed it, which at first seemed promising, before offering nothing more than superfluous concessions along with a request to end the boycott and demonstrations. The various parties continued to forge ahead in the negotiations, and Evers and the others walked away from the meeting with the impression that a favorable agreement had finally been reached. He even relayed his enthusiasm to New York.[20]

In one of many instances of recalcitrance, however, city leaders would not let the NAACP have its victory. The next day, Nosser denied in a press conference that the city had cowered to the ultimatums of the NAACP. Courtesy titles, the unshakable verbal tradition at the center of the daily racial etiquette, posed a major sticking point for white leaders. Nosser told the press that he and the board of aldermen "will never" consent to the NAACP demand "to ask city employees to address anyone as Mr., Mrs., or Miss." Local blacks, he said on another occasion, were simply "being bullied around" and they were "scared to death to express an opinion," which Nosser believed would be in accord with his own. He and other city officials had never tried to hide their contempt for the NAACP negotiators, especially Evers, an outsider who openly endorsed the idea of blacks arming themselves. Ironically, Nosser believed the bullies were the black leaders, not the police or white segregationists like himself who had for generations systematically constricted black aspirations.[21]

A similar attitudinal myopia came from the Mississippi Sovereignty Commission in an unsolicited proposal for solving the city's problems. In a letter to Nosser, commission director Erle Johnston suggested that the city take the offensive and put counterdemands on the black community. Apparently informed by the myth of cultural inferiority, Johnston proposed that the city insist that blacks "take advantage of free health services to control and stamp out" the "high incidence" of venereal disease that was likely found in their community. He believed that black leaders should "guarantee" that the "hundreds of Negro couples" living in common-law arrangements become "better citizens morally" by binding their relationships legally. He also suggested that the leadership be required to take steps to reduce the school dropout rate, which would in turn reduce the rate of juvenile "thievery and other misdemeanors." Finally, he wanted black leaders to "encourage cleaniness [sic] and sanitation in the Negro residential areas."[22]

If Johnston thought that the black community lacked the awareness and incentive to deal with social maladies—real rather than perceived maladies—he was wrong. Activists were frustrated at every turn when blacks tried to convince whites like Johnston and Nosser that it was Jim Crow, not some cultural impediment, that blocked the way to a better quality of life. The most difficult task required of a successful struggle for equality was getting those who hoarded opportunities to not just share them, to not just act and behave differently, but to think in unfamiliar ways, that is to recognize and question culturally programmed modes of logic and reason. But to do this would require the oppressor to take the perception of the oppressed. The organized efforts of blacks would fail to get whites to take a cognitive leap of this magnitude even as their efforts would prevail in other important ways.

There is no evidence that Nosser ever took that leap. Nor did he adopt Johnston's suggestions. In their own way, Natchez officials remained recalcitrant, which increasingly came at the expense of local merchants. By Thanksgiving, it had grown obvious that the boycott had expanded from a small core to the entire black community. As Thomas Reed, a city alderman at the time, remembered it: "Blacks for the first time showed they had economic power." More specifically, they had purchasing power, and they recognized that the white merchant's dependence on their collective patronage was an effective means of persuasion. Many were tired of freely giving back what blacks worked so hard to squeeze out of whites. To maids who cleaned an entire week for a paltry ten dollars and laundry workers who put in sixty hours for twelve dollars, civil rights was as much about low wages and menial jobs as about segregation and disfranchisement, as much about economics as about dignity. The white man, who for so long had taken for granted blacks' collective patronage, could now suffer from their collective protest. Despite constant threats of economic reprisals and mass firings, black Natchez remained united.[23]

Some folks in the white community tried to show that they also could unite and exercise a similar kind of power. Businesses laid off black employees and many housewives joined in support by dismissing their maids. To limit the effectiveness of the boycott, the local chapter of the Americans for the Preservation of the White Race (APWR) organized a "counter-boycott." Established regionwide, the APWR was founded in Natchez after a group of middle-class whites became disillusioned with the Citizens' Council's lack of aggressiveness. In accord with its charter, signed by Governor Ross Barnett in 1963, the APWR sought to "unite the white man" in the cause of racial self-respect and "PRIDE." Its most important task locally came in early November during the NAACP boycott. With newspaper advertisements, fliers, and rallies, it launched a "Buy In Natchez" drive that encouraged whites locally and in nearby Louisiana communities to support Natchez's beleaguered merchants. On Saturdays, APWR car pools transported shoppers from Jackson, a two-hour drive away. Nosser endorsed the campaign. He and the Chamber of Commerce had grown sensitive to the national media's claim that Natchez had become the site of the "first successful Negro boycott" in Mississippi. By December, two dozen businesses had closed their doors.[24]

With Christmas approaching, the NAACP held Natchez and the business community in its clutches. Local civil rights activity received a tacit nod of support from the national level when House Republican Leader Gerald Ford canceled a white-only party luncheon scheduled that November in Natchez. Feeling the pressure of the boycott and apparently rattled by the negative press, city officials and a group of business leaders worked out an agreement with Evers and the NAACP on November 29. Twenty-three merchants, representing only one-fifth of the business community, said they would begin hiring and promoting blacks into salesclerk positions. The city promised to hire four more black police officers in addition to the existing two, to desegregate city-operated public facilities, and to lift segregation barriers in the public schools. On the issue of courtesy, city employees were to be instructed to refrain from using demeaning terms such as "boy," "uncle," "auntie," and "hoss." To the Delta Ministry and the FDP, the agreement lacked suitable concessions and a solid pledge of commitment. But Evers engineered a mass-meeting vote in support of lifting the boycott and demonstrations, and a few days later, Nosser's public announcement of the settlement made the national wire services. With obvious bias, the national NAACP public relations director described the agreement as "far more meaningful than any settlement ever achieved as the result of a direct action program by the Negro community in any other southern city." By February, the city and most of the businesses had demonstrated a good-faith effort to comply with the agreement. Satisfied with those efforts, the NAACP shifted to the selective boycotting of merchants who continued discriminatory practices.[25]

* * *

Natchez blacks had won a major victory, but Klan harassment and Klan rallies in municipal parks never stopped. In the midst of the boycott in late October 1965, Shead Baldwin was arrested in Rolling Fork while driving back to Natchez from a mass meeting in Clarksdale. After posting a $200 cash bail for "driving without a license, improper equipment, improper parking, and disobeying an officer," Baldwin returned to Natchez to learn that the NAACP headquarters had been burglarized. Missing were the branch records, which included meeting minutes and the membership list. A year later, the records were filed with the Mississippi Sovereignty Commission after having somehow landed in the hands of a commission investigator.[26]

The violence persisted as well. On June 10, 1966, three white men in a late-model Chevrolet picked up Ben Chester White, a black plantation caretaker and longtime employee of the family of Adams County supervisor James Carter, on the pretense of needing help finding a lost dog. Sixty-seven years old and semiretired, White had no connection to civil rights activity. Unknown to him, at least two of the men were members of Mississippi's most murderous Klan group, the White Knights. According to later testimony, the four drove to a country store and bought two beers and a Coke for the white men and a "red pop" for the black man. From there they proceeded down an isolated road and stopped the car on a bridge crossing Pretty Creek in the Homocitto National Forest. Two of the men climbed out of the car with guns, then ordered White from the backseat. White looked at the men and asked, "Oh Lord, what have I done to deserve this?" "Nothing," said one of the white men, but you "got to [be] got rid of." White prayed, then slumped back in the car as the same man emptied a full cartridge of eighteen bullets from his rifle. The other man standing outside the car then raised a shotgun and blasted into the lifeless form, opening White's skull and sending brain matter throughout the car. The killers dumped White's remains in a creek and, in an attempt to destroy evidence, set the car on fire.[27]

White's alleged killers were James L. Jones, Claude Fuller, and Ernest Avants. Avants had been implicated in the 1964 beating of Bruce Payne, Fuller had made a an unsuccessful bid for a constable seat a few years earlier, and all three were employees at International Paper. Accounts of the White killing are conflicting. One version of what happened tells of the three white men rustling cattle belonging to James Carter. Worried that White may have seen them, they then killed him to silence a witness.[28] Another version has the three looking for a "nigger to kill," any "nigger," as part of a broader scheme of southern white resistance.[29] Martin Luther King had come to Mississippi that June to resume James Meredith's Memphis-to-Jackson March against Fear after a sniper's rifle shot felled the lone activist. The three Adams County men, calling themselves the Cottonmouth Moccasin Gang, hatched a plot to kill a local black, draw King to Natchez in protest, and then assassinate the civil rights leader. King never came. More reliable evidence indicates that White was a victim of an impulsive race murder, and his only offense was his blackness.[30]

Whatever the reason for White's death, Jones was overcome with remorse and went to the sheriff with a confession.[31] Four days after the murder, he and the other two men were arrested, and all three were arraigned for first-degree murder. For once, the justice system seemed to be working in accord with the Fourteenth Amendment, not as the white South deemed. But when Jones went to trial in September 1967, after having wasted in jail and the hospital for fourteen months, a hung jury assured his release.

Avants was tried in December before a jury that included three blacks. The defendant's legal team was headed by the famed Klan attorney Travis Buckley. No novice in murder trials, Buckley had defended White Knights imperial wizard Sam Bowers in the cases involving the killing of the three civil rights workers in Neshoba County and that of Vernon Dahmer, a Hattiesburg civil rights leader. Buckley outclassed the state prosecutors, who, to at least one juror, appeared indifferent about winning a conviction. On the first vote, the jury rendered a verdict of not guilty. The district attorney never pursued the cases against Avants's two cohorts. The White family later won a million-dollar civil suit against the trio but could never collect on the judgment.[32]

The unbridling of violent forces in Natchez was attributable in large measure to misguided civic leadership. Officials argued that the violence was the work of a few rough-natured "rednecks," who came from beyond the county line in reaction to demonstrations precipitated by meddling outsiders, the real troublemakers. That belief was conveyed to the white community when police arrested only blacks for curfew violations and only civil rights demonstrators for disorderly conduct, not Klan demonstrators or their officious goon squads. By contrast, few arrests and no convictions were made in all the incidents of beatings, bombings, and murders. Chief Robinson made the preposterous claim before a 1965 Civil Rights Commission investigating team that the Klan was not active in Natchez, though he acknowledged that the grand dragon lived in his city and that he personally had attended a rally, which he said "impressed" him. He also said no violence accompanied the campaign to desegregate public facilities; yet his own police beat civil rights workers in his presence. Whether fact or not, it was believed in both black and white neighborhoods that some of Robinson's men wore badges during the day and white hoods at night and that most were Klan sympathizers, including Robinson. Law enforcement officials' old habit of dismissing black testimony and the failure to protect blacks and prosecute their assailants forced the black community to arm itself and seek protection from outside sources.[33]

The denial and dismissals that opened the way for violence came in equal volume from the mayor's office. Nosser regarded mass demonstrations as incendiary demands on a harmonious society. He was right when he told the Civil Rights Commission that the northern students of SNCC and the black protesters disturbed local whites and thus jeopardized peace between the races. And he was right when he said whites would not tolerate sudden change in the social order and that one cannot reconstruct the ways of generations of people "overnight." But he was wrong when he said the Civil Rights Act precluded the need for demonstrations because blacks only had to "let the people know" if they were "dissatisfied." He did not understand that blacks were trying to do just that with petitions and marches, and doing so because officials like him would neither enforce the law nor negotiate reasonably with black leaders. Nosser also failed to see the paradox of his logic when he conceded that only six hundred blacks were registered voters; that not a single black was part of his government, which represented a population that was 51.9 percent black; and that a new black school had been added to the segregated school system—ten years after *Brown*. He could not comprehend that for these reasons blacks had been unable to attain a better place in society by earning it, as he believed they should do, as opposed to demanding it. Beyond his comprehension, and that of most whites, was the reality that blacks were in fact demanding the opportunity to *earn* a better place.[34]

The white rank and file of all classes was accountable as well for creating an environment ripe for Klan terrorism. Most of white Natchez was not aggressively antiblack, but the vast majority remained quietly hostile to the idea of racial equality. When the black churches burned, when the beatings escalated, and when the murders recurred, silence dropped over the white community. Only bomb blasts in the heart of the city moved the lethargic white masses, provoking a few rhetorical protests. Perhaps most whites were too "busy with their lives, trying to make a living," as one white recalled, to pay much attention. All whites to some extent were conditioned by the system created by their forebears to accept, if not defend, its integrity and to believe in the contentment of blacks. "When civil rights came along, a lot of us were shocked," said a white Natchez woman. "I was shocked to find black people we knew participating in the marches, because we didn't know they were unhappy. That's strange to say." That was the reality of white people. For so long had their society been telling them that all was fine between the races, fine with "our Negroes," that many whites came to believe their own deception.[35]

In no way, by contrast, was the white populace as a whole unconscious of the threat of change. White people were involved enough to excommunicate anyone among them who publicly condemned the treatment of blacks and the injustices of white supremacy. The Klan and its terrorist ways offended the sensibilities of most whites, but by maintaining their silence and not taking action against the violence, most whites unwittingly condoned it. "All that is needed for evil to succeed," said one Natchezian, paraphrasing the eighteenth-century philosopher Edmund Burke, "is for good people to say nothing." Communal silence amounted to communal consent, for the white community wanted what the Klan was trying to protect: the continued unquestioned operation of caste society. The movement was about more than the struggle for freedom. For blacks, it was about the social recognition of their culture, a culture not unlike that of whites, and the progress and possibilities that would come with that recognition. That was a thought too frightening for whites, who feared for the supremacy of their own culture. The black cultural threat and the entire white culture itself—its traditions and symbols, its program of education, its history—reinforced the appeal of segregation.[36]

A few whites saw through the lie of social harmony and dismissed the threat of cultural degradation. Some of them even spoke out and became involved. Those who did were generally perceived to endanger the racial order of things and were singled out for public humiliation and scorn, if not worse.

A local white housewife named Marge Baroni was one of the few who did not shrink from moral convictions that ran counter to the social norm. She not only decried racial segregation, she immersed herself as deeply into the operations and activities of the movement as any local black. She was identified in hate literature as "one of the white women who patted Charles Evers on the back." She was active enough for the Mississippi Sovereignty Commission to keep a file on her. The costs of her involvement were considerable: the loss of local white respectability and virtually every white friend she had.[37]

There were others, some involved and some not, who paid a similar price. Forrest Johnson, a lawyer by profession, published a liberal weekly, the *Miss-Lou Observer,* that irked extremists. He and his family endured harassing telephone calls and hate mail, and he made good copy for the hate literature routinely dropped on the front lawns in the white neighborhoods. One group calling itself the Mississippi White Caps, after the vigilante group of the late nineteenth and early twentieth centuries, labeled Johnson "one of the most treacherous white men we have ever come across." In one of its handbills, the White Caps accused Johnson of secretly supporting the "northern agitators" and of selling out his country "for the almighty dollar." The same literature identified by name white men it claimed maintained conjugal relationships with or routinely availed themselves of black women, a practice—though older than segregation—that bred a dangerous familiarity between the races. A tire salesman who greeted black customers with a handshake, a flagrant violation of the racial etiquette, was also worthy of the White Caps' derision.[38]

Some who ventured from the mainstream of racial thought and behavior encountered similar derision in the white church. Churches of the South were typically conservative institutions that produced and sanctioned stalwarts of the status quo, not radicals advocating social change.

God was a gradualist, and so his followers also should be. As exemplars of society, the clergy, the deacons, and the faithful were responsible for the transmission of proper moral and ethical values to the wayward and the young. The world outside the protective structure of family and church was sinful and dangerous. Put simply, the church served as a sanctuary for perpetuating a vital and functional moral framework and value system consistent with white culture.

Black culture, in other words, should be kept in its place. As black culture evolved under the conditions of freedom following the Civil War, separate from the careful guidance of whites, the myth of its inadequacy acquired a new saliency. The physical emotionalism and spontaneity exhibited in black worship, for instance, reinforced white perceptions of the inherently humble, childlike, and superstitious black. Black religion's emphasis on the afterlife, and the pomp and ceremony and expense that went into black funerals, struck whites as a defective arrangement in priorities.[39]

At the same time, southern whites had their own peculiar religious habits, ones related to race. Whites believed that racial separation fell within God's earthly plan, and they read the parable of talents in a way that biblical truth was given to the white axiom that God had not created the races with equal ability. Faithful clergymen had been following this distinctly southern white exegesis since slavery and thumping the Bible to the tune of Jim Crow for as long as anyone could remember. Traditionally, the southern white minister's racial attitudes had been a crucible of character and leadership before the congregations. That was never more true than in the 1960s. Exceptions existed, but the lives of those persons were made difficult for their exceptionalism.[40]

One white cleric supporting the movement at his peril was Father William Morrisey, who pastored the black Holy Family Catholic Church. He was also the vice-president of the local NAACP. Morrisey spent several weeks during the fall of 1965, after the Metcalfe bombing, recovering in the hospital from a cardiac condition and missing much of the excitement on the streets. But a year before, he had played an instrumental role in the desegregation of Natchez's all-white Catholic school, and by mid-October of the next, he was out of the hospital and back as a full participant in the movement. Charles Evers called him "the less-known hero of our whole era." White segregationists, Catholics among them, denounced Morrisey for deeds Evers called heroic.

The intractable also turned their scorn on other liberal clergymen. Two were Elton Brown and Summer Walters. Neither was a firebrand or a radical, but in January 1963 they put their names to the "Born of Conviction" statement with twenty-six other Mississippi Methodist ministers. The statement called for congregations to live up to the Methodist Church's book of discipline, which endorsed free-speaking pulpits, open services, and continued support of public schools (as opposed to opening church schools to avert desegregation). Jesus Christ, the document read, "permits no discrimination because of race, color or creed." Aftershocks of the signing were felt throughout the state when opposing Mississippi Methodists pledged their commitment to segregation. The powerful Mississippi Association of Methodist Ministers and Laymen (MAMML) accused the "Born of Conviction" signers of a misguided attempt to use the church as "an instrument of social change." Removing segregation "from our society," a MAMML bulletin warned, "would be like erasing the center stripe from the highway. The consequences would be destructive." To learn how so, one need only look at the Congo, where "wholesale rape, murder, and pillage have been the fruits of the doctrine of racial equalitarianism." For the "Methodist Misfits" who spoke their conscience, there too would be consequences, which their individual congregations provided in the form of private hells on earth.[41]

Elton Brown was pastor of Lovely Lane Methodist Church when he stoked the flames of dissension. His church drew its membership of some three hundred from the surrounding community of Morgantown, a working-class suburb that blacks called "Klux's Den." Brown signed the "Born of Conviction" statement knowing it was in keeping with church law, and he saw nothing radical about his actions. Others did. Within days, Klan leaflets were scattered about the chapel. In his sermon the Sunday after the statement became public, he explained his reasons for giving it his endorsement. He told the congregation that he had "come to feel from studying the Bible and my own convictions and reverence for God that [the races are] equal." He believed that the church had a mission to serve as a "healing agent" when society was in "turmoil," and he had "strong feelings" that the Methodist Church had failed in that mission. The membership listened in tense silence; there were no outbursts of hostility. Only one member raised the subject following the service, a "big ole guy" who worked at Armstrong. He thanked Brown for the sermon and mentioned how exasperated he had become with the overt racism at the tire plant.[42]

The man's words were encouraging. Brown believed he could depend upon a "very good" lay leadership for support even as some of the congregants expressed their concerns with his actions. Local Baptists, who exhibited less equivocation than others on the race question, called on his members, asking how they intended to deal with the wayward pastor Brown. The standoff reached a critical point when Brown pushed Lovely Lane's official board for an open-service policy. In a meeting in which clashing viewpoints led three members to walk out, the board voted to go with Brown's position. Lovely Lane's open-service policy brought no black worshipers, despite the fears of many whites. As victories tend to go, the one at Lovely Lane included a casualty list of some thirty-five disaffected members, who left to organize a new congregation with other dissenting Christians.[43]

Across town at the church of fellow "Born of Conviction" signer Summer Walters, the congregation's unity resulted in the exodus of only one family, the Walterses. Walters had assumed the assistant pastorship at Jefferson Street Methodist Church in June 1961 at the age of twenty-six. A native of Magee, Mississippi, he took a bachelor's degree from Millsaps College in Jackson, Mississippi, a highly respected Methodist-affiliated institution. He met Betty, a Mobile, Alabama, native, in Jackson, and they married and had one child. Immediately upon earning a master's degree at Yale Divinity School, Walters was hired by unanimous vote of board of the Jefferson Street Methodist Church.[44]

Located on one of the original grid streets in the heart of Natchez, Jefferson Street Methodist Church was a historic landmark included on guided tours of the city. With heavyset concrete columns supporting a stately pediment, its architectural harmony with area mansions was immediately evident. Its worshipers came from the city's upper echelon— professionals, business executives, and old-family scions living in some of the mansions. Well liked by the members and highly valued for his work in rebuilding the church's education program, Walters completed his first year with a renewed contract and pay raise. Walters liked and respected his pastor and embraced the membership; yet he believed that the southern entrenchment in tradition, so apparent in the congregation, was self-defeating. As he saw it, the church had a responsibility to set an example of God's true meaning of brotherhood. Concern about talk in the church of organizing private schools prompted Walters to endorse the "Born of Conviction" statement. He had expected the statement to stir controversy, but he had not been ready for the firestorm that erupted.[45]

The young minister quickly learned that white Natchez would make him a victim of his moral convictions. Publicity surrounding the statement brought letters from all parts of Mississippi and the nation. Even though more letters were supportive than condemnatory, many of his own congregants spurned him. A January 9, 1963, letter from a member of the Jefferson Street official board rebuked the associate pastor for being thoughtless in his actions, which "can accomplish no good for our church. . . . Regardless of whether you stay in Natchez or move to 'Timbuktu,' the damage is done." The board member went on to denounce federal activism, school integration, communists, and "psychology, sociology, welfare minded individuals." Telephone threats came in even greater numbers than recriminating letters. Walters feared for the safety of his family, to the point of hesitating to leave his wife and child at home alone at night. The bishop in Jackson sent no comforting words. Instead, he accused Walters and the other "Methodist Misfits" of being troublemakers who had embarrassed him and the church.[46]

Life in the church turned hellish for Walters and his family. He even questioned his choice of a career in the clergy, or at least one in Mississippi. At a February 5 meeting of the official board, he learned that the answer to that question rested with others. In a special vote, the board decided against renewing Walters's contract, which did not expire until June 1963. It gave no reason for his dismissal. Walters scrambled to salvage his career. After arranging a transfer to a church in Indianapolis, Walters joined the ranks of nineteen of the "Born of Conviction" signers who left their Mississippi churches, forced out either by order of the lay leadership or by unbearable hostility from the congregation.[47]

Whites typically expected their church leaders to be like the Reverend Dr. Bondurant in Ellen Douglas's *A Family's Affair*. In her fictitious Homochitto, a prospective Presbyterian deacon confesses his concern about the opposition mounting against a local pastor who spoke his conviction on integration. Bondurant explains that the church's first responsibility is to "protect its own integrity," not that of a minister who strays from his flock. "The Southern church has a mission," the good reverend continues, placing a paternal hand on the shoulder of his communicant. "We must stand for the Word of God and preach Christ Crucified. We must stem the tide of modernism and turn back the Anti-christ."[48]

In Natchez and elsewhere in Mississippi, the Antichrist came in the devilish form of civil rights activism. Shoring up against the rising "tide" of modernism following the passage of the 1964 Civil Rights Act, Natchez's white churches replaced their ushers with bouncers who would eject "undesirable" worshipers, such as blacks and white demonstrators. Whites overreacted. Although a few churches were visited, blacks showed little temptation to abandon their community's central cultural institution, which provided them with spiritual, social, and political fulfillment in a way that white churches could not. Most whites never grasped the extent of the loyalty within the black community to its own institutions. As a result of its rigidness, white southern Protestantism was unable to serve as a unifying bridge between the races and in some cases perpetuated rather than prevented racial violence.[49]

Violence brought the black community together in an unprecedented denunciation of the mythic harmonious society. That was the society embraced by white churches, Mayor Nosser, white business and civic leaders, and the larger white citizenry. Before the Metcalfe bombing, many blacks had also been captives of the myth. Increasing numbers began breaking away from the myth or began expressing its fallacies that others had long known. The bombings and shootings and killings had freed their minds and their voices. Yet even after the demonstrations and the boycott, violence continued at a level of madness, and from the black perspective, the agents of racial terror operated with impunity.

That was a viewpoint that could hardly be disputed after another bomb shook the city on February 27, 1967. Again, it came from the tire plant. Wharlest Jackson, a past treasurer of the Natchez NAACP,[50] worked late, leaving in the middle of the evening shift, about eight. George Metcalfe—still active despite a bad leg and eye—car pooled with Jackson, who normally inspected his truck after every shift for signs of tampering. But Metcalfe was not riding with Jackson that day, and his absence, as well as a pouring rain, apparently tempered Jackson's caution. Forgoing the usual inspection, Jackson pulled his Chevrolet pickup out of the parking lot, steered it toward home, and drove several blocks before a bomb attached to the frame below the driver's seat exploded. Jackson fared worse than had Metcalfe nineteen months earlier. Metal sheeting from the floorboard ripped up and into Jackson's body, thrusting his feet over his head. Death came instantly. Hearing the blast from home not far away, thirteen-year-old Denise Jackson ran toward the explosion and found her father's twisted body lying in the road. The truck was lodged against a power pole. "That's a night I shall never forget," said Shead Baldwin twenty-six years later. "It was a hurting situation."[51]

The next day, nearly every high-ranking official in the county condemned the killing of the thirty-seven-year-old Korean War veteran and father of five. The city and Armstrong together put up a $37,000 reward. But since the reward would be paid only after a conviction, many called it a poor inducement. "[E]verybody knows," the outspoken Father Morrisey was quoted saying, "you can't get a conviction here for a white man killing a Negro." That night, some two thousand blacks marched "through darkened streets" to the tire plant. "You could have easily poured Natchez in the river, the way people came out and was frustrated," said Baldwin. Governor Johnson called the bombing a "heinous and senseless murder." He also said the march on Armstrong was "foolish" and "intimidating to innocent people." He did not say the same about the nearly four years of racial violence that had been visited on Natchez blacks. Officials commenting on the Jackson killing seemed more worried about the image of the state and the Natchez community than about the loss of a human life. In early March, NAACP Executive Director Roy Wilkins led a funeral procession of hundreds to the national cemetery in Natchez, where Jackson was buried.[52]

Jackson's killers were never caught, despite the governor's assurance otherwise. Few in the black community doubted that the bombing had been the work of the Klan and that Jackson had been set up when he was asked to work late, just as Metcalfe had done in 1965. Two days before his death, Jackson had been promoted to a position previously held by a white man; he had been active in local demonstrations, and after the Metcalfe bombing, he carried on the fight against discrimination at Armstrong. "I didn't know his job was so important," his widow was quoted saying, "that somebody had to kill him." Company officials denied the killing had been an inside job. Most of the barriers of segregation at the plant had been removed by 1967, and blacks were included in the seniority system that once privileged whites with the best jobs. Many blacks before Jackson in fact had been promoted to traditionally white jobs without incident. But if Armstrong had abolished the racial divisions of labor, and had done so despite the protests of many whites, Jackson along with Metcalfe had played a role in that change.[53]

Desegregating the manufacturing plants had been a painstaking and protracted effort. At Armstrong, the cafeteria was the first Jim Crow tradition to go. "At first the black was scared to go in there," said Samuel Stewart of the cafeteria when it opened to both races. "Before he'd [Metcalfe] get off, he'd go in there and eat breakfast. And the blacks there, they would follow, follow Metcalfe. So that kind of built the rest of the courage up." Eventually, the cafeteria closed because few whites continued to patronize it. When the "colored" water fountains were removed, proposals were made to install paper-cup dispensers in their place. Some whites brought in their own bottled water taken from backyard wells. Stewart said that in some cases "that water turned yellow, and they would drink it anyway." Many whites were equally apprehensive about integrated restrooms and showers, and some chose to go home dirty with carbon black rather than share shower facilities with their once-segregated coworkers.[54]

Desegregating jobs was one of the most difficult changes for both races to accept. Blacks wanted better paying positions desperately, but assertiveness before whites was not a lesson learned from previous generations. It was difficult to discard the self-image of being a trespasser in the white domain. At International Paper, blacks could be fired for simply sitting in a work truck. So when Albert Harris was appointed the first black to drive one, he was doubtful about his new opportunity. "I was kind of funny [apprehensive]," he said, "because you know at that time, they was laying on the road, catching folks, and beating them to death, and all that kind of stuff. I went on ahead and drove it, but I was scared [at night] coming home, boy." At Johns-Manville, James C. Anderson was the first black promoted to a white job, and like Harris, he was ambivalent about being a pioneer on the integration frontier. Some white coworkers made his new job difficult by sabotaging his work and by withholding team support. But Anderson, who had participated in the marches, said the movement had given him a voice—"I would speak out for my job"—and he learned to "push, fight, and argue" for it.[55]

Change in the factory workplace was clearly a black-worker initiative. Consistent with past policy, the union locals usually offered minimal relief on matters with "racial overtones." Ironically, years before civil rights organizations came to Mississippi, unions recognized the link between political power and worker interests and conducted voter registration drives among the memberships. Those drives rang with language that later followed in the civil rights movement. "Time to Wake Up! 'Freedom-Vote Friday,'" read one union handbill distributed in Natchez in 1954. "You will be treated like a HUMAN BEING at all times." To some white union members, Klan and non-Klan alike, worker rights and civil rights, and the voter initiatives behind each, were animals of a different stripe. The national unions that had originally brought increased wages to Mississippi whites seemed to be turning against their local white members in the 1960s. In 1964, Mississippi AFL-CIO president Claude Ramsey publicly announced his support of a color-blind franchise, linking labor's progress to that of blacks, and he condemned the practices of the Citizens' Council and "other extremist groups." In protest, the United Papermakers and Paperworkers Union local in Natchez withdrew its membership from the Mississippi Labor Council.[56]

If union locals rendered little or no tangible help, they did provide an example. As union men, black workers gained experience and lessons in the power of organization, witnessed their locals file legal suits to seek recourse for unfair treatment, and voted to establish a voice in matters of concern. In essence, the union shop provided a sense of job protection that emboldened potential activists and showed them that ordinary people could effect change. The human strength and the local leadership of the civil rights crusade in fact came, not from black ministers, but from black industrial workers. Black workers/activists established a beachhead at the manufacturing plants, and in response, the Klan turned that prized terrain into a defensive front line. Because the manufacturing plants underscored both economic opportunity and Jim Crow, Metcalfe, Jackson, and the others bridged civil rights with labor rights.[57]

From the beginning, fair employment was a central concern in the Natchez civil rights movement. Following the Metcalfe bombing in 1965 and invigorated by the ongoing protests, thirty black female employees walked off the job at Natchez Steam Laundry. A typical workweek lasted fifty-four hours and brought them a thirty-cent hourly wage. COFO and the NAACP supported the women by organizing a boycott of the laundry and by coordinating meetings with union organizers. One AFL-CIO representative told the women, "Labor and civil rights are brothers. I'm certain they cannot be separate." Unity in this case won the strikers minimum wages.[58]

A similar struggle was waged a year later. George Metcalfe and Shead Baldwin sent a letter to the Natchez school board requesting that the hourly wage of cafeteria workers, who were mostly black, be raised to one dollar an hour. "[W]e cannot survive under the present salary," the employees petitioned in a separate letter to the superintendent of education. After school officials said a raise was impossible, sixty cafeteria workers walked out, and the NAACP prepared for a citywide business boycott. Among the leaders in the strike was Edith Jackson, a cafeteria worker and NAACP member who was quickly becoming a veteran demonstrator. Still haunted by the boycott of a year before, a group of businessmen then met with the school board and urged that it reconsider its position. The employees got their raise, but the cafeterias reduced their staff and failed to rehire all the striking workers.[59]

Goals were not always reached, but the lives of Natchez blacks began to change significantly in the 1960s. The impetus for a new and better life came with the help of outside organizations and institutional pressures, including federal legislation and court decisions. Some organizations, such as labor unions, were less helpful than others, and despite squabbling within and between some of the civil rights groups, Natchez blacks gained the knowledge and experience of open protest, learned they could unite their energy behind a boycott and be effective, and acquired the ballot.

For whites, the changes of the 1960s made it clear that what had been true in the past could no longer be taken for granted. The boycott and the mobilized black community put the lie to black contentment and the rhetoric of racial harmony. Many whites began to admit that segregation had been wrong, that blacks were unfairly treated. But all knew that the control of society no longer rested solely with whites, who felt their grip on society slipping as blacks took control over their own lives. For each slip, there was an incremental decline in the sense of what was familiar and predictable, the marrow of society's sense of security. Whites now had to share power in local affairs with their fellow black citizens, who often called in federal reinforcements. That alignment, that dependence alone seemed like ample evidence that black culture was not fit to rise to a level that would sustain civilized society's values. With the future no longer so predictable, whites proceeded cautiously, no longer so clearly informed by the past, searching for ways to protect white culture while accepting, oftentimes grudgingly, the black hand joining the white hand on the levers of power.

The events in Natchez have been described as "the last major mobilizing campaign of the Mississippi movement." That may have been true for the 1960s and for the SNCC and the FDP, but not for the local people. Their movement continued into the subsequent decades. While victories had been scored on the voting rights and social segregation fronts, the march along the path to equality and freedom continued apace. Lying ahead was the battle over the disputed terrain of public schools.[60]

CHAPTER SEVEN

THE HIDDEN CURRICULUM
School Desegregation

"Right over there. That's Sadie V. Thompson school," said the man pointing across the street, incredulous that the inquirer could be so nearsighted. "The big, brick building." Opened in 1954 as the new black high school, Thompson had been a model for black schools and white schools alike. Nearly forty years after its construction, time had diminished its once noble presence. The grounds around the school were unkept and shaggy, the parking lot had more potholes than asphalt, and the building's once-bright red brick had weathered to a dull pastel.

No longer part of the public-school system, Thompson now served as the headquarters for Adams County Head Start. More than Thompson had changed over the years. A ten-foot chain-link fence cordoned it off from the crime that had recently invaded the surrounding neighborhood, where cautious residents had barred their windows and doors.

Inside, Thompson's vast auditorium was empty and unused, with paint peeling from its walls. Up a flight of stairs, raucous sounds carried through the hallway from a group of thirty or so preschoolers standing in a single-file line outside their classroom. With limited success, the teacher tried to restrain their activity. All the children were black, as were the teachers, except one. In the school's office, a half-dozen women and one man were busy with paperwork, telephones, and the copy machine.

Many of these women were veterans of the local civil rights marches and demonstrations of the 1960s. The director herself had worked alongside Charles Evers, George Metcalfe, and Wharlest Jackson. Her mission, and that of all the Head Start women, had not changed since the 1960s—to enhance opportunities for a better life for their families and the children of generations that followed. The director was emotional when talking about "the movement"—the beatings, killings, and hate. From her office in the hand-me-down school in the rugged neighborhood, she lamented that progress had come only in bits and pieces.

THE dedication ceremony of Sadie V. Thompson High School would later be remembered as a proud moment in Natchez history. Dressed in their finest, important people turned out to attend the January 2, 1954, event. The school they came to behold was more impressive than its neighbor, Natchez College, whose campus it shared. Gleaming with newness and prepossessing in size, the two-story, red-brick structure housed thirty classrooms, fully equipped science laboratories and home economic facilities, and a "spacious auditorium" separate from the cafeteria and gymnasium. Thompson cost three-quarters of a million dollars, more than any other Natchez school to that date. Built to replace Brumfield School, the black high school of 1920s vintage, Thompson was a welcome sight from the perspective of both blacks and whites.[1]

The black community cherished the school. Many adults had never seen the inside of more than a dingy one-room rural schoolhouse. Now they and their children had a public facility that compared favorably to anything whites had, a school that answered their educational aspirations, something even whites might envy and covet. Locals would come to call the new school simply, Sadie V. The abbreviated name had a smart, lyrical sound that reflected a certain communal endearment. "Over to Sadie V.," one might say, or, "I'm for Sadie V." It evoked a sense of community worth, optimism, and even empowerment.[2]

The new school elicited a different kind of pride within the city's white power structure. Chronologically bookended by the construction of two black elementary schools, Sadie V. formed the centerpiece of a campaign to improve black schools in Adams County. That campaign signaled a new direction in the white paternalistic ethos—that of trying to fulfill the equality part of the segregationist doctrine known as separate but equal.[3] Giving confirmation to the notion that the city was moving in the right direction, an article published in *U.S. News and World Report* a month later described Sadie V. as a sign of "steady improvement" in Natchez race relations.[4]

To the woman who lent her name to the new high school and who spoke at the dedication ceremony, racial progress must have seemed more halting than steady. During her last twenty-six years as an educator, Sadie V. Thompson headed Brumfield School, which served all twelve grades. As principal, she held her teachers and students to the same elevated standards she set for herself. She was walking testimony to black cultural values, most specifically attitudes toward education. Blacks rebuffed many white institutions, such as churches, but they very much wanted what whites had when it came to schools: a stimulating environment that provided a decent education. Since 1903, Thompson had made it her life's work to give the black children of Natchez some approximation of that.[5]

She was a private woman who revealed little about herself. A Canadian by birth and educated in the North, she had light skin and straight hair. Though sometimes referred to as Mrs. Thompson, she never married. She lived a short walk from Brumfield in a cheerful two-story Queen Anne–style home, somewhat in contrast to her reserved nature. Except for graying hair, Thompson never seemed to grow past age fifty-five or so. Yet it was hard to imagine her ever being younger. A stout woman, she was a solid, sturdy force that moved only upon its own will. As a disciplinarian, she projected a similar image to the students. "If she said no, she never said yes," recalled Theresa Lewis, a former Thompson student. But the matronly principal was stern because she cared deeply about the children and about preparing them for the coming difficulties of adult life. It was in those later years that former students came to appreciate her most, to recognize how she had deftly worked the white-controlled system for their benefit.[6]

That benefit, however, came at a cost. The gift of white patronage that Thompson delivered to her students required a reciprocation, which usually meant paying deference to the segregationist cause. She always negotiated with the white leadership on its own terms, extracting concessions in ways that would have made the white man feel ever so noble in fulfilling his social obligations to his black supplicants. Challenging the system overtly and directly would not have brought supplies and books for her students and pay raises for her faculty. Like the black professional leaders of her time, she moved with cautious but sure footing in both communities, sustaining that precarious balance between winning trust and esteem from whites and maintaining both among her own people.[7]

Thompson was the universal favorite among both races to be honored as the new school's principal emeritus. As featured speaker at the dedication ceremony, she showed humility and made clear the identity of her benefactors. "During the entire time that I have been in Natchez," she said, "the white citizens have never spoken one unkind word or caused one unkind deed for me or my work. . . . The school board has also been most kind and generous in all my askings." It was a speech that whites in the audience undoubtedly fitted to their idea that interracial community harmony was compatible with segregation. Whites, of course, established the parameters—the allowances and restraints—of social harmony and segregation. The state-of-the-art black high school represented the allowances; the restraints came in the continued tradition of segregation. When the speeches concluded that evening, the audience adjourned for two scheduled open house tours—one for whites, the other for blacks.[8]

Four months after the dedication ceremony, the Supreme Court handed down the *Brown* decision outlawing segregation in public schools. The ruling for implementing the complicated procedure of desegregation came a year later in *Brown* II. The procedures for remedy invited delay tactics and challenges with which any first-year law student, much less a wily practitioner of the legal system, could have a field day. Justice was not automatic. It required individual blacks to bring suit against local school boards, which in most cases were all white, and blacks suing whites was less common in the South than snow on a magnolia blossom. The Supreme brethren ruling in *Brown* II also unintentionally aided southern obstructionists by requiring that Court orders and decrees be carried out with "all deliberate speed." The verbiage was ambiguous, and segregationists took it to mean slow.

The southern states had anticipated a desegregation ruling as early as World War II. Before that, the doctrine of separate but equal had been the best friend of segregationists, the essential legal backbone of their social system. But through a succession of court cases beginning in the 1930s, the NAACP turned the doctrine into the white South's achilles heel. The courts were telling schools and state legislatures—decades after the fact—that they had not been living up to their side of the bargain in separate but equal. In some cases where states had not provided equal opportunity in higher education, the courts compelled white colleges to open enrollment to blacks. Southern officials convinced themselves and their constituents that open enrollment would not happen at the grade-school level; that could be prevented if the states brought black schools up near the level of white schools. In economic language, parity meant that the costs of maintaining separate schools would climb even higher.[9]

That fact was not lost on Mississippi lawmakers. Beginning in 1953, the state, in cooperation with local school districts, launched a massive overhaul of black school systems. In legislation passed in a special session that year, plans were drawn to achieve equity in salaries, school plant facilities, transportation, and academic curriculums. Initially, lawmakers refused to back their plans with appropriations. They instead approved a state constitutional amendment permitting the abolition of public schools in case of federal interference. Going the way of the state electorate, Adams County voters rallied in support of the amendment by a margin of more than three to one. Two years later, after *Brown* eviscerated the separate-but-equal doctrine, the legislature passed an $88-million biennial appropriation for the "equalization" program.[10]

Driving the overhaul initiative was the widespread fear of federally imposed desegregation. The one thing worse than racial mixing itself was racial mixing by federal mandate. State officials hoped that improving black schools would encourage "voluntary segregation"—blacks remaining in their own schools—and deter desegregation demands and lawsuits. If equalization failed to accomplish its essential goals, state and local officials could still exercise their legal power to shut down the public schools. In the midst of all this, the *Natchez Democrat* observed: "Only by improving negro education can we hope to stem the tide of integration."

That viewpoint flowed forth from the speeches at the Sadie V. Thompson dedication ceremony. The last speaker, the president of the white Mississippi State Baptist Convention, said that the new black high school "not only answers the problem of Natchez but of the entire South."[11]

White Natchez indeed followed the regional and state calculations on school equalization. In 1951, the *Natchez Democrat* endorsed a $2-million bond issue to fund the rehabilitation of black schools, even though white taxpayers believed they were underwriting a disproportionate share of the cost of black education already. The newspaper acknowledged that whites would have to bear the financial costs of the bond issue, but admonished that they "should do so without undue groaning, for this is the price of separate schools." Voters approved the bond and others that followed, along with a plan to merge the county and city school systems under one board of supervisors. The merger was designed to save taxpayers money and at the same time allow for the consolidation and improvement of rural black schools. To circumvent local and federal forces of desegregation, Natchez between the years 1953 and 1964 added two new elementary schools, one junior high, and one high school to its roster of black schools.[12]

Natchez was doing more than paying lip service to improving black education. As early as 1955, a state board of education survey conducted before the merger concluded that city fathers indeed had made impressive strides in upgrading black schools, though they were still short of perfect parity with white schools. Not faring as well was the Adams County government. The survey commended the city for the recent construction of Sadie V. Thompson High School, while withholding praise for the county, which had no black high school. The county devoted eight months to the school year for blacks and whites, and the city provided a nine-month term for both. During the 1954–55 school year, Natchez budgeted $134.57 per black student and $176.64 per white student, 31 percent more. The county spent more than three times as much on white education ($340.26 per student) as it did on black ($110.92 per student). Classes in Natchez black schools averaged twenty-nine students compared to twenty-six in white classes.[13] In the county, there were three white schools, with an average of one teacher for every twenty-five students; there were thirty-one schools for blacks, with a 1:34 teacher-student ratio.[14]

A sad physical example of racial inequality was the pathetic and unsafe condition of school buildings for rural blacks. The county owned only three of the black schools in the mid-1950s; blacks and white planters owned the majority. Many were makeshift schoolhouses, little more than wooden shacks settled haphazardly on brick foundation piers and showing the weight and bulge of time. Sheeted in galvanized metal or tar paper, leaky roofs covered drafty walls and floors. Outdoor pit-toilets and well-water cisterns were as commonplace as broken window-panes; all were like insignias designating the building's rank within the local architectural hierarchy, somewhere near the bottom. Some schools lacked lights, chalkboards, or water and depended on handmade furnishings and coal- or wood-burning stoves. Six buses transported black students to these county schools, while twenty buses served an equal number of white students.[15]

Even with the aggressive school-building program of the 1950s, Natchez's black schools never measured up to white schools in terms of plant facilities, equipment, or teacher qualifications. Christened a model public school, Sadie V. Thompson, like the other black schools, used books and desks passed down from white schools. As late as 1965, the school district in Natchez and Adams County was spending twice as much on office, janitorial, classroom, and physical education supplies for the white schools as for the blacks schools. The next year, the state board of health repeatedly cited Brumfield School for poor bathroom and kitchen conditions. If whites thought parity could be achieved despite segregation, many blacks knew otherwise.[16]

Although white officials were sometimes willing to address disparate conditions, their cooperative tenor invariably fell out of harmony when it came to complying with federal court rulings on school desegregation. Whites may have tolerated new schools and teacher pay raises, but when the school board vetoed the Natchez NAACP's 1955 petition to desegregate schools in accordance with *Brown* and the Natchez newspapers published the names of the petitioners, whites made clear how little they would cooperate. All might have been regarded as a routine defense of the system if the threat of integration was not so real, if the power of the federal government was not behind it, and if the hidden goal of blacks was not believed to be racial mixing. As the *Democrat* wrote in 1952, "If they want to mix, it is because they are confusing equality of opportunity with social equality."[17]

Blacks and whites characterized school desegregation differently. Whites related it to federal interference, blacks to a historically disparate education system. Blacks as a rule embraced the American commitment to education. During Reconstruction, black lawmakers were among the chief supporters behind the Mississippi legislative establishment of public schools in 1870. A symbol of freedom, education would relieve the burdens of illiteracy and the drudgery of rural black life, and it would open a path to the fruits of a better existence—if not for oneself, then for one's children. Coming at great personal expense, the benefits of formal education were indeed recognized, if not always accessible.[18]

For the few fortunate, black schools provided an enclave of professional employment for teachers and administrators that contributed to racial autonomy, unity, and strength. Yet esoteric comfort came at the expense of cross-cultural experience. Public education removed black culture from the mainstream of American life, providing a stepping-stone to nowhere outside the enclave or into the larger world, the white world, of privilege and opportunity.[19] The black ceiling of success was despairingly low, and the resources of black schools were such that few students would ever reach even that ceiling's limited height. Walled away in their separate schools, blacks struggled against terrific odds to find meaning in life at the lower strata of a racially divided world. Whites rarely recognized the quiet struggle on the other side of that wall they had constructed to keep the cultures apart, thus theirs protected. Instead, they fixated on the academic inadequacies of black students and teachers and linked those inadequacies as cause, not consequence, of the physical and fiscal conditions of black schools, ignoring their own apathy and indifference as the true causal source.

Whites were the ones who devalued black education. Parity in schools represented to whites a waste of resources because they believed blacks lacked the drive, commitment, and ability needed to reach the academic level of whites. Dismal literacy and school-attendance rates—the effects of which were manifested in nearly every verbal and business interaction between whites and blacks—seemed proof that blacks neither valued education nor deserved better schools. Even those blacks who showed talent could encounter white doubts about the need for anything more than a basic education for blacks. When Ozelle Fisher's mother decided to go to college and become a teacher, the white woman who employed her questioned the decision, pointing out that blacks needed only a high-school education to teach.[20]

Discouraging achievement and denying opportunities perpetuated myths about the black desire and the social need for a decent education. Closely related to these myths was the false proclamation about who paid for public education. White Mississippians, including many from Adams County, contended that blacks did not pay enough taxes to justify greater expenditures on their public education. Vexed by what he saw as a lack of appreciation from the black community for the state's new commitment to black education, one local white summed up the issue in the context of the southern white's ultimate fear: "Response of our colored friends has been disheartening. We hear no acknowledgement of the millions that have been spent for them; we do not hear from some of their leaders that Courts and Schools and Old Age Pensions are not enough—that we must mix the two races into one race and put Civilization itself in peril."[21]

To this man, and to so many other whites, "the Colored People had nothing to be taxed." Ramshackle schoolhouses were the sum of their contributions to public coffers. The irony of this argument was that the relegation of blacks in southern society to menial work reduced their income and their tax contribution. In actuality, as the research of historian Neil McMillen has shown, black Mississippians paid more than their fair share in taxes and even shouldered part of the costs for white schools. The old elitist mantra that poor people do not pay taxes because they do not own property could not have been more wrong. Any landlord worth his/her salt priced the rent to cover expenses, including property taxes. When the tax collector visited the landowner, the landowner in turn visited the renter.[22]

Although fought mostly within the courts and given little attention by COFO activists, school desegregation was central to the civil rights agenda of local blacks. When on August 19, 1965, George Metcalfe presented a new petition to the school board, he accompanied it with the request that the names of the sixteen petitioners not be made public, as had happened a decade before. He wanted "to protect the signers from possible reprisal and harrassment [sic]." But the petition became part of the public domain at the time it was submitted, R. Brent Forman, board chairman, noted in the record. Even if the board had wished to honor Metcalfe's request, it had no power to withold the petition from the press. In its next meeting, the board voted to reject the petition and to hire an attorney to prepare for a desegregation lawsuit launched by the Justice Department. The very next day, the two local newspapers published the names and addresses of the signers, and a few days later, a bomb nearly took Metcalfe's life.[23]

Such efforts to prevent integration kept a dual school system operating in Natchez for more than a decade after the Supreme Court had spoken in *Brown*. In the 1963–64 school year, Mississippi was the only state in which some form of desegregation had not occurred at the grade-school level. The next year, a scant one thousand Mississippi black students, 0.4 percent of their numbers statewide, attended school with whites. None did so in Natchez. Every fall well into the 1960s, the *Democrat* listed the separate registration schedules for the black and white schools.[24]

The tendency to cling to the past was exhibited by the city's leadership. After the national spotlight illuminated Natchez's racial discord following the August 1965 Metcalfe bombing, an investigating committee of the U.S. Commission on Civil Rights called several Natchez citizens to testify before its body. Civil rights activists, Klansmen, and city officials from Natchez joined other Mississippians outlining the civil rights conflict in their state. Dual school systems were a point of issue. When Mayor John Nosser took the commission's hot seat, he seemed to believe as always that he traveled the logical middle road and that all would be right if the others would follow. Unable to grasp the truth that lay beyond his convoluted reality, the mayor created a "very vicious circle," one commissioner said, when he defended continued black disfranchisement on the grounds of poor education and still operated separate and disparate school systems. The commission's inability to understand the logic of separate equality apparently dumbfounded Nosser. So he resorted to a meaningless defense, pointing out that every poor white and poor black family got a turkey on Thanksgiving; that kindly gesture was

ᴗ, than could be said about the treatment of blacks in
ᴗᴗer and other Natchez officials stood by their conviction
ᴗgation and discrimination were mutually exclusive, that the
ᴗ did not beget the latter. Yet, as Nosser spoke, larger forces were
ᴗsy dismantling the traditions born of his conviction.[25]

The convoluted logic and the persistent denial of Nosser and the others
would serve as a pliable facade over the inevitable for just so long. The
August following the enactment of the 1964 Civil Rights Act, the
Catholic Church in Mississippi became the first to pierce that facade
when Bishop Richard O. Gerow issued an edict requiring the desegregation of the first grade in Catholic schools across the state. Though encountering opposition from outside as well as from within the church,
Monsignor Thomas Joseph Fullam faithfully set in motion the new edict
at Cathedral Schools of Saint Mary's Parish in Natchez.[26] The next year,
seventeen days before the Metcalfe bombing, Fullam announced during
Sunday service that every grade at the elementary and secondary levels
would be open to "qualified Catholic students" of all races. In the midst
of the full drama of civil rights demonstrations and counterdemonstra-
tions, the parish instituted the new school desegregation policy. It also
jeopardized its enrollment of some 700 students in grades K through 12.[27]

Several blocks away, Holy Family voluntarily sacrificed students from
its own enrollment of some 400 for the cause of desegregation. The all-
black parish, headed by Father Morrisey, was part of the Josephite order
in Baltimore, from which Morrisey took directives, and was therefore independent of the Natchez-Jackson diocese that oversaw Saint Mary's
and Cathedral Schools. A large, apple-shaped bald man with a booming
voice, one that tended to unnerve some of the students, Morrisey was in-
tensely committed to human and civil rights, even at the expense of his
congregation's school. Upon word that Cathedral would open its enrollment, Morrisey began contacting parents to persuade them to send their
children to Cathedral, cautioning them that the children would be thrust
into an uncertain, if not unfriendly, environment. Ultimately, Cathedral
accepted fewer black students than the number Morrisey and the Holy
Family parents tendered.[28]

Only eleven entered the white Catholic school that year, which meant
that most of them sat alone in classrooms full of whites. One of the new

black students was Sophronia Hall, a third grader whose father, Joseph Hall, participated in the local civil rights demonstrations. When Morrisey telephoned looking for volunteers, Hall agreed to send all four of his daughters. Claiming classes were full, Cathedral accepted only two, Sophronia and her sister Angie, who was entering the second grade. (The next year, the other sisters were admitted.) Sophronia was fortunate to have another black classmate in her grade, for she went on to spend ten mostly stressful years at Cathedral. The nuns tried to make her feel welcome, but it required the animosity of only a few children to make her experience at Cathedral unpleasant. The name calling and insults—"nigger," "you stink," "you don't belong here"—were routine, as was the alienation in the lunchroom and on the playground. Her experience at Cathedral improved by her high-school years; she made a few friends, and one year she was chosen class favorite. But incidences of harassment and rejection continued nevertheless. Even some of the kids who tried to be nice came across as "condescending." Their friendliness seemed, she said, "more forced; it wasn't natural." She valued the superb academic education Cathedral gave her, yet regretted missing the socialization experience she would have enjoyed at Holy Family and that she later found at Xavier University. She never felt fully connected to the student body or integral to the institution. Acceptance by whites too often meant a rejection of her blackness.[29]

Like the white students, Saint Mary's parishioners proved not to be blind followers of the church, especially on the issue of race. Monsignor Fullam tried to mediate interparish financial, faculty, and religious education disputes, and at the same time, he watched enrollment drop from 710 in 1964 to 360 in 1967. The monsignor and his supporters waited out the hard times, purposely keeping the black enrollment low. By the early 1970s, after the public schools had finally implemented desegregation plans and whites began departing for private schools en masse, enrollment would rebound to over 600.[30]

The parish leadership's deference to central authority at the diocese in Jackson was not the style of public-school officials. In violation of *Brown* and the 1964 Civil Rights Act, they perpetuated the dual system for as long as possible. In 1965, the Justice Department took them to court on the complaints of the U.S. attorney general, George Metcalfe, and other local blacks. The Natchez case followed on the legal coattails of *Singleton v. Jackson,* a June 1965 landmark decision ordering the abolition of the dual school system in Jackson, Mississippi.[31] On October 2, 1965, Judge Harold Cox ruled against Natchez school officials in accordance with *Singleton.* But the National Guard at the time was trying to restore order in the streets of Natchez, and Cox, always unfailingly sympathetic to the white position, gave the school district until the next school year to begin the process of desegregation: six grades that year and the remaining six the following year.[32]

The foot-dragging in Natchez reflected a regionwide hostility to federal law. When *Brown* was a full ten years old, dual school systems remained the norm in the states of the lower South. Only 2.25 percent of black children attended school with white children, which after factoring in population growth meant that more black children were enrolled in segregated schools in 1964 than in 1954. White southerners had gone to great lengths to render ineffective the remedy provisions in *Brown* II. Some whites closed down public schools altogether, as did Virginians in Prince Edward County. Most adopted freedom-of-choice plans, which allowed students to attend the school of their choosing. Those plans simply lifted legal barriers of segregation without providing any effective means to end the dual school system. The first black students who entered white schools in Natchez did so under a freedom-of-choice plan like that operating in 98 percent of Mississippi's school districts.[33]

Mississippi's U.S. senator John Stennis was a chief backer of freedom of choice. His constituents believed that the plan represented an ingenious way to fend off federal intrusions and to preserve separate schools. Under the open-enrollment system, the burden of implementing the transition fell squarely on the shoulders of black parents and black students. Whites had no incentives to attend black schools, stigmatized as zoos of disorderliness and academic incompetence. Even blacks acknowledged that their schools offered an inferior learning environment that dampened expectations for academic and occupational success. When black students looked at the white schools, they saw a pathway to the mainstream opportunities for which they longed. They also saw the familiar face of hostility. More often than not in the case of blacks, personal choice yielded to community pressure to stay in one's place.[34]

Bogus in its meaning and application, freedom of choice was the first stage of three in an integration process that spanned more than two decades in Natchez. Before blacks could exercise their choice to transfer to a white school, they had to be selected by that school, and only top-rated students were awarded a choice. Contrary to white fears, there was no mad rush of predatory blacks to take over the white schools. Only a small percentage of blacks dared to enroll in Natchez's white schools and be cast in the role of interloper, and no whites, of course, chose to attend black schools. Nor did desegregation unleash a legion of lecherous black "bucks" eager to assault every white man's daughter, as Klan literature strewn across lawns in white neighborhoods warned. The small number of blacks in white schools (the exact number is unclear), in fact, belied the term "integration." Even so, an unusually high number, 415 white students (nearly 10 percent), withdrew during the 1966–67 school year. By contrast, only 47 black students, representing less than 1 percent of the black student body, withdrew during the same period. While white Natchezians nursed their fears over the unknown consequences of desegregation, few showed compassion for the black students who entered a domain where for a dozen years since *Brown* they were told bluntly, and sometimes violently, that they were not welcome.[35]

One of the first black students to step foot in the white domain was Betty Williams, a bright twelve year old who loved the challenge of schoolwork. Natchez born and reared, Betty could trace her lineage to early nineteenth-century Adams County slaves. Until her mother's generation, her family lived on the same rural ground on which their enslaved forebears had labored. Betty's mother took all eight years of education the county schools offered and later vowed that her own children would have more. She moved to Natchez and as a single mother raised three girls. Like so many black women of her generation and background, she worked as a maid.[36]

Betty was her youngest child, born in the year the Supreme Court gave imprimatur to southern delays with its words "all deliberate speed." After six years of school, neither Betty nor any of her friends had ever seen the inside of a white school. But the demonstrations and marches and violence in Natchez that occupied those same years were the signs of a society being wrenched free from its past. When the open-enrollment plan was announced, Betty's mother allowed her daughters to choose their schools and then supported their decisions. While one of Betty's sisters opted to transfer to the white high school, the other preferred to stay at Thompson. Betty decided to attend the all-white Martin Junior High, which was within walking distance of her house. Theresa Lewis, principal at Susie B. West, the black school Betty attended under the old system, recommended only the brightest students for transfer, knowing that the white schools would screen them first. She also chose those who she believed "could take care of themselves in any situation." Betty was one of her choices, and although Betty was hesitant about leaving her friends behind, Lewis assured her that superior educational opportunities awaited at Martin.[37]

Rain fell the morning of the first day of school. That alone seemed a bad omen to a twelve year old already somewhat frightened by the historical drama in which she was partaking. Black parents escorted their children to school that morning and remained on hand, as unsure about what might develop as were the white parents who were present. The handful of black students lined up outside the school and readied to enter. Uniformed police officers flanked the campus grounds, and the faculty as well stood extravigilant of violence. After the white students were settled in their classes, the newcomers were allowed to enter. Betty was the first. There were no incidents. For the first several days, black parents continued to escort their children to school, eventually leaving them on their own but not alone. The children walked to and from school in groups, leaving and picking up the black children attending the elementary school en route. Occasionally, a racial slur was hurled from the window of a passing car or school bus, but nothing more than what any Natchez black child routinely endured.[38]

At her new school, Betty was the only black in all her classes except one. She saw others only in the lunchroom or during physical education class. Teachers generally welcomed her presence, and most of the white students accepted her, though an expected few exhibited animosity toward their new classmate and her race in general. Betty learned in later years that some of the white students secretly competed with her in class, trying not to let the new black girl do better than they. Once Betty settled into the routine of her new school, she experienced a "kind of rude awakening," she said. "I realized it is true. They do have a head start on us." She was surprised, for instance, to learn that her white classmates had studied science every year. In the black school, Betty had taken science only once in six grades because of a lack of books. Nor had she ever read from a brand-new textbook, like those at Martin. Another daunting contrast was the library, which housed a larger collection in a more impressive facility than the one at West.[39]

Similar impressions struck John West, who transferred to Natchez High that same year. West was the youngest son of George West Sr. and the grandson of Susie B. West, namesake of the school that Betty Williams had previously attended. John's father would become Natchez's first black city alderman since Reconstruction. He would die in office, and his second son would then take his seat in city government. The oldest son, George Jr., was the first black in the twentieth century appointed to the local school board, and he would later become the board's first black chairman. With all these firsts in the West family, death threats were common during the heyday of civil rights activity and when the senior West served on the board of aldermen. Knowing the way such threats were sometimes carried out, John inspected for a bomb under the hood of the family car every morning before his father drove him to the white school.[40]

With his father encouraging him to follow his own wisdom, John had come to a decision about transferring to Natchez High in the months before the 1967 school year began. That summer, he visited the white high school and liked what he saw. It had an open, airy feel to it. The chemistry and biology laboratories were better equipped than those at Thompson, and the teachers at Natchez High had reputations for being more qualified. As an athlete, West made note of the sports facilities. "I saw fiberglass [basketball] backboards I had never seen before. I saw a white guy pole-vaulting; I had never seen that before. A track field that looked like a track field, and a parquet [gymnasium] floor." Only thirteen years old and the white community's answer to educational parity, Thompson High had grown overcrowded and fallen into "disrepair." "There was so much traffic," said West, "folks just walking down the hall, some of them smoking cigarettes. I just wanted a change of pace."[41]

West entered Natchez High in his junior year. His departure from Thompson for the white school brought resentment from some of his former classmates. As a member of an upper-class black family, he prequalified as a snob, regardless of his true demeanor, but the transfer convinced some blacks that he did indeed consider himself better than they and that he was trying to be something that he could never be, something they would never want to be, white. From his new white classmates at Natchez High, he got a mixed reception. "Some were indifferent," he said. Others felt the social pressure to be "standoffish." Being too friendly with West risked eliciting accusations of being "a nigger lover or whatever," said West. "I had a few altercations, not many." The white students nicknamed John "Spook" and even captioned one of his yearbook photographs with the name, as if the mutual acceptance (acquiescence on his part) of the nickname mitigated the epithet and sanitized the racist symbols that the white teenagers had inherited from their parents.[42]

In his senior year, John was the only black on the varsity basketball team, and sports brought the hope of some sense of social leveling. John felt actually liked by his white classmates only when on the court. Road trips, when he was frequently denied service in restaurants and use of gas-station restrooms, brought an unexpected benefit: they exposed his teammates to life from the black perspective. One incident that surprised even John happened after he arrived at the Eola Hotel for the team's annual dinner. When John asked a black waiter for directions to the banquet room, so deep was the impress of racial conventions that the waiter handed him a waiter's jacket and told him to put it on.[43]

The year John, Betty, and others desegregated the public schools brought another victory for improved black education. In June 1967, the first black joined the membership of the school board, but as usual, progress had not come without a struggle.

Local blacks first tried for an appointment to the five-member board the year before when one of the county's two appointees prepared to end his term. Fearing that black activism might succeed in securing the first black appointment, an ad hoc delegation of white women went before the county board of supervisors to urge the reappointment of the incumbent, John Stowers, who was also on the board of trustees of a local all-white private school. At a subsequent meeting, the Natchez NAACP and other activist groups submitted several names of black candidates for Stowers's post. Revealing a liberal consciousness never before displayed in local governmental affairs, county supervisor Jake Brown moved to nominate George West Sr. for the post. Brown preceded the motion with a lengthy statement, calling on his fellow board members to show the "courage and conviction" to appoint a black. He contended that the black community warranted a representative on the board since its children accounted for more than half of the student body in the public schools. "Let's not be forced to integrate the School Board," as in the case of the schools, he said in a strategic appeal to pride. Brown finished with a touching tribute to the senior West and the West family, but his nomination failed to draw a second. The board proceeded with the appointment of a white business executive instead. Six months later, Brown lost his reelection bid in the August primary.[44]

Whites were still making the rules, but the black community was no longer willing to allow politics as usual to go unanswered. The day after the West rejection, 80 percent of the black student body walked out of schools in protest. At the same time, the NAACP intensified the business boycott organized after the Metcalfe bombing. Local blacks had learned the power of demonstration to attract the attention of the white powers that be, and they held that attention for a year. When the term of one of the city's school-board appointees expired in March 1967, black leaders representing the NAACP, the Adams County Democratic Club, and the Natchez Business and Civic League turned to the board of aldermen and presented a list of prospective candidates. The board scarcely hesitated before reappointing the white incumbent. This kind of dismissive indifference was familiar to the black leaders, and the reappointment came as no surprise. The black leaders pointed out that as part of the boycott settlement a year before, the city had promised to appoint a black to the school board. Mayor Nosser later said the promise had not come with a definite date of fulfillment.[45]

Still, the board of aldermen attempted to make concessions. It voted to require all persons, black and white, doing business with the city to be addressed with courtesy titles—another overdue promise. Alderman Tony Byrne, a young politician who demonstrated a degree of moderation on race matters, nominated Robert D. Mackel, of Robert D. Mackel and Sons Funeral Home, for appointment to the local civil service commission. The board confirmed Mackel. Byrne also entered into the record his pledge to vote for a black appointee to the city's next vacant spot on the school board. The board of aldermen then offered to make a preliminary appointment and confirm the appointee the following March when the next school-board member's term expired.[46]

Byrne found the indoctrination into local government equivalent to a baptism by fire. Before the meeting, the aldermen had agreed to appoint George West Jr., a newly minted black attorney, to the school board. Alderman Randall Ferguson, who like Byrne revealed a streak of fair-mindedness on race issues, nominated West. Although West had gotten a nod of approval from sovereignty commission director Erle Johnston, there had long before been pressure to appoint a member of a prominent white family, which reportedly had strong ties to the Klan. The aldermen then looked for a compromise in the reappointment of the incumbent, R. Brent Forman, the longtime chairman of the school board. Byrne went along with the majority and in the process left the black community feeling betrayed. After the meeting, Byrne went home to hostile phone calls from blacks and whites. One of the latter promised that harm would come to Byrne's family for "putting that 'nigger' on the civil service commission." Byrne had to take the threat seriously and so joined the routine of many blacks who checked their cars each morning for bombs.[47]

Black leaders had left the meeting feeling like cheated sharecroppers at the year-end settle. Shead Baldwin called the aldermen's actions "just another run-around," and he reminded the elected officials that blacks now had the vote and could make the difference in an individual's reelection. Tired of compromises and excuses, he and others consolidated the support for another business boycott. But the black community did not have to wait another year for an appointment to the board, and white elected officials did not have to test the power of enfranchised blacks. That April, the aldermen appointed George West Jr. to the school board, effective March 1 of the next year, 1968. Then in June, a school-board member died, opening the way for an early confirmation of West.[48]

Even as segregationists began to lose some battles, the war still raged in their favor. Just how powerless blacks had been and were still was clearly seen after blacks climbed high enough to look out over the territory of white omnipotence. Its vastness was imposing. Blacks had to not only gain political power to compete with whites, they had to spread their empowerment to the reach of that territory's every corner. Winning a political appointment was a mere footstep, albeit an important one, upon the territory; wielding influence in public policy was a reach yet to be attained. This became particularly evident when one contemplated the realities of school desegregation. One year after West's appointment and after Betty Williams transferred to Martin, seven of Natchez's fifteen schools were all black, and the others predominantly white. Of 5,500 enrolled black students, roughly 500, or 9.8 percent, attended integrated schools. No full-time faculty members taught outside their race's domain. Similar figures could be cited for most other Mississippi school districts.[49]

Action on the part of the federal government was required to bring the white South's "all deliberate speed" evasion to an end. In the 1968 case of *Green v. School Board of New Kent County, Virginia,* the Supreme Court struck down the fraud of freedom of choice and shifted the burden of desegregation from blacks to local school boards, which the Court ordered to take affirmative steps toward terminating dual school systems.[50]

Taking its cue from the Supreme Court, the Fifth Circuit Court of Appeals in July of the next year informed twenty-four Mississippi school districts, including the Natchez–Adams County district, that freedom of choice had failed and that the time had come to develop plans for unitary school systems. The decision reversed the orders of Judge Cox allowing the continued use of the freedom of choice system. In none of the twenty-four districts had a white student ever attended a traditionally black school. Following the appellate court ruling, the U.S. Department of Health, Education, and Welfare quickly came forward with plans that called for complete and immediate integration. Beginning in the fall, students were to be assigned to schools according to zones redrawn by the HEW.[51]

In a four-to-one vote, the school board in Natchez rejected the plan. The HEW had provided erroneous and faulty zoning coordinates, the board argued, and its proposal would put black majorities in twelve of the fourteen school buildings. That result would lead to mass faculty resignations and student withdrawals that would "completely destroy the education system." The school board then submitted its own plan, which allowed for the integration of schools over a two-year period, six grades at a time. Elementary schools would keep girls and boys together; and at the secondary level, students would be segregated by sex.[52]

George West stood as the lone dissenter against the board's plan. As the school board's only black member, he was prone to enter into the minutes-long statements outlining an alternative view to a majority decision. His was a voice that the black community had never had on the school board. West was no fan of federally forced integration though; to him, successful integration required the willingness of whites "to come to our neighborhoods." But whites had already shown an unwillingness to attend the traditionally black schools, and as long as the majority of the indigenous population continued to deny the legitimacy of black complaints, the South could not solve its problems of racial inequality itself. The HEW plan should therefore be followed, West argued; any alternative plan of the board's making would represent "a continued effort toward the perpetuation of segregation."[53]

That appeared to be happening at the national level after the Nixon Justice Department appealed to the Court on behalf of Mississippi schools and won a delay. Desegregation forces, which included the NAACP, quickly regrouped. With the help of Hugo Black, the courtly Alabama liberal who at eighty-three was the Supreme Court's oldest associate justice and senior member, they got their case to the head of the Supreme Court's fall docket. On October 29, 1969, a unanimous Court in *Alexander v. Holmes* overturned the lower court's delay and declared that "'all deliberate speed' for desegregation is no longer constitutionally permissible." In mid-December, the Fifth Circuit Court of Appeals ordered Mississippi schools, once and for all, to integrate student bodies and faculties by the end of the Christmas break.[54]

Administrators, teachers, and staff in Natchez worked through the holiday to coordinate reassignments according to mandated zoning parameters. It was "a logistical nightmare," said Charles Kempinska, who was principal at Morgantown Junior High at the time. All eleventh and twelfth graders were assigned to the former white high school, renamed South Natchez-Adams High. Thompson was converted into one of four junior highs. One of the white junior highs, Anchorage, became North Natchez-Adams High, where all tenth graders were sent. White principals headed the high schools with black assistant principals. One was Robert Lewis, who was demoted from his former position as principal of Thompson.[55] Many high-school faculty became "roving teachers," spending part of their day at each school while keeping much of their classroom materials in their cars. All teacher workshops, meetings, and seminars were desegregated. With most objecting to the HEW plan, forty-six teachers resigned before the end of the school year.[56]

The student body suffered its own losses. Just before the Christmas break, School Superintendent D. Gilmer McLaurin announced that a survey of parents indicated that 84 percent of the students would be returning to public schools. The estimate could not have been much more accurate, but nearly all the students not returning were white. The student body dropped by 1,630 (16 percent) from a 10,101 total, representing an attrition that had begun in the fall and that came mostly from the secondary schools. In January, whites accounted for 31 percent of the public-school student body, compared to nearly 50 percent in 1964. In drawing up desegregation plans before Christmas, HEW officials had anticipated a 46-percent white student body at the high schools. Only 641 whites (35 percent) returned to the high schools along with 1,168 blacks, and many apparently wondered to what they were returning.[57]

The transition from the old and familiar to the new and uncertain was abrupt, confusing, and intrusive. Both races sacrificed something, but blacks gave up the most. Aside from being bused across town, blacks gave up their football, basketball, and baseball teams, cheerleading squads, and marching bands. Black homecoming queens, valedictorians, and salutatorians all but disappeared. During the freedom-of-choice days, Natchez High discontinued proms, dances, and baccalaureate services; none were reinstated at the new South Natchez-Adams High School. Sacrificed as well were black cultural role models from leadership positions; black principals were demoted to assistant principals, and many senior teachers were shifted out of supervisory posts. The loss of this leadership meant that blacks could no longer tailor the classroom curriculum to black interests. Black students had new access to highly qualified white teachers, and while most teachers were dedicated to black and white students alike, not all teachers were sensitive to the needs of black students trying to cope in a new environment. Not as well prepared academically as the white students, black students sometimes encountered impatience instead of understanding from the teachers to whom they had to prove themselves.[58]

Moreover, blacks bore the mark of the intruder in a sometimes hostile setting. Now, if a classmate called one of them "nigger," "spook," "burr head," "spear chucker," or any other of a vast assortment of racial epithets, that classmate was probably white. The disparaged black would have to endure humiliation or fight, and with the latter came the risk of expulsion. Said John West: "My daddy told me, 'If they call you a nigger, walk away. If they talk about your momma, walk away. If they lay a hand on you, knock the hell out of them and call me.'"[59]

White students identified with many of the black responses. One student summed up the 1969–70 school year as a "mess." Whites got their first feel of the disparity in public schools upon discovering that many of the classes they had been taking were not available in the formerly black schools. Most students took the change "all in stride." Other high-schoolers were angry because they were forced to give up their school name, the Rebels, and choose new school colors with their new class-mates. An assistant editor of the school newspaper, *Echoes,* lamented, "No longer will there be Rebels, Bucks, Does, Rebelettes, Buckettes, the Victorian, or Echoes." No longer allowed to stay either was the school mascot, Colonel Reb, the gray-clad symbol of the Confederacy, honorable enough to whites. But to blacks, he suggested a longing for slave days. Since a large number of the white students departed for private schools or dropped out, seniors felt their class had been gratuitously "cut off in the middle of the year," as *Echoes* coeditor Pete Haley phrased it. "We are unfortunate, in that, as an intact class, we have only a single semester of memories."[60]

Though impatient with the burdens of change, the students generally accepted integration. There were the few expected fights and quarrels, and there were certain students, black and white, who hated the whole of the other race. At the other extreme, some white students clumsily tried to compensate for the evident racial hostility and went to great lengths, sometimes interpreted as condescending, to welcome and accept their new black classmates. In general, students of both races felt the pressure from racial peers to socialize only with their own. As a consequence, the student body usually segregated at open gatherings, such as between classes and in the school cafeteria, which many whites avoided altogether. But the self-imposed segregation usually derived from the comfort of being among those with whom one had the most in common, known since kindergarten, lived with in the same neighborhood, or shared ideas and perceptions.[61]

The Klan alone could not be blamed for sabotaging a smooth transition to a unitary system, as school and city leaders would have their followers believe. While the Klan literature warning of lustful blacks did have its intended effect of alarming some students, many others saw through the rhetoric to find the absurd. To them, the principal stokers of racial tension were the white parents who picketed the schools, taunted teachers and students, withdrew their children against their children's will, flouted authority, and with their alarmist rumors raised the specter of a race riot. White and black students alike watched the parents in dismay. Wrote *Echoes* assistant editor Alyson Coyle in January: "Perhaps the greatest threat to the continuance of school is agitation from the outside. If parents and other outsiders would leave the schools alone, the enrollment might not be so low." Classmates regarded themselves as "pawns in some sort of political process." Nor were black parents above the scrutiny of their own children. Some believed that the adults overreacted to the potential of violence and made even more difficult the unenviable role of trespasser. Burnette Brudgewater, a 1974 graduate of North Natchez-Adams High,[62] remembered "having watched the adult counterparts panic so much, it instilled a fear in us."[63]

The parents of both races indeed seemed to overreact. At racially separate meetings with school officials in February, black and white parents were given a chance to air their grievances. At the white meeting, complaints took the form of nearly every fear and vile belief about black culture found in the white culture's catalog of racial myths. Some parents said they were alarmed by reports that the black students were tormenting white students. One man claimed his daughter had been surrounded by eight black boys in the school cafeteria. Parents had heard stories about marauding gangs of blacks preying upon lone white boys in restrooms. The parents accused black students of brazenly cursing the other children and teachers, complained about a lack of classroom discipline, and spoke of portending racial violence. They insisted that teachers and administrators step up policing efforts, and they discussed the possibility of posting uniformed law-enforcement officers on school campuses.[64]

Black parents came to their meeting with their own complaints. Blacks contended too that students of the other race tormented their children. They blamed white parents for condoning the harassment and for teaching their children racial hatred. There were rumors that white teachers referred to blacks as monkeys and forced black children to use "sir" and "ma'am," when the same forms of address were not always required of white children. There was also the issue of the parents' meetings. The black adults joined with George West Jr. in arguing that the racially separate parents' meetings set a bad example for the children trying to cope in integrated settings. If the parents could not come together, it was reasoned, how could they expect the same of the children. White officials said that the racially charged grievances warranted segregated meetings.[65]

The racial tension was spawned in the rub between the expected behavior of blacks and what actually occurred. Quickly fading since the Metcalfe bombing nearly five years earlier was the image of the black standing before the white with hat or apron in hand, eyes fixed upon the ground, and head nodding in assent while lips imparted the obliging "yes, sir" or "yes, ma'am." The complaints aired at the school meeting were of the sort that for decades blacks had kept hidden beneath an agreeable countenance—the linchpin in the harmonious society. Seemingly overnight, the countenance had changed, and not only that of a few leaders but that of nearly an entire community. The new countenance questioned and argued; it even betrayed suspicion, and from the lips freely flowed words such as "demand," and "challenge," and "no"—untempered by the deferential sir or ma'am.

Whites missed the deferential "Negro" who shuffled to the beat of white supremacy. With the civil rights movement, blacks transformed the social system that had necessitated the compliant "Negro," and in the process they changed themselves and their image. To whites at the school meeting and elsewhere, nearly the entire black community appeared to have gone to hell in a handbasket of uppity nonsense. This was a reflexive way of thinking, first excited across synapses generations earlier and in each generation since. It was unfair to pin that inflammatory label, uppity, upon black parents who simply showed strength in their convictions in ways similar to, and sometimes less hostile than, those of white parents.

Blacks, as a result, found themselves explaining to their racial others their real objective in integration. Many whites could not conceive of the black objective in school integration as anything but a shortcut to "social equality," artificially achieved by intermingling as alleged equals with whites. Blacks, however, had the same vision as the Irish, Italian, Polish, and Jewish immigrants of the late nineteenth and early twentieth centuries, who saw their children's upward social mobility dependent upon a decent education. Integration meant simply incorporation into institutions that provided entree to the American Dream, where through luck and pluck, as the saying and idea went, one might achieve economic security. Many whites, especially rabid segregationists, believed, however, that one of those institutions was the white family and that entree came via the bedroom of the fair maiden of southern white culture. But the culture that admired itself more than did others was flattering itself with such thoughts. Blacks were no more or no less interested in socially or physically intermingling with the other race than were whites, and blacks had no designs on private white institutions such as family and church.

Excerpts from the following open letter from Mississippi black teachers to the white community provide revealing testimony of black aspirations in an open society: "We do not crave to belong to [white] churches and social clubs. . . . We do crave an opportunity to have a fair chance and succeed. We do crave an opportunity to have good schools for our children so that they may become intelligent, self-supporting, self-respecting citizens. We do not want our people to fill your jails, your penitentiaries, and your hospitals; but we do want them to be able to work and earn an honest living in Mississippi."[66]

Many whites by the late 1960s were coming around to accepting this stated position. But they regarded the white schools, though public venues, as private domains. "No question about that," said Elliot Trimble. In a state and community where continuity generally transcended change, students typically attended schools with their siblings, first cousins, and distant cousins. The schools were frequently those that their parents, and even grandparents, claimed as their alma maters. Walker Percy described the private nature of public schools when he wrote that the familial boundary "of this society came to coincide with the actual public space which it inhabited." When the justice department compelled the enrollment of James Meredith at Ole Miss in 1962, Percy noted, "it was as if he had been quartered in their [whites'] living room."[67]

The reaction was no different eight years later in Natchez. With the Court's decision to integrate Natchez schools in 1970, whites felt that the federal government seized control of the schools by some perverse right of eminent domain and, even worse, ungated a black invasion of a familial institution. By right of the most immediate sovereign, if by nothing else, whites believed, the public schools came under local jurisdiction. Whites had conceived the public-school system, built it, financed it, and until recently, lorded over it.[68]

But now in integrated schools, they were a minority in their domain. Their children attended classes with, not a select few blacks, but the children of the whole population and, as whites saw it, with black culture exhibited at its worst. Segregated schools had served two parallel purposes. One was to prevent physical interaction between the children of the races. Segregationist organizations blanketed the state with inflammatory literature, some with alarming images and all carrying the imprimatur of Thomas Dixon's ghost, warning against the dire consequences of school integration: racial mongrelization. No loving white parent, the literature either implied or expressed, would want to open the front door to a black boy—a schoolmate—calling on his/her daughter. That message nearly became the basis of public policy with the Natchez–Adams County School Board's failed proposal to segregate the secondary schools by sex, a policy that embodied the ancient white fear that oversexed black males lusted wildly for white females.

The second and equally important purpose of school segregation, preventing cultural interaction, paralleled the barriers against physical interaction. Whites had never been able to stop a cultural exchange between blacks and whites, though a consensus to do so probably never existed. Whites consciously accepted from black culture what they considered worthy and enriching and unconsciously absorbed some traits they considered otherwise. By and large, though, whites preferred a unilateral exchange, blacks learning from whites. The reputed immoral nature of blacks was to be contained with segregation laws and separate institutions. Bill Hanna said, "A majority of the [white] people that I knew felt that [school] integration would diminish white culture because it would bring white culture down toward the [perceived] level of black culture."[69]

At first blush, there appears to be an unexplained incongruity in the idea that the supposedly inferior culture could debase the supposedly superior one. But segregated schools had helped ensure that whites would continue to stand upon their higher cultural ground. Schools were regarded as an institutional extension of the family, a wholesome environment that continued the task begun within the home of teaching the culture's values and ideals to the culture's progeny, upon whom the culture's future survival depended. The character-building role in any American school, said John Dewey, was the hidden curriculum behind its academic role. In the South, building character in the context of biracial society, said Bill Hanna, was "the nature of segregation. That's where family values are centered, in the church and school." From the white perspective, the supreme horror of school integration was that it brought white children at an impressionable age into close and prolonged contact with black children and faculty and their lower standard of values. One white Natchezian said simply that white parents did not want their children associating with children from an "amoral family that didn't know who their daddy was." There was an unspeakable image in white parents' minds of their progeny being unduly treated to exhibitions of uninhibited sexual behavior, teenage pregnancy, stealing, knifings, lazy study habits, and unbridled truancy. Black teachers posed less physical danger than did the students,[70] but whites presumed that black teachers were academically inferior educators and poor role models of character and values—the adult products of the allegedly lesser culture. Rather than risk subjecting his children to the corruptions of integrated schools, one Natchezian preferred an extreme, if not ironic, alternative. "If my choice for my children is immorality or illiteracy," he wrote in reference to school integration, "I won't hesitate to choose the latter."[71]

With such comments, whites displayed their prejudices toward and their ignorance of black culture. Whites knew that their own race held no exclusive on individual intelligence and good behavior, but when blacks exhibited these positive traits, there existed a disjunction between what the white mind was conditioned to think and what was real. The rowdy, disruptive, academically indifferent black eased the mental conflict, if not the emotional fears, of integration, as did the many academically ill-prepared blacks. Both then reaffirmed white beliefs about a pathological black culture. It was easier and more natural to bend toward the familiar—that which sustained a preexisting idea—than toward the unfamiliar—such as the novel idea of the black culture holding promise. Natural or not, this habit of mind was perhaps the chief obstacle to the goals of school desegregation and black equality.[72]

It was also the very reason for the original creation of separate private-school systems. Mississippi had only five nonsectarian private schools in the 1964–65 school year. In 1971, 106 private, segregated grade schools operated in the state. Throughout the region, private academies, as they were called to suggest academic prestige, increased tenfold between 1964 and 1971. These institutions were the incarnation of lost private domains and the ultimate expression of the fear of white cultural decline. To avoid the myriad consequences of integration, white parents pooled their resources and organized all-white private schools in continuing pursuit of preserving their conception of a wholesome learning environment for their children. White Mississippi cast private schools as one of its best hopes for survival of the culture and its children's future.[73]

The first private school in Natchez organized in response to integration was Adams County Private School (ACPS). Its founding in the early 1960s was attributable largely to the efforts of the Americans for the Preservation of the White Race (APWR). In segregationist literature disseminated in white Mississippi neighborhoods, the APWR portrayed school integration as "*genocide*," "*race murder*," and "*legalized kidnaping.*" ACPS was the brainchild of Rowland Scott, a Natchez accountant and state president of the APWR. Scott organized a board of trustees for the school, many of whom were members of his white-supremacist organization. The board's legal advisor served in the same capacity for the Natchez Citizens' Council. The board president, Ernest Parker, a wealthy oilman, cattle farmer, and White Knight, was implicated in, but never indicted for, the murder of Henry Dee and Charles Moore, the two young civil rights workers found near Natchez in 1964 during the hunt for the three Neshoba County victims.[74]

In 1962, the trustees secured a state charter for a nonprofit educational corporation. The "Ladies" of the APWR held fund-raising barbecues and raffles for the new school, housed in a vacated Baptist church in the enclave of Morgantown. At one barbecue, the featured speaker was Judge Jack Wallace, brother of Alabama Governor George Wallace. In

September 1965, ACPS announced that it would begin taking applications for enrollment and would operate under a nonsectarian policy. Catholics and Jews were welcome. Tuition was $250 a year, and parents were eligible for a $185 grant from the State Educational Finance Committee, created by the legislature to promote private schools and to circumvent integration. In 1969, the federal courts declared such state-supported grants unconstitutional, and ACPS made arrangements with two local banks willing to lend money for tuition. ACPS offered eight grades in the 1966–67 school year and operated two buses. As was true with private schools in general, its expenditures were less than that of public schools, it was dependent on tuition, and its library reflected its financial shortcomings. Yet, state accreditation for Mississippi's private schools was typically awarded immediately. ACPS received its in April.[75]

Many of the parents who enrolled their children in ACPS were not aware of its connection to the APWR. While most probably would not have considered themselves racists, they shared the segregationist group's views about integration. The reasons for sending one's children to a private school varied, but underlying all was the fundamental fear of cultural commingling. There were, of course, the "hot-headed racists" who would allow racial interaction only in incidences that clearly delineated white supremacy and that limited familiarity between blacks and whites. For more moderate parents, the greater concern was maintaining high standards of academic quality. Ironically, it took integration to provoke many whites into acknowledging the inferiority of black schools. Since Mississippi schools consistently ranked near the bottom nationally, white parents found the preservation of educational standards in Natchez even more important. Their public schools had frequently been recognized as among the best in the state, and private schools seemed the only opportunity to continue the teaching of solid academic skills. At the same time, private schools restored values not directly related to race, including school prayer, which was outlawed in public schools in 1963.[76]

The loss of neighborhood schools was another principal reason parents sent their children to private schools. Parents of both races put great stock in the value of neighborhood schools. They represented continuity, security, neighborhood affiliations, and local autonomy. With federal authorities effectively assuming control of the Natchez school district, parents were unsure of the fate of neighborhood schools. Whites believed at the same time that they had lost local control to meddlesome outsiders. Said high-school principal Robert Barrett, "The first thing everyone was being told, 'Open your mouth, you're going to take this dose of medicine whether you like it or not.'"[77]

Among the least agreeable patients were white women. Their role as perpetuators of the culture had depended on the sacredness of two major institutions outside the family, churches and schools. Federally mandated school integration was a prescription for disaster in their efforts to raise their children in the proper way and in a fitting environment. "You're able to choose the friends you're associated with socially, but you're not able to choose your classmates," said one Natchez mother. "We wanted that freedom to choose who our child would sit next to in school." Their eyes cast federal authorities in the role of tyrannical usurpers of the parental responsibility to decide "what was best for our children." Some saw themselves as having "been stripped of all of our rights." Said another mother, "I cried." As a result, many parents diverted time, energy, and interest from the public schools to private schools.[78]

The latter were created in the image of the white public schools before integration. For every twenty students at ACPS, there was a qualified teacher, 20 percent of whom held master's degrees. In the wake of the school integration order, ACPS offered all twelve grades to accommodate an enrollment of more than 600, up from under 400 the year before. A new building went under construction on a thirty-four-acre site at a cost of $1.2 million. It had twenty-nine classrooms, a fully equipped science laboratory, wood shop, a home-economics class, and a sizable gymnasium/auditorium. The school's shop teacher designed the new building. The board of trustees' president ran heavy equipment. The new assistant principal joined parents doing interior finish work, including laying the gym's parquet floor. With the new building complete, the school was rededicated in the fall of 1970 with a new name, Thomas Jefferson Schools. Thomas Jefferson had football, basketball, and baseball teams, a marching band, school yearbook and newspaper, everything students had enjoyed in the public schools—including the personal commitment that many white parents withdrew from the public schools along with their children. Thomas Jefferson also offered something the public schools did not: morning devotional, school prayer, and religious clubs.[79]

Despite its thriving existence, Thomas Jefferson's lifespan was a short one. In 1973, the trustees sold the school and its sizable debt to the Council School Foundation of Jackson, the educational arm of the Citizens' Council. The sale belied the local autonomy that was so dear to parents and administrators in the struggle over public-school integration. Central authority now resided with a bureaucracy in Jackson. In January 1977, that bureaucracy determined that Thomas Jefferson had become a financial liability and sold the school facilities to an investment group, which closed the school's doors permanently. Parents felt betrayed. The council had taken away a vital part of their lives, something they themselves had created from the common resolve of a shared goal.[80]

Natchez's other private schools absorbed most of Thomas Jefferson's more than 600 disaffected students. In 1974, 22 percent of the Adams County student population of approximately 10,500 attended private schools, roughly 10 percent above the state average. Slightly under 500 students went to the integrated Cathedral school. The Episcopal Church's Trinity Day School (known as the school of the Natchez old-family elite) maintained an enrollment slightly over 400. The church had operated a kindergarten since the late 1950s and opened an elementary school when the Supreme Court outlawed prayer in public schools. Trinity gradually added grades as public-school integration sent whites fleeing to private schools, eventually offering all secondary grades. The last of the major private schools, Adams County Christian School (ACCS), opened in 1969 when local white Baptist churches joined in opposition to public-school integration. In the 1974–75 school year, more than 680 students attended ACCS. Following the closing of Thomas Jefferson, ACCS enjoyed a record high enrollment of some 800 students in grades kindergarten through twelve. Through the 1970s until the late 1980s, the ratio of public- to private-school students remained relatively constant. The private schools educated approximately the same number of white students as did the public schools.[81]

That figure might have been much larger if not for certain "stop-gap" measures taken by Natchez public-school officials. School administrators and teachers worked hard to make white students feel comfortable in an integrated environment, hoping that some students would share news of good experiences with concerned parents. On the legal side, the school board went back to court in the spring of 1970 and proposed school-zone changes and the restoration of all three grades in the two high schools. The board claimed that the new plan would correct enrollment and racial imbalances caused by white flight and would save the school system $38,000 in operating costs. The Fifth Circuit Court of Appeals approved the changes in August. But in terms of correcting racial imbalance, the outcome of rezoning contradicted the school board's claims. Natchez blacks would return to court in the 1980s to challenge a pattern of resegregation, advancing the desegregation process to a third stage.[82]

Betty Williams and John West would again be caught in the fray, not as students but as parents, and they had a special history to share with their children. West graduated from Natchez High in 1969, one of the first blacks to do so. When he walked across the platform during commencement ceremonies, his older brother, school-board member George West Jr., presented him his diploma. They were pioneers.[83]

Williams graduated four years later from South Natchez-Adams High School at the top of her class. She was one of three students, and the first ever black, to speak at graduation. She was neither class valedictorian nor salutatorian. Those honors were casualties of integration. There was no senior prom either, or a ten-year reunion in 1973. Some alumni held private celebrations, but none invited her. After graduation, Williams won a scholarship to a college in Kentucky. But higher education for her ended when she was forced to return to Natchez to care for her ailing mother, who had retired from her career as a domestic with no pension or health benefits. For Williams, school integration was not enough to allow her to fulfill lifelong aspirations. Her higher education plans were preempted by unresolved issues—the poverty of the larger black population and the legacy of racial discrimination.[84]

The continuing struggle for improved black education, begun in the days of Ms. Sadie V. Thompson, reflected that legacy. With the events of school desegregation in the late 1960s and early 1970s, the black community demonstrated that a new era of mass intolerance for racial injustice had arrived in Natchez. Still, the climb out of a history of privation and discrimination was a slippery one. The dual public-school system that redeveloped in the 1970s, much on the order of the old, survived through the next decade. It was no mere coincidence that whites held fast to segregated schools. Beyond the family, they were the repository of cultural norms, their very preservation necessary if civilization was worth saving. Natchez entered the post–civil rights movement period with many issues of race unresolved. Blacks continued their collective struggle for social and political equality, and whites continued theirs for cultural dominance.

THE SHADOW OF JIM CROW

The white principal leaned back and gazed out across the high-school courtyard. He sat in the same chair he had occupied two decades earlier when the school system implemented court-ordered integration. Comparing those days to the present, he entered into two hours of conversation.

He left his principal's job once before, in 1977, when he took an administrative position in Greenville. He came back to Natchez recently with the idea of retiring. But the public schools were beset with problems, and he decided he could help. He now worked for a man who had once worked for him as assistant principal and who presently served as Natchez's first black school superintendent.

The principal's perception of the public-school problems was summed up in three words: "The system's broke." He was referring to the legal and educational systems collectively. As he saw it, the system first showed signs of trouble when it failed to prevent white flight to private schools. His school had been 80 percent white in the 1970s; now it was 80 percent black. White community support had followed the white student exodus. Talented teachers left as well. They left because the system, in their minds, broke, and the system broke because they all left.

According to the principal, the broken system permitted the rate of teenage pregnancy to flourish. The principal said thirty-nine of his students were pregnant, all of them black. "I've got one girl who almost delivered last week. Her water broke. Fourth young one, by four different fellows. She's seventeen." Twenty years ago he would have told the girl, "Now, you're beginning to show a little bit. Call mother." He added, "But now her civil rights would be infringed on. The system is broke. What are we perpetuating?"

What was not being perpetuated, in his mind, were values once considered the most important in American society. By the principal's reckoning, the majority of the students ate free lunches, including some who could afford to pay: "That youngster comes out with that tray, they've got hundred-dollar Nike shoes on. The system's broke. Until we can get that kid to come out with that tray and say, 'Whoa, wait a minute. I'm paying for my lunch today,' we're not going to cure where we are right now. We've got a void right now of caring, self-respect, self-esteem, self-worth. I call that a big void. We've got to break a cycle. We've got generations that don't know anything but that Aid to Dependent Children check.

"When I say these things, I know I sound so prejudiced I know it stinks. I'm not prejudiced. We've got generations that come through that chow line, 'Momma got free lunches. I'm gonna get free lunches.' Nothing is free in this world. We had the same thing twenty-one years ago."

The broken system was responsible for the principal's most prodigious problem: discipline in the classroom. There was a time, the principal said, "when I could open this drawer and pull that paddle out and tell you because you told Miss Jones to go to hell I'm going to warm your britches up. And mommas and papas loved it rather than what I do now. Now, I've got to go through six due-process approaches [to suspend troublemakers]."

From the principal's perspective, it seemed at times that violence filled discipline's void. "If I had a scuffle that broke out, I'd go out there once again trying to keep two kids from killing themselves. So why do they care about life when they don't care about nothing?" Pulling a confiscated modified carving knife from his lap drawer, he said, "I'm trying to avoid that from going through one of them—or me.

"So I'm dealing with something here that reflects right back to twenty-one years ago: cultural difference."

THE civil rights struggle of the 1960s changed Natchez. Some people said for the best; others said for the worst. All agreed, though, that blacks expressed their discontent with discrimination with greater fortitude and dispatch than before. That new assertiveness was apparent one bright May afternoon in 1980 when Natchez blacks led the largest protest march since the Wharlest Jackson bombing in 1967, with more than two thousand people. The march surged like a river through the streets, overflowing onto sidewalks, as it pushed its way downtown, where it spilled around the front steps of the courthouse and covered half a city block. The march had begun with speeches in the parking lot of an abandoned shopping center off Pine Street, where John Nosser once owned a store. The shopping center was leveled now, just as the system of Jim Crow that Nosser had supported was leveled. The speakers, some of whom gave a new face to the local black leadership, said Jim Crow lingered, nevertheless, in the schools, in the economy, in the Old South traditions, and in the legal system.[1]

It lingered, they said, in the shooting of Terry Thornburg, a twenty-five-year-old black man from a local family. It was that incident that brought the protesters together. Thornburg had gone into a convenience store on Homochitto Street, allegedly stolen a pack of cigarettes, and then scuffled with the white owner before the owner's wife pulled a gun and shot Thornburg dead. The young man was no saint, many in the community admitted. He had been in trouble of this kind before. But his actions had not warranted the taking of his life. When one of the speakers, Phillip West (of no relation to the George West family), held up a petition and called for signatures, little coaxing was required to enlist supporters. The crowd moved forward with a readiness not exhibited by so many during the 1955 and 1965 school desegregation petition drives, when white intimidation still had a stranglehold on black collective action. The people in the former Nosser parking lot that day wanted all Natchez to know that the black community demanded justice in the Thornburg case.[2]

The day before the big march, Judy Ann Reeder had been charged with manslaughter for the shooting death of Terry Thornburg. Many blacks felt that the charge should have been murder. At Reeder's July trial, mostly blacks filled the courtroom. An eyewitness to the shooting told the court that Reeder "put two hands on the pistol. She didn't say nothing. She just pulled the gun and fired and the bullet hit Terry in the back." A pathologist report confirmed that Thornburg died from loss of blood from a gunshot wound in the back. When Reeder took the stand to defend herself, she told the prosecutor that she yelled "stop" twice as Thornburg wrestled with her husband. The shoplifter ran to the door, she said, and she shot him, though not with the intent to kill. The prosecutor asked if she had to shoot to save her life. "No sir, I didn't," she said. "But my husband is my life too, and I felt like I had to protect him." Following closing arguments, the jury of ten whites and two blacks deliberated for two hours and returned a verdict of not guilty.[3]

The jury's decision sent protesters into the streets again. With roughly three hundred joining in, the march was much smaller than the one in May. As before, it climaxed with a rally at the courthouse. Natchez NAACP President Phillip West, who had spoken at the May assembly, told the crowd that the protest was about more than the Reeder verdict. He encouraged blacks to organize to "deal with the businesses that don't hire us . . . with the stores that don't hire us . . . [with] the Adams County Public School system . . . [with] the Natchez Police Department that takes advantage of our black officers." He concluded by saying, "We intend to deal with all facets of Natchez where white people have misused the black community. . . . We should not let the death of Terry Thornburg be in vain."[4]

More than a decade after the local civil rights struggle, blacks such as West felt the frustration of unreconstructed racial attitudes and discriminatory behavior. To whites, relations were good between the races as long as blacks were not demonstrating or boycotting. Blacks had different ideas. Said one black letter-writer to the *Democrat* after the Thornburg shooting: "A good relationship suggests that we are free from fear; free to pursue a course of self-determination, without attempts being made to block that course. Free from suspicion where freedom of association can be enjoyed, without fear of peer retaliation. That we are free to live in any location, without being awakened by a 30-foot cross burning in the yard, or finding that everyone has left the block in mass exodus."

Natchezians had yet to achieve completely that sort of "good relationship" in 1980. Progress had been made, but never without confronting familiar reactionary forces. For blacks, the struggle for equality and fair treatment, for equal humanity, lumbered laboriously forward in the aftermath of the 1960s civil rights movement.[5]

From the standpoint of some whites, the Thornburg incident validated the old prognosis that the liberal revolt of the 1960s would unseat society and send it into decline. The robbery itself was another frightening example of a reported rise in the crime rate, which in the four years preceding the Thornburg incident had more than doubled. The majority of the crime emanated from the black neighborhoods, where Jim Crow once kept it contained, and now it was spreading into the larger community. "If it wasn't for the colored people," said one local white expressing the sentiment of many others, "there wouldn't be any crime." Why did blacks so passionately protest for the justice of a common criminal, many whites asked, when they could better use their energies to divert illicit impulses of people like Terry Thornburg into respectable endeavors. Eight years later, a white reader aired this very opinion in the *Democrat*: "Just imagine, if the time and energy used to organize boycotts and produce racially divisive speeches were devoted to helping black children. What could be accomplished?"[6]

It was a matter of priorities in this new era of voting, civil rights, and government welfare, and the letter writer and legions of other whites believed blacks had theirs askew. A disproportionate number of blacks seemed to be failing to use their newly acquired civil rights in a constructive way. Instead, whites generally believed, they were turning more freely to federal agencies for civil rights protection and welfare handouts, exploding the size of government in the process. The black victories in the 1960s seemed to unleash the worst traits in the victors, especially youths. They were no longer deferential toward their white superiors, but were instead bolder in demanding rights that seemed ill-suited to them, and they seemed too hasty in organizing mass protest.[7]

If Natchez society's advance toward racial progress was slow, entrenched white attitudes were the major obstacle to change. The myths that informed social constructions of blackness and the idea of cultural difference, the very racial myths that were alive and prevalent in the days of Jim Crow, found fertile ground in the new era of black political empowerment. It was an era to which the struggle for civil rights and school desegregation had been less than a revolutionary prelude.

During the earlier struggles, Natchez blacks acquired a new voice in local affairs that was broadcast through various mediums. Boycotts, rallies, marches, and petitions, powerful tools of the 1960s, opened up new mediums: biracial committees, city and county board meetings, letters to the editor, and the ballot. In the political arena, blacks raised their voice first to win the appointment of George West Jr. to the school board in 1967. Before the end of the decade, they had successfully demanded the inclusion of blacks as election workers. In 1973, blacks used their new voter strength to elect the first black city alderman, George West Sr., since Reconstruction days. The senior West ran unopposed in his first re-election bid, and in 1984, the city named a street for the veteran leader. In 1979, blacks elected Barney Schoby, who had been the first black Adams County supervisor in the twentieth century, to the State House of Representatives. That same year, Phillip West was elected to the county board of supervisors. Mary Toles of the NAACP captured a justice court judgeship in 1982 on the strength of black votes. In 1988, the city aldermen appointed a black police chief. A year later, two blacks sat on the five-member school board, and the county board of supervisors revealed an identical ratio.[8]

None of these advances had come easily, and black empowerment had its limitations. Although blacks accounted for a slightly larger portion of the city population, a greater number of whites consistently registered to vote. Blacks typically needed a 60 percent or greater voting majority in a district to elect one of their own, even when two or more blacks did not divide the ticket. Blacks occasionally charged voting fraud, but such allegations were never sustained by voting officials or the courts. Of the city's six-member board of aldermen in 1989, one member was black. Two years later, voters elected Theodore "Bubber" West, second son of George West Sr., to sit as the board's second black member. The power of blacks in economic affairs was comparatively less. In 1989, only two blacks sat on the Chamber of Commerce's twenty-three-member board of directors. As a result of political inexperience and indifference and old feelings of fear, Natchez blacks as late as 1990 were still underrepresented in city leadership.

Although black political gains seemed somewhat stifled, black protest remained ever aggressive. It was led primarily by a generation that during the 1970s assumed leadership from the older civil rights warhorses. Like many of those veterans, and unlike the professional-class leadership of earlier years, the new group of leaders generally rose from unassuming backgrounds. Phillip West, for example, was the seventh of twelve children born to plantation workers. At one point, West's father owned a truck and hauled timber off surrounding plantations, which sold their reserves to IP, Johns-Manville, and other manufacturing plants. For some ten years, he operated a juke joint in the Franklin Street area—the kind of place that would have been off limits to the likes of the Mackel and Dumas children. After graduating from all-black Sadie V. Thompson High School in 1964, Phillip West headed to Chicago, returned after a few months, attended Alcorn State University, and then took a job at Armstrong. He worked at the tire plant from 1968 to 1971, excepting a short stint in the military. When he left Armstrong, a Klan presence still sullied the workplace.

West came of age in the years of heightened black activism, and the times proved to be infectious. He marched with black Natchez after the Metcalfe bombing. At Alcorn, he participated in student demonstrations. At Armstrong, he stood up to a suspected Klansman who tried to intimidate black workers; West was a junior supervisor at the time confronting a white laborer. Soon after, the local draft board called up West's number, and he always wondered whether the Armstrong incident was related in some way. After receiving a discharge for a medical condition and returning to Armstrong, West filed a complaint with the Equal Employment Opportunity Commission stating that he was assigned to a position of lower status than before. The complaint was never sustained. In 1969, West made his debut in the local newspaper when he complained from the audience at a school-board meeting that black students in the public schools were being treated in "a racist manner." In what appeared to be a strange coincidence, one of his brothers was drafted a few days later. In 1974, West became president of the Natchez NAACP, and he was generous with words such as "demonstrations" and "boycott" that sent shivers through the white community. Some people said that West would return the city to the tumultuous 1960s. West said, "We never left the sixties."[9]

The young leader always felt that the white community misunderstood his intentions. He was true to the philosophy of nonviolence, but whites tended to see him as militant. He attributed that confusion in part to his appearance. Upon birth, he claimed, the Lord fixed a scowl on his countenance that made him look permanently antagonistic. In his early adult years, he wore an Afro, as did Barney Schoby, and together they cast the appearance of a pair of angry black militants ready to set the city in flames. Like Schoby, West always spoke his mind, tended to be more critical than complimentary, and rarely hesitated to sound charges of racism or to show contempt for whites suspected of impeding black progress. At a city aldermen's meeting in 1983, he lashed out against the emotional foundation of white tradition, and the city's sacred motto, when he proclaimed: "We are tired and fed up with seeing progress stymied by a philosophy of maintaining, 'where the old south still lives.'" Barney Schoby so habitually upbraided whites with epithets and insults that the *Democrat* accused him of making obscene language one of his "personal trademarks."[10]

The political philosophy and sometimes discordant approach of the new black leadership grated against conservative principles. The approach of West and Schoby represented a sharp contrast to the supplicating ways of the defunct professional-class leadership with which whites were familiar and which they preferred. Said one white Natchezian of the new black leadership: "If we had more George West [Sr.]s, we wouldn't have what we have now. And we ain't got much." The vitriolic demands of blacks such as Phillip West and Schoby struck whites as inflammatory, and they often questioned the sincerity of the black leaders' convictions. The leaders were outspoken about establishing hiring and promotion policies in the police, fire, and other city departments based on racial balances, as opposed to the merit system whites claimed to favor. When the new black leadership fought fiercely for 65 percent or greater black majorities in half the voting districts, whites complained that they would be unfairly disfranchised to compensate for black political lethargy.[11]

More than anything else, boycotts were the bane of the white community. After blacks learned the extent of their purchasing power from the 1965–66 boycott—from which many whites said the city never fully recovered—they launched four other successful boycotts over the next twenty-five years. At the 1978 state board meeting of the NAACP held in Natchez, Phillip West proclaimed that boycotting white businesses was "the best weapon the NAACP can utilize against racism." As the usual targets of boycotts and demonstrations, whites felt victimized by what they considered excessive caviling, which was nothing more than a fraudulent means of bypassing traditional routes to progress and uplift— hard work, determination, and patience. From the white side of the struggle, boycotts and demonstrations undermined racial harmony by disrupting the natural process of individual accomplishment and advancement.[12]

Both West and Schoby were seeking that natural process for blacks. They wanted Adams County and Natchez to be a better place to live, as did any public servant worthy of his or her office. They wanted better roads, better public services, and better economic opportunities that would keep people, black and white, in the area rather than drive them away. West recognized, in ways that all the white officials combined never had, that the local citizenry included blacks and that years of discrimination had left their community lacking in public services and economic resources. He wanted the white community to thrive as well, but no longer at the expense of the black community. In other words, gravel roads were unsuitable when white areas had asphalt, and cow pastures were an insult when white neighborhoods had lighted ball fields.[13]

Blacks no longer brooked such insults from whites. A confrontation at the December 1, 1975, meeting of the Adams County Board of Supervisors was indicative of the wedge driven between blacks and whites in an era of black political empowerment. The black-operated Adams-Jefferson Improvement Corporation (AJIC) requested $12,000 in supplemental funding from the supervisors. The AJIC was a nonprofit organization that administered federal programs in Adams and Jefferson Counties, such as Head Start. Most of the requested money was to go toward operating expenses; $3,000 was for matching federal funds to purchase minibuses to transport elderly poor citizens to the doctor, grocery, and bank. The request led to a "polite disagreement" between Barney Schoby, the lone black supervisor, and Sammy Cauthen, one of the white board members, that continued through a series of three meetings.[14]

Cauthen opposed the request for the bus. He argued that the county already provided $190,000 a year for social programs. Too much, he said. He favored taking "care of the peoples' tax dollars." He praised the AJIC's work, but added that "too many people rely on the government to feed them, clothe them and transport them." As Cauthen saw it, food stamps and Aid to Dependent Children made too many employable people complacent. "They had rather leech off the government" than work. He complained also about "welfare Cadillacs." Wait at the food-stamp office long enough, he said, and some recipient defrauding the government will eventually drive up in one. As for the money for the buses, Cauthen said, "When I was younger, you had to walk. I don't care whether you were white or black or purple."[15]

Schoby said he was sympathetic toward the poor. He himself once had been forced to seek welfare and, like most blacks, he "hated it." "There aren't enough jobs to go around," he said. "We've got senior citizens shut in on $140 a month fixed income." He added that the sick and infirm could not walk long distances, and as a result of society's indifference, they lacked necessary medical attention. At one meeting, an elderly black man stood up and said, "It seems to me that because this is a black group [in attendance] the board tries to dodge around and jump the track." Phillip West, representing the NAACP, suggested Cauthen's views did not represent the sentiment of his constituency, "especially black people." Schoby agreed, saying the supervisors "certainly haven't displayed leadership."[16]

At the third and final meeting, it became evident that a compromise between the white and black leaders was unlikely. The board president, Jimmy Carter, employer of the late Ben Chester White, broke a tie vote to reject the AJIC additional funding request. The quarreling at the board meetings reflected continuing divergent views on the reasons for poverty. In the decades after the civil rights marches, blacks believed that the social conditions of the black community were in large part the result of attitudes and a society that were slow to change. They considered lingering economic, political, and social injustices as the principal cause of their problems with poverty, illiteracy, single motherhood, and crime. Recalcitrant whites could not accept that argument as anything more than a contrived deflection from what had always been the problem—black culture—which was weakened even more so by paternalistic government social programs. Twenty percent of all Adams County black families in 1970 received federal assistance under the federal government's Aid to Dependent Children (welfare), and two decades later, in a new era of equal opportunity, that figure had increased to 29 percent. Here was statistical proof to whites that blacks were not culturally equipped to go it alone and that the policies of an abiding federal bureaucracy undermined initiative, presumably a nonexistent trait in black culture.[17]

Black and white views also diverged on the proper role of government in a society trying to overcome racial problems of the past. Cauthen articulated the two greatest fears of southern whites: federal aggrandizement and black empowerment. As seen through the distorted prism of white reality, blacks and federal officials had formed a conspiratorial partnership soon after World War II that set the South on an apocalyptic course. That partnership matured during the civil rights movement, when it brought dire consequences to the southern way of life. Now whites were fighting blacks for control of the wheel in their attempt to steer society back to a course charted by whites, only to find that the wheel was not easily won. Blacks had a say in matters now, and when they spoke emphatically, whites flinched. The problems and concerns of the black community could no longer be ignored or smoothed over by the fraud of patrician beneficence as they had been before. Wherever racial discrimination endured, conflict was likely to erupt.

Outside of local politics, Natchez blacks squared off with the white establishment in some familiar arenas. In 1977, for instance, John Scott filed a class-action discrimination lawsuit against International Paper Company, where he had been employed since 1950. Scott charged that as a result of the company's hiring and promotion practices and its "non-bona fide seniority system," blacks had been systematically excluded from the better-paying and more respected supervisory and skilled positions. Scott's suit came in the wake of a similar complaint that the NAACP filed with the Justice Department the year before. In effect, IP had violated Title VII of the Civil Rights Act of 1964, which prohibited employment practices based on sex and race. Natchez blacks were always quick to show their gratitude for the economic opportunities that the manufacturing companies provided, and many blacks were beginning to enjoy in the 1970s and 1980s something with which few had been familiar: a retirement pension. Still, they did not allow gratitude to compromise equality, and they were often quick to point out vestigial problems of discrimination.[18]

In the days after the disappearance of Jim Crow signs, that discrimination was never more obvious than in the hard, grinding poverty that persisted in the black community. Poverty itself is color-blind, but in Natchez, economic injustice revealed an unambiguous racial bias that withstood even the best of economic conditions. The world of the dispossessed was clearly the kingdom of blacks. Sixty percent of their families in Adams County remained beneath the poverty line in 1970, representing 87 percent of all poor families. By the end of the 1980s, the general economic condition of blacks had improved only slightly. In 1989, 79.3 percent of the families below poverty level came from the black community, half of which were impoverished. Single black women heading households suffered the worst. More than 80 percent of their families lived in poverty in 1970, and their numbers accounted for 91 percent of all poverty-level female-headed families.[19]

Deliverance from reduced circumstances came with decent employment opportunities, which continued to elude so many of the poor. Blacks in Adams County filled only one-fifth of all managerial and professional positions as late as 1990. As had so long been their fate in southern society, they still dominated the ranks of unskilled workers, more than two to one over whites. Increasing numbers were finding work in the growing service industry, at fast-food restaurants, grocery stores, and discount retail chains, in the type of jobs that were once exclusively white but that at minimum-wage rates could not support a family. Nearly one-third of all working black women made their living as domestics, and another 27 percent took work in the nonprivate cleaning and food service trades. In the late afternoons and early evenings, an ancient ritual repeated itself when black domestics streamed out of white homes and neighborhoods in a daily exodus to their own community.[20]

The headwaters of racial discrimination that fed such streams had also given rise to John Scott's class-action lawsuit. Not surprisingly, IP denied the plaintiffs' claims. The company did consent to a pretrial settlement though, promising to revamp the promotion system and open more traditionally white positions to blacks. It also agreed to pay the plaintiffs $412,000 in compensatory back pay. Scott returned to court in

1985 claiming IP had not lived up to its agreement in the original settlement, and the plaintiffs in the Scott case were forced to seek new concessions from the paper company.[21]

By this time, the invisible hand of the marketplace had reached out and pulled Natchez into a national economic recession. Unemployment in the 1980s soared as high as 17 percent and never dropped below double-digit figures. Problems first began when the bottom dropped out of a small but significant oil boom many Adams County landowners and mineral-lease holders had been riding since the 1970s. Industries that had migrated to the South for its cheap labor, low cost of living, and employer-friendly labor and environmental laws were moving to offshore locales providing even more favorable conditions. Natchez plants that remained downsized their workforce. In 1986, IP announced that it was reducing its payroll of one thousand employees by four hundred. That same year, Armstrong laid off one hundred employees from its already shrunken corpus of labor.[22]

A year later, Armstrong's corporate headquarters issued wrenching news that it planned to close the plant altogether. Hustling to save the hub of Natchez's manufacturing base, local businessmen and Armstrong employees bought and reopened the plant as Fidelity Tire Company. At its peak, the new company would employ five hundred, less than half of Armstrong's workforce in better days. Characteristic of the diminishing state of Natchez's manufacturing industry in general, Fidelity would never match Armstrong's pay scale, overtime opportunities, and benefits of earlier years. It was the same story played out in the industrial cities of the Great Migration to the North—Chicago, Detroit, Buffalo, Youngstown, and others. Just as better-paying skilled and supervisory positions were opening to blacks, factories began closing or exporting their labor requirements.[23]

In part due to John Scott's lawsuit, and despite the economic turndown, industrial jobs were more open to blacks than before. One found considerably less openness, however, in white churches. Christianity in some congregations proved that it had not transcended the days of Jim Crow. When congregants of a three-church circuit in Adams County ousted their pastor Karl Mertz in 1978, they staged a sequel to the drama performed in Methodist churches during the "Born of Conviction" affair in the 1960s. A Mississippi native, Mertz assumed the pastorship of Old Washington Methodist Church—where the old slave balcony still existed—and two other churches in June. Four years earlier, he had been a schoolteacher on the Mississippi Gulf Coast when he entered his name into a race for a congressional seat. The rangy thirty year old styled himself as a "New South" candidate with human-rights values. After his bid for public office failed, Mertz went on to complete a Th.D. at the Vanderbilt School of Divinity. Adams County was his first pastorship appointment.[24]

It was an odd match. Mertz had written his dissertation on race relations in the church, and on that issue he clearly leaned far enough to the left to fall quickly into bad graces with his congregations. The catalyst of his eventual removal came in an August sermon titled "One Can Not Be a Christian and a Segregationist, Too." In it, Mertz criticized both state conference and local congregational attitudes and practices on race—including the maintenance of the all-white church membership on his circuit and the segregated private schools to which many congregants sent their children. "There are, and always have been, two societies in Natchez," Mertz told his congregations, "one white and one black. . . . Most ministers, both black and white, are more concerned about preserving their own pulpits and pay than promoting racial justice and reconciliation." Then in perhaps a self-destructive move, he criticized his boss, the bishop in Jackson, for making "ministerial appointments under the leadership of culture, not the Holy Spirit."[25]

The sermon was icily received. In the evening three days later, a delegation of men from the Old Washington congregation called on Mertz with the news that they were planning a visit with the bishop to ask for the minister's removal. Six days after the sermon, representatives from the Pastor-Parish Relations Committee informed the bishop in Jackson that Mertz's sermons "have not met with the satisfaction of the congregations." In early September, the bishop relieved Mertz of his pastorship with the questionable claim that the dismissal had nothing to do with race.[26]

Mertz's future with the church remained uncertain until the annual state conference the following June. Shaw Gaddy, who had been pastor of Old Washington in the early 1950s and had been known to preach radical sermons then, spoke in support of Mertz. It was a noble but fruitless effort. By a three-to-one margin, 150 ministerial delegates voted to eject Mertz from the Mississippi ministry. By that time, the embattled minister had already begun to question his "real sense of calling," just as Summer Walters had done sixteen years earlier. Also like Walters, he preferred that the fate of his career in the Mississippi Methodist Church be determined by the will of God, not by the will of reactionary mortals. Mertz became yet another casualty of intractable earthly views on the race question. As it had been the case since Reconstruction, the sacred venue of the white church continued to endure in its racial isolation.[27]

In another one of Natchez's sacred venues, schools, the battleground opened between blacks and whites in the most explosive conflict of the post–civil rights decades. Blacks made it clear in the late 1960s that they would scrutinize the operation of public schools closely and would sound their dissent when dissatisfied. They did so almost immediately after the Christmas 1969 school-integration court order. In 1972, the Natchez NAACP filed a petition in federal court citing the segregated conditions that had redeveloped in Natchez public schools. North Natchez High and Prince Street Elementary had all-black enrollments, and only a handful of whites attended Thompson Junior High. The total student body in Natchez schools was 68 percent black; yet the faculty was 54 percent white. There were five black and ten white principals. Of forty-seven new teachers hired in recent years, eight were black. By 1980, Thompson had no white students. At North Natchez High School, one white student appeared in the 1985 yearbook, and ten of the fifty-two teachers were white. Resegregation of this sort in public schools was unusual in districts where private academies had not siphoned off nearly all the white students, and that had not yet happened in Natchez.[28]

The predominantly white schools remained havens of white heritage and pride that pandered to white students. At the same time, they revealed an indifference to and ignorance of black concerns with those attitudes. In the early 1970s, the allegiant, white sounds of "Dixie" were broadcast over the intercom system at desegregated South Natchez High, and modern-day redeemers restored Colonel Reb as school mascot. Black students also took offense at the administrative decision to ban high-school proms as official functions, lest blacks and whites engage in a level of social interaction deemed too intimate and dangerous. If and when proms were held, as Betty Williams learned, they were done so privately and generally at the exclusion of blacks. One fall football season, the NAACP marched on the South Natchez High's stadium in protest of the selection process of the homecoming queen, which favored whites with their majority numbers.[29]

Blacks had the option of partaking in white celebrations at official functions or truncating their social life at school. With either choice, they felt cheated. The circumstances of continuing discrimination and resegregation gave the Ford Justice Department in the early 1970s little choice but to oppose a school-board request to remove Natchez schools from federal court oversight. Blacks welcomed the Justice Department support, but found in it little encouragement for change. Under both Democratic and Republican administrations, the Justice Department looked the other way while Natchez effectively reconstructed a dual school system. School officials claimed that they operated the system in accordance with federal school zoning guidelines and blamed resegregation on shifting demographics and white flight. Some parents moved their entire families across town to avoid a traditionally black school or across the river to Vidalia, Louisiana, and its predominantly white schools. Other parents consulted zoning maps before enrolling their children under a relative's, friend's, or a bogus address that placed them in a majority-white school zone. Hoping to shut off the drain to private schools, public-school officials refused to "play policeman" when parents carried out their subterfuge.[30]

Zone jumping, as this practice was called, began soon after the 1969–70 desegregation order. The practice could hardly be discouraged when local officials got into the act, as did Natchez alderman Joe Bonner. The *Democrat* reported that Bonner had enrolled his children in the predominantly white McLaurin School, using the address of a rental house he had purchased under his wife's name. Bonner's father-in-law, Clarence Eyrich Jr., the school-board chairman, said he "really couldn't say" where his grandchildren lived. Ten months later, Bonner's children were still enrolled at McLaurin, even though the family had not moved.[31]

Once an unquestioned fact in the lives of most white children, choosing to go to public school now came after hard decision making. White parents were ambivalent about the benefits of public schools. They heard horror stories about student violence against teachers and other students, and not all the stories were false. In January 1979, at nearly all-black Thompson Junior High, a seventh grader was arrested for carrying a gun, and in a separate incident, an eighth grader was stabbed. At all-black North Natchez High, a fight between two boys resulted in the stabbing death of one. In 1989, the estranged husband of a black teacher at Northside Primary School held nineteen kindergartners hostage while he raped two teachers and shot his wife. Such incidents seemed to validate the dire predictions of whites who believed that integration would "draw down the education system" and subject their children to pathological behavior.[32]

More than a few Natchez blacks agreed with some of the assessments whites made about public schools in the aftermath of court-ordered desegregation. They pointed to "the erosion of standards of academic performance and discipline" in some of the schools. One black letter-writer to the *Democrat* said parents and administrators lacked "the courage to insist on tough standards" and "balk at insisting that incompetent teachers [black and white] be weeded out." Another black letter-writer went so far as to say that "a deeper decline in the education of black students was brought about when the school system had to follow the federal mandate to integrate." The letter writer was voicing his complaint about a growing lack of discipline, which he blamed on judges and social workers who "have intervened and set guidelines for parents on rearing children." Many blacks agreed with whites that student insolence was on the rise. Thompson Junior High principal Freddie Johnson, who spent the first eighteen years of his education career in Natchez black schools, said the single greatest problem schools faced with integration was "discipline of black students." Teachers could no longer use corporal punishment by the 1980s, and many white teachers were afraid to punish black students or were just indifferent to problem students.[33]

Public-school officials winced at the negative publicity. With private schools establishing a foothold in Adams County, as they did elsewhere in Mississippi, public schools no longer had a lock on the student market. Administrators worried that the image of unsafe conditions would send whites seeking refuge in comparatively safer private schools. Losing students meant losing federal and state funding based on enrollment. "We worked *hard* to maintain white students," said Claude Porter, who started with Natchez schools in 1953 and served as superintendent from

1977 to 1988. A devoted educator, Porter made high academic standards his top priority, above integration. Under his leadership, the public schools actively sought the best-qualified teachers, preferring those with graduate degrees. It was a policy, according to Porter, that later "got me into trouble," since the teachers who were most academically qualified were usually white.[34]

Scholastically, Porter's policies worked at some schools, even as there were reports of eroding standards at others. Throughout the 1970s and 1980s, Natchez public schools attained top accreditation ratings from the Southern Association of Colleges and Schools. Students at some of the traditionally black schools benefited, as did whites. Black North Natchez High students in the 1980s consistently scored higher on graduation testing than their rivals at mostly white South Natchez High, refuting an old stereotype about black intelligence (but not dismantling white attitudes about integration).[35]

With such positive reports, the black community found itself in a quandary over the issue of resegregation. For the most part, blacks had struggled for integrated schools to establish equality in educational opportunities, not interracial social interaction. Even with the redevelopment of segregation, many blacks felt that substantial progress toward equality had been made. They saw few benefits in sharing schools with whites. Blacks once again had their own administrative and faculty leaders, sports teams, marching bands, cheerleading squads, and homecoming queens. They did not have to tolerate the sometimes uncomfortable presence of whites; nor did they have to feel they were the source of discomfort for others. In their own schools, they were free of white racism, arrogance, and officiousness. Blacks too worried about the dilution of culture. Just as whites embraced their own racial and cultural identity under the schoolhouse roof, blacks naturally felt more secure in their cultural identity as African Americans in an environment that nurtured that identity, free of white restraints.[36]

Other blacks believed that the benefits of integration outweighed the drawbacks. They raised the time-honored arguments that the retention of all-black schools encouraged disparities in school plant facilities and equipment, that blacks as usual would, as one black school administrator put it, "get the neck of the chicken." In 1983, the NAACP complained that the upkeep of Thompson Junior High had fallen behind that of the mostly white schools. The organization also claimed that the better black teachers were assigned to the white schools. Many black parents feared that if black and white children remained isolated from each other, another generation of whites would grow up harboring the same old myths about blacks. A black letter-writer wondered how white children would otherwise "learn that blackness of the skin has nothing to do with right or wrong, success or failure, morality or immorality, rather it's a blackness of the heart that causes a person to perpetuate the idea that incompatibility, incompetence and inferiority are exclusively characteristics of blacks." Supporters of integration reasoned that it was better for children to find compatibility at a young age than for them to wait until they are adults confronting each other in the integrated workplace. They hoped also to share with whites the idea that differences in people did not have to be obstacles to unity and equality.[37]

The most vociferous opponents of resegregation were Barney Schoby and Phillip West. Throughout the 1970s and 1980s, the two leaders constantly sparred with school officials. As early as 1973, they called for the consolidation of the high schools and two of the junior highs to correct growing racial imbalances. They accepted Porter's emphasis on educational quality as a fraud that contradicted the intent of the 1969 court decision. They were especially critical of his policy to retain white enrollment at all costs. Porter had argued that integration would create upheaval in the white community and provoke white flight. In response, West charged school officials with "the misuse of black people in order to appease the white community." Upheaval in the white community was a white problem related to destructive racial attitudes, which were responsible for the educational disparity to begin with and for which blacks should no longer have to suffer. Some Natchezians, black and white, suggested that Schoby and West were too often impetuous in their attacks against the white leadership, especially in their unrestrained accusations of racism; politics and a hunger for power, it was said, fed their crusades.[38]

In this highly charged atmosphere, a seemingly isolated incident in 1987 became a spur for black anger and protest, which ultimately led to a major change in the school system. In November, Lonnie and Carolyn Nichols complained to the school board that the Martin School principal, Robert Owen, had threatened their ten-year-old son with detention for sitting with his white classmates in the school cafeteria. The board promised to look into the matter, but eleven days later the Nicholses said that no one had yet contacted them in regard to an investigation. Schoby, West, and other black leaders summoned a press conference in which they denounced school officials for their inaction and called for the resignations of Porter and Owen. Whites saw the separation of the classmates as a routine disciplinary measure, but to blacks it was symptomatic of more fundamental problems in the school system. The Schoby and West group maintained that Porter was "in another world" when it came to the concerns of 67 percent of the student body. The next day, West announced that the black leadership was strongly considering a boycott of schools and businesses.[39]

On December 2, the school board unanimously adopted a statement refuting the Nicholses' claim and supporting Porter and Owen. A school investigation concluded that the Nichols boy and two white students were separated in the cafeteria for disruptive behavior. Owens had followed standard procedure, and the next day, the students were allowed to sit together again. The investigation's conclusions made sense to friends and colleagues who knew Owen as a quiet and affable man who cared deeply about all his students. Since the early days of school desegregation, there had been legitimate reports of white teachers breaking up interracial gatherings in lunchrooms and elsewhere. But for Owen to behave in such a manner contradicted the character of a man who himself socialized with blacks. Blacks and whites both suspected that the Nichols complaint had been hijacked by the NAACP and unfairly politicized.[40]

Some black leaders did seem to ignore the veracity of the Nichols incident in pursuit of a larger goal. The evening of the day of the school-board statement, approximately three hundred blacks and fifty whites gathered at Zion AME Church. In a scene reminiscent of a 1960s civil rights rally, people held hands and sang songs, while speakers energized the crowd. West and Schoby confirmed that their complaint had never been specifically about the Nichols case. The real problems of concern were resegregation and school disparity. They reiterated the demand for the resignations of Porter and Owen and added a call for the departure of the entire school board, including its two black members. They gave school officials two days to meet their demands or risk a school and business boycott.[41]

The school-board members refused to resign. Nor did they ask for the resignations of Porter and Owen. They averted a boycott by agreeing to meet with the black leaders. Their first meeting ended at an impasse, and black leaders again made a public demand for resignations. Then Theodore Johnson, one of the black board members, wrote a letter to the *Democrat* acknowledging that Natchez blacks had "legitimate and valid grievances" against the operation of the school system, and he provided a list of discrepancies ranging from school-zone jumping to the number of blacks in South Natchez High School's choir.[42]

Board officials again met with black leaders. This time the two parties reached an agreement. School officials consented to the implementation of an affirmative action plan with a 50-percent-placement goal for black teachers and administrators. They also agreed to appoint a biracial committee to correct the disparity in school plant facilities and another to make school operation recommendations to the superintendent's office; to award 30 percent of all school business to minority vendors and contractors; to promote Willie Hoskin, the only black assistant superintendent, to first assistant; to hire an impartial body to investigate the Nichols incident and to determine whether Porter and the school board were guilty of discrimination; and to fire those persons identified as guilty. The parties signed the agreement, which the board of aldermen and the county supervisors were to sanction.[43]

But the agreement fell apart quicker than it had come together. The resulting incident smacked of what happened when John Nosser in 1965 backed out of the twelve-point agreement with the NAACP in apparent fear of dismantling southern traditions. This time, those who reversed themselves came from the black side of the struggle. At a rally the night of the agreement, West and Schoby and two other black leaders called for a full-scale boycott of white businesses. "You must understand . . . the history of what has been done over so many years," West told the crowd. As a result, "we think of white people like the United States thinks of the Russians." The announcement of the boycott stunned the white community. City and county officials had not been given the chance to meet to endorse the agreement. The seeming impetuosity of the decision to boycott confirmed suspicions that West and Schoby and other boycott leaders were motivated by selfish ambitions. All were elected officials, and according to the *Democrat*, they had acknowledged staking their political futures "against a successful outcome of the crisis."[44]

As with past demonstrations, the boycott deepened the division between blacks and whites. This time it also divided the black community and the NAACP. The breach within the civil rights organization cut a vague line along generations, with older blacks, including those who had been leaders during the 1960s demonstrations, more likely to oppose the aggressive tactics of West and Schoby. The boycotters did receive an important endorsement from one 1960s leader, Charles Evers, who was now mayor of Fayette, Mississippi. Boycott backers contended that the original demands of the black leaders had been watered down in negotiations, that the promised investigation could easily be whitewashed, and that change in school-system leadership was needed regardless. But many others believed West and Schoby had been too hasty in their call for a boycott. NAACP President Mary Toles, who described herself as part of "the old moderate realm," though she was a contemporary of West and Schoby and shared their ideology, said she respected the purpose of the boycott, but would have used it as a "last resort." She agreed that problems persisted in the school system, and she held the school board responsible for the present turmoil. But she noted, "We in the NAACP are not school board bashers." She obviously was not speaking for West and Schoby, also members of the NAACP.[45]

Despite the split in the black community, the boycott was effective. It reminded too many whites of the Christmas boycott that followed the Metcalfe bombing in 1965. Feeling unfairly targeted and resentful toward West and Schoby, businesses reported a sharp drop in sales and announced that they consequently would not be hiring their usual complement of Christmas help. The Chamber of Commerce said the business community was being "punished for something they have no control over." Responding to the boycott, the school board voted four to one to revoke the agreement with the black leaders. A *Democrat* editorial urged the school board to proceed with addressing the problems in the agreement, despite the impasse. A faction within the NAACP led by Toles asked the school board to do the same. It also requested that the Justice Department reopen the school desegregation suit originally filed against Natchez in 1965. It did so at the end of February, and West and the Nicholses, by now calling themselves the Concerned Citizens, followed a few days later with a companion suit.[46]

The boycott continued, however. West and Schoby wanted resignations. Toles, who supported the spirit of the boycott, believed that the majority-black school system needed either a majority-black school board or a black superintendent. Then in a surprise move, Porter resigned on March 10, citing the decision as best for himself, his family, and the public schools. Years later, recognizing that he was part of the problem but still proud of his record of maintaining high educational standards, Porter said, "One of my weaknesses was I was an educator, not a politician. I was interested in the schools."[47]

Just as the city was trying to shake the effects of the boycott, an extremist from the other side presented himself. Nine days after Porter's resignation, a flamboyant Jackson attorney named Richard Barrett, who had a track record of association with white-supremacist groups, led an antiboycott rally of some three hundred whites on the courthouse grounds in Natchez. The city had attempted to stop the rally, but when Barrett filed suit, the city backed down. Barrett referred to himself as a "pro-majority activist" opposed to "mobs running by the law of the jungle." At the rally, he spoke about tyranny by the minority and called the boycotters "tyrants, haters and oppressors." He and his supporters carried signs that read, "Bust Boycott," "Free Natchez," and "Back Porter." Barrett's rally embodied the concerns of a growing number of disgruntled whites who conceived that black civil rights had come at the expense of white rights. Blacks understood that whites tended to confuse constitutional and legal rights with fleeting caste privileges. To this end, an equal number of blacks, which included Schoby and West, met the antiboycott rally with their own signs, which read, "We Will Be Free," "We Will Be Here when You're Gone," and "We've Paid Our Dues." Schoby declared that the rally helped unite the black community.[48]

Contradicting that assertion, the boycott began falling apart after Porter's resignation. Charles Evers withdrew his support, stating that the boycotters' demands were no longer clear since Porter was out. One of the four boycott leaders pulled out to devote more time to his county supervisor duties. In July, the school board named a new superintendent, Melvin R. Buckley, an education professor from Northeastern Louisiana State University. Schoby denounced the appointment, insisting that it should have gone to a black applicant. West withheld his opinion to give

Buckley a chance to remedy the school system's problems. In September, the school board elected George West Jr. chairman, in place of the retiring Clarence Eyrich. The boycott finally collapsed.[49]

During the same months, the lawsuit moved forward. In July 1989, the U.S. district court ordered Natchez school officials to proceed immediately with a Justice Department desegregation plan. It called for the consolidation of the two high schools (grades ten through twelve) into the South Natchez High facility. The North Natchez High campus would convert to a middle school for all students in grades seven through nine. Two days later, the school board officially approved the plan. Mayor David Armstrong, who supported it, expected many whites to depart from the public schools. In classic political doublespeak, he said, "I don't know that's going to happen, but realistically I know it's going to happen."[50]

With the beginning of the new school year, it seemed that history was repeating itself. The cast included many of the same faculty and staff from 1970. White flight was significant but not massive. The high school lost approximately 20 percent of its white students, or fewer than 150. A considerable number of the students were children of parents who had pioneered the same transition nineteen years earlier, and the responses were nearly the same. Describing the change as "chaos," many students blamed adults—parents, administrators, and politicians—for the disruption in their lives. Seniors complained about having to "sacrifice" their final and most cherished year in school. Students dealt with overcrowding, confusion, new teachers and classmates, and classroom mix-ups.[51]

Students also lost the school of their identity. At Natchez High, the school colors were changed to reflect one each from the old high schools. Colonel Reb was banished once again—along with the Confederate flag—and replaced by a bulldog. A junior-high teacher who had been through the 1970 transition said the children were angry over having lost their own schools and being crowded into a single facility. Unlike 1970, she said, "Every child that came through the [classroom] door was mad, everyone, black and white." Although an advocate of integration, she believed, as did so many others, that the abolition of neighborhood schools was the greatest loss both races suffered in 1970 and 1989.[52]

To many parents, integration in 1989 was a haunting flashback to 1970 when they had been students. The memories of losing their identifiable schools, principals, model teachers, and so much else were bitter ones for a number of parents who had supported desegregation before incurring that loss. As adults, they were ambivalent about the same thing happening to their children. Former North Natchez High principal Oscar Reed echoed many when he said, "Integration for the sake of integration is no good." White parents harbored the same concerns their parents had before them. The specter of diminished education quality, riots, violence, cultural intermixing, and "young black bucks" loomed once again. Looming even larger were new fears about drugs and gang violence on school campuses. Remembering the alarmist reactions of their parents in 1970 and coming of age after Jim Crow, when racial discrimination was no longer openly tolerated, many white parents tried to keep an open mind about integration, and many failed.[53]

The outcome of past efforts (1955, 1965, 1970) to integrate the public schools was a prelude to the final stage, which ultimately failed as well. It was no coincidence that Natchez private schools thrived after 1989. Whites had little choice but to share the political process, the workplace, and even historical interpretation with blacks. Private schools, however, offered whites an alternative to sharing a public venue. Within a decade's time, enrollment in the local private academies grew 73 percent, and with that increase, the public schools experienced a drop not only in enrollment but in local and state funding. They also lost strong community support, one of "the biggest problems" for the school system, according to an assistant supervisor. Like many communities across Mississippi and the South, Natchez accommodated a dual system of a post–Jim Crow sort, which included virtually all-white private academies and nearly all-black public schools. By the time of the 1989 court order, the third stage in the battle over public schools, the continuing story of school desegregation in Natchez had evolved into an epic.[54]

Similar conflicting impulses of change and continuity also clashed over white Natchezians' most beloved institution: the Pilgrimage. As had always been the case, whites enjoyed a near monopoly in the Pilgrimage's economic windfall. With oil and manufacturing industries suffering, the Pilgrimage had emerged by the late 1980s as the city's top business, generating roughly $5 million a year in revenues. The tourist trade built around this commercialization of history provided nearly 1,400 jobs and a $9.7-million payroll in 1986, and put $890,000 in local government coffers. Said the *Democrat* news editor in 1989, "Until we can woo industries, until oil prices go up again . . . we must depend on history—and the tourists it attracts—to keep the economy alive." Each of the owners of homes on the tour, all of whom were white, took in several thousand dollars every year. Nearly all of the merchants and motel and restaurant owners who saw a big chunk of the tourist dollars were white. But the locals who bused tables, directed parking, trimmed flower gardens, waxed floors and furniture, and peddled pralines on street corners were almost always black.[55]

Natchez blacks had always been conflicted over the economic and cultural benefits that they realized from the spring event. On the one hand, it offered the black community an economic opportunity. On the other hand, it was emblematic of the long and unending economic disparity between blacks and whites. Expressing the hidden feelings of so many Natchez blacks, Phillip West proclaimed the Pilgrimage "a detriment to black/white relations. . . . Blacks get nothing out of the tours other than a few minimum wage jobs." Harden Wallace, a longtime president of the Natchez Business and Civic League, offered the same observation with a different eloquence: the money "don't hardly leave after it gets into the big houses."[56]

As public history, the Pilgrimage was similarly offensive to blacks. The re-creation of the glory days of the antebellum white South conjured up an image in black minds of something different from gallant young men and pristine belles. "When I look at the big houses, Melrose, and the fan [punka]," said Theresa Lewis, "I'm thinking about a small black doing that [under his master's eye], and if he didn't do it right, he'd get a whipping." One black letter-writer to the *Democrat* understood the white cultural meaning and the social implications of the "revival of the Old South" as a way "to continue the old traditions." Through this "activity [whites] attempt to instill those ideas in each succeeding generation." He concluded with the observation that whites "cannot seem to understand that [the Old South] is as dead as the 'third Reich'!"[57]

Like whites, blacks recognized a cultural value in preserving the past. The visible family tree of some blacks may have been rootless beyond a generation or two, sustained by little more than oral tradition and cut off by unrecorded slave demographics and insufficient record keeping, the names and lives of ancestors who existed before emancipation lost in mystery. But the whole of the black experience was not inconsequential—not to blacks. Even in the days of segregation, they managed to surmount impediments of Jim Crow society to seek an equivalent to the sustenance whites took from history. During the 1940s and 1950s, Audley Mackel, who reorganized the local chapter of the NAACP in 1940, often spoke of the lessons of history in the "motivational" speeches he delivered at area black churches. In one speech, he revealed a deeper understanding of history's cultural function than that of Pilgrimage cofounder Katherine Miller, for Mackel told rapt congregants of the deceit inherent in the white version of the past.

> History is written in such a fashion as to distort the real facts concerning the contribution made by Negroes[,] and our environment is so constructed as to cause most of us to unconsciously concieve [sic] the idea that our civilization, rather the civilization in which we live, started in America. . . . The Caucasians have distorted facts in history by omission and commission until History as we recieve [sic] it is more or less propaganda. We must emphasize the contributions made by the Black Man. We must let our youth know the facts and at best a large number will become the victims of white man's supeority [sic] complex. The so called American civilization is no more than a continuation of the initial stage of man regardless of creed or color.[58]

Others shared Mackel's insight. Equally mindful of the deceit of history were black schoolteachers who deviated from the standard "segregationist" textbooks to incorporate lessons on the black experience. Particular emphasis was given to local black figures such as Hiram Revels, John R. Lynch, Robert Wood, Richard Wright, and many other successful landowners, politicians, and professionals. Negro history week was celebrated every February in the black schools as late as 1969, when the federal court ordered the abolition of Natchez's dual school system. Throughout the year, teachers brought into their classrooms black history books, such as Carter G. Woodson's old standard *The Negro in Our Time,* and related articles from magazines and black newspapers, such as the *Chicago Defender* and *Pittsburgh Courier.* As for

Pearl Guyton's white-supremacist history text, *Our Mississippi,* retired black educator Theresa Lewis said, "I tell you exactly what happened to that history book in my classroom; it just stayed on the shelf."[59]

Beyond the black community, black history had a limited public. Before the 1990s, for instance, most local whites knew nothing of Natchez's most renowned native and historical figure, Richard Wright. The historical memory of blacks was quite different from that of whites, and difference of any sort could lead to conflict. As long as black history was rendered nonessential, just as were black civil rights and liberties, differences were avoided and the continuous operation of an artificially harmonious society was assured. For memory can, to quote historian Edward Ayers, "divide as much as unite. . . . Memory makes the cultural political, the political cultural; memory makes present conflicts revolve around questions about the past."[60]

One can also argue that memory empowers. Black history began to emerge from its underground existence following the passing of Jim Crow in the 1960s. When blacks sought recognition of it in the public realm, black history threatened the social dominance of white culture, its values, ideals, and priorities. Indeed, black-white conflicts came to revolve around questions about the past, and at times, history became contested battleground.

In subsequent decades, history remained an issue in the search for a common meaning of equal access and opportunity. Whites had been puzzled ever since blacks first showed their antipathy for the Pilgrimage in the 1960s. Since the Pilgrimage extolled the positive images of wealth, gallantry, and gaiety and evoked communal pride, Natchez whites presumed that others felt the same as did they. Blacks should be willing to wrap bandanas around their heads, dress in calico, and portray spiritual-singing cotton pickers; it was all accurate history, as whites saw it, and therefore not offensive. "It was beautiful," said a garden club president of the spirituals blacks once sang in a pageant tableau. "It sent a chill up my spine to listen to them. . . . I don't know why they stopped."[61]

The answer could be found in the traditional attitude and language of some pageant officials. In 1986, for example, they found themselves entangled in a racial controversy that made national news when the pageant committee prohibited a black student of a local dance troupe from

participating in one of the pageant tableaux. The committee cited historical authenticity as its reason, maintaining that only whites would have
been part of the nineteenth-century soiree that the tableau was depicting.
Ironically, the committee dismissed the fact that since blacks pulled out
of the pageant in the 1960s, whites had on more than one occasion performed in black face and females routinely danced in male dress. Pilgrimage faithfuls denied charges of discrimination. "We have tried to get
the colored people back since the NAACP took them out in the 1960s,"
said the Natchez Garden Club president. She suggested creating a tableau "showing one of the darkies' balls—that's the one I've always wanted
to do." She explained, "In these balls, the darkies would be given access to
one of the antebellum homes, and they would have great parties."[62]

To many Natchezians, the "darkie" comment reflected a gratuitous,
at the least careless, choice of words. Some blacks took heart in knowing
that the "darkie" comment came from a generation that was soon to
pass in the garden clubs, even as it reflected the failure of some whites to
appreciate or understand black sensitivities to racial language of this
kind. Some whites made the argument that the term "darkie balls" represented common language of the Old South and that Natchez's prominent free-black barber William Johnson, author of one of the antebellum
South's most important diaries, wrote of these events using the same verbiage.[63] But words of this sort translated into power, while at the same
time language commonly used and considered socially acceptable symbolized an inequitable distribution in power. As blacks understood, even
if whites did not, speaking in historical context did not justify the use of
particular language since that context was created from the historical
perspective of only one group, the group in power. Additionally, Johnson's perspective was inconsistent with that of the larger black community of his day, for he was a slaveholder and an elitist who embraced the
values of the white world as he aspired to be accepted into it.

As Natchez moved into the final decades of the twentieth century, the
Pilgrimage prospered even as it remained largely unchanged in content,
style, and mythic message. One Natchez black observed, "There are
Ante-Bellum minds as well as Ante-Bellum structures here." Recognizing
that the white understanding of the black historical perspective lagged
behind the advancing tourist industry, black Natchez mustered forth an

intensified determination to instill public history with the black experience. In January 1986, blacks broke with the white past and publicly honored their own history with Natchez's first Martin Luther King Day parade. Few whites attended the parade, and the local chapter of the NAACP called for a boycott of the virtually all-white Natchez Mardi Gras parade in February. In response to white accusations of economic tyranny, blacks pointed out that the King parade had been all but ignored by whites, including the local newspaper, the Chamber of Commerce, the mayor, and the sheriff, who traditionally participated in other parades.[64]

Two years later, a coalition of black leaders collided with a wall of united white opposition when they petitioned to rededicate Pine Street in central Natchez in the name of Martin Luther King Jr. A long asphalt band that stretched across the city from antebellum homes in a white neighborhood, past black businesses and homes and several miles out to Anna's Bottom in the rural environs, Pine Street appealed to the petitioners as a symbol of race and class unity consistent with King's own social philosophy. Resistance forces included many self-identified liberal whites, who argued that the historic value of the 152-year-old street should be preserved in its name. Blacks made a similar argument about King. After eight months of rejected counterproposals, the city board of aldermen voted to rename the northern half of Pine Street, occupied by mostly black businesses and residences, and to retain the original name for the southern section, where whites lived. Mary Toles, NAACP chapter president, described what many believed to be the divisive implications of the decision when she said, "I think the action of the board reflects a tale of two cities."[65]

In the black "city," the memory of the slain civil rights leader served as a springboard for instituting a broader revision of local public history. When Congress considered a bill in 1988 to convert a Natchez plantation into a national historic park, black county supervisor Phillip West traveled to Washington to support the bill on the condition that the black community would share the economic benefits of the new park. Local blacks also wanted assurances that history at the park would not be showcased in the same "moonlight and magnolia" image for which the Pilgrimage was known. To this end, blacks and many local whites successfully lobbied for the park to include the house of William Johnson.[66]

Clearly, some among the traditional guardians of history were beginning to open their minds to a fuller, more complete image of the past. The idea to preserve the William Johnson house had been put into motion by the all-white Preservation Society of Ellicot Hill when it bought the house in 1976 from Johnson's descendants. An outgrowth of the Natchez Garden Club, the Preservation Society was chaired by Margaret Moss, then garden club president. Acquiring the Johnson house was an important, though nonaggressive, first step toward the public recognition of black history. Johnson represented a "safe" black historical figure because his own life as a slaveholder confirmed the cultural choices of the dominant racial group. Frequently, whites held up—and still do—Johnson and other successful blacks of the nineteenth century as evidence of a history of racial tolerance in Natchez. Despite the questionable record on race of both the city and Johnson, the black community recognized the historical importance of the barber of Natchez. Once Johnson was publicly acknowledged, observed Duncan Morgan, a black Natchezian dedicated to historic preservation, black history "could not be denied." With the precedent of that history, blacks affirmed their more recent struggle against racial intolerance.[67]

Occupying a central role in the federal acquisition of the William Johnson house was the Historic Natchez Foundation. Created by the Natchez Historical Society, the foundation was formed in 1974 for the purpose of preserving historic structures other than privately owned mansions. With the appointment of Ron Miller, a North Carolina social liberal, the foundation's role quickly expanded to include recapturing the ethnic history of Natchez. Miller found support in a board of directors reflecting Natchez's biracial society, as well as in the efforts of California State University historian Ron Davis and an inexhaustible reinforcement of students researching and writing about Natchez. No other biracial institution in Natchez did more than the foundation to enrich local public history with the black experience. Mimi Miller of the foundation, for instance, developed a black-history tour that the Natchez Convention and Visitors Bureau adopted after hiring its first African American tour director in 1991.[68]

There were a number of other local efforts to discover black history that complemented the National Historic Park and the Historic Natchez Foundation. Thelma Williams, who hailed from local stock, opened the

Mostly African Market in 1988 after organizing Project Southern Cross, a summertime educational enrichment program for local children that included learning about Natchez's black heritage. Founded in 1990, an annual Natchez Literary Festival helped bring local fame to Richard Wright, whereas he once enjoyed only international fame. Evidence of a growing market for black history in Natchez encouraged a small group of black women in 1990 to organize the Natchez Association for the Preservation of Afro-American Culture (NAPAC). "The idea was that locally we ought to be able to tell our own story," said Mary Toles, one of the founders of NAPAC and the first president. Pursuing a proposal that had been floating around Natchez since the airing of the miniseries *Roots* in 1977, NAPAC opened a museum of African American culture, in part to show that the black experience was "not that far from the total American experience."[69]

In 1990, blacks even rejoined the Pilgrimage. In cooperation with the garden clubs, the choir of the black Holy Family Catholic Church added the African American perspective to Pilgrimage events with the gospel presentation "Southern Road to Freedom." Unlike the spirituals that were part of the Pilgrimage during the days of Jim Crow, this performance did not ask believers to accept worldly troubles in exchange for heavenly bliss. It instead offered, to quote the 1998 Natchez Spring Pilgrimage brochure, "a stirring musical tribute to the struggle and victory of the African-American [slave] experience in Natchez."[70]

The acknowledgment in the Pilgrimage brochure was a small, though significant, public recognition of the black historical experience. Recognizing a struggle of a century earlier, however, was different from recognizing the modern-day struggle for political and civil rights. The actions of long-dead ancestors may no longer have been so faithfully defended, perhaps even looked at critically, but evaluating one's own behavior from the perspective of a racial counterpart was still beyond the ability of a significant number of whites. Like the hunter on the riverbank in *Eyes on the Prize*, whites were continually challenged to look at life in ways never conceived.

The challenge came largely from blacks, who no longer allowed the white perspective to dominate in ways it had before. Yet publicly legitimizing the black historical experience also reinforced the idea of cultural difference, which in turn increased the emotional distance between blacks and whites. Amidst all the change precipitated by blacks, a major thread of continuity that held back racial progress was the social construction of race. In a match against time, race was equally persistent, and associating race with culture made the idea of race more real. The very idea of race took sustenance from those everyday things considered the very stuff of culture, such as family, worship, leisure, work, and history. With the black community reeling from the effects of single-motherhood, multigenerational welfare dependency, crime, violence, and drugs, many whites striving for open-mindedness during the twilight decades of the twentieth century were beset by an inherent impulse to generalize about race and culture in the ways of their predecessors. Still at stake for whites was far more than political and economic power. At stake was the future of society and the culture upon which it was built. With that came the white compulsion to protect schools, churches, and heritage from the "plague" of black culture.

This was the image blacks had to bear. Southern society had in fact been built upon the pillars of black culture as much as any other. Knowing that the long memory of segregation and its legacy of discrimination were more real than the history portrayed by the Pilgrimage, blacks carried forth the struggle for equal humanity and cultural respect against the myths, misperceptions, omissions, and deceptions of the past and the present. Even after blacks removed the rigid guidelines of the caste system described so eloquently by Davis and the Gardners in 1941, the past's impact on the generations born after Jim Crow was indisputable. Breaking down physical barriers of discrimination, disrupting the artificiality of social harmony so that democracy could work, was a step short of breaking down racial attitudes embedded in history. That history continued.

LEAVING NATCHEZ

I have left Natchez for the last time on several occasions now, always thinking that this study is finally ready to be put to bed. But invariably, I find myself going back. Each time I do, I am witness to the unceasing forward motion of history. Natchez never waits during my absences. It continues to grind ahead on its course to wherever, and when I return I have to scramble to catch up.

The first time I left Natchez "for the last time" was as a graduate student in 1994. A friend and I had gone there one week that winter. She worked a booth at a gun and knife show, while I cloistered myself in a room at the historic Eola Hotel to put the final touches on the dissertation from which this book evolved. Though cramped and noisy, the hotel room offered a pacifying view of the the Mississippi River and the evening sun sinking into the Louisiana Delta. The disharmony between the accommodations and the view seemed the perfect setting for completing an arduous yet satisfying labor. The last day in town, though, brought a reminder that Natchez's story would never be complete.

That morning, we went for breakfast at the local Shoney's restaurant. While waiting to be seated, we stood behind a young black couple. With menus in hand, the white hostess approached the couple and politely offered the obligatory, "Smoking or nonsmoking?" The couple answered nonsmoking. The hostess apologized and said that nonsmoking was full. The couple agreed to take smoking and then trailed off behind the hostess.

When she returned, the same question was presented to us. We said something to the effect of, "Since you don't have any nonsmoking, we'll have to take smoking." The hostess smiled and replied cheerfully, "Oh, I have some nonsmoking." She then turned to lead us to a table as my suspicion about what we might have witnessed began to rise. Looking over her shoulder, the hostess said in reference to seating the black couple, "I did that for a reason." Shocked that she might be confirming my suspicion, and that she apparently presumed that because we were white we would accept being taken into her confidence and would consent to her subterfuge, I demanded to know her "reason." Flustered, she tried to assure us. "It's not that," she said. "It's not that." Without being specific, she said that the couple knew the waitress in the nonsmoking section and that they were not on good terms. Stewing at our table over what to believe and what to do and thinking of the surreptitious segregation recently exposed at Denny's restaurants, I noted that the entire nonsmoking section was all white. The restaurant's several black diners ate in the smoking section.

When I returned to Natchez two years later, I went again to the Shoney's. I have been back several times, in fact, and there has never been any sign of institutionally imposed segregation. On each visit, the smoking and nonsmoking sections have been integrated with blacks and whites. The hostesses have always been black, as have most of the wait staff, leaving me always wondering about the state of racial affairs in Natchez.

Whatever we had witnessed years before, one thing is now certain. Shoney's staff reflects an apparent norm in Mississippi's and Natchez's service industry today. Throughout the state, the employees at fast-food restaurants and retail chains are predominantly black. These jobs in themselves represent a step up from the type of work limited to blacks during Jim Crow (work in which they still dominate), but not a step out of the minimum-wage trap. One sometimes wonders whether blacks are still consigned to service work not unlike that of preceding generations.

Many white Mississippians would take exception to such an assessment. They would argue that the complexion of the service-industry workforce is the result of limited economic opportunities. The less-reconstructed white would say that most blacks aspire to, or are capable of, nothing better. Bleeding-heart bureaucrats, they might add, fail to realize this, and affirmative-action programs give unqualified blacks priority to jobs in all levels of government. Blacks, in other words, have nothing to complain about.

Yet, like whites, blacks in Natchez and elsewhere in Mississippi do have complaints, even as conditions improve. While better than in many places, North and South, race relations in Natchez are a mixed bag of good and poor. There is an inspiring cordiality in the daily interactions between the races. The "sir"s and "ma'am"s so common in southern speak flow from white to black as easily and naturally as from black to white. There is a sense among both races that the mutual presence of black and white is as essential to the community as to the printed page; one would not be whole without the other.

Despite the cordiality and the interracial sense of community, some habits of the old racial etiquette have yet to be broken. Adams County was once crisscrossed by scores of unnamed roads. To aid emergency vehicles, the county, as did other rural communities across the country a few years ago, named the roads and installed signs. In many instances, a road was given the name of one of its longtime residents. I traveled to many of those roads to interview people, and sometimes the interviewee was the namesake of the road on which that person lived. In one case, the interviewee was white, and the road carried his surname. In another case, the interviewee was black, and the road carried that person's name—his first name. I then began to notice that some of the roads in Adams County had last names and others had first names.

Traveling these roads and others, one learns that Natchez is not always a unified and peaceable kingdom. Blacks remain suspicious of white motives and whites remain suspicious of black culture. Although many locals would disagree, a low-level conflict between the races seems to continually simmer, occasionally heating up to the level of eruptions like those of the past.

Education is one sad example of where battles persist. Looking at the public schools in Natchez and Adams County today, seeing that they barely meet accreditation standards, one is inclined to describe them bluntly as a train wreck. This evaluation is unfair to those administrators, teachers, staff, and students who struggle against the eroding currents of white abandonment. The enrollment in public schools at this writing stands around 5,300 students, slightly more than half the enrollment in 1964, before the sluggish process of desegregation began. Private-school enrollment is around 2,000 and is virtually all white, save for a few blacks recruited for their athletic talent. The public schools are left with a small minority of whites and a level of support from the white community that reflects this minority. Parents who pay $3,000 or more per child in private-school tuition are not apt to offer financial support to public schools outside of ad valorem taxes. Sympathetic state legislators in turn have seen fit to protect private-school parents with a law that requires 65 percent of the voters to approve an increase in school taxes, a near impossibility within a culture that possesses a fundamental disdain for any kind of tax.

In short, the public schools cannot compete with the private schools, and as was the case before, blacks suffer the most. Betty Christmas, who was Betty Williams when she was among the first to desegregate the local schools in the 1960s and whose own children today attend the Natchez public schools, summed up the consequences of this competition for black education: "I was treated better twenty something years ago than [schoolchildren] are now. The quality of education was better because I was getting just what the whites were getting."[1]

Since white flight has turned the public schools into a predominantly black institution, blacks make the argument that they should oversee operation of the schools. To this end, many blacks show a battle-ready devotion to their leaders. In the spring of 1998, for instance, the school board in a racially divided three-to-two vote declined to renew the contract of the school superintendent, Willie Hoskin. Hoskin, who is black, replaced Melvin Buckley, whose own contract the school board chose not to renew in 1993. Hoskin's forced departure outraged many blacks. The Reverend Leon Howard, who was involved in the 1987–89 desegregation efforts, threatened to throw Natchez into yet another pitched battle between blacks and whites when he called for a boycott of white businesses—except Wal-Mart, Kmart, and Kroger—to "end the so-called school board's racism." The boycott never materialized. Many other blacks, especially parents with children in the public schools, agreed with the white school-board members that Hoskin's effectiveness had passed and that a change was due.[2]

Like Hoskin, the first black school superintendent, other black firsts are now gone. With his public and legal careers plagued by charges of sexual harassment, insurance fraud, and disbarment, George West Jr., the first black school-board appointee and board chairman, resigned in 1993. Eddie Jones was dismissed as Natchez's first black police chief of the twentieth century, but only after he was allowed to accrue enough years to qualify for full retirement. Phillip West ran for mayor in 1996 but met defeat. He then won election to the state House of Representatives. Some whites privately say that to get rid of West they had to vote him out of the county.

While many old segregationists remain, they tend to maintain a low profile. Some prefer it that way. In this decade in which the state of Mississippi is apparently trying to make amends for its past civil rights record by finally rendering justice against leading racists such as Byron De La Beckwith and Sam Bowers, no one has ever been arrested for the Metcalfe and Jackson bombings. In the fall of 1999, the investigative work of *Newsday* reporter Stephanie Saul, who wrote on civil rights murders that never brought convictions, encouraged the Adams County sheriff's office to reopen the file on Jackson's death. The ABC news program *20/20* piggybacked on Saul's work and produced a segment on Ben Chester White and his alleged murderers. ABC's hired consultant Don Simonton, a graduate student at the University of Mississippi, discovered that the White incident had occurred on federal property, suggesting that the U.S. Justice Department could bring federal charges against the alleged killers, originally indicted on state charges, and circumvent the rule of double jeopardy. With this revelation, the Justice Department reopened the 1966 case, and in June 2000, Ernest Avants, the only surviving member of the trio previously charged, was indicted for White's murder.

Still other segregationists are more perplexing than before. E. L. McDaniel, former Ku Klux Klan grand dragon, appeared ever the opportunist when he endorsed Charles Evers's 1971 Republican campaign for governor. McDaniel and his former lieutenant L. C. Murray joined their darker brother of conservatism for a fund-raising barbecue in Fayette, clasped hands on a stage before thousands of blacks, and sang "We Shall Overcome."[3] Although part of a paradoxical coalition, McDaniel had apparently come to realize what many Natchezians are now learning: that "whites are not one big solid block of white," to quote Mimi Miller of the Historic Natchez Foundation, "and that blacks are not one solid block of black." No longer as involved in politics, McDaniel now operates a security company in Natchez.

Common ground between the races is unlikely to be found at the ballot box or on the school campus. Many locals also doubt that it will come on Sunday mornings, the most segregated time in the South, as the saying goes. There are still whites today, I am told, who will walk out of church if a sermon turns to the subject of race and interracial cooperation. Preferring their own churches, blacks are also responsible for the continuing ritual of separation.

Yet religion does have possibilities. One day it may rise above its inglorious history and bring the races together. The supremacist strain that runs through the white idea of brotherhood has begun to lose its edge as the two races come to realize that southern black and white doctrines of Christianity share a common conservatism. In an age of expanding secularism, a religious backlash could unite blacks and whites in a common cause, such as restoring prayer in schools.[4]

For such a unification to be lasting, however, the white cloud of myth that still shrouds black culture will have to be set aflight. That can only be done through new lessons in history, to which Natchezians seem to be increasingly receptive. Natchez-Adams High School's Colonel Reb has been permanently laid to rest and the buoyant sounds of "Dixie" no longer rise from the public schools. While casualties of white flight, the disappearances of both are also examples of the significant ongoing advances toward making Natchez's public history more racially inclusive.

The perception of how far Natchez has left to travel on its journey of progress generally differs between the races. Inside city hall one will not find any acknowledgment of the city's only black mayor, Robert Wood, among the collection of mayoral pictures on a boardroom wall. While today black city employees groom the grounds of (Confederate) Memorial Park and while on the front lawn of city hall rests a headstone dedicated to Tripod, a three-legged cat who was once the city's mascot, there is no commemorative marker in Natchez dedicated to Wharlest Jackson or to Ben Chester White. Yet both are memorialized at the Southern Poverty Law Center in Montgomery, Alabama.[5]

The continuing racial divide in public history is probably most evident in local parades. Today, as in the early years, few whites outside of local officials and tourists attend the Martin Luther King Day parade every January and even fewer participate. In February 1998, I was in Natchez for a conference during the city's Mardi Gras Parade. Although a poor imitation of its more-famous counterpart in New Orleans, it draws thousands. It was a bright and mild winter afternoon when I attended. Spectators frolicked on the sidewalks as a stop-and-go procession of floats, school bands, antique cars, motorcycles, and other participants pushed its way up Main Street. The next day, local blacks held along the same route Natchez's first parade commemorating Black History Month. Somehow, no one at the conference, including the local hosts, was aware of this new parade, even though much of the conference was devoted to local black history. The only whites I saw on the sidewalks were Natchezians going about their daily business and tourists and conference attendees puzzled by what appeared to be an esoteric event, unannounced and sparsely attended. Perhaps the event organizers moderated their public-relations efforts in anticipation of white participation amounting to nothing more than tokenism.

There is never any question that Natchez's grand houses will continue to draw crowds during Pilgrimage. Unlike other southerners, Natchezians have not occupied themselves with a debate over the Confederate battle flag. Their equivalent to the controversial Southern Cross is the antebellum mansions. They remain a powerful symbol of a bygone era of a supreme white civilization as well as a major tangible source of revenue for the white community. Signature figures of the continuing economic disparity are bandana-clad black women who sell homemade pralines on the tree-shaded drives of Pilgrimage tour homes. Even as they assume stereotyped roles, these women exhibit an entrepreneurial resourcefulness that other blacks are trying to bring to public history. As black tour guides tell visitors, the big mansions may symbolize oppression and disparity, but they are also the product of many skilled black craftsmen, as much a part of the local black heritage as of the white heritage. In them, one can find an admirable history of sacrifice, fortitude, and survival.

Each initiative toward making public history in Natchez more racially inclusive represents another victory of the African American experience and, one might add, a victory for history itself. Neither victory will come without a struggle. The praline seller in her period costume is more familiar, and therefore more acceptable, to local whites than is the black tour guide's elaboration on slave days. The black story is told separately in parades and special events and generally before black audiences. As remarkable as blacks and white tourists find Natchez's black history, white tour guides typically refrain from elaborating on, much less interpreting, the enslavement of ancestors of local citizens. The National Historic Park set a local example in the 1990s by incorporating the black experience into its various tours and programs. Yet even a token reference to slavery or black life remains an oddity at other home tours. Even after the Pilgrimage added the black presentation "Southern Road to Freedom" to its repertoire of events, the history portrayed in the Confederate Pageant retains its lily-white character.

Inclusive history in Natchez is not about proportional representation or bashing the white race. It is about honesty, completeness, liberation, and legitimizing the historical identity of a traditionally ignored group in a city where history so profoundly shapes social mores. History need not always feel good to serve a positive cultural purpose, for the distance Natchezians traveled to get to the era of civil rights from a system of slavery portrayed realistically harsh is farther than the distance from a system of slavery mythicized as benign and beneficent.

Natchezians are slowly coming around to this idea, even as the races remain for the most part emotionally divided. As long as whites believe that black culture is inferior, as long as whites fear black history as a condemnation of their own past, as long as blacks regard white history and historic preservation as an attempt to reconstruct a stratified social order, as long as those who control history control society, history in Natchez will remain contested terrain. But in the days when public history conveyed a pleasing harmony, neither blacks nor whites could make legitimate claims to a truthful, liberating past.

Since the 1960s, Natchez blacks and whites have made their own history. While it has brought truth and liberation, it includes forty years of conflict that far into the future will inform perceptions each group has of the other. Democracy could not work in Natchez without healthy conflict, equality could never be realized, and Natchez would fall again into a false social harmony. Racial progress is sometimes painful, but it would be less so and would come more rapidly if all knew that black culture and white culture are less in conflict than in harmony with each other.

NOTES

ABBREVIATIONS

ACBS   Adams County Board of Supervisors
ACCS   Adams County Christian School
ACPS   Adams County Private School
AJIC   Adams-Jefferson Improvement Corporation
APWR   Americans for the Preservation of the White Race
BAWI   Balance Agriculture with Industry
CMA   Confederate Memorial Association
COFO   Council of Federated Organizations
FDP   Freedom Democratic Party
FIS   Freedom Information Service Library, archives in the posses-
            sion of Jan Hillegas, Jackson, Mississippi
FWP   Federal Writers Project
GCMR   Garden Clubs of Mississippi Records
HNF   Historic Natchez Foundation, Natchez, Mississippi
MAMML   Mississippi Association of Methodist Ministers and Laymen
MDAH   Mississippi Department of Archives and History
MIC   Mississippi Industrial Commission
MOHP   Mississippi Oral History Program
NAACP   National Association for the Advancement of Colored
            People
NAPC   Natchez Association for the Preservation of Afro-American
            Culture
NBA   Natchez Board of Aldermen
NBCL   Natchez Business and Civic League
NGCR   Natchez Garden Club Records
NPA   Natchez–Adams County Public Schools Administration Of-
            fices, Natchez, Mississippi
NSMSSD   Natchez Special Municipal Separate School District Records
SCF   Mississippi State Sovereignty Commission Files, MDAH
SLA/GSU   Southern Labor Archives, Georgia State University

SNCC   Student Non-Violent Coordinating Committee
UDC   United Daughters of the Confederacy
UDCP   United Daughters of the Confederacy Papers
UKA   United Klan of America
UMASC   Department of Archives and Special Collections, John Davis
         Williams Library, University of Mississippi

INTRODUCTION

1. *Eyes on the Prize: America's Civil Rights Years, 1954–1965*, episode 5: "Mississippi: Is This America? (1962–1964)" (Boston: Blackside, 1986), television documentary.

2. Robert Ezra Park, *Race and Culture: Essays in the Sociology of Contemporary Man* (Reprint, New York: Free Press, 1964; Glencoe, Ill.: Free Press, 1950), 3–8, 115. See also David K. Shipler, *A Country of Strangers: Blacks and Whites in America* (New York: Alfred A. Knopf, 1997), x.

3. These conclusions have been drawn from more than one hundred interviews conducted for the study and countless hours of informal conversation with white Natchezians and other white Mississippians. A number of scholarly readings have also facilitated the formulation of these conclusions, including David Theo Goldberg, *Racist Culture: Philosophy and the Politics of Meaning* (Cambridge: Blackwell Publishers, 1993); and Bronislaw Malinowski, "Man's Culture and Man's Behavior," in his *Sex, Culture, and Myth* (New York: Harcourt, Brace, and World, 1962), 196–222. See also W. J. Cash, *The Mind of the South* (New York: Knopf, 1941), 94–102; Guion Griffis Johnson, "The Ideology of White Supremacy," in *The South and the Sectional Image*, edited by Dewey W. Grantham Jr. (New York: Harper and Row, 1967), 56–78; Elvin Hatch, *Theories of Man and Culture* (New York: Columbia University Press, 1973), 13–73; George C. Stocking Jr., *Race, Culture, and Evolution: Essays in the History of Anthropology* (New York: Free Press, 1968); Park, *Race and Culture*; Ronald T. Takaki, *Iron Cages: Race and Culture in Nineteenth-Century America* (New York: Alfred A. Knopf, 1979).

4. Richard Wright, *Black Boy* (New York: Perennial Library, 1989), 14; Vernon J. Williams Jr., *From Caste to Minority: Changing Attitudes of American Sociologists toward Afro-Americans, 1896–1945* (New York: Greenwood Press, 1989); Lee Baker, "From Savage to Negro: Anthropology and the Construction of Race, 1896–1954" (Ph.D. diss., Johns Hopkins University, 1994). Social scientists also talked about a damaged black psyche. See Daryl Michael Scott, *Contempt and Pity: Social Policy and the Image of the Damaged Black Psyche, 1880–1996* (Chapel Hill: University of North Carolina Press, 1997).

5. Pierre L. van den Burghe, *Race and Racism: A Comparative Perspective* (New York: John Wiley and Sons, 1967), 13. See also Thomas Sowell, *Race and Culture: A World View* (New York: Basic Books, 1994); S. Davis, *Race-Relations in Ancient Egypt: Greek, Egyptian, Hebrew, Roman* (London: Methuen, 1953); Peter I. Rose, *The Subject Is Race:*

Traditional Ideologies and the Teaching of Race Relations (New York: Oxford University Press, 1968), 32–33; Thomas Gossett, *Race: The History of an Idea in America* (New York: Schocken Books, 1970).

6. Ethnicity in this study is defined as the distinctive characteristics of primarily nationality and culture that identify a group. According to Harvard literary scholar Werner Sollors, the word "ethnicity" first appeared in print in a 1941 book coauthored by W. Lloyd Warner and Paul S. Lunt. Warner was the Harvard mentor of Allison Davis and Burleigh Gardner who initiated their 1930s study of Natchez, later published as *Deep South*, upon which this study builds. See Werner Sollors, editor, *The Invention of Ethnicity* (New York: Oxford University Press, 1989), xii; W. Lloyd Warner and Paul S. Lunt, *The Social Life of a Modern Community* (New Haven: Yale University Press, 1941).

7. Winthrop D. Jordan, *White over Black: American Attitudes toward the Negro, 1550–1812* (Chapel Hill: University of North Carolina Press, 1968), 3–43; Robert F. Berkhofer Jr., *The White Man's Indian: Images of the American Indian from Columbus to the Present* (New York: Vintage Books, 1978); Eric Foner, "Who is an American?" *Culturefront* 4 (winter 1995–1996): 4–12; Badi G. Foster, "Toward a Definition of Black Referents," in *Beyond Black or White: An Alternate America,* edited by Vernon J. Dixon and Badi Foster (Boston: Little, Brown, 1971), 7–22.

8. William Ferris, "Local Color: Fostering an American Sense of Place," *Museum News* (September/October 1996), 47 (quote). On whiteness, see David R. Roediger, *The Wages of Whiteness: Race and the Making of the American Working Class* (New York: Verso, 1994); Grace Elizabeth Hale, *Making Whiteness: The Culture of Segregation in the South, 1890–1940* (New York: Pantheon Books, 1998). For a study of Mississippi's ethnic diversity, see Barbara Carpenter, editor, *Ethnic Heritage in Mississippi* (Jackson: University Press of Mississippi, 1992).

9. K. Anthony Appiah, "The Multiculturalist Misunderstanding," *New York Review* 44 (October 9, 1997): 30.

10. Joel Williamson, *The Crucible of Race: Black-White Relations in the American South since Emancipation* (New York: Oxford University Press, 1984), 35–38, 52–57; C. Eric Lincoln and Lawrence H. Mamiya, *The Black Church in the African American Experience* (Durham, N.C.: Duke University Press, 1990), 1–19, pass.; Paul Harvey, *Redeeming the South: Religious Cultures and Racial Identities Among Southern Baptists, 1865–1925* (Chapel Hill: University of North Carolina Press, 1997), 45–74.

11. On the subject of the "interpenetration" of black culture and white culture in America, see for instance Mechal Sobel, *The World They Made Together: Black and White Values in Eighteenth-Century Virginia* (Princeton: Princeton University Press, 1987); Lawrence W. Levine, *Black Culture and Black Consciousness: Afro-American Folk Thought from Slavery to Freedom* (New York: Oxford University Press, 1977); Charles Joyner, *Down by the Riverside: A South Carolina Slave Community* (Urbana: University of Illinois Press, 1984); and Joel Williamson, *New People: Miscegenation and Mulattos in the United States* (Baton Rouge: Louisiana State University Press, 1995).

12. Jacqueline Jones, *The Dispossessed: America's Underclasses from the Civil War to the Present* (New York: Basic Books, 1992), 10.

13. Park, *Race and Culture*, 81–82; W. E. B. Du Bois, *Souls of Black Folk: Essays and Sketches* (New York: Blue Heron Press, 1953), 166–67. Although generally thought otherwise, racism was not a western invention. For a commentary on this, see van den Burghe, *Race and Racism*, 12. See also Oliver Cromwell Cox, *Caste, Class, and Race: A Study in Social Dynamics* (Garden City, N.Y.: Doubleday, 1948); Roediger, *The Wages of Whiteness;* Barbara Jeanne Fields, "Slavery, Race, and Ideology in the United States of America," in *Region, Race, and Reconstruction: Essays in Honor of C. Vann Woodward,* edited by J. Morgan Kousser and James M. McPherson (New York: Oxford University Press, 1992), 143–77.

14. For a broader look at the cultural reinforcements of segregation, see Hale, *Making Whiteness.*

15. Thomas Holt, "Marking: Race, Race-making, and the Writing of History," *American Historical Review* 100 (February 1995): 1–20.

16. Theodore G. Bilbo, "World War II: Increasing Racial Tension," in I. A. Newby, *The Development of Segregationist Thought* (Homewood, Ill.: Dorsey Press, 1968), 142 ("The white"); *Natchez Democrat,* August 6, 1948 ("For"); Stark Young, "The South Presents Its Design for Living," *New York Times Magazine* (January 17, 1937), 4–5, 25 ("South").

17. Allison Davis, Burleigh B. Gardner, and Mary R. Gardner, *Deep South: A Social Anthropological Study of Caste and Class* (Reprint, Los Angeles: The Center for Afro-American Studies, University of California, 1988; Chicago: University of Chicago, 1941). Saint Clair Drake also conducted field research for the study. Oliver C. Cox criticized the application of the Hindu system to an American, arguing that one was based on consent the other on force. See his *Caste, Class, and Race.* See also van den Burghe, *Race and Racism,* 10.

PROLOGUE

1. Wright, *Black Boy,* 14.

2. Don Simonton to Jack Davis, March 30, 1998, e-mail in possession of author.

3. Probably the best and least sensational of the many popular histories of the Natchez Trace is Jonathan Daniels, *The Devil's Backbone: The Story of the Natchez Trace* (New York: McGraw-Hill, 1962).

4. *Mississippi: The WPA Guide to the Magnolia State* (reprint, Jackson: University Press of Mississippi, 1988; New York: Viking Press, 1938), 237; Don Simonton e-mail.

5. Gus J. Requardt, "A Paean of Praise for the Great State of Mississippi," June 14, 1968, Hough Papers, MDAH.

6. *The Code of the City of Natchez, Mississippi, 1954* (Natchez, Mississippi), Section 10, City Charter.

7. The *Woodville Republican,* June 3, 1933; *Jackson Daily News,* May 29, 1933; *Natchez Democrat,* June 3, 4 ("because"), 1933; Davis et al., *Deep South,* 559–63.

8. *Natchez Democrat,* June 4, 1933.

9. For a black perspective on this idea, see Anthony Walton, *Mississippi: An American Journey* (New York: Vintage Books, 1997); and Clifton L. Taulbert, *Once upon a Time when We Were Colored* (Tulsa, Okla.: Council Oak Books, 1989).

CHAPTER ONE

1. In 1948, the Mississippi state legislature considered, and eventually tabled, a bill requiring radio stations to open and close the day's broadcast with the playing of "Dixie." *Time,* April 5, 1948, 25.

2. Interview with Virginia Beltzhoover Morrison, by author, March 27, 1993; "Historical Year Book, Mississippi Division, United Daughters of the Confederacy, 1937–1938," box 1, United Daughters of the Confederacy Papers, 1896–1954 (no. 1293) (hereafter cited as UDCP), MDAH.

3. Interview with Bill Hanna, by author, July 2, 1992; "Concise Sketch of Robert E. Lee," *Over the Garden Wall,* January 1952, 12; "Historical Year Book, Mississippi Division."

4. Quoted in Harnett T. Kane, *Natchez on the Mississippi* (New York: William Morrow, 1947), 343.

5. Cash, *The Mind of the South,* x; *Natchez Democrat,* December 17, 1933 ("we"); *Jackson Daily News,* December 14, 1985 ("Young").

6. For a discussion of memory, its relation to history, and its social purpose, see David P. Thelen, editor, *Memory and History* (Bloomington: Indiana University Press, 1990).

7. Margaret Walker Alexander, "Natchez and Richard Wright in Southern American Literature," *The Southern Quarterly: A Journal of the Arts in the South* 24 (summer 1991): 171.

8. *The WPA Guide to Mississippi,* 238 (quote); Father Le Petit, "The Jesuit Relations and Allied Documents," in *A Place Called Mississippi: Collected Narratives,* edited by Marion Barnwell (Jackson: University Press of Mississippi, 1997), 231–35; Kane, *Natchez on the Mississippi,* 2–6; "Tracing Natchez," *American Heritage,* July/August 1988, 24–26; Hodding Carter, *Lower Mississippi* (New York, Toronto: Farrar and Rinehart, 1942), 235, 252; William Scarborough, "Lords or Capitalists? The Natchez Nabobs in Comparative Perspective," *Journal of Mississippi History* 75 (September 1988): 239–67; D. Clayton James, *Antebellum Natchez* (Baton Rouge: Louisiana State University Press, 1968), 136–61.

9. "Surget Name Legend in Homes at Natchez," newspaper clipping, n.d., Cherry Grove subject file, MDAH; Scarborough, "Lords or Capitalists?" 239–67; Interview with Grace M. S. MacNeil, by Charlotte Capers, July 10, 1973, MDAH; Interview with Grace MacNeil, by author, November 23, 1992; James, *Antebellum Natchez,* 136–61.

10. Stark Young, *So Red the Rose* (New York: Charles Scribners' Sons, 1934), 8 ("the society"); Frances Trollope, *Domestic Manners of the Americans* (New York: Vintage Books, 1960), 19 ("sweet"). See also "Natchez, Belle of the River," *Colonial Homes,* January–February 1986, 54.

11. James, *Antebellum Natchez*, 101–35.

12. Steve Power, *The Memento: Old and New Natchez, 1700–1897* (Louisville, Ky.: F. C. Nunemacher Press, 1897), 64 ("regal"); James Roark, *Masters without Slaves: Southern Planters in the Civil War and Reconstruction* (New York: W. W. Norton, 1977), 148; Edward L. Ayers, *The Promise of the New South: Life after Reconstruction* (New York: Oxford University Press, 1992); Michael Wayne, *The Reshaping of Plantation Society: The Natchez District, 1860–80* (Urbana: University of Illinois Press, 1990), 31–52; Ronald L. F. Davis, *Good and Faithful Labor: From Slavery to Sharecropping in the Natchez District, 1860–1890* (Westport, Conn.: Greenwood Press, 1982); Elizabeth Dunbar Murray, *Early Romances of Historic Natchez* (Natchez: Natchez Printing and Stationery, 1938), 16–17.

13. Fox hunting was a popular pastime of many Adams County whites up through the mid–twentieth century. Many residents held membership in the Louisiana-Mississippi Fox Hunters Association and approached the sport in the spirit of English tradition, with fine steeds, a crowd of beagles, and the fox hunter's panoply—boots, jodhpurs, red jacket with tails, and riding helmet. *Natchez Democrat*, December 6, 1939.

14. Carter, *Lower Mississippi*, 252 ("persistent"); Power, *The Memento*, 25 ("chivalrous").

15. See Lee Glazer and Susan Key, "Carry Me Back: Nostalgia for the Old South in Nineteenth-Century Popular Culture," *Journal of American Studies* 30 (April 1996): 1–24. For the northern origins of Old South popular themes, see Patrick Gerster and Nicholas Cords, "The Northern Origins of Southern Mythology," *Journal of Southern History* 43 (November 1977): 567–82.

16. Robert Penn Warren, "The Legacy of the Civil War: Meditations on the Centennial," in *A Robert Penn Warren Reader* (New York: Random House, 1987), 274 (quote). For a discussion of how traditions among other western cultures serve to inculcate values and norms of behavior, see Eric Hobsbawn and Terence Ranger, editors, *The Invention of Tradition* (Cambridge, England: Cambridge University Press, 1983).

17. Although I do not use in this narrative the term "social memory," a heuristic concept recently emerging in southern history, I attempt to explore in my examination of myths in this and subsequent chapters ideas that interest historians of social memory, ideas such as the social and cultural basis upon which memory is shaped, its influence in turn upon society and culture, and on social group unity, identity, conflict, and reality. My central interest is reality, a product of experience and memory, a product itself of myth, perception, and truth. Scholars of race relations have typically ignored the reality, or discounted its legitimacy or relevance, of whites and substituted a researcher's reality or an academic formula to explain intergroup dynamics. For a brief but interesting discussion of social memory, see Scot A. French, "What Is Social Memory," *Southern Cultures* 2 (fall 1995): 9–18.

18. Literature most influential in this discussion of myth and crisis has been Robert Penn Warren, "The Legacy of the Civil War"; William H. McNeill, "The Care and Repair of Public Myth," in *Myth and the American Experience*, edited by Nicholas Cords and Patrick Gerster (New York: Harper Collins, 1991), 2: 435–45; John Hellmann, *American Myth and the Legacy of Vietnam* (New York: Columbia University Press, 1986); Friedrich

Nietzsche, *The Use and Abuse of History,* translated by Adrian Collins (Indianapolis: Bobbs-Merrill, 1957).

19. Power, *The Memento,* 64.

20. *Natchez Democrat,* August 6, 1948.

21. *Natchez Democrat,* April 27, 1912 (quotes through "resort"). See also Melody Kubassek, "Ask Us Not to Forget: The Lost Cause in Natchez, Mississippi," *Southern Studies* 3 (fall 1992): 159; Power, *The Memento,* 52 ("dark").

22. Power, *The Memento,* 51–52, 57–59, 68 (quotes); "A Brief Historical Sketch, concerning the Origin of Memorial Day in Mississippi," box 2, Daughters of Confederate Veterans Papers, MDAH; *Natchez Democrat,* April 26, 27, 1888.

23. Gaines M. Foster, *Ghosts of the Confederacy: Defeat, the Lost Cause, and the Emergence of the New South, 1865–1913* (New York: Oxford University Press, 1987), 128–31.

24. Power, *The Memento,* 51–56; *Natchez Democrat,* April 23, 26, 27, 1889; Kubassek, "Ask Us Not to Forget," 160–61.

25. Kubassek, "Ask Us Not to Forget," 166 ("feminization"); Roark, *Masters without Slaves,* 46–50, 89–90, 149–50; Drew Gilpin Faust, "Altars of Sacrifice: Confederate Women and the Narratives of War," *Journal of American History* 76 (March 1990): 1200–1228.

26. Faust, "Altars of Sacrifice," 1204. See also her *Mothers of Invention: Women of the Slaveholding South in the American Civil War* (Chapel Hill: University of North Carolina Press, 1996). Anne Frior Scott, *The Southern Lady: From Pedestal to Politics, 1830–1930* (Chicago: University of Chicago Press, 1970), 37–44, pass.; Catherine Clinton, *The Plantation Mistress: Woman's World in the Old South* (New York: Pantheon Books, 1982), 87–109. For a commentary on the concept of separate spheres, see Linda K. Kerber, "Separate Spheres, Female Worlds, Women's Place: The Rhetoric of Women's History," *Journal of American History* 75 (June 1988): 9–39; Karen J. Blair, *The Torchbearers: Women and Their Amateur Arts Associations in America, 1890–1930* (Bloomington: Indiana University Press, 1994), 1–11.

27. "Historical Year Book, Mississippi Division" (quote); "Monthly Historical Programs for the United Daughters of the Confederacy and Children of the Confederacy, 1917," box 1, UDCP; "Program of the Forty Fifth Annual Convention of the Mississippi Division of the United Daughters of the Confederacy," box 1, UDCP; Mary B. Poppenheim et al., *The History of the United Daughters of the Confederacy* (Raleigh, N.C.: Edwards and Broughton, 1925), 135–41; *Natchez Democrat,* July 27, 1950.

28. "Programs, Mississippi Division, United Daughters of the Confederacy," 1968, box 18, Roane Fleming Byrnes Collection, UMASC.

29. Poppenheim et al., *History of the United Daughters of the Confederacy;* Foster, *Ghosts of the Confederacy,* 172; Angie Parrot, "'Love Makes Memory Eternal': The United Daughters of the Confederacy in Richmond, Virginia, 1897–1920" in *The Edge of the South: Life in Nineteenth-Century Virginia,* edited by Edward L. Ayres and John C. Willis (Charlottesville: University Press of Virginia, 1991), 224.

30. Mrs. Lucian H. Raines, "United Daughters of the Confederacy: Origins, History,

and Growth," *Confederate Veteran* 6 (September 1898): 452 ("the selection"); Kubassek, "Ask Us Not to Forget," 158; "Historical Year Book"; "Monthly Historical Programs"; "Outline of Historical Study for the Mississippi Division of United Daughters of the Confederacy, 1911–1912," box 1, UDCP. Regionally, the United Confederate Veterans, along with other associations and white southerners committed to the legacy, concerned themselves with the "correct" history lessons. See Rollin G. Osterweis, *The Myth of the Lost Cause, 1865–1900* (New York: Archon Books, 1973), 111–17; Foster, *Ghosts of the Confederacy,* 108, 188.

31. "List of Natchez Chapter, No. 304," n.d., box 1, UDCP ("Good"); National Daughters of the American Revolution, *Natchez Chapter 3-040-MS, Yearbook, 1977–1980,* Daughters of the American Revolution Papers, MDAH; *Natchez Democrat,* February 28, 1939 ("qualities"); Natchez Chapter, Daughters of the American Revolution, *Yearbook, 1968–1971.* For an interesting examination of textbook censorship in Texas by the UDC and other keepers of the legacy, see Fred Arthur Bailey, "Free Speech and the 'Lost Cause' in Texas: A Study of Social Control in the New South," *Southwestern Historical Quarterly* (January 1994): 452–77. Bailey argues that textbook censorship in the early twentieth century represented a "neo-Confederate crusade" to preserve aristocratic authority.

32. Schools in Old Natchez District file, Amanda Geisenberger Collection, George Armstrong Public Library, Natchez. A lengthy description of history courses in Natchez schools is also discussed by an educator in the *Natchez Democrat,* February 23, 1964. For another example, see ibid., October 19, 1965.

33. Minutes, Mississippi State Textbook Rating and Purchasing Board, pass., Textbook Division, Mississippi State Department of Education, Jackson, Mississippi; "Recommendations and Suggestions from Teachers' Workshop, August 26–30, 1963, Natchez–Adams County Public Schools," Social Studies Workshop, ringbinder, NPA; Frances Fitzgerald, *America Revised: History Schoolbooks in the Twentieth Century* (Boston: Little, Brown, 1979), 47.

34. For an analysis of American history textbooks, see Fitzgerald, *America Revised;* Richard Shenkman, *Legends, Lies, and Cherished Myths of American History* (New York: William Morrow, 1988); Diane Ravitch, *The Troubled Crusade: American Education, 1945–1980* (New York: Basic Books, 1983), 90–91, 107, 298–300; James W. Loewen, *Lies My Teacher Told Me: Everything Your American History Textbook Got Wrong* (New York: New Press, 1995).

35. Minutes, Textbook Rating and Purchasing Board, May 23, July 1, 1940, October 3, 1952.

36. *Jackson Daily News* clipping, n.d., Textbook Commission subject file, MDAH ("one-world-ism"). See also "Screening Urged as Pro-Integration Books are Found," *Jackson Daily News,* March 2, 1956. *Jackson Daily News,* September 6, 1959 ("that Negro"); "Mississippi Mud," *Time,* May 16, 1960, p. 65 ("clean"). See also Margaret Gibbs, *The DAR* (New York: Holt, Rinehart, and Winston, 1969), 210–11; James Silver, *The Closed Society* (New York: Harcourt, Brace, and World, 1963), 65–66; Frank Smith, *Congressman from Mississippi* (New York: Pantheon Books, 1964), 255, 269. In 1963, authors Jack Nelson and Gene Roberts in *The Censors and the Schools* called the DAR "the

most formidable adversary of free speech" during the height of the textbook screening era in the 1950s and 1960s. Quoted in Peggy Anderson, *The Daughters: An Unconventional Look at America's Fan Club—The DAR* (New York: Saint Martin's Press, 1974), 106–7.

37. See C. Vann Woodward, *The Burden of Southern History* (Baton Rouge: Louisiana University Press, 1968); and F. Gavin Davenport Jr., *The Myth of Southern History: The Historical Consciousness in Twentieth-Century Southern Literature* (Nashville: Vanderbilt University Press, 1970).

38. Guyton's book was first published under the title, *The History of Mississippi: From Indian Times to the Present Day* (Syracuse: Iroquois Publishing, 1935); Pearl Guyton, *Our Mississippi* (Austin, Tex.: Steck, 1959); Interview with Katherine Blankenstein, by author, August 29, 1997; Interview with Bettye Jenkins, by author, March 26, 1993; Interview with Ruth Tiffee Jordan, by author, January 28, 1993; Virginia Beltzhoover Morrison interview.

39. Guyton, *History of Mississippi;* Minutes, Textbook Rating and Purchasing Board, February 7–8, November 4–7, 1949, October 3, November 20–22, 1952.

40. Guyton, *Our Mississippi,* pass. Another history text on the approved list revealed a similar interpretation of Reconstruction. See Richard Aubrey McLemore and Nannie Pitts McLemore, *The Mississippi Story* (River Forest, Ill.: Laidlaw Brothers, 1959).

41. See Thomas Dixon, *The Clansman* (New York: Doubleday, Page, 1905), and *The Leopard's Spots: A Romance of the White Man's Burden, 1875–1900* (New York: Doubleday, Page, 1902). For a provocative analysis of Dixon, see Williamson, *The Crucible of Race,* 140–76, pass.

42. "Recommendations and Suggestions from Teachers' Workshop"; Natchez Special Municipal Separate School District (hereafter cited as NSMSSD), *Report of Self-Evaluation: Submitted to the Visiting Committee of the Southern Association of Schools and Colleges* (Natchez, 1965), vol. 2, sec. 12, MDAH (quotes). See also "Recommendations and Suggestions from Teachers' Workshop."

43. *Natchez Democrat,* October 11, 1940.

44. Bettersworth's textbook was first published in 1959 under the title, *A History of Mississippi* (Austin, Tex.: Steck-Vaughn, 1959), and was later titled *Your Mississippi;* Minutes, Textbook Purchasing Board, November 9, 13, 1964, November 12, 1968. See also Wilson F. Minor, "Conflict and Change in Mississippi," *Harvard Education Review* 45 (February 1975): 114–19; and Jason Berry, "Speaking Directly to the Young," *Nation,* April 12, 1975, 441–42.

45. Minutes, Textbook Purchasing Board, November 9, 13, 1964, 12, 1968, November 4, 1974; Bill Minor, "Textbook Battle: Civil War vs. Civil Rights," *Jackson Capitol Reporter* September 6, 1979, 3 ("a'safe'").

46. Minutes, Textbook Purchasing Board, January 14, February 11, 1975, February 13, 1979, August 12, December 17, 1980; James Loewen and Charles Sallis et al., *Mississippi: Conflict and Change* (New York: Random House, 1974); Minor, "Textbook Battle"; *Jackson Clarion-Ledger,* April 3, 1980; July 24, 1981; *Greenville Delta Democrat-Times,* July 24, 1981. The last edition of the Bettersworth history text, published in 1981, devoted only three pages to the civil rights struggle and all but overlooked racial discrimination. See

John K. Bettersworth, *Mississippi: The Land and the People* (Austin, Tex.: Steck-Vaughn, 1981).

47. See John Ray Skates and David Sansing, *Mississippi Life: Past and Present* (Jackson: Magnolia Publishing, 1980). Interview with David Sansing, by author, June 18, 1996.

48. Minutes, Textbook Purchasing Board, December 17, 1980.

49. See John W. Blassingame, "Using the Testimony of Ex-Slaves: Approaches and Problems," *Journal of Southern History* 41 (November 1975): 473–92; Jerre Mangione, *The Dream and the New Deal: The Federal Writers' Project, 1935–1943* (Boston: Little, Brown, 1972), 263–65; Gary R. Mormino, "Florida Slave Narratives," *Florida Historical Quarterly* 66 (April 1988): 399–419.

50. Interview with Jan Hillegas, by author, August 12, 1993; George Rawick, Jan Hillegas and Ken Lawrence, editors, *American Slave: A Composite, Mississippi Narratives,* supp., pt. 1, ser. 1, vol. 6 (Westport, Conn.: Greenwood Publishing, 1977), xci–xvi; Ken Lawrence, "Oral History of Slavery," *Southern Exposure* 1 (winter 1974): 84–86.

51. William Ransom Hogan and Edwin Adams Davis, editors, *William Johnson's Natchez: The Ante-Bellum Diary of a Free Negro* (Baton Rogue: Louisiana State University, 1993), xiii; Hillegas and Lawrence, *Mississippi Narratives,* supp., pt. 1, ser. 1, vol. 6: lxxx–lxxxi; *Natchez Democrat,* April 13, 1965; November 2, 1935; "Recommendations and Suggestions from Teachers' Workshop"; Katherine Blankenstein interview; "Glamorous Natchez," promotional brochure, Natchez Pilgrimage Papers, MDAH; "Mississippi Book Review," *Mississippi News and Views* 25 (March 1965): 25.

52. Winthrop D. Jordan, *Tumult and Silence at Second Creek: An Inquiry into a Civil War Slave Conspiracy* (Baton Rouge: Louisiana State University Press, 1993), 131–33; Hillegas and Lawrence, *Mississippi Narratives,* supp., pt. 2, ser. 1, vol. 7: 569.

53. Hillegas and Lawrence, *Mississippi Narratives,* supp., ser. 1, pt. 1, vol. 6: xciii–xciv; and pt. 2, vol. 7: 572.

54. For an examination of the ill-fated conspiracy that Davenport spoke about, see Jordan, *Tumult and Silence.*

55. Rawick, *The American Slave* (Newport, Conn.: Greenwood Publishing, 1972), 7: 43; Hillegas and Lawrence, *Mississippi Narratives,* supp., pt. 2, ser. 1, vol. 7: 572; Ibid., supp., pt. 3, ser. 1, vol. 8: 91–99. Even the best of historians may become victim of corrupted historical data. In his otherwise absorbing study of the Adams County slave conspiracy, Winthrop Jordan mistakes the Davenport fabrication as historically accurate. See Jordan, *Tumult and Silence,* 133.

56. Edith Wyatt Moore, "Wild Flowers" (Moore quotes); "History of Natchez," 18–23; and "Heroes and Heroines," WPA Project Files, RG 60, MDAH; *Natchez Democrat,* April 13, 1965, November 2, 1935.

57. For discussions of Cavalier literature, see William R. Taylor, *Cavalier and Yankee: The Old South and American National Character* (New York: George Braziller, 1961), 177–93; Lawrence J. Friedman, *The White Savage: Racial Fantasies in the Postbellum South* (Englewood Cliffs, N.J.: Prentice-Hall, 1970), 57–76.

58. Young to Donald Davidson, July 4, 1992, *Stark Young, a Life in the Arts: Letters, 1900–1962,* John Pilkington, editor (Baton Rouge: Louisiana State University Press, 1975),

1209. On southern fiction and the Civil War, see John Pilkington, "The Memory of War," in *The History of Southern Literature,* edited by Louis Rubin (Baton Rouge: Louisiana State University Press, 1985), 356–62.

59. Young, *So Red the Rose,* 34 (quote); Executive board minutes, November 26, 1935, March 6, 1936, box 1, Natchez Garden Club Records (hereafter cited as NGCR), MDAH; "'So Red the Rose' Written in the South," newspaper article, February 20, n.y., in Natchez Garden Club Scrapbook, Natchez Garden Club Archives, Magnolia Hall, Natchez, Mississippi; John Pilkington, *Stark Young* (Boston: Twayne Publishers, 1985), 2–4, 120; Donald Davidson, "Theme and Method in *So Red the Rose,*" in *Southern Renascence: The Literature of the Modern South,* edited by Luis D. Rubin Jr. and Robert D. Jacobs (Baltimore: Johns Hopkins Press, 1953), 262–77.

60. *Book Review Digest, 1934,* 1053 ("special"); Stark Young to Donald Davidson, July 4, 1952, *Stark Young: Letters,* 1209 ("whole"); Pilkington, *Stark Young,* 124 ("I"). See also Davidson, "Theme and Method," 256.

61. Young, *So Red the Rose,* 150–51.

62. Davidson said that not until he visited Natchez did he understand *So Red the Rose.* See *Stark Young: Letters,* 1210 n.

63. See Louis D. Rubin Jr. *The Wary Fugitives: Four Poets and the South* (Baton Rouge: Louisiana State University Press, 1978), 205–8.

64. Davidson, "Theme and Method," 264 ("battle"); Young, *So Red the Rose,* 386 ("the debasement").

65. Pilkington, *Stark Young,* 386.

66. Davidson, "Theme and Method," 275; Walter Sullivan, "The Southern Novelists and the Civil War," in *Southern Renascence,* 120–22; Stark Young to Norma Long Brickell, June 11, 1934, *Stark Young: Letters,* 533–36; Pilkington, *Stark Young,* 119 ("I"), 121–23, 124.

67. Davidson, "Theme and Method," 276–77 ("literature"); Alexander, "Natchez and Richard Wright," 171 ("The world").

68. Pilkington, *Stark Young,* 128.

69. For a study of the persistence of the Lost Cause well into the twentieth century in the regional imagination, particularly in literature, see Thomas L. Connelly and Barbara L. Bellows, *God and General Longstreet: The Lost Cause and the Southern Mind* (Baton Rouge: Louisiana State University Press, 1982).

CHAPTER TWO

1. Katherine Grafton Miller, *Natchez of Long Ago and the Pilgrimage* (Natchez: Rellimak Publishing, 1938), 37.

2. Ibid., 5.

3. Interview with Marty Nathanson, by author, March 26, 1993.

4. David Donald quoted in Charles Sallis, "Images of Mississippi," in *A Sense of Place:*

Mississippi, edited by Peggy W. Prenshaw and Jesse O. McKee (Jackson: University Press of Mississippi, 1979), 69.

5. *New York Times,* March 17, 1935 ("a sense"); "A Page from *Gone with the Wind,*" *Boston Herald American,* March 25, 1979 ("During"); Elmer T. Peterson, "The Old South Lives Again!" *Better Homes and Gardens,* February 1938, 34–50; *Natchez Democrat,* March 4, 1972. According to Miller, the Pilgrimage's slogan was borrowed from George Nealy of the New Orleans *Times-Picayune,* who wrote, "Natchez, where the Old South still lives and where shaded highways and antebellum homes greet new and old friends." See Mrs. J. Balfour Miller, "Natchez Is a Fairy Story," n.d., MDAH.

6. Ronald Miller and Mary M. Miller, *Natchez National Historical Park, Historic Resource Study* (Historic Natchez Foundation, 1997), 47–48 ("garden"). See also Frederick Law Olmsted, *Cotton Kingdom: A Traveler's Observations on Cotton and Slavery in the American Slave States* (New York: Alfred A. Knopf, 1953), 422–25. "Natchez' First Pilgrimage," *Over the Garden Wall,* March 1955, 4 ("most"); Unsigned letter to Roberta Seiferth, February 20, 1941, Correspondence, box 3, NGCR; "Statement of the Natchez Garden Club," n.d., Natchez Pilgrimage Papers, MDAH; "Petticoat Peace Quiets Quarreling Natchez," *American Weekly,* August 16, 1942, 8; Miller, "Natchez Is a Fairy Story"; Interview with Ruth Audley Britton Wheeler Beltzhoover, by Graham Hicks, August 4, 1981, MDAH; "How the Pilgrimage Came About," *Natchez Club Affairs* 1 (March 1935): 11–13; Bern Keating, "The Old South Comes Alive in Natchez," *50 Plus,* March 1987, 61–66.

7. Natchez Garden Club minutes, March 3, 12, April 13, 1931, Natchez Garden Club Archives; Program, "Garden Club of Mississippi, Second Annual Convention, Natchez, Mississippi, March 19, 20, and 21, 1931," box 2, Garden Clubs of Mississippi Records (hereafter cited as GCMR), MDAH; Louise La Barr Garrett, Garden Clubs of Mississippi History, box 1, GCMR.

8. The Natchez Garden Club to Natchez Rotary Club, November 16, 1931, Correspondence 1931 file, box 2, NGCR; "Petticoat Peace Quiets Quarreling Natchez," 8; Beltzhoover interview; Kane, *Natchez on the Mississippi,* 337–42; "How the Pilgrimage Came About," 11.

9. Miller, "Natchez Is a Fairy Story" ("to"); *Jackson Clarion-Ledger,* March 25, 1984 ("They"); see also December 18, 1984.

10. Natchez Association of Commerce to Katherine G. Miller, November 10, 1931, Correspondence 1931 file, box 2, NGCR; R. A. McLemore to National Trust, March 17, 1971, Mrs. J. Balfour Miller subject file, MDAH; *Natchez Democrat,* January 1, 1930, February 10, 1933; Interview with Mary Louis Goodrich, by Graham Hicks, January 27, 1982, MDAH; Bette Barber, *Natchez' First Ladies: Katherine Grafton Miller and the Pilgrimage* (New York, 1955).

11. Miller, "Natchez Is a Fairy Story" ("agog"); Katherine Miller Scrapbooks, HNF; "Natchez Pilgrimage Week: 1933 Project of the Natchez Garden Club," report, n.d., Natchez Pilgrimages 1935–1950 subject file, MDAH; Garden Clubs of Mississippi, *First Year Book,* 1931–1932, 21, GCMR; "Natchez' First Pilgrimage," 4–5; *Natchez Democrat,* March 27, 28, 1932.

12. *Birmingham News,* clipping, n.d., Miller Scrapbooks ("royal"); Executive board minutes, May 27, 1937, and August 24, 1938, box 1, NGCR; *Mississippi Homes and Gardens* (1948), box 4, GCMR; Interview with Rebecca Fauntleroy Benoist, by Graham Hicks, August 16, 1981, MDAH; Mary Louis Goodrich interview; Katherine Blankenstein interview; Eleanor Roosevelt to Mrs. Miller, March 12, 1939, Miller Scrapbooks; *Natchez Democrat,* February 28, 1939, January 9, 1981, April 3, 1983, July 9, 1989; *Jackson Clarion Ledger,* March 25, December 18, 1984; *Jackson Daily News,* February 2, 1947; *Washington Post,* April 3, 1977; "Petticoat Peace Quiets Quarreling Natchez," 8.

13. David Glassberg, *American Historical Pageantry: The Uses of Tradition in the Early Twentieth Century* (Chapel Hill: University of North Carolina Press, 1992), 269.

14. "Natchez Pilgrimage Week" ("hardly"); Peterson, "The Old South Lives Again!" 34–35 ("Old"); *Natchez Democrat,* February 10 ("intelligence"), April 12, 1933; Interview with Troy B. Watkins, by author, July 13, 1992; Interview with Thomas J. Reed, by author, September 14, 1993; Letter from the Adams County Board of Supervisors (hereinafter cited as ACBS), n.d., Resolutions file, box 4, NGCR.

15. In later years, this objective was incorporated into the charter of the Natchez Garden Club. See Mrs. J. F. Schmidt to Mrs. T. A. Berry, April 8, 1966, Correspondence, box 4, NGCR.

16. Katherine Miller to the Mayor and Aldermen of the City of Natchez, November 25, 1930, Miller Scrapbooks ("beautification"); Garden Clubs of Mississippi, *Year Book,* no. 2, 1933–1934, box 3, GCMR; "A Tribute to the Original Members of the Natchez Garden Club," Miscellany file, box 2, and executive board minutes, June 25, 1942, NGCR; Verbie Lovorn Prevost, "Roane Fleming Byrnes: A Critical Biography" (Ph.D. diss., University of Mississippi, 1974), 105 ("civic").

17. Ibid.; Executive board minutes, February 22, 1951, NGCR ("to"); Katherine Blankenstein interview; Ben Arthur Davis to Mrs. Miller, September 23, 1932, in Miller Scrapbooks ("doing").

18. Katherine Grafton Miller, "Reflections from Yesterday for Tomorrow," Pilgrimage Garden Club president's report, 1942, in author's possession. See also R. A. McLemore to National Trust.

19. "Petticoat Peace Quiets Quarreling Natchez," 8; Mary "Mimi" Warren Miller, "Paying Homage in Natchez," *Reckon* 1 (fall 1995): 62–71; Executive board minutes, March n.d., November 1, 1935, April 16, June 9, 1936, May 27, 1937, NGCR; "Statement in regard to the ideas of certain members of the Garden Club on the question of giving 75 percent of the Pilgrimage profits to the Pilgrimage Home-owners," and Annie Barnum to Mrs. Ferriday Byrnes, August 30, 1935, and Petition, August 26, 1935, all in Natchez Pilgrimage Papers. Application for Membership in the Garden Clubs of Mississippi, January 9, 1937, Applications file, box 1; and Application for Membership in the Garden Clubs of Mississippi, box 3, GCMR. *Jackson Clarion-Ledger,* December 18, 1984; *Washington Post,* April 3, 1977.

20. Stark Young to Ella Somerville, July 21, 1949, *Stark Young: Letters,* 1107 (quotes); Proceedings memorandum, November 17, 1937, Natchez Pilgrimage Papers; "Petticoat Peace Quiets Quarreling Natchez," 8; Rebecca Fauntleroy Benoist, Katherine Blankenstein,

and Mary Louis Goodrich interviews; Kane, *Natchez,* 346–48. Executive board minutes, March 13, 1936, March 24, 1941, October 14, 1946; *Natchez Garden Club v. The Pilgrimage Garden Club,* April 1941, Legal papers, box 7; Mrs. W. A. Sullivan to Stark Young, June 2, 1941, Correspondence, box 3; and Lawrence Abrams to Mrs. W. A. Sullivan, April 11, 1941, roll 4, ser. 3 (B-1508), all in NGCR.

21. Troy B. Watkins interview; J. Oliver Emmerich, "Collapse and Recovery," in *A History of Mississippi,* edited by R. A. McLemore (Hattiesburg: University and College Press of Mississippi, 1973), 106.

22. Troy B. Watkins interview ("Renaissance"); *Report of Self Evaluation; Natchez Democrat,* March 13, 1962, November 12, 1970; *Jackson Clarion-Ledger,* March 26, 1978; *Washington Post,* April 3, 1977; "Great Comeback," *Over the Garden Wall,* September 1955, 6 ("probably").

23. Many of the scholarly studies of Natchez architecture are terribly flawed. The sources with which one should use caution include J. Frazier Smith, *White Pillars: Early Life and Architecture of the Lower Mississippi Valley Country* (New York: William Hellman, 1941); James, *Antebellum Natchez,* 239–41; James C. Bonner, "Plantation Architecture of the Lower South on the Eve of the Civil War," *Journal of Southern History* 11 (August 1945): 370–80. The most accurate study on Natchez architecture is Ronald Miller and Mary W. Miller, *The Great Houses of Natchez* (Jackson: University Press of Mississippi, 1986); and Miller and Miller, *Natchez National Historical Park.*

24. Smith, *White Pillars,* 117 ("at"). Constructed in 1812, Auburn was actually the first home of this design in Natchez. See Miller and Miller, *Natchez National Historical Park,* 30–31.

25. Miller and Miller, *Natchez National Historical Park,* 115–17; Kane, *Natchez,* 166–69; Grace MacNeil interview; Nola Nance Oliver, *Natchez: Symbol of the Old South* (New York: Hastings House Publishers, 1940), 10–13.

26. *Birmingham News,* clipping, n.d., Miller Scrapbooks ("houses"); Oliver, *Natchez,* dust jacket ("vanished"); Davenport, *Myth of Southern History,* 34 n.

27. Margaret Mitchell, *Gone with the Wind* (Garden City, New York: Garden City Books edition, 1954), 266–67, 277, 287–88. On this subject, see also Davenport, *Myth of Southern History,* 34 n.; Troy B. Watkins interview.

28. Stark Young to Claribel Drake, February 2, 1935, Stark Young Letters, MDAH; Prevost, "Roane Fleming Byrnes," 115; Bonner, "Plantation Architecture"; *Stark Young: Letters,* 119 (quote); Stark Young to Julia Young Robertson, March 18, 1935, *Stark Young: Letters,* 586, and 617 n.

29. Steven H. Scheuer, editor, *Movies on TV, 1988–1989* (New York: Bantam Books, 1987), 729 ("history"); Darden Asbury Pyron, *Southern Daughter: The Life of Margaret Mitchell* (New York: Oxford University Press, 1991), 370–72 ("know").

30. For a discussion of Greek Revival architecture of the Old South, see Smith, *White Pillars.*

31. Carter, *Lower Mississippi,* 234, 251 ("as"); Thomas Craven, "Culture of Natchez," newspaper clipping, n.d., in scrapbook, Accretion, box 1, NGCR ("culture-seekers").

32. Peterson, "The Old South Lives Again!" 34 (quote). Executive board minutes,

March 26, April 23, 1936; "The Confederate Pageant," *Over the Garden Wall,* March 1955, 6–9; "Seventh Annual Pilgrimage Tour Guide," 1938; and "Natchez Pilgrimage Guide," 1947, all in NGCR.

33. "A Mansion," *Over the Garden Wall,* March 1955, 11 ("enchanted"); "The Confederate Pageant, 1992," Confederate Pageant program guide, in author's possession (other quotes).

34. "Confederate Ball: 9th Annual Pageant of the Original Natchez Garden Club, March 24–April 7, 1940," box 3, GCMR; Miller, "Natchez Is a Fairy Story"; Ruth Audley Beltzhoover interview. Some whites regarded the Old South luminaries as religious saints and martyrs. See Charles Reagan Wilson, *Baptized in Blood: The Religion of the Lost Cause, 1865–1920* (Athens: University of Georgia Press, 1980), 25.

35. Carolyn Vance Smith, *Secrets of Natchez: From a Journalist's Notebook* (Natchez: Plantation Publishing, 1984), 9–17.

36. Interview with Anabel Young Maxie, by Graham Hicks, August 25, 1981, MDAH; Interview with Mary Jane Beltzhoover, by author, March 27, 1993; Virginia Beltzhoover Morrison, Katherine Blankenstein, and Rebecca Benoist interviews; *Natchez Democrat,* April 2, 1969; Attendance at the Confederate Pageant, by author, March 27, 1992.

37. Anonymous interview ("trying"); Natchez Board of Aldermen (hereafter cited as NBA) minutes, September 10, 1940; *Code of the City of Natchez, Mississippi, 1954,* Chapter 24, "Tourist Guides" ("cultural"); Mayor W. J. Byrne to Mrs. W. A. Sullivan, October 8, 1940, and Mrs. W. A. Sullivan to Honorable W. J. Byrne, October 23, 1940, Correspondence, box 3, NGCR. The city ordinance still exists, and Pilgrimage Tours administers the exam.

38. Carter, *Lower Mississippi,* 234, 251.

39. Davis, *Good and Faithful Labor,* 59–62 ("waving"); Mrs. Harry C. Ogden to Mrs. Hanun Gardner, September 9, 1938, box 3, Henrietta Henry Papers, MDAH ("perfect"); Miller and Miller, *Natchez National Historical Park,* 111; Ronald L. F. Davis, *The Black Experience in Natchez* (Eastern National Park and Monument Association, 1994), 133; James M. McPherson, *Battle Cry of Freedom: The Civil War Era* (New York: Ballantine Books, 1989), 626–38; Kane, *Natchez,* 274–75; Oliver, *Natchez,* 92.

40. Newspaper clipping, n.d., Miller Scrapbooks ("of"); Miller, *Natchez Long Ago,* pass.; Mencken quoted in David L. Cohn, "Natchez was a Lady," *Atlantic Monthly,* January 1940, 14. See also Mencken's "The Anglo-Saxon," in *The Vintage Mencken,* edited by Alistair Cooke (New York: Vintage Books, 1955), 127–37; "The Confederate Pageant, 1992" ("an").

41. Morton Rothstein, "The Changing Social Networks and Investment Behavior of a Slaveholding Elite in the Ante-Bellum South: Some Natchez 'Nabobs,' 1800–1860," in *Entrepreneurs in Cultural Context,* edited by Sidney M. Greenfield, Arnold Strickon, and Robert Aubrey (Albuquerque: University of New Mexico Press, 1979), 67–68 (quote); Scarborough, "Lords or Capitalists?" 239–67; James, *Antebellum Natchez,* 136–61.

42. Georgia Willson Newell and Charles Cromartie Compton, *Natchez and the Pilgrimage* (Southern Publishers, 1935), 5, 39 ("It"); Peterson, "The Old South Lives Again!" 34–50 ("modern"); *New York Times,* March 17, 1945.

43. Kane, *Natchez,* 337–41. See also Newell and Compton, *Natchez and the Pilgrimage.* Cohn, "Natchez Was a Lady," 15 ("the last").

44. Wayne, *The Reshaping of Plantation Society,* 75–109; Kane, *Natchez,* 335. See also Cohn, "Natchez Was a Lady," 15; Editorial, *Over the Garden Wall,* April 1950, 2; Newell and Compton, *Natchez and the Pilgrimage,* 39; John Gunther, *Inside U.S.A.* (New York: Harper and Brothers, 1947), 802–03; Power, *The Memento,* 32.

45. Alice Walworth Graham, *The Natchez Woman* (Garden City, N.Y.: Doubleday, 1950), 218–20.

46. See Editorial, *Over the Garden Wall,* 2.

47. *Jackson Daily News,* December 14, 1985.

48. Joanne V. Hawks, "A Historical Assessment," in *Rituals: The Importance of Family in the Development of Mississippi Society,* edited by Joanne V. Hawks and Mary Emma Graham (Jackson: Mississippi Committee for the Humanities, 1986), 3–5 ("families"); Mary Emma Graham, "Family as a Literary Theme," in ibid., 6–8; "What Shall Children Do with Their Parents?" *Over the Garden Wall,* February 1949, 13, 19; Willie Morris, "A Sense of Place and the Americanization of Mississippi," in *A Sense of Place,* 3–13; Walker Percy, "Mississippi: The Fallen Paradise," *Harper's,* April 1965, 166–71; Sam Jones, narrator, 1994 Confederate Pageant, Natchez, Mississippi.

49. *New York Times Book Review,* July 8, 1962, 18 (quotes); Walton, *Mississippi,* 25–28.

50. Ellen Douglas, *A Family's Affair* (Boston: Houghton Mifflin, 1961), 40–41.

51. Ibid., 33. In a draft of the novel, Douglas recrafted the passage about poverty and aristocracy a number of times, indicating that the idea carried importance in describing Homochitto society. See Ellen Douglas Manuscript Collection, box 36, folder 90-34-36-8a, UMASC.

52. Douglas, *A Family's Affair,* 33, 37, 40–41.

53. Ibid., 36–37, 433.

54. Ibid.

55. Power, *The Memento,* 8, 13, 14.

56. Cohn, "Natchez Was a Lady," 15.

57. "Ten Commandments of the Modern Wife," *Over the Garden Wall,* October 1947, 5 (quote). For a discussion of the Victorian origins of this so-called domestic ideology, see Nancy F. Cott, *The Bonds of Womanhood: "Woman's Sphere" in New England, 1780–1835* (New Haven: Yale University Press, 1977); and Barbara Welter, "The Cult of True Womanhood: 1820–1860," in *The American Family in Social-Historical Perspective,* edited by Michael Gordon (New York: Saint Martin's Press, 1978), 313–33. For a commentary about domesticity in southern society, see Scott, *The Southern Lady;* Clinton, *Plantation Mistress.* Clinton offers the most insightful and, consequently, valuable examination of the thesis of southern women as keepers of culture.

58. Blair, *Torchbearers,* 120–30.

59. Newell and Compton, *Natchez and the Pilgrimage,* 23 (quote); *Memphis Commercial-Appeal,* February 23, 1941. Interview with Marion Kelly Ferry, by Graham Hicks, November 17, 1981, Interview with Clarence C. Eyrich Sr. and Clarence C. Eyrich

Jr., by Elliot Trimble, August 12, 1981; and Interview with Mr. and Mrs. Joseph F. Dixon, by Graham Hicks, n.d., all in MDAH.

60. *Memphis Commercial-Appeal,* February 23, 1941; "Natchez Pilgrimage Week," Natchez Pilgrimage brochure, 1933, box 7, folder 68, James Allen and Family Papers, MDAH; *Natchez Democrat,* March 15, 26, 1933; February 25, 1987; Allison Davis, "The Negro Church and Associations in the Lower South," June 1940, Carnegie-Myrdal Study, The Negro in America, Schomberg Collection Negro History, reel 5, 42–43, 68.

61. *Natchez Democrat,* clipping, n.d., Miller Scrapbooks ("creditable"); Mary P. McVeigh, "Negro Spirituals," *Over the Garden Wall,* April 1952, 20 ("A cherished").

62. *Natchez Democrat,* December 1, 1934 ("Nature"), May 6, 1936 ("Another"); Interview with Elliot Trimble, by author, September 17, 1993.

63. Interview with Dolores George [pseud.], by author, July 17, 1996; Interview with Charlotte Mackel Harrison, by author, December 22, 1996; Interview with Mary Toles, by author, May 2, 1998; Library of Congress Copyright Certificate, April 23, 1936, issued to Julia Walker Harrison for "Heavenbound Pilgrims," copy in author's possession; Natchez Pilgrimage brochures, 1965 and 1966, Natchez Pilgrimage Papers. Seventh Annual Pilgrimage Tour Guide, 1938, and Natchez Pilgrimage Guide, 1947, in Publicity and Promotions file; Executive board minutes, November 15, 1933, box 1; and Check Stubs file, box 11, all in NGCR.

64. Natchez Pilgrimage Historical file, box 7, NGCR ("Possible Evidence").

65. Ethel L. Fleming, "Achievements and Social Conditions of Negroes," Adams County Education, Negro Organizations file, WPA Projects Files, RG 60, box 217, MDAH; Power, *The Memento,* 13.

66. See Jacquelyn Dowd Hall, *Revolt against Chivalry: Jessie Daniel Ames and the Women's Campaign against Lynching* (New York: Columbia University Press, 1979); Donald L. Grant, *The Anti-Lynching Movement: 1883–1932* (San Francisco: R and E Research Associates, 1975). For a firsthand account, see Jessie Daniel Ames, *The Changing Character of Lynching, 1931–1941* (Atlanta: Commission on Interracial Cooperation, 1942).

67. Interview with Ruth Dumas, by author, August 19, 1992; Marty Nathanson interview; *Jackson Clarion-Ledger,* July 3, 1979; Davis et al., *Deep South,* 38–39, 457–58; "Democracy in Mississippi," *Crisis* 34 (November 1927): 296; "Deep in Dixie: Race Progress," *U.S. News and World Report,* February 26, 1954, 53–4; U.S. Commission on Civil Rights, *Hearings before the United States Commission on Civil Rights,* Administration of Justice, February 16–20, 1965 (Washington, D.C., 1965), 2: 69.

68. *Natchez Democrat,* August 6, 1948; Robert Penn Warren, "Segregation," in *Robert Penn Warren Reader,* 245–46. See also Davis et al., *Deep South,* 15–24.

69. Elliot Trimble interview ("have"); Davis et al., *Deep South,* 19–20; John Dollard, *Caste and Class in a Southern Town* (Madison: University of Wisconsin Press, 1988), 88; Elizabeth Dunbar Murray, *My Mother Used to Say: A Natchez Belle of the Sixties* (Boston: Christopher Publishing, 1959), 188–89. See also Power, *The Memento,* 31–33.

70. Power, *The Memento,* 14.

71. On these various points, see Dollard, *Caste and Class in a Southern Town,* 134–72;

Joel Kovel, *White Racism: A Psychohistory* (New York: Pantheon Books, 1970); Clinton, *Plantation Mistress;* Welter, "The Cult of True Womanhood."

72. *Natchez Publishing Company v. Dunigan,* No. 39135, Supreme Court of Mississippi, May 24, 1954, found in *Southern Reporter,* 2d ser. (Saint Paul, West Publishing, 1954), 72: 681–87.

73. Nietzsche, *The Use and Abuse of History,* 10; Cohn, "Natchez Was a Lady," 14.

CHAPTER THREE

1. Charlotte Mackel Harrison interview; Anne Moody, *Coming of Age in Mississippi* (New York: Dial Press, 1968), 213, 215 (quote); Neil R. McMillen, *Dark Journey: Black Mississippians in the Age of Jim Crow* (Urbana: University of Illinois Press, 1989), 20–21.

2. Charlotte Mackel Harrison interview.

3. Vernon Lane Wharton, *The Negro in Mississippi, 1865–1890* (Chapel Hill: University of North Carolina Press, 1947), 229, 68 n.

4. Interview with Jerold Krouse, by author, July 10, 1997.

5. Ibid.

6. Ibid.; Zeev Chafets, *Members of the Tribe: On the Road in Jewish America* (New York: Bantam Books, 1988), 21–24.

7. Although it has been criticized for being too simplistic, the two-caste model of Davis and the Gardners succeeds in describing Natchez race relations in the days of segregation. For a negative evaluation of this model, see especially Vernon J. Williams, *From a Caste to a Minority: Changing Attitudes of American Sociologists toward Afro-Americans, 1896– 1945* (New York: Greenwood Press, 1989), 160–71.

8. Williamson, *New People,* 82; Howard N. Rabinowitz, *Race Relations in the Urban South, 1865–1890* (Urbana: University of Illinois Press, 1980), 249; Davis et al., *Deep South,* 245–46.

9. *Population in the United States in 1860* (GPO 1864); Davis, *The Black Experience in Natchez,* 47–60; James, *Antebellum Natchez,* 163, 180; Ira Berlin, *Slaves without Masters: The Free Negro in the Antebellum South* (New York: Vintage Books, 1976), 137. See also Edwin Adams Davis and William Ransom Hogan, *The Barber of Natchez* (Baton Rouge: Louisiana State University Press, 1973); Hogan and Davis, *William Johnson's Natchez;* Miller and Miller, *Natchez National Historical Park.*

10. Davis and Hogan, *Barber of Natchez;* Hogan and Davis, *William Johnson's Natchez.*

11. Michael Telesca, "Black Politicos of Reconstruction Era Natchez," research paper, California State University at Northridge, 1993, HNF; Wharton, *The Negro in Mississippi,* 167; McMillen, *Dark Journey,* 37; Davis, *The Black Experience in Natchez,* 188–90; Miller and Miller, *Natchez National Historical Park,* 125; Eric Foner, *Freedom's Lawmakers: A Directory of Black Officeholders during Reconstruction* (Baton Rouge: Louisiana State University Press, 1996), xvii, 235.

12. John R. Lynch, *The Facts of Reconstruction,* edited by William C. Harris (Indianapolis: Bobbs-Merrill, 1970), 46–47; Davis, *The Black Experience in Natchez,* 188–89; Miller and Miller, *Natchez National Historical Park* 123–24; Wharton, *The Negro in Mississippi,* 159–63, 172–80; Loewen and Sallis et al., *Mississippi: Conflict and Change,* 154; Telesca, "Black Politicos of Reconstruction Era Natchez"; Foner, *Freedom's Lawmakers,* 138–39, 180–81.

13. Davis, *The Black Experience in Natchez,* 195–200; Miller and Miller, *Natchez National Historical Park,* 124; Williamson, *New People,* 81–83; McMillen, *Dark Journey,* 22.

14. *Natchez Democrat,* November 11, 1981 (quote); Lynch, *The Facts of Reconstruction,* 137–46, 169–85, 261–68; McMillen, *Dark Journey,* 38–57; Wharton, *The Negro in Mississippi,* 181–215; Davis, *The Black Experience in Natchez,* 192; Miller and Miller, *Natchez National Historical Park,* 125; Telesca, "Black Politicos of Reconstruction Era Natchez."

15. *Polk's Natchez City Directory, 1950–1951* (Richmond, Va.: R. L. Polk, 1950); Wharton, *The Negro in Mississippi,* 129; McMillen, *Dark Journey,* 168–70; Leon F. Litwack, *Trouble in Mind: Black Southerners in the Age of Jim Crow* (New York: Alfred A. Knopf, 1998), 250.

16. *Polk's Natchez City Directory, 1950–1951;* Taylor Branch, *Parting the Waters: America in the King Years, 1954–1963* (New York: Simon and Schuster, 1988), 16.

17. Williamson, *New People,* 95; Davis et al., *Deep South,* 38–42.

18. Charlotte Mackel Harrison interview; Interview with Mary Miller, by author, December 12, 1997; Davis et al., *Deep South,* 33–7; *Progressive Preservation* 17 (spring 1995); *Daily Mississippian,* May 4, 1992.

19. According to the will of the subject in question, who shall remain anonymous, he died a single man. To his companion and two sons, he left separate sums of money. Each son also inherited a house.

20. Anonymous interviews.

21. Interview with Joseph Dumas, by author, August 18, 1992; Ruth Dumas and Dolores George interviews; Interview with Walter Mackel, by author, July 8, 1997; Interview with George F. West Jr., by author, July 10, 1997; Charlotte Mackel Harrison interview.

22. Davis et al., *Deep South,* 214–16, 234–35; 243–48; McMillen, *Dark Journey,* 19–23.

23. George F. West Jr. interview; Interview with John West, by author, October 29, 1993; "Charter of Incorporation of Natchez Business and Civic League," March 10, 1952, Harden Wallace Center, Natchez, Mississippi; *Natchez Business and Civic League, Twenty-Second Annual Awards Banquet,* February 21, 1997, program, in author's possession.

24. *Polk's Natchez City Directory, 1950–51;* Charlotte Mackel Harrison and Mary Miller interviews; "Brumfield School," National Register of Historic Places Registration Form, HNF; *Baton Rouge Morning Advocate,* August 14, 1990; Leedell W. Neyland, *Unquenchable Black Fires* (Tallahassee, Fla.: Leney Educational and Publishing, 1994); *Natchez Democrat,* August 14, 1985, July 12, 17, 1990.

25. Interview with Androse Mackel Banks, by author, December 8, 1997; Interview with Audley M. Mackel Jr., by author, December 8, 1997; Charlotte Mackel Harrison and Walter Mackel interviews.

26. Interview with Frank Robinson, by author, December 11, 1997 (quote); Interview with Duncan Morgan, by author, December 11, 1997; Androse Mackel Banks, Ruth Dumas, and Charlotte Mackel Harrison interviews; Field notebook, 2, 8–10, 39–40, box 31, Allison Davis Papers, Special Collections, University of Chicago Library.

27. Androse Mackel Banks, Dolores George, Charlotte Mackel Harrison, Walter Mackel, and Duncan Morgan interviews.

28. *Natchez Democrat,* December 30, 1983.

29. Androse Mackel Banks, Ruth Dumas, Dolores George, Charlotte Mackel Harrison, Audley M. Mackel Jr., Walter Mackel, Duncan Morgan, and Frank Robinson interviews; Lawrence Adams to Roane F. Byrnes, April 6, 1962, box 19, Byrnes Collection; *Natchez Democrat,* September 15 ("necessary"), October 1, 1960, January 22, 1961, December 30, 1983 ("The first").

30. "Easter Sunday Baseball," newspaper clipping, n.d., *Bluff City Bulletin,* December 8, 1965, and broadside, n.d., all in box 19, Byrnes Collection.

31. Interview with Shead Baldwin, by author, September 17, 1993; Interview with Phillip West, by author, May 1, 1998; Audley M. Mackel Jr. interview. A newspaper article credits Robert Williams of Natchez with organizing black youth baseball. *Natchez Democrat,* December 30, 1983. Mackel pointed out in an interview that his efforts actually preceded those of Williams.

32. For further examination of this subject, see Jack E. Davis, "Baseball's Reluctant Challenge: Desegregating Major League Spring Training Sites, 1960–1963," *Journal of Sport History* 20 (fall 1992): 144–62.

33. Androse Mackel Banks, Ruth Dumas, Dolores George, Charlotte Mackel Harrison, Audley M. Mackel Jr., Walter Mackel, Duncan Morgan, and Frank Robinson interviews; *Natchez Democrat,* October 26, 1950, April 4, 8, 16, 21, 1953, March 18, 1954.

34. Joseph Dumas, Ruth Dumas, Dolores George, and Frank Robinson, interviews; Interview with Harden Wallace, by author, December 11, 1997; Robert W. Shumway, "Physicians and Surgeons of Natchez, Adams County, Mississippi," Residents file, HNF; *Natchez Business and Civic League* program; "Frank Robinson on Dr. Banks," n.d., videotape, Mostly African Market, Natchez, Mississippi; *Natchez Democrat,* April 15, 1989.

35. *Natchez Democrat,* April 15, 1989.

36. Androse Mackel Banks and Charlotte Mackel Harrison interviews; Audley M. Mackel Sr., "Let the Works That I Have Done Speak for Me," edited by Androse L. Mackel Banks, unpublished manuscript, The Rinky Dinks, 1997, in the possession of Audley M. Mackel Jr., Chicago, Illinois; NBA minutes, May 10, 1938; A.W. Dumas to Board of Education, n.d., school board minutes, 1915–1920, MDAH; Brumfield School, National Register of Historic Places registration form, HNF.

37. NBA minutes, May 10, 1938.

38. Zack J. Van Landingham to Director, Mississippi State Sovereignty Commission,

March 18, 1959, State Sovereignty Files, MDAH ("front"); Anonymous and George F. West Jr. interviews.

39. Anonymous interview (quote).

40. Field notebook, 6–7, 8–10 ("That's"); Anonymous interview ("some").

41. On this subject, see Glenda Elizabeth Gilmore, *Gender and Jim Crow: Women and the Politics of White Supremacy in North Carolina, 1896–1920* (Chapel Hill: University of North Carolina Press, 1996).

42. In recent years, historians have taken a new interest in the subject of class divisions in the black community after slavery, first explored by E. Franklin Frazier in his *Black Bourgeoisie* (New York: Free Press, 1957). See also Willard B. Gatewood, *Aristocrats of Color: The Black Elite, 1880–1920* (Bloomington: Indiana University Press, 1990); Earl Lewis, *In Their Own Interest: Race, Class, and Power in Twentieth-Century Norfolk, Virginia* (Berkeley: University of California Press, 1991); Joe W. Trotter, *Coal, Class, and Color: Blacks in Southern West Virginia, 1915–1932* (Urbana: University of Illinois Press, 1990); George C. Wright, *Life behind the Veil: Blacks in Louisville, Kentucky, 1865–1930* (Baton Rouge: Louisiana State University Press, 1985).

43. Ethel L. Fleming, "Negroes' Activities, Natchez," n.d., Adams County Education, Negro Organizations file, WPA Projects Files, MDAH; Joseph Dumas, Ruth Dumas, Dolores George, and Charlotte Mackel interviews; *Mississippi,* July/August 1991, 501.

44. On the subject of women and a service ethic, see Charles Harris Wesley, *The History of the National Association of Colored Women's Clubs: A Legacy of Service* (Washington, D.C.: The Association, 1984); Elizabeth L. Davis, *Lifting as They Climb: The National Association of Colored Women* (Washington, D.C.: National Association of Colored Women, 1933); Gilmore, *Gender and Jim Crow;* Evelyn Brooks Higginbotham, *Righteous Discontent: The Women's Movement in the Black Baptist Church, 1880–1920* (Cambridge: Harvard University Press, 1993).

45. Joseph Dumas, Ruth Dumas, Dolores George, Charlotte Mackel Harrison, and Audley M. Mackel Jr. interviews; Adams County Poll Books, HNF; Field notebook, 2–5, 8–10, 40; Executive board minutes, NGCR; R. L. McLean, "Boy Scouts of Natchez," *Over the Garden Wall,* September 1947, 13, 20; *Natchez Democrat,* December 25, 1931, April 15, 1989.

46. Compiled from numerous interviews; "Be Proud of Your Race," Roane Byrnes speech, n.d., box 19, Byrnes Collection.

47. Leo E. Turitz and Evelyn Turitz, *Jews in Early Mississippi* (Jackson: University Press of Mississippi, 1995), 11; Louis Lettes, "On the Verge of Extinction: Small-Town Jewish Communities in the Deep South" (Senior thesis, Princeton University, 1986), 12–14; Kenneth Hoffman, "The Jews of Natchez," n.d., research paper in possession of the Museum of the Southern Jewish Experience, Jackson, Mississippi, 2; "The Natchez Jewish Experience," documentary video, 1994, Museum of the Southern Jewish Experience.

48. On early Jews in Savannah, see Mark I. Greenberg, "Creating Ethnic, Class, and Southern Identity in Nineteenth-Century America: Jews of Savannah, Georgia, 1830–1880" (Ph.D. diss., University of Florida, 1997). On the southern Jewish experience, see es-

pecially Eli N. Evans, *The Provincials: A Personal History of Jews in the South* (New York: Atheneum, 1974); Leonard Dinnerstein and Mary Dale Palsson, editors, *Jews in the South* (Baton Rouge: Louisiana State University Press, 1973); Nathan M. Kaganoff and Melvin I. Urofsky editors, *"Turn to the South": Essays on Southern Jewry* (Charlottesville: University Press of Virginia, 1979); David Goldfield, "A Sense of Place: Jews, Blacks, and White Gentiles in the American South," *Southern Cultures* 3 (spring 1997): 58–79.

49. Turitz and Turitz, *Jews in Early Mississippi,* 11–12; Abram Leon Sachar, *A History of the Jews* (New York: Alfred A. Knopf, 1965), 299–308; Lettes, "On the Verge of Extinction," 21; Hoffman, "The Jews of Natchez," 3–10; "The Natchez Jewish Experience."

50. Mannie, Morris, and Alek Krouse, family videotape, n.d., in the possession of Jerold Krouse, Natchez, Mississippi; Jerold Krouse interview; Sachar, *A History of the Jews,* 299–308.

51. Krouse family videotape; Jerry Krouse interview.

52. Ibid.

53. Lettes, "On the Verge of Extinction," 36–40; Hoffman, "The Jews of Natchez," 3, 7; "The Natchez Jewish Experience"; Aunt Sister, *Family Stories Retold for Frank, Isaac, Margaret, and Henriette* (New York, 1929), 16; Margaret England Armbrester, *Samuel Ullman and "Youth"* (Tuscaloosa: University of Alabama Press, 1993), 19–21.

54. "Clifton Heights District Elements," National Register of Historic Places inventory-nomination form, n.d., HNF.

55. "Of Passover and Pilgrimage: The Jewish Experience in Natchez," exhibit, B'nai Israel synagogue, Natchez, Mississippi (quote); Hoffman, "The Jews of Natchez," 10; Lettes, "On the Verge of Extinction," 25; Evans, *The Provincials,* 61–68; Aunt Sister, *Family Stories,* 1–5, 15; Charter of Incorporation, Natchez Chapter, Daughters of the Confederacy, UDCP; "The Natchez Jewish Experience"; Thomas Reber, *Proud Old Natchez: History and Romance* (Natchez Printing and Stationery, 1909), 39–41.

56. Interview with Elaine Lehmann, by author, August 28, 1997; Interview with Robert Lehmann, by author, August 28, 1997; Interview with Jay Lehmann, by author, August 28, 1997, and May 21, 1998; Marty Nathanson and Jerold Krouse interviews; Minutes, March 20, 1947, Natchez Temple Sisterhood Meeting Minutes Book 1940 to 1948, Temple B'nai Israel Archives, Natchez, Mississippi; Chafets, *Members of the Tribe,* 22–3.

57. On the subject of intermarriage and southern Jews, see Evans, *The Provincials,* 183–91.

58. See for instance Melissa Fay Greene, *The Temple Bombing* (New York: Fawcett Columbine, 1996).

59. Special meeting minutes, October 18, 1947, and Congregation meeting minutes, March 30, 1948, in Congregation Meeting Minute Book, 1935–1957, and Simon Wiener to Milton Abrams, January 28, 1958, Miscellaneous Correspondence, 1923–1989 folder, box C3, Temple B'Nai Israel Archives; Krouse family videotape; "The Natchez Jewish Experience"; *Natchez Democrat,* November 5, 11, 1947, November 28, 29, 30, 1949.

60. Jerold Krouse, Elaine Lehmann, Jay Lehmann, Robert Lehmann, and Marty Nathanson interviews; *Memoirs of George W. Armstrong* (Austin, Tex.: Steck, 1958); Leon

Abrams to Dear Friend, March 22, 1949, Raffle folder, box C4, Temple B'nai Israel Archives; *Natchez Democrat,* November 10, 27, 1942, November 5, 11, 1947, November 28, 29, 30, 1949; Hoffman, "The Jews of Natchez," 10–11; Lettes, "On the Verge of Extinction," 25.

61. Gunther, *Inside U.S.A.,* 802–3 (quote); Katherine Blankenstein interview; Jerold Krouse, Elaine Lehmann, Jay Lehmann, Robert Lehmann, Mary Miller, and Marty Nathanson interviews; Krouse family videotape; "The Natchez Jewish Experience"; Stephen J. Whitfield, "Jews and Other Southerners: Counterpoint and Paradox," in *"Turn to the South,"* 76–104.

62. Jerold Krouse, Elaine Lehmann, Jay Lehmann, and Robert Lehmann, interviews; Krouse family videotape; "The Natchez Jewish Experience"; Interview with E. L. McDaniel, by Orley B. Caudill, August 12, 1977, vol. 493, Mississippi Oral History Program (MOHP), University of Southern Mississippi; Neil R. McMillen, *Citizens' Council: Organized Resistance to the Second Reconstruction* (Urbana: University of Illinois Press, 1971), 22–23.

63. Jerold Krouse interview; *Natchez Democrat,* October 18, 1965.

64. Katherine Blankenstein interview.

65. Whitfield, "Jews and Other Southerners," 104; Lettes, "On the Verge of Extinction," 72, 82; Hoffman, "The Jews of Natchez," 10–11.

66. On the subject of southern Jews and segregation, see Dinnerstein and Palsson, *Jews in the South,* sec. 5; Evans, *The Provincials,* ; 291–331, pass.; Mark H. Elovitz, *A Century of Jewish Life in Dixie: The Birmingham Experience* (Tuscaloosa: University of Alabama Press, 1974), 163–75; Greene, *The Temple Bombing.* For Mississippi, see Jack Nelson, *Terror in the Night: The Klan's Campaign against the Jews* (New York: Simon and Schuster, 1993).

CHAPTER FOUR

1. "Armstrong Tire and Rubber Company: 20th Anniversary, 1939–1959," company pamphlet, n.d., UMASC; *Natchez Democrat,* October 12, 1949.

2. NBA minutes, November 16, 1937, January 6, 1938. For an examination of Armstrong site selections, see Cheryl Marie Flory, "Locational Decisions in the Rubber Tire Industry: An Analysis of the Armstrong Rubber Company" (Master's thesis, University of Vermont, 1977), 22–24.

3. *The Natchez Mill* (Natchez: Ketchings, n.d.) ("the mellowness"); Mrs. W. A. Sullivan to Vivien Leigh, December 12, 1940, Correspondence, box 3, NGCR; *Natchez Democrat,* March 22, 1949 ("In"); Elliot Trimble interview. In 1959, Armstrong's annual payroll was $5 million. "Armstrong Tire and Rubber Company: 20th Anniversary," 5; Ernest J. Hopkins, *Mississippi's BAWI Plan: Balancing Agriculture with Industry, an Experiment in Industrial Subsidization* (Atlanta: Federal Reserve Bank of Atlanta, 1944), 46–48.

4. See the comments of David Cohn on the "unwritable codes" of black and white in-

teraction in James C. Cobb, editor, *The Mississippi Delta and the World: The Memoirs of David L. Cohn* (Baton Rouge: Louisiana State University Press, 1995), 6.

5. See Broadus Mitchell and George Sinclair Mitchell, *The Industrial Revolution in the South* (Reprint, New York: Greenwood Press, 1968; Johns Hopkins Press, 1930), 133; Allen Tullos, *Habits of Industry: White Culture and the Transformation of the Carolina Piedmont* (Chapel Hill: University of North Carolina Press, 1989), 12–13; Victoria Byerly, *Hard Times Cotton Mill Girls: Personal Histories of Womanhood and Poverty in the South* (Ithaca: ILR Press, 1986); Bruce J. Schulman, *From Cotton Belt to Sunbelt: Federal Policy, Economic Development, and the Transformation of the South, 1938–1980* (New York: Oxford University Press, 1991), 90. For a discussion of blacks in postbellum southern industry, see Herbert R. Northrup and Richard L. Rowan, *Negro Employment in Southern Industry* (Philadelphia: University of Pennsylvania, Wharton School of Finance and Commerce, 1970); Claude H. Nolen, *The Negro's Image in the South: The Anatomy of White Supremacy* (Lexington: University of Kentucky Press, 1967), 190–95.

6. Occupation and neighborhood were the "meaningful solidarities among" lower-class whites, according to the Davis research team. See Davis et al., *Deep South,* 81, 431 n.

7. Davis et al., *Deep South,* 431 n.

8. Interview with Sargent Butler, by author, September 1, October 19, 1992; Interview with James Anderson, by author, August 25, 1992; Interview with James C. Anderson, by author, July 24, 1992; Interview with Robert Carroll, by author, August 25, 1992; Interview with Albert Harris, by author, August 11, 1992; Interview with Robert Latham, by author, June 30, 1992; Earl L. Bailey, *A Look at Natchez: Its Economic Resources* (University, Miss.: Bureau of Business Research, University of Mississippi, 1953), 60–65; William Lincoln Giles, "Agricultural Revolution, 1890–1970," in McLemore, *History of Mississippi,* 211.

9. Interview with Horace Harris Jr., by author, August 18, 1992; James Anderson, James C. Anderson, Sargent Butler, and Robert Latham interviews. For a discussion about detaching from the land for the factory, see Tullos, *Habits of Industry,* 12–13, 19, pass.; and James C. Cobb, *Industrialization and Southern Society, 1877–1984* (Lexington: University Press of Kentucky, 1984), 3–4, 68–98.

10. Sargent Butler interview.

11. Sargent Butler interview; Interviews with Lejoy McCoy, by author, November 19, December 11, 1992; Interviews with Maria Washington, by author, November 23, December 11, 1992; Interview with Estella Polk, by author, October 20, 1992; Interview with Adolph Butler, by author, November 19, 1992; Grace MacNeil interview; "Contract of Lease," Aventine Plantation, sharecropper lease, January 1923 file folder, MacNeil-McKittrick-Surget Papers, MDAH.

12. Sargent Butler interview. Actually, the national minimum wage in 1968 was $1.40 an hour. Butler may have been mistaken about his pay rate when the mill closed. James Anderson confirmed the pay rate at Natchez Hardwood Company in the late 1940s. Sargent Butler and James Anderson interviews. See *Labor Law Reporter: Federal Wage-Hours* (Chicago: Commerce Clearing House, 1990), 1: 39404; and P[eter] T. Burns to

A. M. Collins, June 30, 1955, box 235, Woodworkers District Four Records, 1943–1959, Southern Labor Archives, Georgia State University (hereafter cited as SLA/GSU).

13. James Anderson, Sargent Butler, Robert Carroll interviews; Interview with Lillian Carter, by author, September 1, 1992; Interview with Samuel Stewart, by author, January 22, 1993; James W. Silver, *Running Scared: Silver in Mississippi* (Jackson: University Press of Mississippi, 1984), 20.

14. James Anderson, Sargent Butler, Robert Carroll, and Lillian Carter interviews. Interview with Frank Osgoode [pseud.], by author, November 19, 1992. Davis and the Gardners found that caste sanctions were less "thoroughly applied" at the planing mills than with timber gangs and levee crews. Davis et al., *Deep South,* 439.

15. James Anderson, Sargent Butler, Lillian Carter, and Frank Osgoode interviews. I. A. Newby makes a similar argument in his examination of the relationship between white workers and textile-mill owners in the Carolinas and Georgia. See I. A. Newby, *Plain Folk in the New South: Social Change and Cultural Persistence, 1850–1915* (Baton Rogue: Louisiana State University, 1989). "Workmen's Account Books," Andrew Brown-Rufus F. Learned Sawmill Company Papers, UMASC.

16. James Anderson, James C. Anderson, Sargent Butler, Robert Carroll, Lillian Carter, Frank Osgoode, and Samuel Stewart interviews.

17. On the idea of blacks squandering money, see Davis et al., *Deep South,* 358. In 1940, blacks constituted 66 percent of the Adams County workforce. *Sixteenth Census of the United States: 1940.*

18. Sargent Butler, Robert Carroll, and Lejoy McCoy interviews.

19. Farm and domestic service workers were not covered under federal minimum-wage standards until 1978. *Labor Law Review,* 1: 39404.

20. Like Butler, James Anderson still plants a garden. He also raises chickens and hogs. James Anderson, James C. Anderson, Sargent Butler, Robert Carroll, Lillian Carter, Frank Osgoode, and Samuel Stewart interviews; Interview with Gerard Stanton, by author, July 24, 1992.

21. Lillian Carter interview; *Sixteenth Census of the United States: 1940.* Black women and domestic service are discussed in Jacqueline Jones, *Labor of Love, Labor of Sorrow: Black Women, Work, and the Family from the Civil War to the Present* (New York: Basic Books, 1985), 127–34. On the subject of marriageable black men in Adams County, see Jack E. Davis, "Deep South Reencountered: The Social Basis of Race Relations in Natchez, Mississippi, Since 1930" (Ph.D. diss., Brandeis University, 1994), 67–91.

22. Lillian Carter interview.

23. Ibid.; *Natchez Democrat,* June 12, 1935 ("350"), September 23, November 14, 1937.

24. Frank Osgoode interview. On soybeans, see Marie M. Hemphill, *Fevers, Floods, and Faith: A History of Sunflower County, Mississippi, 1844–1976* (Indianola, Miss.: 1980), 677–78.

25. Lillian Carter and Frank Osgoode interviews. See also Sidney Fant Davis, *Mississippi Negro Lore* (Jackson, Tenn.: McCowat-Mercer, 1914), 10.

26. Lillian Carter and Frank Osgoode interviews.

27. James Anderson, Sargent Butler, Robert Carroll, Lillian Carter, Albert Harris, and Frank Osgoode interviews.

28. James C. Anderson, Robert Carroll, Lillian Carter, and Horace Harris Jr. interviews.

29. Davis et al., *Deep South*, 431, 478–86; Ibid., abridged edition (Chicago: Phoenix Books, 1965), iix. For a general study of the early years of the tire industry in America, see Daniel Nelson, *American Rubber Workers and Organized Labor, 1900–1941* (Princeton: Princeton University Press, 1988).

30. James C. Cobb, *The Selling of the South: The Southern Crusade for Industrial Development, 1936–1980* (Baton Rouge: Louisiana State University Press, 1982), 8–11; Bill P. Joyner and John P. Thames, "Mississippi's Efforts at Industrialization: A Critical Analysis," *Mississippi Law Journal* 38 (May 1967): 468–80; Ralph J. Rogers, "The Efforts to Industrialize," in McLemore, *History of Mississippi,* 2:233–49; Robert S. McElvaine, "Claude Ramsey, Organized Labor, and the Civil Rights Movement, 1959–1966," in *Southern Workers and Their Unions, 1880–1975: Selected Papers, The Second Southern Labor History Conference, 1978,* edited by Merle E. Reed and Leslie F. Hough (Westport, Conn.: Greenwood Press, 1978), 111; Flory, "Locational Decisions in the Rubber Tire Industry," 36. For a look at some examples of BAWI critics, see Donald C. Mosely, "The Labor Union Movement," in McLemore, *History of Mississippi,* 2:250–73; "A Supplement to the Statement on Farm Tenancy Submitted to the Governor's Commission on Farm Tenancy by the Executive Council, Southern Tenant Farmer's Union," October 10, 1936, Southern Tenant Farmers' Union subject file, MDAH; Cobb, *Selling of the South,* 16; *Indianola Enterprise-Tocsin,* June 6, 1936.

31. *Natchez Democrat,* November 3, 1937 (quote); Schulman, *From Cotton Belt to Sunbelt,* 91; Flory, "Locational Decisions in the Rubber Tire Industry," 6, 24, 54; State Board of Public Welfare, "Acceptance Resolution," November 9, 1932, box 3, Schwartz and Stewart Company Papers, 1866–1944, MDAH; *Natchez Democrat,* January 2, 1930, May 6, June 22, 1933, February 2, 1935, February 5, 1938; *Fifteenth Census of the United States: 1930; Unemployment,* 1: 557–58; *Sixteenth Census of the United States: 1940; Agriculture, Mississippi.*

32. Moore, "History of Natchez"; *Natchez Democrat,* January 28, March 23, 25, 26, June 20, 1930, July 18, 1931 (quote), March 28, July 11, 13, 1933.

33. NBA minutes, August 31, 1937, November 16, 1937; "Report of the Election Commission, November 12, 1937," read into the NBA minutes, January 6, 1938; *Natchez Democrat,* August 26, September 18, November 3, 13, 1937; Hopkins, *Mississippi BAWI,* 46–48; Cobb, *Selling of the South,* 59; Harry O. Hoffman to S. B. Laub, September 8, 1937, Mississippi Industrial Commission (hereafter cited as MIC) Records, RG 13, MDAH; "Minutes of Recessed Meeting of the Mississippi Industrial Commission," January 7, 1938, MIC Minute Book 2, August 1937–January 1938, 66–87; and "Minutes of Recessed Meeting," April 8, 1938, MIC Minute Book 3, February 1938–December 1938, 3–30, MDAH; James A. Walsh, *The Armstrong Rubber Company: Seventy Years of Progress in the Tire Industry* (New York: Newcomen Society, 1982), 13.

34. Flory, "Locational Decisions in the Rubber Tire Industry," 32–37; Schulman, *From Cotton Belt to Sunbelt,* 65; "Application of the Town of Natchez, Mississippi, for the Certificate of Public Convenience and Necessity for Industrial Development, no. 10," October 5, 1937, MIC Minute Book 2, August 1937–January 1938, 23–27, RG 76, MDAH; NBA minutes, October 19, 1937; S. B. Laub to Harry Hoffman, September 4, 1937 (quote), and Lemuel P. Conner to H. O. Hoffman, October 5, 1937, MIC Records; Cobb, *Selling of the South,* 116.

35. Schulman, *From Cotton Belt to Sunbelt,* 65–66; Joyner and Thames, "Mississippi Efforts at Industrialization," 476–80. Recruitment strategies across the South prioritized the white male worker. See Cobb, *Industrialization and Southern Society,* 81–84. For an examination of New Deal policy toward women as workers, see Susan Ware, *American Women in the Twentieth Century: Holding Their Own* (Boston: Twayne Publishers, 1982), 21–53; and Susan Ware, *Beyond Suffrage: Women in the New Deal* (Cambridge: Harvard University Press, 1981). For the New Deal and blacks, see Harvard Sitkoff, *A New Deal for Blacks: The Emergence of Civil Rights as a National Issue: The Depression Decade* (New York: Oxford University Press, 1978); and Raymond Wolters, *Negroes and the Great Depression: The Problem of Economic Recovery* (Westport, Conn.: Greenwood Press, 1970).

36. Nelson, *American Rubber Workers and Organized Labor;* Schulman, *From Cotton Belt to Sunbelt,* 65–66; Harry O. Hoffman to Hugh L. White, September 29, 1936, MIC Records; Interview with Robert Fly, by author, September 7, 1992; Interview with Myrtle Graves, by author, January 27, 1993; Ruth Tiffee Jordan interview; George F. West Jr. interview; James Anderson, Robert Latham, Walter Mackel, Gerard Stanton, and Samuel Stewart interviews.

37. Ruth Tiffee Jordan interview; *Natchez Democrat,* June 5, 1942, March 2, 1944, January 14, 1945, March 3, 1946, January 12, 1949; Mississippi Agricultural and Industrial Board, *State of Mississippi: Balancing Agriculture with Industry,* second report to the Legislature, 1948, 15; and fifth report to the Legislature, 1954, 10, MDAH.

38. NBA minutes, May 29, 1946, April 29, 1949; Interview with Joseph Hall, by author, July 9, 1997; Harden Wallace, Albert Harris, Horace Harris Jr., Robert Latham, Walter Mackel, Samuel Stewart, and George F. West Jr. interviews.

39. Robert Latham interview.

40. Ibid.; Gerard Stanton interview; Interview with Anna Nethers [pseud.], by author, January 27, 1993; Interview with Thomas Nethers [pseud.], by author, January 27, 1993; Interview with E. Malcolm Graves, by author, January 29, 1993; Interview with Russell Parsons, by author, January 27, 1993; Interview with Jack Whitehead, by author, January 28, 1993.

41. Robert Latham interview. The national minimum wage at the time was forty cents an hour, which suggests that the war economy boosted pay scales. *Labor Law Reporter,* 39404.

42. Robert Fly, Ruth Tiffee Jordan, and Robert Latham interviews.

43. Samuel Stewart interview; *Natchez Democrat,* January 18, 1942.

44. On work experience as a determinant of the racial division of labor in southern tex-

tile mills, see Gavin Wright, *Old South, New South: Revolutions in the Southern Economy since the Civil War* (New York: Basic Books, 1986), 158, 185–97.

45. Albert Harris interview; Davis et al., *Deep South,* 428–29. On market pressures and employment practices, see Wright, *Old South, New South.* On the assumed role of superiority in even the most equal of economic conditions between blacks and whites, see Jacqueline Jones, "Encounters, Likely and Unlikely, between Black and Poor White Women in the Rural South, 1865–1940," *The Georgia Historical Quarterly* 76 (summer 1992): 333–53.

46. James Anderson, Robert Fly, Joseph Hall, Horace Harris Jr., Ruth Tiffee Jordan, Robert Latham, Walter Mackel, Gerard Stanton, Samuel Stewart, and George F. West Jr. interviews.

47. James Anderson interview.

48. James C. Anderson and Samuel Stewart interviews.

49. Anna Nethers interview.

50. Mary Jane Beltzhoover and E. Malcolm Graves interviews.

51. Robert Fly interview.

52. Cohn, "Natchez Was a Lady," 14; Bill Hanna, E. Malcolm Graves, Myrtle Graves, and Troy B. Watkins interviews; *Natchez Democrat,* January 1, 1930, December 6, 1976; Davis et al., *Deep South,* 79; Jones, *The Dispossessed,* 45–70, 205–32.

53. Nola Vance Oliver, "Snobocracy," *Over the Garden Wall,* March 1955, 20; Davis et al., *Deep South,* 63, 74–79, 251. The conclusions in this paragraph also have been drawn from the various oral histories compiled for this study.

54. Anna Nethers [pseud.] interview. Nethers said that her father acquired the property by way of a homesteading program. Most likely it was a FSA loan, which were made available in 1937, the same year her father purchased his new property. See George B. Tindall, *The Emergence of the New South, 1913–1945* (Baton Rouge: Louisiana State University Press, 1967), 424–25; and Sidney Baldwin, *Poverty and Politics: The Rise and Decline of the Farm Security Administration* (Chapel Hill: University of North Carolina Press, 1968). Don E. Albrecht and Steve H. Murdock, *The Sociology of U.S. Agriculture: An Ecological Perspective* (Ames: Iowa State University Press, 1990), 126–27; Walter W. Wilcox et al., *Economics of American Agriculture* (Englewood Cliffs, N.J.: Prentice-Hall, 1974), 383–86; *Natchez Democrat,* June 18, 1933.

55. Anna Nethers [pseud.] and Thomas Nethers [pseud.] interviews; Davis et al., *Deep South,* 80.

56. E. Malcolm Graves, Myrtle Graves, Anna Nethers [pseud.], and Thomas Nethers [pseud.] interviews. On rural children and work, see Tullos, *Habits of Industry,* 58, 76; and Jones, *The Dispossessed,* 98–99, 159, 161.

57. E. Malcolm Graves, Myrtle Graves, Anna Nethers [pseud.], and Thomas Nethers [pseud.] interviews.

58. Anna Nethers [pseud.] and Thomas Nethers [pseud.] interviews. The strong nuclear family of the poor white and the value-oriented environment among that group described in J. Wayne Flynt, *Poor but Proud: Alabama's Poor Whites* (Tuscaloosa: University of

Alabama Press, 1989), 211–13; and Lee Rainwater, Richard P. Coleman, and Gerald Handel, *Workingman's Wife: Her Personality, World, and Life Style* (New York: Oceana Publications, 1979), 103–13. See also Tullos, *Habits of Industry,* 13–15, pass.

59. Anna Nethers [pseud.] and Thomas Nethers [pseud.] interviews.

60. Robert Fly, E. Malcolm Graves, Myrtle Graves, Anna Nethers [pseud.], Thomas Nethers [pseud.], Russell Parsons, and Jack Whitehead interviews. Interview with James Ray Bradshaw, by author, January 28, 1993.

61. Other whites interviewed expressed the same sentiment of tradition as a basis of racial attitudes. E. Malcolm Graves, Myrtle Graves, Ruth Tiffee Jordan, Anna Nethers [pseud.], Thomas Nethers [pseud.], Russell Parsons, Troy B. Watkins, and Jack Whitehead interviews.

62. Roediger, *The Wages of Whiteness;* David L. Cohn, *Where I Was Born and Raised* (Notre Dame: University of Notre Dame Press, 1967), 148–49; Williamson, *The Crucible of Race,* 50–52.

63. Robert Fly, E. Malcolm Graves, and Russell Parsons interviews; B. M. Wofford and T. A. Kelly, *Mississippi Workers: Where They Come from and How They Perform* (Tuscaloosa: University of Alabama Press, 1955), 61–91.

64. James C. Anderson and Gerard Stanton interviews.

65. Troy B. Watkins interview; *Natchez Democrat,* September 2, 1947, September 1, 1985 ("working"); *Jackson Daily News,* May 14, 21, 1947; McElvaine, "Claude Ramsey," 110, 140 ("I"); Subcommittee on Migration and Subsidization of Industry, American Federation of Labor, *Subsidized Industrial Migration: The Luring of Plants to New Locations* (Washington, D.C.: American Federation of Labor, 1955), 72; Mosely, "The Labor Union Movement," 267; J. Wayne Flynt, "The New Deal and Southern Labor," in James C. Cobb and Michael Namorato, edited by *The New Deal and the South* (Jackson: University Press of Mississippi, 1984), 67–68.

66. *Jackson Daily News,* July 16, 1939 ("absolutely"); *Natchez Democrat,* July 16, 1939; *Mississippi Labor Federationist,* July 21, 1939 ("from"); Mosely, "The Labor Union Movement," 253–55.

67. Flynt, "The New Deal and Southern Labor," 69–70; Schulman, *From Cotton Belt to Sunbelt,* 39–62; Robert Fly, Ruth Tiffee Jordan, and E. Malcolm Graves interviews; Interview with Vergy Mullins, by author, February 3, 1993; *Natchez Democrat,* November 29, 1945. George Bentley to J. M. Jones Lumber Company, June 10, 1946; George Bentley to Natchez Stave Company, June 10, 1946; George Bentley to Secretary of Labor, January 30, 1947; "Agreement, R. F. Learned and Son, Natchez, Mississippi," July 17, 1946; "Report of Results of NLRB Elections," October 25, 1946; Wilson and Company Box Factory, Natchez, Mississippi, and International Wood Workers of America, Local S-440, CIO, National Labor Relations Board, case no. 15-R-1664; all documents in box 234, Woodworkers District Four Records, SLA/GSU.

68. AFL, *Subsidized Labor Migration,* 61; Schulman, *From Cotton Belt to Sunbelt,* 6, 7, 28, 176, 177; Robert Fly interview; Ray Smithhart to Robert L. Fly, October 20, 1958, box 2162, Mississippi AFL-CIO Records, 1947–1986, SLA/GSU.

69. Ruth Tiffee Jordan ("A bunch"), E. Malcolm Graves ("dedicated") interviews. Whether Armstrong or local antiunion civic and business leaders initiated the police raids is unclear. Robert Fly and Shead Baldwin interviews.

70. Claude E. Ramsey to Rayford Huff, October 26, 1964, box 2162, Mississippi AFL-CIO Records, SLA/GSU (quote); Flynt, "The New Deal and Southern Labor," 85; James C. Anderson, Robert Fly, Ruth Tiffee Jordan, Robert Latham, Samuel Stewart, and Harden Wallace interviews; "Armstrong Tire and Rubber Company: 20th Anniversary," 8. "Agreement between the Armstrong Rubber Company, Southern Division Natchez, Mississippi, and Local No. 303 of the United Rubber, Cork, Linoleum, and Plastics Workers of America," July 22, 1965; and "Agreement," July 31, 1967, both in Local 303 of the United Rubber, Cork, Linoleum, and Plastics Workers of America Union Hall Collection, Natchez, Mississippi. Bruce Nelson, "Organized Labor and the Struggle for Black Equality in Mobile during World War II," *Journal of American History* 80 (3) (December 1993): 952–88.

71. Robert Fly and Robert Latham interviews. Throughout the South, blacks were recognized as good union members. See Flynt, "The New Deal and Southern Labor," 64, 85–88.

72. The results of the 1947 strike are unclear from oral testimony and a search of labor records and other sources. In December 1946, the union negotiated a three-cent hourly wage increase. E. L. Stanford to Doyle Dorsey, December 16, 1946, box 234, Woodworkers District Four Records.

73. Doyle Dorsey to Robert L. McKnight, December 30, 1946; George Bentley to Secretary of Labor, January 30, 1947; George Bentley to Doyle Dorsey, July 3, 1947; all in box 234, Woodworkers District Four Records. James Anderson, Sargent Butler, and Robert Carroll interviews (quotes); *Natchez Democrat,* June 24, 28, July 12, 13, 1947. On the postbellum labor struggle in the Natchez district, see Davis, *Good and Faithful Labor,* 89–99.

74. For one analysis of modernization and race in Mississippi, see Stephen J. Whitfield, *A Death in the Delta: The Story of Emmett Till* (New York: Free Press, 1988), 133.

75. Robert Latham interview.

76. James C. Anderson and Robert Carroll interviews.

77. Other blacks interviewed said that working in industry beside whites awakened them to the extremes of racial discrimination. James Anderson (quote); James C. Anderson, Sargent Butler, Robert Carroll, Joseph Hall, Albert Harris, Robert Latham, Samuel Stewart, and George F. West Jr. interviews.

CHAPTER FIVE

1. The standard-bearer study of the southern political response during this period is Numan V. Bartley, *The Rise of Massive Resistance: Race and Politics in the South during the 1950s* (Baton Rouge: Louisiana State University, 1969). See also Dewey W. Grantham,

The South in Modern America: A Region at Odds (New York: Harper Collins, 1994), 194–23. For Mississippi, see the autobiographical account of Frank Smith in his *Congressman from Mississippi*. See also John Dittmer, *Local People: The Struggle for Civil Rights in Mississippi* (Urbana: University of Illinois Press, 1994), 19–40; and Kenneth Williams, "Mississippi and Civil Rights, 1945–1954" (Ph.D. diss., Mississippi State University, 1985).

2. *Natchez Democrat,* February 10, March 14, 20, 21, September 4, 1948.

3. Ibid.

4. Ibid.; Address by Governor Fielding L. Wright, July 13, 1948, Governor Fielding L. Wright Papers, RG 27, MDAH; Cecil L. Sumners, *The Governors of Mississippi* (Gretna, La.: Pelican Publishing, 1980), 122–25.

5. U.S. Commission on Civil Rights, *The Voting Rights Act: Ten Years after* (Washington, D.C., January 1975), 43; U.S. Commission on Civil Rights, *Hearings,* Jackson, Mississippi, vol. 2; Adams County Poll Books, 1951–1954, HNF; *Natchez Democrat,* August 6, 1948 ("are"); June 30, 1954 ("are"), July 25, 1956. Elliot Trimble interview; Interview with James W. Crumpton, by author, September 14, 1993; Interview with V. J. Stephens, by author, September 14, 1993; Interview with Summer Walters, by author, September 24, 27, 1993; Interview with John D. Johnson, by author, September 15, 1993; Thomas J. Reed interview; Johnson, "The Ideology of White Supremacy, " 56–78; Smith, *Congressman from Mississippi.* Even Mississippi racial moderate Hodding Carter referred to blacks as "culturally retarded people." See Hodding Carter, *Southern Legacy* (Baton Rouge: Louisiana State University Press, 1950), 133. See also the works of two other influential Mississippians, Dunbar Rowland, *Mississippi View of Race Relations in the South* (Jackson, Miss.: Harmon Publishing, 1903); and Alfred Holt Stone, *Studies in the American Race Problem* (New York: Doubleday, 1908).

6. *Natchez Democrat,* July 28, 1948 (quote); Smith, *Congressman from Mississippi,* 120–21; Bartley, *The Rise of Massive Resistance,* 28–46; Grantham, *The South in Modern America,* 200–202; William F. Winter, "New Directions in Politics, 1948–1956," in McLemore, *History of Mississippi,* 7: 140–53.

7. F. Glenn Abney, *Mississippi Election Statistics, 1900–1967* (University, Miss.: Bureau of Governmental Research, 1968), 22; Winter, "New Directions in Politics," 143–44; *Natchez Democrat,* November 2, 1947, August 11, September 4, October 22, November 3, 1948. On Dixiecrats, see Kari Frederickson, "The Dixiecrat Movement and the Origins of Massive Resistance: Race, Politics, and Political Culture in the Deep South, 1932–1955" (Ph.D. diss., Rutgers University, 1996).

8. *New York Times,* August 24 ("the silk"), April 19, 1956; *Natchez Democrat,* June 6, July 13, August 12, 15, 1952. *Memphis Commercial Appeal,* clipping, n.d.; Katherine Miller to Fred [?], August 27, 1952, Miller Scrapbooks, MDAH. Perry W. Howard, the delegation chairman, was a legal resident of Jackson, Mississippi, who practiced law in Washington, D.C. See Winter, "New Directions in Politics," 147–49. Stephen Cresswell, "Who's Who in Mississippi's Opposition Political Parties, 1878–1963," unpublished manuscript, 1994, p. 172, MDAH.

9. *Natchez Democrat,* July 30, 1952.

10. *Natchez Democrat,* June 6, July 13, August 12, 15, November 2, 4, 1952. Newspaper clipping, n.d., and photograph of Republican Headquarters in Natchez, 1952, Miller Scrapbooks. Barber, *Natchez' First Ladies,* 7–8.

11. Whitfield, *A Death in the Delta,* 73; Grantham, *The South in Modern America,* 219; Winter, "New Directions in Politics," 149; *Natchez Democrat,* November 15, 1952 ("smashing"); Abney, *Mississippi Election Statistics,* 24.

12. *Natchez Democrat,* October 7, 1953, May 18 (quote), 19, 21, June 8 (quote), 1954; *Natchez Times,* June 6, 1954, August 6, 1955. A comprehensive and stimulating study of the *Brown* decision is Richard Kluger, *Simple Justice: A History of Brown v. Board of Education and Black America's Struggle for Equality* (New York: Vintage Books, 1977). See also Robert L. Carter, "The Warren Court and Desegregation," and other essays in *The Warren Court: A Critical Analysis,* edited by Richard H. Sayler et al. (New York: Chelsea House, 1968), 46–57; and L. Brent Bozell, *The Warren Revolution: Reflections on the Consensus Society* (New Rochelle, N.Y.: Arlington House, 1966), 41–57.

13. *Natchez Democrat,* May 12 ("mingling"), 21 (other quotes), 1954; *Natchez Times,* August 5, 7, 9, 12, 1955; Elliot Trimble interview.

14. Hodding Carter III, *The South Strikes Back* (Garden City, N.Y.: Doubleday, 1959), 43 ("If"); McMillen, *The Citizens' Council,* 61, 175 ("God's"), 179, 209; James Graham Cook, *The Segregationists* (New York: Appleton-Century-Crofts, 1962), 11–114; Memorandum, Mr. Current to Board of Directors, December 13, 1954, supp., pt. 1, reel 2: 646, National Association for the Advancement of Colored People Papers (hereafter cited as NAACP Papers), University of South Florida Library, Tampa, and Lamont Library, Harvard University; "Report of Board of Directors for the month of January, 1955," February 14, 1955, supp. to pt. 1, reel 2: 719, NAACP Papers; Char Miller, editor, "The Mississippi Summer Project Remembered—The Stephen Mitchell Gingham Letter," *Journal of Mississippi History* 47 (November 1985): 291.

15. As early as September 1954, the NAACP petitioned the school board in Walthall County, Mississippi, to desegregate its schools. As in the other cities petitioned later, the petition was rejected. *Southern School News,* September 3, 1954; Dittmer, *Local People,* 29.

16. Saint Clair [Drake] to Juanita [Jackson], January 4, 1937, select NAACP Branch Files, 1913–1939, NAACP Papers; Miscellaneous correspondences, Natchez, Mississippi, NAACP Branch files, NAACP Papers, Library of Congress (hereafter cited as Natchez NAACP Branch Files). See specifically William Pickens to A. M. Mackel, April 24, 1940. Davis, "The Negro Church and Associations," 146, 149; Fleming, "Negroes' Activities, Natchez"; *Natchez Democrat,* March 14, 1930; Dittmer, *Local People,* 29.

17. Androse Mackel Banks, Audley M. Mackel Jr., Walter Mackel, and George F. West Jr. interviews; Interview with Thelma Williams, by author, July 9, 1997; "Service of Triumph," Audley Maurice Mackel Sr. obituary leaflet, in the possession of author.

18. Ibid.; A. M. Mackel to NAACP, September 1, 1938, Natchez NAACP Branch Files; "When Is a Man a Man," in Mackel Sr., "Let the Works That I Have Done Speak for Me."

19. David Bacon and A. M. Mackel to Brent Forman, July 25, 1955, in board of trustees special meeting minutes, August 9, 1955, NSMSSD Records, NPA (quote); Gloster B. Current to A. M. Mackel, August 23, 1955, Natchez NAACP Branch Files; Shead Baldwin

interview; V. J. Stephens interview; *Southern School News,* August 1955; *Natchez Democrat,* July 19, August 7, 10, 1955, June 9, 1957; *Natchez Times,* July 26, 27, 1955; Carter, *The South Strikes Back,* 29; McMillen, *The Citizens' Council,* 28; Cook, *The Segregationists,* 56–7.

20. *Jackson Daily News,* August 5, 1955 ("scores"); Anonymous interview ("to"); *Natchez Times,* August 5 ("ignorant"), 7, 12, 1955; *Natchez Democrat,* September, 24, 1955; Whitfield, *Death in the Delta,* ix ("intellectual"). See Tom P. Brady, *Black Monday: Segregation or Amalgamation . . . America has Its Choice* (Winona, Miss.: Association of Citizens' Council, 1955).

21. Elliot Trimble interview; *Natchez Democrat,* August 10, 1955; *Natchez Times,* August 10, 1955. Investigative report, March 2, 1961; D. G. McLaurin to Douglas Shands, September 21, 1955, March 17, 1959; Zack J. Van Landingham to S. C. Craft, March 17, 1959; Zack J. Van Landingham to Director, State Sovereignty Commission, March 18, 1959; all from the Mississippi State Sovereignty Commission Files (hereafter cited as SCF), MDAH.

22. J. P. Coleman to Brent Forman, August 8, 1955, in school board minutes, August 9, 1955, NSMSSD; "Petition Signers Request Their Names be Withdrawn," SCF; Interview with Mamie Lee Mazique, by author, September 17, 1993; James C. Anderson, Lillian Carter, Horace Harris Jr., Harden Wallace, and Shead Baldwin interviews; "Report of Board of Directors for the Month of January 1955," NAACP Papers, 719; *Natchez Democrat,* August 7, 10, 22, 1955; Dittmer, *Local People,* 48, 50–51.

23. Joseph Hall, Troy B. Watkins, Androse Mackel Banks, Shead Baldwin, Mamie Lee Mazique, V. J. Stephens, Harden Wallace, and Thelma Williams interviews; *Natchez Democrat,* September 24, 1955. Zack J. Van Landingham to W. R. Priester, March 17, 1959; D. G. McLaurin to Douglas Shands, September 21, 1955; Zack J. Van Landingham to Director, State Sovereignty Commission, July 7, 1959; Zack J. Van Landingham to File, December 14, 1959; all SCF.

24. Natchez Branch to Mr. Roy Wilkins, memorandum, n.d. (probably September 1965), White Resistance and Reprisals, 1956–1965, NAACP Papers; *Los Angeles Daily Journal,* clipping, n.d., provided by Charlotte Mackel Harrison.

25. Nixon joined the Monrovia, California, NAACP during his 1946 congressional campaign against incumbent Jerry Voorhis, who reputedly had familial ties to the Ku Klux Klan. When Nixon allowed his membership to lapse is unclear. See Roger Morris, *Richard Milhous Nixon: The Rise of an American Politician* (New York: Henry Holt, 1990).

26. Abney, *Mississippi Election Statistics,* 27; *Natchez Democrat,* January 7, April 4, 13, November 7, 1956 August 3 (quote), September 14, October 18, 30, November 13, December 25, 1960, June 1, 8, 1961, November 27, 1962.

27. James W. Crumpton, John D. Johnson, Thomas J. Reed, and Elliot Trimble interviews; Interview with Willie Hall, by author, August 11, 1992; Anonymous interview ("the colored"); Carter, *The South Strikes Back,* 12–15; Roane F. Byrnes to Hon. John Stennis ("victim"), February 7, 1966, box 19, Byrnes Collection; *Natchez Democrat,* March 20, 1948, January 1, 1963, April 26, September 9, 1964, October 12, 1965; *Jackson Clarion-Ledger,* October 22, 1965.

28. Joseph A. Sinsheimer, "The Freedom Vote of 1963: New Strategies of Racial Protest in Mississippi," *Journal of Southern History* 55 (May 1989): 217–44; Neil R. McMillen, "Black Enfranchisement in Mississippi: Federal Enforcement and Black Protest in the 1960s," *Journal of Southern History* 43 (August 1977): 365; "Natchez, Mississippi, Background Report," November, 8, 1965, app. A, reel 65, Student Non-Violent Coordinating Committee Papers (hereafter cited as SNCC Papers), Martin Luther King Jr. Center for Nonviolent Social Change, Atlanta; Shead Baldwin interview; *Natchez Democrat,* September 1, 1963; *Jackson Daily News,* October 23, 1964; Dittmer, *Local People,* 203–4. William Dennis Ware statement, August 25, 1964; "Statement on Events in Natchez, Miss.," November 1, 2, 1963; Newspaper clipping, n.d., all in Beatings I file, Freedom Information Service Library (hereafter cited as FIS), Jackson, Mississippi (quotes).

29. House Committee on Un-American Activities, *The Present-Day Ku Klux Klan Movement,* Report by the Committee on Un-American Activities, 89th Congress, 1st session, 29–30, 71–72, 109, 359; Michael Newton and Judy Ann Newton, *The Ku Klux Klan: An Encyclopedia* (New York: Garland Publishing, 1991), 4, 371, 607–08; Sally Belfrage, *Freedom Summer* (Charlottesville: University Press of Virginia, 1990), 39, 105; Doug McAdam, *Freedom Summer* (New York: Oxford University Press, 1988), 75; Miller, "The Mississippi Summer Project Remembered," 291; Don Whitehead, *Attack on Terror: The FBI against the Ku Klux Klan in Mississippi* (New York: Funk and Wagnalls, 1970), 221–22; "Adams County People Associated with Right-Wing Activities," data compiled by Jan Hillegas, in possession of author; *Muhammad Speaks,* September 25, 1964, in Natchez file, FIS; *Reporter,* December 2, 1965.

30. E. L. McDaniel interview, MOHP.

31. Ibid.

32. Ibid.; U.S. Commission on Civil Rights, *Hearings,* 2: 152–56; Investigative report, April 23, 1965, SCF. "The Principles of the United Klans of America Knights of the Ku Klux Klans" (Natchez, n.d.); "K.K.K. Brings Real Facts to the Surface," United Klans of America, Inc., Knights of the Ku Klux Klan, Realm of Mississippi (Natchez, n.d.), both in Mississippi folder, box 1, Ku Klux Klan Collection, UMASC. Newton and Newton, *The Ku Klux Klan,* 4, 371, 607–8; *Natchez Democrat,* October 10, November 16, 1964, May 5, 1966, July 9, 1989. Natchez Jews and Catholics were on occasion the target of hate literature but never the target of Klan violence. For an example of hate literature, see *Natchez Democrat,* April 26, 1964. Klan violence against Mississippi Jews was generally carried out in Jackson and Meridian by Sam Bowers's White Knights. See Nelson, *Terror in the Night.*

33. *Natchez Democrat,* October 10, 1964.

34. Anonymous interview (quote).

35. *Bluff City Bulletin* April 14, 1962 (quote), box 19, Byrnes Collection; "Negro People Qualify to Vote," NBCL broadside, 1952, Harden Wallace Center, Natchez, Mississippi; Harden Wallace interview. Incident summary, September 25, 1964; Untitled report, September 25, 1964; and Janet Jemmott to Jesse Harris, January 26, 1965, in FIS. "Name of Committee Chairmans," March 19, 1969, Natchez NAACP Branch Files.

36. Edwin King, unpublished autobiography (excerpts in possession of author), 11–16. "Miss. Troops in Natchez, NAACP Calls for March," White Resistance and Reprisals,

1956–1965, pt. 20, reel 2, NAACP Papers. Incident summaries, May 5, June 1, 1965; and "What Then???" League of Concerned Colored Citizens handbill, in FIS. Shead Baldwin, Joseph Hall, and Harden Wallace interviews; Moody, *Coming of Age*, 298; Robert Coles, *Farewell to the South* (Boston: Little, Brown, 1972), 56; Evers and Szanton, *Have No Fear*, 141–88; *Bluff City Bulletin*, October 17, 1964, Byrnes Collection; Lincoln and Mamiya, *The Black Church*, 204–12.

37. Gloster B. Current to Charles Evers, January 22, February 3, 1965, Natchez NAACP Branch Files; "List of Negro Churches and Church Buildings Burned in Mississippi," SCF; Shead Baldwin, Lillian Carter, and Mamie Lee Mazique interviews; *Natchez Democrat*, February 16, 1985, July 9, 1989.

38. Mary Toles interview; Shead Baldwin, Lillian Carter, and Mamie Lee Mazique interviews; "Miss. Troops in Natchez," NAACP Papers; Charles Evers, *Evers* (New York: World Publication, 1971), 130–34; *Natchez Democrat*, February 16, 1985, February 1, 1987 (quote), July 9, 1989.

39. U.S. Commission on Civil Rights, *Hearings*, 2: 86–90, 104–08.

40. Ibid. (quote); Case report, Sheriff's Department, Natchez, Mississippi, February 16, 1964, SCF; Interview with J. T. Robinson, by Stephanie Saul, April 27, 1998.

41. U.S. Commission on Civil Rights, *Hearings*, 2: 86–90, 104–08.

42. Ibid., 96–103.

43. U.S. Commission on Civil Rights, *Hearings*, 2: 90–96, 104–08; Case report, Sheriff's Department, Natchez, Mississippi, February 16, 1964, SCF; Archie Curtis statement, August 23, 1964, Case Studies in Intimidation file and incident summary, August 2, 1964, FIS. COFO publication no. 3, and "Natchez, Mississippi, Background Report," SNCC Papers. *Natchez Democrat*, August 6, 1964; Adams County Poll Book, Jefferson Hotel Precinct, District 4, 1951–1954, HNF; *Jackson Clarion-Ledger*, November 7, December 18, 1964, June 18, 1989; Nelson, *Terror in the Night*, 11; Whitehead, *Attack on Terror*, 99–100; Civil Rights Education Project, *Free at Last: A History of the Civil Rights Movement and Those Who Died in the Struggle* (Montgomery, Ala.: Southern Poverty Law Center, n.d.), 64–65.

44. Incident summary ("every"), July 21, 1964 , FIS; U.S. Commission on Civil Rights, *Hearings*, 2: 73 ("If"). The best history of the Summer Project of 1964 is found in Dittmer's *Local People*. See also McAdam, *Freedom Summer*, and Howard Zinn, *SNCC: The New Abolitionists* (Boston: Beacon Press, 1964). For excellent personal accounts see Belfrage, *Freedom Summer*; Moody, *Coming of Age*; William McCord, *Mississippi: The Long Hot Summer* (New York: W.W. Norton, 1965); and David Harris, *Dreams Die Hard* (Markek, N.Y.: Saint Martin's Press, 1982).

45. Incident summaries, August 14, 15 (quote), 19, 1964, FIS; U.S. Commission on Civil Rights, *Hearings*, 2: 104–08; Dorie Ladner affidavit, reel 65, SNCC Papers. "Natchez, Mississippi, Background Report," SNCC Papers; "Report on Mississippi State Sovereignty Commission (1964–1967)," State Sovereignty Commission folder, Paul B. Johnson Jr. Papers, RG 27, Box 1135, MDAH. *Natchez Democrat*, August 15, September, 15, 27, October 3, 18, 1964; *Jackson Clarion-Ledger*, June 18, 1989; *Jackson Daily News*, May 5, 1964; Dittmer, *Local People*, 353; McAdam, *Freedom Summer*, 276.

46. *Natchez Democrat*, March 2, 9, 1960; March 3, 31, August 11, 13, 14, 15, 23, September 5, November 8, 1963; May 26, June 16, September 1, November 1, 4, 5, 1964.

47. James W. Crumpton, John D. Johnson, Marty Nathanson, Thomas J. Reed ("government"), V. J. Stephens, and Elliot Trimble interviews; *Natchez Democrat*, October 23, 1960 ("destructive"); Ibid., March 2, 9, 1960, February 1, July 1, December 11, 1962, February 3, August 11, 13, 14, 23, September 5, October 17, November 8, December 3, 1963 ("Civil"), April 14, September 1, November 4, 5, 1964, February 26, July 25, 1965 (quote), November 1, 1981.

48. Thomas J. Reed interview.

49. Interview with Peter Rinaldi ("black"), by author, March 27, 1992; Gunther, *Inside U.S.A.*, 803 ("We"); Davis, "The Negro Church and Associations," 32; James W. Crumpton, E. Malcolm Graves, John D. Johnson, V. J. Stephens, Elliot Trimble, and Summer Walters interviews; *Natchez Democrat*, July 1, 1962, February 26, 1964. On the theme of transposing cultural images, see Toni Morrison, *Playing in the Dark: Whiteness in the Literary Imagination* (New York: Vintage Books, 1993).

50. "Sworn Written Applications for Registration" ("duties"), reel 65, SNCC Papers; U.S. Commission on Civil Rights, *Hearings*, 2: 69. "Mr. Saltzman—Notes—Natchez, Mississippi," February 1965, George Green[e], Mrs. Mamie Lee Mazique, Annie Pearl Avery, George Metcalfe, Walter Anderson, app. A, reel 65, SNCC Papers. "Report of the Secretary for the Board of Directors," June 13, 1955, supp., pt. 1, reel 2, NAACP Papers. Untitled report, February 8, 1965; "Negroes Were Deterred," report, n.d., Natchez file, FIS. U.S. Commission on Civil Rights, *Voting in Mississippi: A Report of the United States Commission on Civil Rights, 1965* (Washington, 1966), 31–40; Adams County Poll Book, Jefferson Hotel Precinct, District 4, 1951–1954; McMillen, "Black Enfranchisement," 351–53; Robert Latham, James Anderson, Shead Baldwin, Lillian Carter, and Mamie Lee Mazique interviews; Interview with Edith Jackson, by author, September 17, 1993; *Natchez Democrat*, February 9, 1962, February 13, 1963, July 9, 1964.

51. James C. Anderson interview.

52. SNCC research, October 25, 1965, reel 65, SNCC Papers.

53. NBA minutes, January 11, 1966.

54. U.S. Commission on Civil Rights, *Hearings*, 2: 108–29; Interview with Shaw Gaddy, by author, July 8, 1992; Shead Baldwin, Mamie Lee Mazique, V. J. Stephens, Elliot Trimble, and Troy B. Watkins interviews; *Natchez Democrat*, May 23, 1952, January 24, April 29, May 1, May 10, 1964 (quote).

55. Incident summaries, August 19, September 2, 14, 1964, FIS; U.S. Commission on Civil Rights, *Hearings*, 2: 108–29; NBA minutes, December 28, 1965; *Chicago Daily News*, clipping, n.d., SCF; *Natchez Democrat*, September 15, 16, 1964; Interview with Barbara Cannes [pseud.], by author, August 28, 1997; Interview with Wilbur Cannes [pseud.], by author, August 28, 1997; Katherine Blankenstein interview.

56. Incident summary, September 25, 1964, FIS; NBA minutes, December 28, 1965; Katherine Blankenstein interview; *Natchez Democrat*, September 26, 1964; *Jackson Clarion-Ledger*, September 27, 1964; *Time*, October 15, 1965, 31–32.

57. *Natchez Democrat*, September 2 ("highly"), October 3, 18 ("our"), 24, 29, 1964;

Jackson Clarion-Ledger, September 27, 1964. Though the *Democrat* typically rebuffed local civil rights affairs, it did condemn the June killing of Medgar Evers in Jackson. See *Natchez Democrat,* June 13, 1963.

58. "Citizens of Natchez–Adams County," handbill, September 13, 1964; "National Association for the Advancement of Colored People," handbill, April 20, 1965, box 19, Byrnes Collection. Shead Baldwin, Edith Jackson, Mamie Lee Mazique, and Peter Rinaldi interviews; Evers and Szanton, *Have No Fear,* 183. Incident summaries, September 2, 4, 10, November 28, 29, December 3, 6, 1964, January 4, 7, 8, March 12, April 23, May 8, 11, 12, 13, 15, 28, 29, 30, 31, June 4, 1965, FIS. *Natchez Democrat,* August 11, 1965 (quote).

59. Annie Pearl Avery affidavit and "Statement of Ophelia Green," January 20, 1965, reel 65, SNCC Papers. McAdam, *Freedom Summer,* 28–34; Shead Baldwin, Edith Jackson, Mamie Lee Mazique, and Peter Rinaldi interviews; Evers and Szanton, *Have No Fear,* 183; Mr. Current to Mr. Moon, December 17, 1964, Natchez NAACP Branch Files; *Natchez Democrat,* May 8, 11, 15, 22, 29, 1965. "Freedom Voice," handbill, n.d.; Annie Pearl Avery, "Natchez, Mississippi Project," report, n.d.; "Natchez Civil Rights Cases Heard before Federal Judge in Vicksburg," January 6, 1965; Janet Jemmott to Jesse Harris, January 26, 1965; "The Natchez Project," handwritten report, n.d.; "Natchez COFO Pickets Arrested," COFO news release, January 9, 1964; "COFO in Natchez Protests Jail Treatment," January 10, 1965; "Natchez Protest," COFO News, January 12, 1965; and Incident summaries, September 2, 4, 10, November 28, 29, December 3, 6 (quote), 1964, January 4, 7, 8, March 12, April 23, May 8, 11, 12, 13, 15, 28, 29, 30, 31, June 4, 1965, all in FIS.

60. Incident summaries, March 6, 9, 1965, FIS.

61. Membership meeting minutes, December 9, 1965, Natchez Garden Club minutes, 1963–67, NGCR; Minutes of the Pilgrimage Board of Directors, August 21, 28, September 23, October 16, November 11, 18, 1964, box 12, NGCR.

62. Mrs. Graham H. Hicks to James T. Robinson, February 20, 1964; Mrs. Graham H. Hicks to John J. Nosser, March 2, 1964; Ellen K. Goodell to Joseph Patterson, August 24, 1964; Joe T. Patterson to Ellen K. Goodell, September 4, 1964; Mrs. J. Fred Schmidt to Board of Directors, December 16, 1965, all box 4, NGCR. Minutes of the executive board of the Natchez Garden Club, July 27, 1966, box 2, NGCR. Alberta Watkins to Jesse Harris, weekly report, February 1, 1965; Incident summaries, March 6, 9, 11, 1965, all FIS. Personal memorandum, "Natchez, Miss.," May 12, 1965, box 19, Byrnes Collection.

63. Bill Ware, "We Need a Political Party to Fight for Our Freedom," November 6, 1965, and "Negroes Tell of Harassment in FDP Hearings in Natchez," COFO News, January 28, 1965, FIS. John West and George F. West Jr. interviews; U.S. Commission on Civil Rights, *Voting Rights Act,* 43, 149–50; *Natchez Democrat,* August 17, 19 (quote), 1965, April 1, 4, 9, 1966, November 1, 1981.

64. Memphis *Commercial Appeal,* July 7, 1964 (quotes). Investigation report, August 13, 1964, and Jackson *Daily News,* October 24, 1964, SCF.

65. Whitehead, *Attack on Terror,* 225–30.

66. "A Proposal for a Program in Natchez,"ca. 1965, app. A, reel 65, SNCC Papers

("one"); "The Ku Klux Klan and Its Story" box 2189, Mississippi AFL-CIO Records, SLA/GSU ("the use"); Interview with Mary Lee Toles, by author, May 2, 1998; Samuel Stewart, Phillip West, Shead Baldwin, Robert Latham, Mamie Lee Mazique, and George F. West Jr. interviews; *Natchez Democrat,* August 28, 29, 1965, July 9, 1989; *Jackson Daily News,* August 28, 1965.

CHAPTER SIX

1. Shead Baldwin, Robert Latham, Mamie Lee Mazique, Samuel Stewart, Mary Lee Toles, Harden Wallace, Phillip West, and E. L. McDaniel interviews; Memorandum, Natchez Branch NAACP to Roy Wilkins, , n.d. (probably September 1965), White Resistance and Reprisals, NAACP Papers; George Metcalfe affidavit, reel 65, SNCC Papers; Charles Horwitz, "Natchez Crisis," October 9, 1965, from FIS records, in author's possession, 8; *Natchez Democrat,* August 28, 29, 1965; *Jackson Daily News,* August 28, 1965.

2. Adams County Poll Book, Courthouse Precinct, District 1, 1951–1954, HNF; Joseph Hall and Walter Mackel interviews; Interview with Joe Frazier, August 29, 1997.

3. Investigation report, Adams County, July 29, 1965, SCF; U.S. Commission on Civil Rights, *Hearings* 2: 152–56; Committee on Un-American Activities, *Present-Day Ku Klux Klan Movement,* 29–30, 71–72, 109, 359; Memorandum, Natchez Branch NAACP to Roy Wilkins, NAACP Papers; Incident summary, July 26, 1964, p. 6, FIS; George Metcalfe affidavit, Council of Federated Organizations Records, MDAH; "Proposal for a Program in Natchez," SNCC Papers.

4. George Metcalfe affidavit, September 4, 1965, in *U.S. v. Natchez Special Municipal Separate School District,* September 7, 1965, Civil Action File 1120 (W); *Natchez Democrat,* August 28, 29, 1965; *Jackson Daily News,* August 27, 1965.

5. Daily reports for Natchez, August 27, 1965, SCF; Shead Baldwin, Robert Latham, Mamie Lee Mazique, Samuel Stewart, Mary Lee Toles, Harden Wallace, and Phillip West interviews; George Metcalfe affidavit, *US v. Natchez;* Louis L. Redding to Roy Wilkins, September 20, 1965, White Resistance and Reprisals, NAACP Papers; *Natchez Democrat,* August 28, 29, 1965; Ibid., July 9, 1989 (quote).

6. Federal Bureau of Investigation report, JN 174–27, August 28, 1965, and Natchez, Mississippi, Police Department report, August 27, 1965, Bombing Case no. 4836-C, FBI Archives, Washington, D.C.; Shead Baldwin, Robert Latham, Mamie Lee Mazique, and Samuel Stewart interviews; *Natchez Democrat,* August 22, 28, 29 (quote), 1965, July 9, 1989; *Jackson Daily News,* August 28, 1965, January 15, 1966; *Republic,* December 2, 1965; Evers, *Evers,* 130–34; Whitehead, *Attack on Terror,* 230.

7. Edith Jackson, George F. West Jr., Shead Baldwin, Joseph Hall, Mamie Lee Mazique, Mary Lee Toles, and Harden Wallace interviews; Lucille Black to Bettye M. Birdie, May 20, 1966, Natchez NAACP Branch Files; Memorandum, Natchez Branch NAACP to Roy Wilkins, NAACP Papers; "Natchez, Mississippi, Background Report," SNCC Papers; Incident summaries, June 1, 4, 5, November 27, 1965, FIS; Davis et al., *Deep South,* 345;

Robert Coles, "Natchez, Lovely Natchez," *New Republic,* February 18, 1967, 32; *Jackson Reporter,* December 2, 1965; "Report by SNCC Field Secretary Eugene Rouse," December 8, 1964, and "Attention!" in Natchez file, FIS; Moody, *Coming of Age,* 298; Evers and Szanton, *Have No Fear,* 185; Coles, *Farewell to the South,* 57.

8. See Evers, *Evers;* Evers and Szanton, *Have No Fear;* Maryanne Vollers, *Ghosts of Mississippi: The Murder of Medgar Evers, the Trials of Byron De La Beckwith, and the Haunting of the New South* (Little, Brown, 1995), 8–18.

9. "Natchez, Mississippi—Six Weeks of Crisis," n.d., Natchez file, FIS; Roy Wilkins to William Booth, September 7, 1965, Gloster B. Current to Phil Savage, transcript of telephone conversation, October 5, 1965, White Resistance and Reprisals, NAACP Papers.

10. "Natchez, Mississippi, Background Report," SNCC Papers ("with"); Evers, *Evers,* 134; Evers and Szanton, *Have No Fear,* 184–85; Edward Pincus and David Neuman, *Black Natchez,* Center for Social Documentary Films, 1966, Rutgers University Library; Coles, *Farewell to the South,* 56–57; Dittmer, *Local People,* 354–55.

11. "Natchez, Mississippi—Six Weeks of Crisis," FIS; Pincus and Neuman, *Black Natchez;* Shead Baldwin, Mamie Lee Mazique, and Thomas J. Reed interviews; *Natchez Democrat,* September 1, 3, 4, 7, 10, November 21, 1965, July 9, 1989; *Jackson Daily News,* August 30, 1965; *Christian Science Monitor,* September 15, 1965; "Petition," August 29, 1965, Natchez NAACP Branch Files.

12. News release, Governor Paul B. Johnson, September 1, 1965, RG 27, box 1138, Governor Paul B. Johnson Jr. Papers, MDAH; NBA minutes, September 3, 1965; Pincus and Neuman, *Black Natchez;* Lillian Carter, Shead Baldwin, Mamie Lee Mazique, Mary Toles, Harden Wallace, George F. West Jr., and Phillip West interviews; *Natchez Democrat,* September 3 ("under"), 4, 7, 1965, July 9, 1989.

13. Evers and Szanton, *Have No Fear,* 185 ("Natchez"); *Natchez Democrat,* September 10, 1965 ("mislead"); Pincus and Neuman, *Black Natchez;* Shead Baldwin, Lillian Carter, Mamie Lee Mazique, Mary Lee Toles, Harden Wallace, George F. West Jr., and Phillip West interviews; Incident summary, May 22, 1965, FIS; *Jackson Reporter,* December 2, 1965.

14. John Morsell to Gloster B. Current, October 5, 1965, White Resistance and Reprisals, NAACP Papers; Current to Savage, telephone transcript. "Natchez Civil Rights Cases Heard before Federal Judge in Vicksburg," and "Statements on Jailing in Natchez Demonstrations at Parchman State Prison," October, 1965, FIS. "Natchez, Mississippi—Six Weeks of Crisis," FIS; NBA minutes, September 17, 1965; Shead Baldwin, Edith Jackson, and Mamie Lee Mazique interviews; *Natchez Democrat,* October 2, 3, 5, 6, 1965, December 30, 1983. The treatment of the Natchez demonstrators at Parchman led to one of a number of civil damage suits filed against the prison. See David Oshinsky, *Worse than Slavery: Parchman Farm and the Ordeal of Jim Crow Justice* (New York: Free Press, 1996), 237–39.

15. Current to Savage, telephone transcript ("of"); Roane Byrnes to John Stennis, Byrnes Collection; "Natchez, Mississippi—Six Weeks of Crisis," FIS; NBA minutes, January 11, 1966; "Monthly Report," February 14, 1966, Natchez NAACP Branch Files; Bill Hanna, John D. Johnson, Shead Baldwin, Lillian Carter, Edith Jackson, and V. J. Stephens

interviews; *Natchez Democrat,* October 7, 8, 9, 10; Vollers, *Ghosts of Mississippi,* 244–25. On Harold Cox, see Jack Bass, *Unlikely Heroes* (New York: Simon and Schuster, 1981), 164–67.

16. John Morsell to Gloster B. Current; "Natchez, Mississippi Background Report," SNCC Papers; Incident summary, October 27, 1965, FIS; "Natchez, Mississippi—Six Weeks of Crisis," FIS; Evers and Szanton, *Have No Fear,* 156; Shead Baldwin and Joseph Hall interviews; Dittmer, *Local People,* 356–61.

17. On women and the civil rights movement, see Vicki L. Crawford, Jacqueline Rouse, and Barbara Woods, editors, *Women in the Civil Rights Movement: Trailblazers and Torchbearers* (Bloomington: Indiana University Press, 1993); Belinda Robnett, "African American Women in the Civil Rights Movement, 1954–1965: Gender, Leadership, and Micromobilization," *American Journal of Sociology* 101 (May 1996): 1661–93; "The Voices of African American Women in the Civil Rights Movement," special issue, *Journal of Black Studies* 26 (May 1996).

18. Pincus and Neuman, *Black Natchez;* Evers and Szanton, *Have No Fear,* 156; Gloster B. Current to Priscilla Johnson, April 3, 1952, Frances Baldwin to NAACP, June 13, 1953, Natchez NAACP Branch Files; Shead Baldwin, Lillian Carter, Joseph Hall, Edith Jackson, Mamie Lee Mazique, and Mary Lee Toles interviews.

19. Ibid.; Current to Savage, telephone transcript; Aaron E. Henry to Charles Evers, October 8, 1965, White Resistance and Reprisals, NAACP Papers.

20. "Petition," n.d., "Answer," n.d., and Gloster Current to John Morsell and Henry Moon, October 8, 1965, White Resistance and Reprisals, in NAACP Papers. *Natchez Democrat,* January 1, 1966 ("petition").

21. "Natchez Backs Down on Agreement with NAACP," press release, October 18, 1965, White Resistance and Reprisals, NAACP Papers; *Natchez Democrat,* October 15, 1965 ("will"); *Jackson Clarion-Ledger,* October 22, 1965 ("being").

22. Erle Johnston Jr. to Johnny Nosser, October 14, 1965, SCF.

23. "Miss. Troops in Natchez"; Memorandum, "Natchez Boycott Continues Despite Reprisal Threat," November 6, 1965; and memorandum, "NAACP Warns Natchez Businessmen against Mass Firings of Negroes," November 13, 1966, all in White Resistance and Reprisals, NAACP Papers. Incident summary, November 27, 1965, FIS; Shead Baldwin, Lillian Carter, John D. Johnson, Mamie Lee Mazique, Thomas J. Reed (quote), V. J. Stephens, and Samuel Stewart interviews; *Natchez Democrat,* October 8, 9, 13, 14, 17, 1965; Evers and Szanton, *Have No Fear,* 186.

24. *Natchez Democrat,* November 6, 1965 ("counter-boycott," "first"), July 9, 1966; *Memphis Commercial-Appeal,* May 11, 1964 ("unite"); Charter, Americans for the Preservation of the White Race, State of Mississippi, June 25, 1963, *American Patriot,* November 1964, SCF.

25. Shead Baldwin, Mamie Lee Mazique, Mary Lee Toles, V. J. Stephens, Phillip West, and Elliot Trimble interview; *Natchez Democrat,* December 1, 1964, October 30, 31, November 5, December 4, 5, 11, 12, 1965, January 1, 15, 19, 1966; *Jackson Clarion-Ledger* November 12, 20, December 29, 1965, April 5, 1966. "To the Negro Citizens of Natchez and Adams County," n.d., and Gloster B. Current to Roy Wilkins, November 30, 1965,

White Resistance and Reprisals, NAACP Papers; Henry Lee Moon to Editorial Writers and Columnists, December 8, 1965 (quote), also quoted in Dittmer, *Local People,* 361.

26. Gloster Current to Henry Moon, November 3, 1965, Natchez NAACP Branch Files; Investigation report, October 17, 1966, and meeting minutes, Natchez Chapter of NAACP, March 3 to August 3, 1965, SCF.

27. *State of Mississippi v. James Lloyd Jones,* case no. 6156, trial transcript, HNF, 114–35; Civil Rights Education Project, *Free at Last,* 66, 88; "Order Directing Autopsy," June 12, 1966, Adams County Court Minutes, 9: 246, HNF; Newton and Newton, *The Ku Klux Klan,* 602–03; *Natchez Democrat,* May 8, June 15, 1966; March 28, 1968; Don Simonton, "One Ben Chester White, a Human Being" (Graduate research paper, Center for the Study of Southern Culture, University of Mississippi, 1997). For a discussion of White Knight violence, including the Philadelphia murders, see Nelson, *Terror in the Night,* and Seth Cagin and Philip Dray, *We Are Not Afraid: The Story of Goodman, Schwerner, and Chaney and the Civil Rights Campaign for Mississippi* (New York: McMillan, 1988).

28. Simonton, "One Ben Chester White"; J. T. Robinson interview.

29. Civil Rights Education Project, *Free at Last,* 88.

30. *State of Mississippi v. James Lloyd Jones;* General Docket, State Cases, March 1957 to November 1977, and Adams County Circuit Court Case Files, case nos. 6156, 6157, 6158, HNF; "Some Persons Associated with the Killing of Ben Chester White," data collected by Jan Hillegas, copy in author's possession; "Election Returns, August 2, 1955 to June 25, 1974, A. V. Davis CC," election book in Adams County, Mississippi, voter registrar's office; *Natchez Democrat,* June 15, 1966, April 12, 1967, March 28, 1968; *Jackson Clarion-Ledger,* October 23, 1964, December 9, 11, 1967; Harvard Sitkoff, *The Struggle for Black Equality, 1954–1980* (New York: Hill and Wang, 1981), 212–14.

31. J. T. Robinson, police chief at the time, says Jones came to him with the confession. J. T. Robinson interview.

32. *State of Mississippi v. Ernest Avants,* Adams County Circuit Court, case no. 6157, NHF; Jay Lehmann interview; Whitehead, *Attack on Terror,* 249–54, 274, 304; *Jesse White v. The White Knights of the Ku Klux Klan of Mississippi, et al.,* Southern District of Mississippi, case no. 1197; Civil Rights Education Project, *Free at Last,* 88; George F. West Jr. interview; Simonton, "One Ben Chester White."

33. U.S. Commission on Civil Rights, *Hearings,* 2: 152–66 (quotes).

34. Ibid., 108–29 (quotes). In his annual report to the citizens of Natchez presented December 28, 1965, Nosser made no mention of the racial strife between black citizen and white citizen and seemed oblivious to the concerns of his black constituency. NBA minutes, December 28, 1965.

35. Anonymous interview ("I").

36. Anonymous interview ("all"); Bill Hanna, John D. Johnson, Thomas J. Reed, and Summer Walters interviews; Beatrice Baldwin to State Sovereignty Commission, November 30, 1960, SCF. On the subject of silent white masses, see also Silver, *Closed Society,* 57.

37. "Liberty is a Boisterous Sea, Timid Men Prefer the Calm of Despotism," handbill, n.d., Natchez NAACP Branch Files (quote); Interview with Bartlett Lipscomb [pseud.], by author, July 9, 1997.

38. Bill Hanna and John D. Johnson interviews; "Liberty is a Boisterous Sea" (quote); Charles Evers to Gloster B. Current, March 16, 1965, Natchez NAACP Branch Files.

39. Davis, "The Negro Church and Associations"; *Natchez Democrat,* October 17, 1937; Wayne, *The Reshaping of Plantation Society,* 132–40; Wharton, *The Negro in Mississippi,* 256; J. Julian Chisolm, *History of the First Presbyterian Church of Natchez, Mississippi* (Natchez: McDonald's Printers and Publishers, 1972), 58–59; Ted Ownby, *Subduing Satan: Religion, Recreation, and Manhood in the Rural South, 1865–1920* (Chapel Hill: University of North Carolina Press, 1990), 137; Williamson, *The Crucible of Race,* 47–48.

40. For general studies of race, religion, and segregation, see Everett Tilson, *Segregation and the Bible* (New York: Abingdon Press, 1958); W. J. Cunningham, *Agony at Galloway: One Church's Struggle with Social Change* (Jackson: University Press of Mississippi, 1980); Will D. Campbell and James Y. Holloway, editors, *The Failure and the Hope: Essays of Southern Churchmen* (Grand Rapids, Mich.: Eerdmans, 1972); C. Eric Lincoln, *Race, Religion, and the Continuing American Dilemma* (New York: Hill and Wang, 1984); Kenneth K. Bailey, *Southern White Protestantism in the Twentieth Century* (New York: Harper and Row, 1964); Thomas Daniel Young, "Religion, the Bible Belt, and the Modern South," in *The American South: A Portrait of a Culture,* edited by Louis D. Rubin Jr. (Baton Rouge: Louisiana State University Press, 1980), 110–17; Harvey, *Redeeming the South;* David L. Chappell, "Segregationist Propaganda and Religious Schism" (paper presented at the Gulf South History and Humanities Conference, 1998). For a primary source that offers a white commentary on the attitude of Christian brotherhood, and a source that was widely read in Mississippi and cited as authority, see Clareton Putnam, *Race and Reason: A Yankee View* (Washington, D.C.: Public Affairs Press, 1961).

41. "Born of Conviction Statement," Summer Walters Papers, in possession of author ("permits"), also in MDAH; "Information Bulletin," Summer Walters Papers; Interview with Elton Brown, by author, November 17, 1993; Summer Walters interview; *Natchez Democrat,* January 11, 1963; *Mississippi Methodist Advocate,* January 2, 1963 (other quotes); *Jackson Clarion-Ledger,* January 3, 1963; Silver, *Closed Society,* 58–60; Bailey, *Southern White Protestantism,* 150–51.

42. Shaw Gaddy and Elton Brown interviews.

43. Elton Brown, Shaw Gaddy, and James W. Crumpton interviews.

44. Summer Walters interview; Clyde H. Gunn to Summer Walters, January 18, 1961, and Summer Walters to Clyde H. Gunn, January 23, 1961, Summer Walters Papers.

45. Ibid.

46. Summer Walters Papers; Summer Walters interview; Bailey, *Southern White Protestantism,* 150–51; Silver, *Closed Society,* 58–60; Robert B. Halton to Summer Walters, January 9, 1963 ("can"), and James B. Nichols to Friends, January 7, 1963 ("Methodist Misfits"), Summer Walters Papers; Ethnic Relations file, box 5, J. B. Cain Archives of Mississippi Methodism and Millsaps College Archives.

47. Ibid.; Memorandum, July 11, 1963, Clyde H. Gunn to Summer Walters, August 6, 1963, and Summer Walters to Dr. Selah, December 31, 1964, Summer Walters Papers.

48. Douglas, *A Family's Affair,* 57–59.

49. Ruth Tiffee Jordan, Troy B. Watkins, Elton Brown, James W. Crumpton, V. J. Stephens, and Summer Walters interviews; Charles Duke, "Born of the Spirit," sermon, Broadmeadow Methodist Church, January 20, 1963, Summer Walters Papers; G. T. Gillespie, "A Christian View on Segregation," November 4, 1954, Citizens' Council pamphlet, Summer Walters Papers; Robert B. Halton to Summer Walters, August 6, 1963, and Summer Walters to Dr. Selah, December 31, 1964, Summer Walters Papers.

50. Although non-NAACP materials and oral histories describe Jackson as treasurer at the time of his death, a January 1967 report by the Natchez chapter of the NAACP lists the Reverend Andrew Vanison in this position. George Metcalfe to Roy Wilkins, January 26, 1967, Natchez NAACP Branch Files.

51. Autopsy report, Wharlest Jackson, February 28, 1967, autopsy file box, 1963–1984, HNF; Albert Harris, Shead Baldwin, Joseph Hall, Joe Frazier, Edith Jackson, Robert Latham, Mamie Lee Mazique, Samuel Stewart, and Harden Wallace interviews; *Natchez Democrat,* February 28, March 1, 1967, February 21, 1986; *Memphis Commercial Appeal,* March 1, 6, 1967.

52. *Wall Street Journal,* March 8, 1967, clipping in SCF ("[E]verybody"); News release, February 28, 1967, box 1138, Governor Johnson Papers ("heinous"); Memorandum, Natchez, March 3, 1967, and NAACP bulletin, March 16, 1967, SCF; Shead Baldwin, Robert Fly, Edith Jackson, Robert Latham, Mamie Lee Mazique, and Samuel Stewart interviews; *Natchez Democrat,* February 28, March 1, 2, 3, 1967, February 21, 1986; *Jackson Clarion-Ledger,* March 1, 6, 1967; *Jackson Daily News,* March 3, 1967.

53. "A Proposal for a Program in Natchez"; George Metcalfe and Walter Anderson, in app. A, reel 65, SNCC Papers. Robert Fly, Gerard Stanton, Shead Baldwin, Ruth Tiffee Jordan, Robert Latham, and Samuel Stewart interviews; *Memphis Commercial Appeal,* March 6, 1967 (quote); *Jackson Daily News,* March 3, 1967; *Natchez Democrat,* July 9, 1989.

54. James C. Anderson, Shead Baldwin, Albert Harris, Ruth Tiffee Jordan, Robert Latham, Walter Mackel, Samuel Stewart, and Gerard Stanton interviews.

55. James C. Anderson and Albert Harris interviews.

56. "A Proposal for a Program in Natchez" ("racial"), SNCC Papers. "Speech by Claude Ramsey before the Connecticut AFL-CIO Human Relations Council," June 9, 1964; J. B. Williams to Thomas Knight, October 3, 1964; W. D. Bilbo to Claude Ramsey, October 21, 1964; Rayford J. Huff to Claude Ramsay [*sic*], October 15, 1964, box 2131; Claude E. Ramsey to Rayford Huff, October 26, 1964; Handbill, box 235 ("Time"), all in Mississippi AFL-CIO Records, SLA/GSU.

57. On civil rights and tobacco workers, see Robert Korstad and Nelson Lichtenstein, "Opportunities Found and Lost: Labor, Radicals, and the Early Civil Rights Movement," *Journal of American History* 75 (December 1988): 786–811. Combining civil rights with labor rights became increasingly common decades later in Mississippi. See, for instance, "Fishy Business," special section, *Southern Exposure* 19 (fall 1991): 13–56; Richard Schweid, *Catfish and the Delta: Confederate Fish Farming in the Mississippi Delta* (Berkeley, Calif.: Ten Speed Press, 1992); Michael K. Honey, *Southern Labor and Black Civil Rights: Organizing Memphis Workers* (Urbana: University of Illinois Press, 1993).

58. Phil Lapansky, "Transcription of Tape Documentary of Natchez Laundry Workers Strike," October 17, 1965, Natchez file, FIS (quote). "Proposed Lay-out for Newspaper Ad," n.d.; Handbill, "Boycott Natchez Steam Laundry," n.d.; Newspaper clipping, "Wages Rank High on Negro List," *Christian Science Monitor,* September 15, 1965, all in Natchez file, FIS.

59. Memorandum, Natchez, October 11, 1966, and investigation report, October 17, 1966, SCF. Cafeteria and Janitor Workers to D. G. McLaurin, September 19, 1966 (quote), in school board minutes, NSMSSD, October 8, 1966; Special meeting, board of trustees, NSMSSD, September 7, 24, October 8, November 2, 1966; Petition, Natchez Branch NAACP to Natchez Adams County Public School, September 2, 1966; Regular meeting, board of trustees, October 11, 1966; Committee meeting, joint meeting of the Board of Aldermen, Board of Supervisors, and School Board Committee, October 19, November 2, 1966; "Financial Statement, Natchez–Adams County Public Schools Cafeterias, September 1966," and "October 1966," all in NPA.

60. Dittmer, *Local People,* 361.

CHAPTER SEVEN

1. *Natchez Democrat,* January 3, 1954.

2. Interview with Ozelle Fisher, by author, July 9, 1997; Interview with Robert Lewis, by author, December 12, 1997; Interview with Theresa Lewis, by author, December 12, 1997; Interview with Lillian O. Palmer, by author, July 25, 1992; Walter Mackel and George F. West Jr. interviews.

3. Moody, *Coming of Age,* 196; "Negro Schools," Adams County Education, Negro Organizations file, box 217, WPA Projects Files, MDAH.

4. "Deep in Dixie," 53–54.

5. Androse Mackel Banks, Joseph Hall, Audley M. Mackel Jr., Frank Robinson, Harden Wallace, Ozelle Fisher, Robert Lewis, Theresa Lewis, Walter Mackel, and George F. West Jr. interviews.

6. Ibid.; Thelma Williams interview; Manuscript, Census of Mississippi, 1920.

7. Shead Baldwin, Ruth Dumas, and Lillian O. Palmer interviews; "Deep in Dixie," 53–54; *Natchez Democrat,* January 3, 1954.

8. *Natchez Democrat,* January 3, 1954.

9. The most comprehensive study of the NAACP's legal dismantling of the separate-but-equal doctrine is Kluger, *Simple Justice.*

10. *Southern School News,* September 3, 1954.

11. V. J. Stephens and Elliot Trimble interviews; *Southern School News,* September 3, 1954 ("voluntary"); *Natchez Democrat,* April 10, 1946, September 21, 1949, June 29, 1950, February 1, October 26, 1951, January 11, November 3, 1952, July 5, 1953, January 3 ("not"), April 30, December 24 ("Only"), 1954, July 19, 1955; *Statistical Summary of School Segregation-Desegregation in the Southern and Border States* (Nashville:

Southern Education Reporting Service, 1963–64), 31; McMillen, *The Citizens' Council,* 15–16.

12. Interview with D. Gilmer McLaurin, by author, October 27, 1993; Elliot Trimble and V. J. Stephens interviews; *Natchez Democrat,* April 10, 1946, September 21, November 6, 1949, February 1, May 1, October 26, November 30, 1951, April 18, 1953, December 24, 1954 (quote), June 7, July 19, 1955, October 28, 1956, February 20, December 11, 1957, May 22, 1963, October 28, 1973.

13. According to Robert Lewis and Theresa Lewis, longtime black educators in Natchez, class sizes before the 1950s were much larger, sometimes as large as fifty students.

14. *School Survey: The City of Natchez and Adams County, Mississippi* (Hattiesburg, Miss.: Department of Educational Administration, 1955); *Natchez Democrat,* January 10, 1941, October 18, November 6, 1949, January 11, 1952, March 3, 1953.

15. Ibid.; James Anderson, James C. Anderson, Sargent Butler, Robert Carroll, Lillian Carter, Robert Latham, and Samuel Stewart interviews.

16. A. W. Dumas to Board of Education, n.d., Natchez, Mississippi, Adams County School Board minutes, 1915–1920, MDAH; *Biennial Report and Recommendations of the State Superintendent of Public Education to the Legislature of Mississippi for the Scholastic Years 1919–1920 and 1920 and 1921,* 86, 207, MDAH; "Natchez–Adams County Public Schools Cost of Supplies, August and September 1965," NSMSSD minutes, October 14, 1965, NPA; C. X. Copeland to D. G. McLaurin, February 1, 1966, NSMSSD minutes, March 8, 1966; Mildred S. Topp to J. S. Vandiver, May 2, 1940, Afro-American Education (–1953) subject file, MDAH; Robert Lewis, Theresa Lewis, and George F. West Jr. interviews; *Natchez Democrat,* April 12, 1947, September 20, October 4, 1949.

17. *Natchez Democrat,* January 11, 1952.

18. LeJoy McCoy and Maria Washington interviews; Fleming, "Achievements and Social Conditions of Negroes"; Valerie Grim, "Black Farm Families in the Yazoo-Mississippi Delta: The Brooks Farm Community, 1920–1970" (Ph.D. diss., Iowa State University, 1990), 92. On parental sacrifices made to ensure the education of children, see Hortense Powdermaker, *After Freedom: A Cultural Study of the Deep South* (New York: Viking Press, 1939), 299–300. For black attitudes toward education in Indianola, Mississippi, see also Dollard, *Caste and Class in a Southern Town,* 195–96. For black Mississippians in general, see McMillen, *Dark Journey,* 89–98. For a look at the black drive for literacy in the slave South, see Janet D. Cornelius, *When I Can Read My Title Clear: Literacy, Slavery, and Religion in the Antebellum South* (Columbia, S.C.: University of South Carolina Press, 1991).

19. For an elaboration on this theme, see Williamson, *The Crucible of Race,* 51–52.

20. Ozelle Fisher interview; W. M. Drake, "The Public Schools of Mississippi," Citizens' Council flier, September 9, 1957, box 19, Byrnes Collection; "Report of Monthly Term Reports of Free Schools," 1920, Adams County School Board minutes, 1917–1921; U.S. Bureau of the Census, *Reports by States, Showing the Composition and Characteristics of the Population for Counties, Cities, and Townships, or Other Minor Civil Divisions, 1930,* vol. 3, pt. 1: 1282.

21. Drake, "The Public Schools of Mississippi."

22. Ibid.; Davis et al., *Deep South*, 417–21. See especially McMillen, *Dark Journey*, 72–89.

23. "Petition to the School Board for the Natchez–Adams County Public Schools," in board of trustees minutes, NSMSSD, August 19, September 4, 1965.

24. U.S. Commission on Civil Rights, *Southern School Desegregation, 1966–1967* (Washington, D.C., July 1967), 7; U.S. Commission on Civil Rights, *Public Education*, October 1964 staff report (Washington, D.C., 1964), 130–31.

25. U.S. Commission on Civil Rights, *Hearings*, 2: 115 (quote); Commission on Civil Rights, *Public Education*, 130; *Natchez Democrat*, August 17, 21, 26, 1960, September 3, October 12, 1961, September 13, 1962, December 30, 1963, May 19, 1964.

26. For other studies on the Catholic churches and southern segregation, see Stephen Ochs, *Desegregating the Altar: The Jospehites and the Struggle for Black Priests, 1871–1960* (Baton Rouge: Louisiana State University Press, 1990), and David W. Southern, *John LaFarge and the Limits of Catholic Interracialism, 1911–1963* (Knoxville: University of Tennessee Press, 1993).

27. Mississippi Department of Education, "Nonpublic School Enrollment, 1966–1967," MDAH; Barbara Cannes [pseud.] interview; Charles E. Nolan, *Saint Mary's of Natchez: The History of a Southern Catholic Congregation, 1716–1988* (Natchez: Saint Mary's Catholic Church, 1992), 262–68. Parish bulletin, August 22, 1965, and memorandum from R. O. Gerow, August 6, 1964, Announcements–1964 file, box 1-a-1, Saint Mary's Parish Archives, Natchez, Mississippi.

28. Interview with Sophronia Hughes, by author, July 10, 1997; Barbara Cannes [pseud.] and Joseph Hall interviews; Evers and Szanton, *Have No Fear*, 246–47.

29. Barbara Cannes [pseud.], Joe Hall, and Sophronia Hughes interviews.

30. By the mid-1970s, Cathedral School could not compete with the lower tuition at the other all-white private schools, and enrollment fell again to under 500. Mississippi Research and Development Center, *Nonpublic Schools, 1972–1973*, table 1, and *Nonpublic Schools, 1974–1975*, table 1; Nolan, *Saint Mary's of Natchez*, 262–68; Interview with Sue A. M. Meng, by Amendia Netto, February 4, 1992, MOHP; Barbara Cannes [pseud.], Joseph Hall, and Sophronia Hughes interviews; *Natchez Democrat*, August 10, 1964, August 22, September 8, 11, October 5, 31, 1965.

31. For a study of the *Singleton* case, see J. Harvey Wilkinson III, *From Brown to Bakke: The Supreme Court and School Integration, 1954–1978* (New York: Oxford University Press, 1979), 111–12; Ravitch, *Troubled Crusade*, 166; and Jeanne Marie Middleton, "The History of *Singleton v. Jackson Municipal Separate School District*, Southern School Desegregation from the Perspective of the Black Community" (Ph.D. diss., Harvard University, 1978).

32. *U.S. v. Natchez Special Municipal Separate School District et al.*, case no. 1120, January 28, 1966; U.S. Commission on Civil Rights, *Survey of School Desegregation in the Southern and Border States, 1965–66* (Washington, D.C., 1966), 30; Interview with Claude Porter, by author, November 3, 1993; *Southern School News*, May 1955; *Natchez Democrat*, August 10, 1964, August 22, September 8, 11, October 5, 31, 1965, January 30, September 7, 1966. "Report of Withdrawals, Natchez–Adams County Public Schools,

1966–1967," in Board of Trustees Minute Book, January 1966–December 1968; Executive session, board of trustees, September 9, 1965; Telegram, James N. McCune to R. Brent Forman, September 7, 1965; "Resolution of Board of Trustees of Natchez Special Municipal Separate School District," Natchez, Mississippi, October 14, 1965; Board minutes, September 6, October 8, 1966, all in NSMSSD Records.

33. U.S. Commission on Civil Rights, *Racial Isolation in the Public Schools* (Washington, D.C., 1967)1: 2–7; Commission on Civil Rights, *Southern School Desegregation, 5*; Kluger, *Simple Justice*, 747–78; Hugh Davis Graham, *The Civil Rights Era: Origins and Development of National Policy* (New York: Oxford University Press, 1990), 372–75. For the Virginia story, see Alexander S. Leidholdt, *Stand before the Shouting Mob: Lenoir Chambers and Virginia's Massive Resistance to Public School Integration* (Tuscaloosa: University of Alabama Press, 1997).

34. Mrs. F. B. Byrnes to John Stennis, n.d., box 19, Byrnes Collection.

35. Ibid.; Interview with Robert Barrett, by author, October 27, 1993; Interview with Betty Christmas, by author, October 29, 1993; Interview with Barbara Duck, by author, November 3, 1993; Joe Frazier, Bill Hanna, D. Gilmer McLaurin, and Claude Porter interviews.

36. Betty Christmas interview. Although the court ordered Natchez to begin school desegregation in the fall of 1966, school records are vague about how many or whether any black students attended white schools that year. There were several requests by black students to transfer to white schools, but whether they transferred in the 1966–1967 school year is unclear. Locals interviewed for the study remember the first black students entering in the fall of 1967, the year Betty Williams transferred to a white school.

37. Ibid.; Robert Barrett, and Theresa Lewis interviews.

38. John West interview; Interview with Charles Kempinska, by author, August 27, 1997; Betty Christmas interview. The Natchez school system did not provide school buses for the black schools until 1957. *Natchez Democrat*, July 5, 1977.

39. Betty Christmas interview.

40. John West interview.

41. Ibid.; Interview with Harriet Goodland [pseud.], by author, June 8, 1997.

42. John West interview.

43. Ibid.

44. ACBS minutes, February 7, 9, 14, March 7 (quote), 1966, Board of Supervisors Building, Natchez, Mississippi; Special meeting, board of trustees, NSMSSD, March 8, 1966; "Election Returns, August 2, 1955 to June 1974, A. V. Davis CC," Adams County Courthouse, Natchez, Mississippi; Shead Baldwin interview; *Natchez Democrat*, February 8, 12, March 8, 1966.

45. Special meeting, board of trustees, NSMSSD, March 8, 1966; NBA minutes, March 16, April 11, 1967; Interview with Tony Byrne, by R. Wayne Pyle, 1980, vol. 420, MOHP; Shead Baldwin interview; *Natchez Democrat*, March 9, 1966, March 18, 1967.

46. NBA minutes, March 28, 1967; Shead Baldwin, Tony Byrne, and George F. West Jr. interviews; *Natchez Democrat*, March 18, 29, April 12, 1967.

47. Erle Johnston Jr. to John Nosser, May 9, 1967, SCF; Tony Byrne interview (quote).

48. NBA minutes, March 28, April 11, 1967; Shead Baldwin and George F. West Jr. interviews; *Natchez Democrat,* March 18, 29 (quote), April 12, 1967. Investigative report, June 26, 1967; John Nosser to Erle Johnston, May 3, 1967; Erle Johnston Jr. to File, May 4, 1967, all in SCF.

49. *U.S. v. Natchez,* 417 F2d 852 (1969); *It's Not Over in the South: School Desegregation in Forty-three Southern Cities Eighteen Years After Brown* (Alabama Council on Human Rights, 1972), iv; *Natchez Democrat,* May 2, 1968, May 15, July 11, 18, 31, August 8, 1969.

50. Kluger, *Simple Justice,* 766; Graham, *The Civil Rights Era,* 374; Bob Woodward and Scott Armstrong, *The Brethren: Inside the Supreme Court* (New York: Simon and Schuster, 1979), 40.

51. Commission on Civil Rights, *Southern School Desegregation,* 10–13; *U.S. v. Natchez* (1969); *It's Not Over in the South,* iv.

52. "Objections of the Board of Trustees of the School District to a Proposed Desegregation Plan for the Natchez–Adams County Public Schools Filed by the Department of Health, Education, and Welfare of the United States Department of Education," August 15, 1969 (quote), and "Plan of the Board of Trustees for Desegregation," NSMSSD minutes, August 14, 1969; *U.S. v. Natchez* (1969); *Natchez Democrat,* May 2, 1968, May 15, July 11, 18, 31, August 8, 15, 1969.

53. George F. West Jr. interview; NSMSSD minutes, August 12, 1969; *Natchez Democrat,* August 13, 1969.

54. *Alexander v. Holmes County Board of Education,* 396 US 802, 90 SCt 21 (1969); *Natchez Democrat,* October 30, 1969.

55. Lewis eventually went to North Natchez High as principal.

56. NSMSSD minutes, December 1, 15, 29, 1969; Robert Barrett, Joe Frazier, Charles Kempinska, Robert Lewis, D. Gilmer McLaurin, and Claude Porter interviews; *Natchez Democrat,* August 29, November 4, 11, 12, December 16, 21, 1969, August 18, 1970; Jack Bass and Walter De Vries, *The Transformation of Southern Politics: Social Change and Political Consequences since 1945* (New York: Basic Books, 1976), 30, 187. For a firsthand account of 1970 school integration in another Mississippi community, see Willie Morris, *Yazoo: Integration in a Deep South Town* (New York: Harper's Magazine Press, 1971).

57. NSMSSD minutes, November 17, 1969; "Natchez Special Municipal School District Enrollment and Average Daily Attendance, 5th month, 1969–1970 Session," NSMSSD minutes, February 25, 1970; NSMSSD, "Report on School District Organizations, First Term, 1980–1981 School Year," in Old Court Reports (1989 order) box, NPA; Robert Barrett, D. Gilmer McLaurin, and Claude Porter interviews; *Natchez Democrat,* December 16, 21, 1969, February 14, 1970.

58. Robert Barrett, Shead Baldwin, Betty Christmas, Joe Frazier, Charles Kempinska, Robert Lewis, Theresa Lewis, D. Gilmer McLaurin, Claude Porter, and John West interviews; NSMSSD minutes, December 1, 15, 29, 1969; *Natchez Democrat,* July 30, 1989.

59. John West interview.

60. *Natchez-Adams High School Echoes,* January 1970 ("all"), December 1969

("Cut"), in possession of Bill Hanna; Robert Barrett, Bill Hanna, and Claude Porter interviews; *Natchez Democrat,* July 30, 1989 ("mess").

61. Robert Barrett, Betty Christmas, Barbara Duck, Bill Hanna, Claude Porter, and John West interviews; *Natchez Democrat,* July 30, 1989.

62. In the 1971–1972 school year, the junior and senior years were added to North Natchez-Adams High School.

63. *Natchez Democrat,* July 30, 1989 ("Having"); *Echoes,* January 1970 ("Perhaps"), April 1970; Robert Barrett, Betty Christmas, Barbara Duck, Joe Frazier, Bill Hanna ("pawns"), Charles Kempinska, Robert Lewis, Theresa Lewis, Claude Porter, and John West interviews.

64. *Natchez Democrat,* February 18, 1970.

65. Shead Baldwin interview; *Natchez Democrat,* February 19, 1970.

66. Editorial clipping, *Mississippi Educational Journal for Teachers in Colored Schools* (November 1937), in Afro-American Education (1953) subject file, MDAH. See also black testimonies in Commission on Civil Rights, *Southern School Desegregation,* 59–65.

67. Elliot Trimble interview; Percy, "Mississippi: The Fallen Paradise," 170–71.

68. Interview with Maggie Schimmel [pseud.], by author, October 29, 1993; Interview with Howell Garner, by author, November 3, 1993; Robert Barrett, Barbara Duck, Bill Hanna, Shaw Gaddy, Claude Porter, Thomas Reed, V. J. Stephens, Summer Walters interviews.

69. Bill Hanna and Charles Kempinska interviews.

70. Some blacks believed that black male bandleaders were not transferred to the traditionally white schools to keep them away from white drill-team girls. Anonymous interview.

71. Robert Barrett, Sandra Davidson, Barbara Duck, Howell Garner, Bill Hanna, Charles Kempinska, Claude Porter, V. J. Stephens, Elliot Trimble, Anonymous ("amoral"), John D. Johnson, and Peter Rinaldi interviews; Robert B. Halton to Summer Walters, January 9, 1963 ("If"), Summer Walters Papers, in possession of author and in MDAH.

72. Robert Barrett, Maggie Schimmel [pseud.], Barbara Duck, Howell Garner, Bill Hanna, John D. Johnson, Claude Porter, Peter Rinaldi, V. J. Stephens, and Elliot Trimble interviews; *Natchez Democrat,* December 29, 1961, July 1, 1962.

73. Commission on Civil Rights, *Southern School Desegregation,* 71; James Allen Sansing, "A Descriptive Survey of Mississippi Private, Segregated Elementary and Secondary Schools in 1971" (Ed.D. diss., Mississippi State University, 1972), 12, 41–43.

74. Flier, January 8, 1968, Americans for the Preservation of the White Race subject file, MDAH (Jackson, Mississippi) *The Citizen,* August 1973, 13, 30; newspaper clipping, , n.d., SCF; White Knights of the Ku Klux Klan of Mississippi, list, Governor Johnson Papers, MDAH; *Eagle,* 1972 yearbook (Natchez: Thomas Jefferson Schools), 11, 14, possession of Maggie Schimmel [pseud.]; *Natchez Democrat,* January 24, August 15, November 13, 1965; *Memphis Commercial Appeal,* May 11, 1964.

75. *Mildred Coffey et al. v. State Educational Finance Commission et al., State of Mississippi,* case no. 3906 (1969); Commission on Civil Rights, *Southern School Desegregation,* 74–55, 154–55; Sansing, "A Descriptive Survey," 80–83; *Natchez Democrat,*

January 24, August 15, November 13, 1965, May 9, June 3, 1966, April 28, 1967, August 20, December 7, 1969, January 28, 1970; *The Citizen,* August 1973, 13, 30.

76. Interview with Fred Babb [pseud.], by author, October 27, 1993; Virginia Beltzhoover Morrison, Marty Nathanson, Robert Barrett, Maggie Schimmel [pseud.], Barbara Duck, Howell Garner, Bill Hanna, John D. Johnson, Claude Porter, and V. J. Stephens interviews; Sherwood Willing Wise, "A Case Study for Continuity and Stability in Christian Values" (Jackson: Saint Andrews Episcopal Day School, August 1983), MDAH; *Natchez Democrat,* November 7, 1965, March 23, 1986.

77. Robert Barrett interview.

78. Fred Babb [pseud.], Barbara Duck, Howell Garner, Bill Hanna, John D. Johnson, Claude Porter, V. J. Stephens, and Elliot Trimble interviews; Interview with Lisa Babb [pseud.], by author, October 27, 1993; Anonymous interviews (quotes).

79. Mississippi Research and Development Center, *Nonpublic School Statistics and Enrollments, 1971–1972,* table 1; *The Citizen,* August 1973, 13, 30; Philip Chaffin, Rochelle Chaffin, Sandra Davidson, and Howell Garner interviews; *Natchez Democrat,* September 3, 1967, November 18, 1969, February 22, April 15, 1972, July 6, 1973.

80. Maggie Schimmel [pseud.] and Howell Garner interviews; *Natchez Democrat,* January 22, 1977; *The Citizen,* August 1973, 13, 30.

81. *Nonpublic School Statistics and Enrollments, 1974–1975,* table 1, and *Private School Statistics and Enrollments, 1979–1980,* table 1; *Natchez Democrat,* January 24, 1965, August 4, 1966, November 18, December 7, 1969, June 23, 1974, May 19, 1975, October 19, 1977.

82. NSMSSD minutes, August 17, 1970; Robert Barrett, Joe Frazier, Charles Kempinska, and Claude Porter interviews; *Natchez Democrat,* January 31, March 27, April 21, August 11, 1970, October 13, 1971, June 21, July 4, September 28, October 18, December 9, 1973, March 25, May 10, June 1, 1974, August 15, 22, 31, 1975.

83. George F. West Jr. and John West interviews.

84. Betty Christmas interview.

CHAPTER EIGHT

1. Interview with Mike Willey, by author, May 21, 1998; Mary Lee Toles and Phillip West interviews; *Natchez Democrat,* May 28, 29, 30, 31, July 18, 23, 1980.

2. Ibid.; Douglas D. Smith to D. G. McLaurin, February 12, 1970, and Gary Randall to Mr. McLaurin, January 26, 1970, NSMSSD board minutes, February 25, 1970, NPA.

3. Grand Jury report, Judy Ann Reeder, May 25, 1980, case no. 7289, HNF; *Natchez Democrat,* May 28, 29, 30, 31, July 18, 23, 1980.

4. Mary Lee Toles, Phillip West, and Mike Willey interviews; *Natchez Democrat,* May 28, 29, 30, 31, July 18, 23, 1980.

5. Interview with Francine Brown, by author, May 1, 1998; Shead Baldwin, George F.

West Jr., Mary Lee Toles, and Phillip West interviews; *Natchez Democrat,* June 12, 13, 30 (quote), 1980.

6. Anonymous interview ("If"); *Natchez Democrat,* January 20, 1988 ("Just"); FBI, Uniform Crime Report for the United States, *Crime in the United States 1976* (Washington, D.C.), 97; Ibid., *1982,* 81; Ibid., *1991,* 132.

7. Robert Barrett, Barbara Cannes [pseud.], Wilbur Cannes [pseud.], E. Malcolm Graves, Peter Rinaldi, V. J. Stephens, and Mike Willey interviews.

8. "Election Returns, August 2, 1955 to June 25, 1974, A. V. Davis CC," election book in Adams County Courthouse, Natchez; Mary Lee Toles, George F. West Jr., and Phillip West interviews; *Natchez Democrat,* April 27, 30, 1966, November 11, 1969, November 21, December 22, 1976, January 5, 1977, November 7, 1979, May 14, 16, 27, 1980, June 2, 1982, April 21, July 18, 1984, December 24, 1989. On the new black leadership, see Davis et al., *Deep South,* 345.

9. Phillip West interview.

10. *Natchez Democrat,* March 23, 1983 ("We"), February 7, 1978 ("personal").

11. Ruth Tiffee Jordan, anonymous (quote), Shead Baldwin, Robert Barrett, V. J. Stephens, and Mike Willey interviews; *Natchez Democrat,* February 10, 11, 1976, November 8, 1978, August 8, 1979, February 13, March 12, October 29, November 5, 1980, February 6, 20, 28, May 27, June 1, March 19, 1981, July 14, 15, 25, December 3, 1982, January 7, April 19, 20, May 25, 27, 31, June 2, 7, July 21, 26, August 10, 23, September 3, 24, 1983, March 10, 11, 14, April 7, 10, 14, June 8, July 11, September 20, November 25, 27, December 7, 1984, February 6, 13, December 1984.

12. Mary Miller, Shead Baldwin, Francine Brown, George F. West Jr., Phillip West, and Mike Willey interviews; *Natchez Democrat* August 14, 1978 (quote), March 9, 15, 22, 23, 1979, October 4, 1981, January 20, 1988; *Jackson Daily News,* June 4, 1968.

13. Shead Baldwin, Francine Brown, Mary Miller, Mary Lee Toles, and Phillip West interviews; *Natchez Democrat,* February 21, August 4, 14, September 28, October 6, 9, 27, 1976, June 5, 1977, February 7, 23, May 16, 1978, January 25, 26, 1979, June 6, 1980, January 22, 1982, March 23, 1983, November 12, 1984; Janet Jemmott to Jesse Harris, January 26, 1965, Natchez file and Wats report, November 27, 1965, FIS.

14. ACBS minutes, December 1, 1975, May 12, 1980; *Natchez Democrat,* December 2, 1975.

15. ACBS minutes, December 15, 1975; *Natchez Democrat,* December 16, 1975.

16. Ibid.

17. ACBS minutes, December 19, 1975; Mississippi State Department of Public Welfare, *Annual Report, Fiscal Year 1976–1977,* 5, 10, MDAH; *Natchez Democrat,* December 20, 1975; August 9, 1991.

18. "Final Decree," *John A. Scott, et al. v. International Paper Company, et al.,* Civil Action no. w77–0022, 1–29, John A. Scott Personal Papers, in the possession of John A. Scott, Natchez; Interview with John A. Scott, by author, August 18, 1992. *Natchez Democrat,* September 28, 29, 1973, October 13, 14, 1976.

19. Report of the Mississippi State Advisory Committee to the United States

Commission on Civil Rights, "Welfare in Mississippi," February 1969, MDAH; *Census of the Population: 1970* and *1980* and *1990;* College of Business and Industry, Mississippi State University, *Mississippi Statistical Abstract* (Mississippi State, 1975), 192–93; Ibid. (1980), 274–81; Ibid. (1986), 287–89; Ibid. (1990), 263–75; *Annual Production Report of the Oil and Gas Reservoirs of Mississippi* (Mississippi State Oil and Gas Board, 1990). For a profile of black poverty in the state, see Tommy W. Rogers, "Statistical Poverty in Mississippi: A Profile of the Poor in the Nation's Poorest State," *Mid-South Quarterly Business Review* (1st quarter, 1979), 11–15; and Tommy W. Rogers, *Poverty in Mississippi: A Statistical Analysis* (Jackson: Governor's Office of Human Resources and Community Services, 1977). For a survey of the rising poverty trend for blacks in the U.S. in the post–civil rights decades, see Ann M. Nichols-Casebolt, "Black Families Headed by Single Mothers: Growing Numbers and Increasing Poverty," *Social Work* 33 (July/August, 1988): 306–13.

20. Sargent Butler and Lillian Carter interviews; *Census of the Population: 1970* and *1980* and *1990; Natchez Democrat,* February 20, 1977, August 26, 1982, August 22, 1985, January 21, August 26, 1988.

21. Richard T. Seymour (plaintiff's attorney) to Joyce Margulies (IP attorney), March 4, 1985, Scott Personal Papers; John A. Scott interview; *Natchez Democrat,* September 9, 16, 1986.

22. *Annual Production Report of the Oil and Gas Reservoirs of Mississippi; Natchez Democrat,* February 20, 1977, May 9, August 26, 1982, July 20, December 11, 1983, January 10, 1985, January 17, March 21, 1986.

23. Robert Fly, Robert Latham, Anna Nethers, Thomas Nethers, Samuel Stewart, Jack Whitehead, Ruth Tiffee Jordan, and John A. Scott interviews; *Natchez Democrat,* January 17, March 21, 1986.

24. Interview with Karl Mertz, by author, November 11, 1992; *Biloxi Sun Herald,* June 1, 1975; *Jackson Daily News,* July 27, 1981.

25. Karl Mertz interview; *Natchez Democrat,* September 21, 1978; *Biloxi Sun Herald,* June 1, 1975 (quote); *Jackson Daily News,* June 12, 1979.

26. Karl Mertz interview. Resolution of the Pastor-Parish Committee, Washington, August 26, 1978, and "One Can Not Be a Christian and a Segregationist, Too," sermon, n.d., both in Karl Mertz Papers, in possession of author and in MDAH; *Natchez Democrat,* September 21, 1978; *Biloxi Sun Herald,* June 1, 1975; *Jackson Daily News,* June 12, 1979; *United Methodist Reporter,* May 19, 1979.

27. Karl Mertz interview; Resolution of the Pastor-Parish Committee; "One Can Not Be a Christian and a Segregationist, Too"; *Natchez Democrat,* September 21, 1978; *Biloxi Sun Herald,* June 1, 1975; *Jackson Daily News,* June 12, 1979; *Jackson Clarion-Ledger,* June 13, 1979 (quote); *United Methodist Reporter,* May 19, 1979.

28. Charles Kempinska, Robert Lewis, Theresa Lewis, Claude Porter, Shead Baldwin, Robert Barrett, Mary Lee Toles, and Phillip West interviews; NSSMSD minutes, January 19, 30, 1970; "Report on School District Organization, First Term, 1980–1981 School Year," in Old Court Reports (1989 order) box, NPA; North Natchez High School, *The*

Ram, 1985, HNF; *Natchez Democrat,* June 21, 1973, July 4, 6, September 28, October 18, 1973, March 25, May 10, June 1, 1974, February 11, 1977, March 24, 1982, May 15, 1985.

29. Shead Baldwin, Francine Brown, Betty Christmas, Charles Kempinska, Robert Lewis, Theresa Lewis, Claude Porter, Mary Lee Toles, John West, and Phillip West interviews.

30. Joe Frazier, Shead Baldwin, Robert Barrett, Francine Brown, Charles Kempinska, Robert Lewis, and Theresa Lewis interviews; *Natchez Democrat,* January 31 (quote), March 27, April 21, August 11, 1970, October 13, 20, December 10, 1971, June 21, July 4, 6, September 28, October 18, December 9, 1973, March 25, May 10, June 1, 1974, August 15, 22, 31, 1975, February 11, 1977, November 22, September 7, 1981, March 24, 1982, May 15, 1985, January 7, 1988.

31. *Natchez Democrat,* November 22, 1981.

32. Barbara Duck, Marty Nathanson, Elliot Trimble, Robert Barrett, Charles Kempinska, Claude Porter, and V. J. Stephens, interviews; *Natchez Democrat,* January 16, November 9, 1979, March 17, 1984, December 31, 1989.

33. Betty Christmas, John West, Shead Baldwin, Joe Frazier, and Charles Kempinska interviews; *Natchez Democrat,* February 26 ("the erosion"), March 7 ("a deeper"), 1985; Letter to author from Freddie Johnson, July 11, 1992 ("discipline").

34. Claude Porter interview.

35. Betty Christmas, Betty Duck, Charles Kempinska, Robert Lewis, and Theresa Lewis interviews; *Natchez Democrat,* December 9, 1973, May 1, 1983, May 10, August 30, 1988. Although North Natchez students frequently scored higher on graduation tests than students at South Natchez High, North Natchez students' ACT averages in 1988 (13.8) were 4 percentage points below that of their counterparts at South Natchez (17.3). *Natchez Democrat,* November 27, 1988.

36. Shead Baldwin, Francine Brown, Betty Christmas, Barbara Duck, Robert Lewis, Theresa Lewis, John West, and Phillip West interviews; *Natchez Democrat,* May 15, September 16, 1985.

37. Shead Baldwin, Francine Brown, Charles Kempinska, Robert Lewis, Theresa Lewis ("get"), George F. West Jr., and Phillip West interviews; Freddie Johnson letter; *Natchez Democrat,* March 19, 1981, January 5, 14, 23, 1983, September 16 ("learn"), May 15, 1985, July 14, 1986.

38. Claude Porter, Peter Rinaldi, V. J. Stephens, Mary Lee Toles, and Phillip West interviews; *Natchez Democrat,* February 11, 1977 (quote), December 4, 1987.

39. Claude Porter, Mary Toles, and Phillip West interviews; *Natchez Democrat,* November 13, 25 (quote), 26, 1987.

40. Shead Baldwin, Robert Lewis, Theresa Lewis, Claude Porter, Mary Lee Toles, and Phillip West interviews.

41. Mary Toles and Phillip West interviews; *Natchez Democrat,* December 2, 4, 1987.

42. *Natchez Democrat,* October 22, 1987.

43. ACBS minutes, December 14, 1987; *Natchez Democrat,* December 8, 9, 1987.

44. NBA minutes, December 22, 1987; ACBS minutes, December 14, 1987; Shead Baldwin, Robert Lewis, Theresa Lewis, Claude Porter, Mary Toles, and Phillip West interviews; *Natchez Democrat,* December 4 ("against"), 22 ("you"), 1987.

45. Shead Baldwin, Peter Rinaldi, Mary Lee Toles, and Phillip West interviews; *Natchez Democrat,* December 22, 1987 ("We").

46. *U.S. v. Natchez;* Shead Baldwin, Mary Lee Toles, and Phillip West interviews; *Natchez Democrat,* December 16, 17 (quote), 18, 20, 22, 23, 24, 26, 27, 28, 29, 31, 1987, January 6, 28, 29, February, 2, 4, 25, 26, March 1, 2, 8, 1988.

47. Claude Porter, Mary Lee Toles, and Phillip West interviews; *Natchez Democrat,* March 11, 1988.

48. *Natchez Democrat,* March 2 ("pro-majority"), 15, 20 ("We"), 1988; NBA minutes, March 8, 1988.

49. Mary Lee Toles and Phillip West interviews; *Natchez Democrat,* March 13, 15, 20, April 6, 7, 22, 23, May 1, July 26, August 2, 10, 25, 31, September 9, 1988; *Jackson Clarion-Ledger,* June 18, 1989.

50. *U.S. v. Natchez;* NBA minutes, March 8, 1988; *Natchez Democrat,* March 14, 16, 17, June 16, July 25, 26, 27, 28, 30, August 12, 1989; *Jackson Clarion-Ledger,* June 18, 1989 (quote).

51. *Natchez Democrat,* March 1, 16, 17, April 14, July 25, 26, 27, 28, 29, 30, September 6, 23, November 2, 3, 12, 16, 17, 1989; *Jackson Clarion-Ledger,* June 18, 1989.

52. Shead Baldwin, Francine Brown, Barbara Duck (quote), Joe Frazier, Robert Lewis, Theresa Lewis, Mary Toles, and Phillip West interviews.

53. Bill Hanna, Shead Baldwin, Francine Brown, Joe Frazier, Robert Lewis, Theresa Lewis, Claude Porter, Peter Rinaldi, Mary Lee Toles, Phillip West, and Mike Willey interviews; *Natchez Democrat,* July 27, 28, 30, August 12, September 6, 10, 23, 1989, May 12, 1990; *Jackson Clarion-Ledger,* June 18, 1989.

54. Charles Kempinska interview.

55. Troy B. Watkins, Francine Brown, and Mary Miller interviews; *Natchez Democrat,* May 12, 1983, September 3, 1987, May 22, 1988; *Jackson Clarion-Ledger,* June 18, 23 (quote), 1989; *New Orleans Times-Picayune,* August 21, 1983; *Washington Post,* April 3, 1977.

56. Duncan Morgan, Harden Wallace, Francine Brown, and Phillip West interviews; "Natchez Pilgrimage Week," brochure, 1933, box 7, folder 68, Allen Papers, MDAH; *Natchez Democrat,* March 17, 1975, September 13, 1980, June 14, 1984, March 12, 1988; *Jackson Clarion-Ledger,* June 18, 1989 ("a detriment"); *Atlanta Journal,* April 10, 1988.

57. *Natchez Democrat,* September 13, 1980 ("revival"); Francine Brown, Theresa Lewis, Mary Lee Toles, and Phillip West interviews.

58. Audley M. Mackel Sr., "The Contributions of Negroes in Dentistry to the Advancement of Civilization," in Mackel Sr., "Let the Works That I Have Done Speak for Me,"; Audley M. Mackel Jr. interview.

59. Frank Robinson, Ozelle Fisher, Francine Brown, Robert Lewis, Theresa Lewis, Duncan Morgan, Harden Wallace, and Phillip West interviews.

60. Edward L. Ayres, "Memory and the South," *Southern Cultures: A Journal of the Arts in the South* 2 (fall 1995): 5, 6.

61. Don Simonton to Jack E. Davis, March 30, 1998, e-mail in possession of author; *Natchez Democrat,* October 4, 1978, November 1, 1979; *Jackson Clarion-Ledger,* June 18, 1989 (quote).

62. Peter Rinaldi interview; *Natchez Democrat,* May 17 (quote), 18, 21, June 6, 11, 19, July 23, 1986; *Jackson Clarion-Ledger,* June 18, 1989; *Atlanta Journal,* April 10, 1988.

63. See Hogan and Davis, *William Johnson's Natchez;* and Davis and Hogan, *Barber of Natchez,* 92, 217-18, 241-43.

64. NBA minutes, December 22, 1987; Mamie Lee Mazique, Shead Baldwin, Mary Lee Toles, and Phillip West interviews; *Natchez Democrat,* September 13, 1980 (quote), January 30, February 3, 6, 7, 8, 9, 15, 1986, January 13, 20, 21, 1987, January 14, 15, 1988; Freddie Johnson letter.

65. NBA minutes, August 22, 1989, December 13, 27, 1988; Mary Miller, Mary Lee Toles, and Phillip West interviews; *Natchez Democrat,* December 21, 28, 1988, January 4, 15, February 15, 16, 24, March 2, August 25, 26 (quote), 1989.

66. Mary Lee Toles and Phillip West interviews; "Natchez Historical Park," Historic Resource Study, 1997, HNF; "William Johnson House, National Historic Park," Historic Structure Report, n.d., Ann Beha Associates, Boston, Massachusetts, HNF.

67. Duncan Morgan interview.

68. Board minutes, May 1974, Historic Natchez Foundation, Minutes Book, 1974–1978, HNF; Francine Brown, Mary Miller, Mary Lee Toles, and Phillip West interviews.

69. Thelma Williams, Francine Brown, Ozelle Fisher, Mary Miller, Duncan Morgan, and Mary Lee Toles interviews; *Natchez Democrat,* February 6, 1991 ("not"); *Jackson Advocate,* September 1, 7, 1988.

70. Natchez Pilgrimage program guide, 1998, in possession of the author; Mary Lee Toles interview; *Natchez Democrat,* January 3, March 14, June 6, 9, 1990.

EPILOGUE

1. Betty Christmas interview.

2. *Natchez Democrat,* May 5, 1998.

3. See Vollers, *Ghosts of Mississippi,* 249-50.

4. David Goldfield argues that the strong religious beliefs of white southerners and that commonality with black southerners helped lift the barriers between the races. See David R. Goldfield, *Black, White, and Southern: Race Relations and Southern Culture, 1940 to the Present* (Baton Rouge: Louisiana State University Press, 1990). On this subject in Mississippi, see *New York Times,* December 7, 1993, B8.

5. In all fairness to the city of Natchez, pictures of some white mayors are missing as well. Mayor Butch Brown has asked the Historic Natchez Foundation to help locate photographs of the mayors not represented, including Robert Wood. Mary Miller interview.

INDEX

Arkansas: 28, 101, 106–7

Armstrong, David: 264

Armstrong, George W.: 111

Armstrong Tire and Rubber Company:
115, 116–18, 128–30, 131, 132–34,
136, 137, 140, 141, 143, 144, 146, 159,
165, 166, 177, 180–82, 198, 201,
202–3, 247, 253

Atlanta: 84, 157, 158

Atlanta University: 157

Atlantic Monthly: 74

Audubon, John James: 64

Avants, Ernest: 192–93

Ayers, Edward: 269

Bacon, David: 158, 169

Balance Agriculture with Industry program
(BAWI): 128–31, 132

Baldwin, Shead: 165, 167–68, 171, 183,
184, 185, 188, 192, 202, 205, 225

Bankhead, Tallulah: 68

Banks, John B.: 100–1

Barnett, Ross: 37, 41, 190–91

Barnum, P. T.: 68

Baroni, Marge: 196

Barrett, Richard: 263

Barrett, Robert: 237

Beekman, Rosalie: 109

Beltzhoover, Mary Jane: 136

Bernard, Jessie: 188

Better Homes and Gardens: 68

Bettersworth, John K.: 40–41

Bilbo, Theodore: 9, 149

Black History Month: 279

Black, Hugo: 227

Blacks in Natchez: activism of, 102,
156–57, 159–60, 164–65, 174–76,
180–83, 184–86, 187–92, 194–95,
201–6, 215–16, 218–19, 239–40,
244–45, 246, 247, 248, 250, 251–52,
255–56, 259–65, 260–64, 267, 270,
272–73; ancestry, 85, 88–89, 91, 93, 94,
95; as free blacks, 89–90; as slaves, 25,

26, 27, 44, 61, 75, 90; attitudes toward
education, 5, 7, 95, 96, 97–98, 101–2,
208–10, 214–15, 219, 221–26, 231–32,
234; business community of, 97, 101;
civic organizations among, 99, 101,
104–5; churches of, 162, 164, 165, 167,
174, 185, 195, 278; class structure
among, 88, 90, 91, 92, 95, 98, 103–4;
identifying culture with race, 2; in
Natchez Pilgrimage, 75–79; interracial
relations with whites, 94–95; political
empowerment, 20, 90–91, 92, 100, 206,
223–26, 246–51, 272, 277; poverty
among, 53, 115, 120–21, 123, 124–25,
249, 250–51, 252; upper-class, 84, 85,
86, 87–89, 90–93, 95, 96, 97–98, 99,
100–1, 102, 103–4, 114, 157, 222–23,
247, 248, 269, 271; voting, 17, 90, 92,
98, 105, 153, 164, 170, 171, 176, 194,
245, 246–47, 248; women, 85, 92, 95,
124, 125–28, 131, 145, 171, 187–88,
252, 271–72; working-class, 88, 114,
115–16, 119, 120–28, 130, 131–35,
140, 141, 142–43, 144, 145–47, 165,
180–83, 203–5

Blankenstein, Katherine: 38, 112, 173

Blankenstein, Rodney: 173

Bluff City Savings: 101

B'nai Israel: 108, 110, 111

Bonner, Joe: 256

Boston Herald: 54

Bowers, Sam: 193, 278

Brady, Thomas P.: 159

Brown, Butch: 337 n. 5

Brown, Elton: 198–99

Brown, Jake: 223–24

Brown v. Board of Education: 142, 155,
156, 158, 160, 179, 194, 210–12, 213,
216, 218, 219, 220

Brudgewater, Burnette: 230

Brumfield High School: 97, 102, 208, 209,
213

Buckley, Melvin R.: 263–64, 277

INDEX

International Hod Carriers, Building, and
Common Laborers Union: 142
International Paper Company: 132, 134,
142, 166, 167, 177, 181, 203, 247, 251,
252–53

Jackson Daily News: 158
Jackson, Denise: 202
Jackson, Edith: 205
Jackson (Mich.): 144
Jackson (Miss.): 18, 19, 71, 85, 142,
156–57, 178, 191, 199, 200, 218, 219,
238, 254, 263
Jackson, Nellie: 97
Jackson, Wharlest: 165, 177, 208, 243,
278, 279
Jefferson College: 111
Jefferson County: 249
Jefferson Davis Memorial Hospital: 182
Jefferson Street Methodist Church:
199–200
Jefferson, Thomas: 120, 153, 156
Jews: culture 5–6, 232; settlement in the
United States, 105–6, 232
Jews in Natchez: acceptance by non-Jews,
84, 86, 105, 108, 109–10, 111, 112,
114; anti-Semitism and, 86, 111, 112;
assimilation, 86, 108, 109–10, 111, 113,
114; business community of, 98, 101,
106, 107; discord among, 110–11, 112;
early years of, 105–6, 107–8, 109; interfaith relationships, 85–86, 110; in the
Confederacy, 109; place in social structure, 5–6, 85–86, 87–88, 110, 113, 179;
population, 83, 86, 110; religious life,
107–8, 112–13, role in segregation of,
113, 170; women among, 109; Zionism
and, 110–11
Johns-Manville Company: 132, 134, 135,
142, 181, 203, 247
Johnson, Forrest: 196
Johnson, Freddie: 257

Johnson, Lady Bird: 57
Johnson, Lyndon: 177
Johnson, Paul B.: 36
Johnson, Paul B., Jr.: 174, 185, 202
Johnson, Theodore: 261
Johnson, William: 43, 89, 93, 269, 270–71
Johnston, Clarence (son of William
Johnson): 91
Johnston, Erle: 189–90, 225
Johnston, William R.: 93
Jones, Archie: 183
Jones, Eddie: 277
Jones, Jacqueline: 7
Jones, James: 192–93
Jones, L. H. "Lib": 142–43
Jordan, Ruth Tiffee: 131, 141
Jordan, Winthrop: 292 n. 55

Kane, Harnett T.: 68–69
Kempinska, Charles: 227
Kennedy, John: 161
Kennedy, Robert: 162
Kentucky: 239
King, Martin Luther, Jr.: 187, 193, 270
Knights of Pythias: 109
Krouse, Alek: 106–7, 112
Krouse, Dora: 106–7
Krouse, Jerry: 85–86, 112
Krouse, Mannie: 106, 107, 112
Krouse, Morris: 106–7, 112
Krouse, Samuel: 106–7
Kubassek, Melody: 33
Ku Klux Klan: 39, 111, 112, 162, 163,
164, 165, 166, 170, 173, 175, 177, 179,
181, 182, 185, 192, 193, 194, 195, 198,
204, 216, 220, 225, 229–30, 278

Ladner, Dorie: 168
Latham, Robert: 132, 133, 134, 135,
144–45, 146, 147
Laub, S. B.: 111, 130
Lawrence, Ken: 43

344